REVOLUTION BESIEGED
Lenin 1917–1923

REVOLUTION BESIEGED
Lenin 1917–1923

BY TONY CLIFF

Haymarket
Books

Chicago, IL

The Revolution Besieged: Lenin 1917–1923
© Tony Cliff, 1979

This edition published 2012 by Haymarket Books
P.O. Box 180165
Chicago, IL 60618
773-583-7884
info@haymarketbooks.org
www.haymarketbooks.org

Trade distribution:
In the US, Consortium Book Sales and Distribution, www.cbsd.com
In Canada, Publishers Group Canada, www.pgcbooks.ca
All other countries, Publishers Group Worldwide, www.pgw.com

Cover design by Eric Ruder.

Published with the generous support of Lannan Foundation
and the Wallace Global Fund.

Printed in the United States by union labor.

Library of Congress cataloging-in-publication data is available.

ISBN: 978-1-60846-087-8

10 9 8 7 6 5 4 3 2 1

This is the third volume of Tony Cliff's biography of Lenin.
Although the four volumes follow each other chronologically,
each deals with a specific political period in Lenin's life and so
may be read independently of the others.

SUSTAINABLE
FORESTRY
INITIATIVE

Certified Sourcing
www.sfiprogram.org
SFI-01234

Contents

Foreword

When on the morrow of the October insurrection Lenin calmly declared, 'We shall now proceed to construct the socialist order', he had behind him a quarter of a century of prison, exile, clandestine work and emigration, organizing, educating and leading a party of persecuted revolutionaries, very far from state power. Lenin now had before him five years as leader of the party, in charge of a revolutionary government and the head of a newly established Communist International.

In the long hard years of political work behind him Lenin had been sustained by a great dream – of a new socialist order. For twenty-five years he worked relentlessly towards a goal which seemed far more remote than it actually proved to be; as late as February 1917 he still did not believe that the revolution would come in his lifetime. After their dramatic ascent from obscurity to the summit of power, Lenin and the Bolsheviks faced a host of new, difficult tasks. They had to administer the state of a gigantic, backward country, whose economy was in ruins and which was under attack by 'fourteen armies'. The Bolsheviks had to create a workers' and peasants' army from scratch, and lead it against domestic and foreign armies far better equipped.

On coming to power the party had to change its mode of operation radically from agitating and organizing against a state, to administering a state and leading the workers in doing so. Lenin and the other Bolsheviks never doubted the crucial role of the proletariat in the revolution and its ability to rule, even though it was a class with no experience of power, no standing in society, and no wealth or culture to speak of. The Bolsheviks had great confidence in the creative abilities of the awakened working class. Relying on the iron discipline of the party, forged over many hard years of struggle, and the courage and heroism of the proletariat, Lenin unhesitatingly grasped the helm of the state.

Another new, heavy burden fell on Lenin's shoulders – that of leading the newly founded Communist International. The Russian revolution had massive reverberations abroad. From tiny groups of revolutionary marxists, mass communist parties emerged in a number of countries. It was an extremely arduous task to educate and train the young, inexperienced parties.

The present work spans the period between Lenin's rise to power and his death. Of necessity its canvas has to be much broader than the previous two: Lenin's triple role as leader of the party, the government and of the International has to be documented and analysed.

The relationship between Lenin's biography and the history of the working class is an everchanging one. In *Lenin: Building the Party* I tried to show how Lenin influenced the party and the party influenced the proletariat, as well as how the proletariat created the party and the party shaped Lenin. The political biography of Lenin meshed in with the political history of the working class. The fusion of Lenin's activities with those of the party and the class reached its climax in the revolution of 1917, the subject of *Lenin: All power to the Soviets*. If in the first book the strands of biography and of history did not harmonize completely it was because Lenin had to work his way towards implanting the party in the class, remoulding the party and himself in the struggle to change the working class and transform society. In 1917 the fusion of the biographical and the historical was complete, so that it seems as if Lenin merged completely with the party and the proletariat. He acquired his strength and greatness in 1917 from the strength and greatness of the workers.

In this present volume, the relationship between the biographical and the historical changes again. Following the October revolution, the grim reality of Russian backwardness and peasant conservatism, combined with the tardiness of the international revolution, led to an increasing impotence and inability of the Bolsheviks to shape reality. It was as if the march of events pushed Lenin to the periphery of social life. The biographical element appears very marginal compared with the historical. The weakness of Lenin and his party in the face of overwhelming forces makes this period of his life a tragic one; nevertheless, the sacrifices which he, the party and the proletariat made during this period were not made in vain.

Throughout the Promethean struggle Lenin never wavered in his conviction that the future belonged to Bolshevism. The relatively small proletariat of Russia, in the most difficult circumstances, provided a glimpse of what the international working class can achieve in its fight for freedom, for workers' power.

To Lenin it was clear that the Russian proletariat could not retain state power without the victory of the proletariat in the West. For him the Russian revolution was no more than the first stage of the world revolution. This book describes the efforts, the successes and failures, of Lenin and the Bolsheviks in building a

Communist International and in spreading the revolution. Their success in building a mighty revolutionary international in a very short time was astonishing. However, as history showed, it was impossible to graft Bolshevism speedily on to the parties outside Russia, which had very different traditions. The failure of the grafting process led to the defeats of the revolution of 1918-23. In the main, these defeats were due to the lack of experience of the young communist parties, an immaturity which could have been overcome with the passage of time. Alas, time was short. And so the isolation of the Russian revolution led to the consolidation in the power of the bureaucracy in Russia and to the transformation of the Comintern into a mere appendage of the Kremlin's foreign policy. This completely obliterated the communist parties as tools of revolution (a subject that falls outside the present work).

In this book there are repeated references to mistakes committed by Lenin and the Bolsheviks. Not that Lenin made more mistakes in the final stage of his life than before, but now there was a disproportion between mistake and the consequence. It is precisely in this disproportion that the ebb of the historical movement expresses itself at this stage. Lenin's mistakes in 1917 were overcome by the sweep of the revolution. Now, in 1921-23, with the exhaustion of the proletariat and the rise of the party-state bureaucracy, and with the failure of the revolution in the west, each 'mistake' by the leadership was not made good by events, but accentuated by them.

In the last few years of Lenin's life, the optimistic, heroic elements intertwine inextricably with the tragic: his grasp of the helm of state, party and International becomes weaker and weaker. Consequently, in this volume the crucial dialectic of the biographical and historical elements causes the latter almost to obliterate the former.

Writing this book was extremely difficult, not only because of the conflict between the breadth of the subject – Russia in the international arena, the party, the state and the Communist International – but even more because it is hard to describe an historical tragedy intertwined with personal agony without descending to a pathos foreign to the subject of the book.

For dates before 1 (14) February 1918 I give two dates, the first according to the Julian or 'Old Style' calendar, the second (in parentheses) according to the Gregorian calendar, known as the 'West European' or 'New Style'. The Old Style was abolished and the New Style introduced in Russia on 1 (14) February 1918. For events occurring later only the Gregorian calendar applies.

* * *

I should like to take this opportunity of thanking Mary Phillips, who translated a number of excerpts from German, and Donny Gluckstein for translating from French, and especially Jo Bradley who edited the original four volumes, patiently scrutinizing the text and offering valuable stylistic suggestions. Above all I am indebted to Chanie Rosenberg, who typed different versions of sections of this work innumerable times and the whole work at least three times. But my debt to her is far greater than this: during the six years it took me to write this work she game me unstinting moral support and friendship.

Tony Cliff
London, July 1977 and April 1978

List of Abbreviations

BKP	Balgarskata Komunisticheska Partia (Bulgarian Communist Party)
BSP	British Socialist Party
Cheka	Chrezvychainaia Komissiia pri sovet Narodnykh Komissarov po borbe s Kontrrevoliutsiei i sabotazhem (Extraordinary Commission for Combatting Counter-revolution and sabotage attached to the Council of People's Commissars)
Comintern	Communist International
CPGB	Communist Party of Great Britain
ECCI	Executive Committee of the Communist International
Goelro	Gosudarstvennaia Komissiia po Elekrtifikatsii Rossii (State Commission for the Electrification of Russia)
Gosplan	Gosudarstvennaia Obshcheplanovaia Komissiia (State General Planning Commission)
KAPD	Komunistische Arbeiter-Partei Deutschlands (German Communist Workers' Party)
Kombedy	Komitety Bednoty (Committees of Poor Peasants)
NEP	Novaia Ekonomicheskaia Politika (New Economic Policy)
PCI	Partito Comunista Italiano (Italian Communist Party)
Profintern	Krasnyi Internatsional Professionalnykh Soiuzov (Red International of Trade Unions)
PSI	Partito Socialista Italiano (Italian Socialist Party)
Rabkrin	Narodnyi Komissariat Rabochei i Krestianskoi Inspektsii (People's Commissariat of Workers' and Peasants' Inspection)
RKP(b)	Rossiiskaia Mommunisticheskaia Partiia (Bolshevikov) (Russian Communist Party (Bolsheviks))
RSFSR	Rossiikaia Sotsialisticheskaia Federativnaia Sovetskaia Respublika (Russian Socialist Federal Soviet Republic)
SDF	Social Democratic Federation
SFIO	Section Française de I'Internationale Ouvriére (French Section of the Workers' International – the Socialist Party of France)
SLP	Socialist Labour Party

Sovnarkom	Sovet Narodnykh Komissarov (Council of People's Commissars)
SPD	Sozialdemokratische Partei Deutschlands (German Social Democratic Party)
SR	Sotsial-Revoliutsioner (Social-Revolutionary)
SSSR	Soiuz Sovetskikh Sotsialisticheskikh Respublik (Union of Soviet Socialist Republics)
TsIK	Tsentralnyi Ispolnitelnyi Komitet (Central Executive Committee)
USPD	Unabhängige Sozialdemokratische Partei Deutschlands (German Independent Social Democratic Party)
Vikzhel	Vserossiiskii Ispolnitelnyi Komitet Soiuza Zheleznodorozhnikov (All-Russian Executive Committee of Union of Railwaymen)
VSNKh	Vysshii Sovet Narodnogo Khoziaistva (Supreme Council of National Economy)
VTsIK	Vserossiiskii (Vsesoiuznyi) Tsentralnyi Ispolnitelnyi Komitet (All-Russian (All-Union) Central Executive Committee)

Congresses of the Party, Soviets, Trade Unions and the Communist International

Party Congresses
Seventh: 6-8 March 1918; Eighth: 18-23 March 1919; Ninth: 29 April-5 May 1920; Tenth: 8-16 March 1921; Eleventh: 27 March-2 April 1922; Twelfth: 17-25 April 1923

Soviet Congresses (RSFSR)
Second: 25-26 October (7-8 November) 1917; Third: 23-31 December 1917 (5-13 January 1918); Fourth: 14-16 March 1918; Fifth: 4-10 July 1918; Sixth: 6-9 November 1918; Seventh: 5-9 December 1919; Eighth: 22-29 December 1920; Ninth: 22-27 December 1920; Tenth (Formation of USSR): 23-27 December 1922

Soviet Congresses (USSR)
First: 30 December 1922

Trade Union Congresses
First: 7-14 (20-27) January 1918; Second: 16-25 January 1919; Third: 6-13 April 1920; Fourth: 17-25 May 1921; Fifth: 17-22 September 1922

Communist International Congresses
First: 2-6 March 1919; Second: 19 July-7 August 1920; Third: 22 June-12 July 1921; Fourth: 5 November-5 December 1922

Tony Cliff is a member of the Socialist Workers Party. His earlier publications include *Rosa Luxemburg* (1959), *Russia: A Marxist Analysis* (1963, republished as *State Capitalism in Russia* (1974)), *The Employers' Offensive* (1970), *Lenin* (four volumes 1975-79, of which this book contains volumes 3 and 4), *Neither Washington nor Moscow* (1982), *Class Struggle and Women's Liberation* (1984), and *Marxism and Trade Union Struggle: The General Strike of 1926* (1986, with Donny Gluckstein).

1
The Bolshevik Government's First Steps

On 25 October (7 November) the Bolsheviks took control in Petrograd. When Lenin came out of hiding after nearly four months, he said to Trotsky: 'You know, from persecution and life underground, to come so suddenly into power . . .' – he paused for the right word. 'Es schwindet (it makes one giddy)', he concluded, changing suddenly to German, and circling his hand around his head.[1]

Lenin himself was in doubt as to how long the Bolsheviks would be able to hold power. Capitalist, Menshevik and Socialist Revolutionary circles were convinced that they could not survive for more than a few days. 'We are absolutely certain that the Bolsheviks will not be able to organize state power,' wrote *Izvestiia*, the official paper of the Soviets, whose last issue, the day after the revolution, was still controlled by the Mensheviks and Socialist Revolutionaries.[2]

S.N.Prokopovich, a minister in the Kerensky government, recalled a few years later: 'In Moscow the Rightists said openly: "Only let the Bolsheviks overthrow the power of the provisional government, and then it will be easy for us to cope with them." ' And he added: 'In the camps of both the right and the left I saw almost open rejoicing during those days over the boldness of the Bolsheviks.'[3] Another eye-witness, Stankevich, the Commissar of the provisional government at army headquarters, wrote of the mood on the right in the days after the October revolution: 'The conviction grew with every hour that the Bolsheviks would soon be liquidated.'[4]

The conservative daily *Novoe Vremia* wrote on the morning after the Bolsheviks assumed control:

Let us suppose for a moment that the Bolsheviks do gain the upper hand. Who will govern us then: the cooks perhaps, those connoisseurs of cutlets and beefsteaks? Or maybe the firemen? The stableboys, the chauffeurs? Or perhaps the nursemaids will rush off to meetings of the Council of State between the diaper-washing sessions? Who then? Where are the statesmen? Perhaps the mechanics will run the theaters, the plumbers foreign affairs, the carpenters, the post office. Who will it be? History alone will give a definitive answer to this mad ambition of the Bolsheviks.[5]

One conservative historian remembered: 'I never met anyone who doubted that the overthrow of the Bolsheviks was imminent. The only question was how and when.'[6] *Delo Naroda*, the daily paper of the Socialist Revolutionaries, wrote three days after the insurrection: 'The Bolshevik adventure . . . , like a soap bubble, will burst at the first contact with hard facts.'[7] And John Reed, who moved in a wide variety of social circles, provides similar testimony: 'That the Bolsheviki would remain in power longer than three days never occurred to anybody – except perhaps to Lenin, Trotsky, the Petrograd workers and the simple soldiers.'[8]

The capitalists, Mensheviks and Socialist Revolutionaries miscalculated, because, as the reliable witness Sukhanov points out: 'the Bolsheviks acted with the full backing of the Petersburg workers and soldiers.'[9] Similarly, Martov wrote to Axelrod on 6 (19) November 1917: 'Understand, please, that before us after all is a victorious uprising of the proletariat – almost the entire proletariat supports Lenin and expects its social liberation from the uprising.'[10]

The October insurrection was accompanied by very little resistance from the bourgeoisie; first, because the latter could not bring itself to believe that its 'natural rule' could be challenged by the proletariat; secondly, because it felt so isolated and estranged from the masses. It required the intervention of the Western imperialist powers to give the Russian bourgeoisie faith in itself and to encourage its resistance to Bolshevism.

The Congress of the Soviets
On 26 October (8 November), the Second All-Russian Congress of the Soviets opened at 11.45 p.m. Its social composition was very different from that of the earlier one. The June Congress

was made up very largely of petty bourgeois elements. Intellectuals and army officers had been prominent. The October Congress was both younger and much more proletarian. As John Reed describes it:

> I stood there watching the new delegates come in – burly, bearded soldiers, workmen in black blouses, a few long-haired peasants. The girl in charge – a member of Plekhanov's Edinstvo group – smiled contemptuously. 'These are very different people from the delegates to the first Sezd,' she remarked. 'See how rough and ignorant they look! The Dark People . . .' It was true; the depths of Russia had been stirred, and it was the bottom which came uppermost now.'[11]

The political composition of the second Congress was also very different from that of the first. Whereas the Socialist Revolutionaries and Mensheviks had predominated in the June Congress, now the majority of the delegates were followers of Bolshevism. The Bolsheviks held some 390 seats out of a total of 650. The strength of the Socialist Revolutionaries was estimated variously as between 160 and 190. But these figures are misleading, since the party had split and most of the SR delegates were suporters of the Left SR Party, which was pro-Bolshevik at the time. The Mensheviks, who in June had accounted for more than 200 delegates, were now reduced to a mere 60-70, and these split into a number of groups. The Right SR and Mensheviks could count on less than 100 votes.

The Congress elected a new Executive. This consisted of 14 Bolsheviks, 7 Socialist Revolutionaries, 3 Mensheviks and 1 United Internationalist (from Maxim Gorky's group). The Right SR and Mensheviks at once declared that they would refuse to share executive power with the Bolsheviks.

Martov then mounted the rostrum and declared that the most urgent problem was to overcome the current crisis by peaceful means. The Bolsheviks, recognizing the need to expose the real nature of SR and Menshevik policy, did not oppose Martov's statement, despite the anti-Bolshevik tenor of his speech. 'The Bolsheviks had absolutely nothing against it; let the question of a peaceable settlement of the crisis be made the first item on the agenda. Martov's motion was voted on: against it – nobody.'[12]

However, the Right Mensheviks and Right SR leaders bluntly rejected collaboration with the 'party of insurrection'. Following their statement the entire Right – Mensheviks, Right SR and Jewish Bund – walked out of the Congress.

Martov continued to argue as if nothing had happened, and went on to preach conciliation. Trotsky then rounded on him:

> Now we are told: renounce your victory, make concessions, compromise. With whom? I ask: with whom ought we to compromise? With those wretched groups who have left us or who are making this proposal? But after all we've had a full view of them. No one in Russia is with them any longer. A compromise is supposed to be made, as between two equal sides, by the millions of workers and peasants represented in this Congress, whom they are ready, not for the first time or the last, to barter away as the bourgeoisie sees fit. No, here no compromise is possible. To those who have left and to those who tell us to do this we must say: you are miserable bankrupts, your role is played out; go where you ought to be: into the dustbin of history!
>
> 'Then we'll leave,' Martov shouted from the platform amidst stormy applause for Trotsky.[18]

The meeting went on to elect a new Central Executive Committee of the Soviet Congress (VTsIK), i.e. a legislative committee to operate between sessions of the Congress. The Bolsheviks were allowed 67 seats, the Left SR 29; 20 seats were divided among minor groups, including 6 United Internationalists.

The Congress also set up a new government – the Council of People's Commissars (Sovnarkom). The Left SRs refused to join it, arguing that this would enable them to mediate between the Bolsheviks on the one side and the Right SRs and Mensheviks on the other, so as to promote a wider coalition.

The composition of the Sovnarkum was as follows:

Chairman of the Council – Vladimir Ulianov (Lenin)
People's Commissar of the Interior – A.I.Rykov
Agriculture – V.P.Miliutin
Labour – A.G.Shliapnikov
Army and Navy Affairs – a committee consisting of
V.A.Ovseenko (Antonov), N.V.Krylenko and P.Y.Dybenko
Commerce and Industry – V.P.Nogin

Education – A.V.Lunacharsky
Finance – I.I.Skvortsov (Stepanov)
Foreign Affairs – L.D.Bronstein (Trotsky)
Justice – G.I.Oppokov (Lomov)
Food – I.A.Teodorovich
Posts and Telegraphy – N.P.Avilov (Glebov)
Chairman of Nationalities Affairs – J.V.Dzhugashvili (Stalin)
The post of People's Commissar for Railways was delibera-
tely left open in the hope of reaching an agreement with
the Central Executive Committee of the Railway Workers'
Union (Vikzhel), which was insistent on the formation of a
broad all-socialist government.*

Decrees, Decrees, Decrees . . .

In the first few days and weeks after coming to power,
Lenin dealt with the numerous problems of economic, political
and cultural life, by issuing a series of decrees. Eighteen months
later, on 23 March 1919, he told the Eighth Congress of the
party :

> *Decrees are instructions which call for practical work on a mass
> scale.* That is what is important. Let us assume that decrees do
> contain much that is useless, much that in practice cannot be
> put into effect; but they contain material for practical action,
> and the purpose of a decree is to teach practical steps to the
> hundreds, thousands and millions of people who heed the voice
> of the Soviet government. This is a trial in practical action in
> the sphere of socialist construction . . . If we treat matters in
> this way we shall acquire a good deal from the sum total of our
> laws, decrees and ordinances. We shall not regard them as abso-
> lute injunctions which must be put into effect instantly and at
> all costs.[14]

Lenin's energy knew no bounds.

> Untiringly, he presided, five or six hours at a stretch, over the
> meetings of the Council of People's Commissars, which at that
> period took place every day; he directed the debates passing
> from subject to subject . . . As a rule, the topics of discussion
> were put on the agenda without any previous preparation, and
> . . . always demanding extreme urgency. Very often neither the

---

* See, further, Chapter 2 below.

chairman nor the commissars were familiar with the essentials of a problem until it became the subject of the debate.[15]

Lenin was a strict chairman of Sovnarkom meetings. To this end he drafted the following standing orders:

1. For those making reports – 10 minutes.
2. For speakers, the first time 5 minutes, the second time 3 minutes.
3. To speak not more than twice.
4. On a point of order, 1 for and 1 against, each for one minute.
5. Exceptions by *special* rulings of the Sovnarkom.[16]

At these meetings Lenin had a habit of sending scribbled notes on tiny bits of paper to members of the government asking for information on this or that point. His summary of the discussion was usually the basis for the subsequent decree. Trotsky quite rightly wrote: 'The collection of Soviet decrees forms in a certain sense a part, and not a negligible part, of the Complete Works of Vladimir Ilyich Lenin.'[17]

As there were no precedents, improvisation played a central role in drafting the decrees. Lenin's creative imagination was indispensable to the legislative work. This huge task was carried out under extremely difficult conditions, the founder of the new state having not even the most ordinary facilities for work. Typewriters were a great rarity in Smolny (the headquarters of the Soviets). There were no shorthand writers. The People's Commissars had to write out their decrees and proclamations in their own hand.

Everybody was extremely inexperienced. For instance, the newly appointed Director of the State Bank, S.S.Pestovsky, describes in his memoirs how he happened to get the job. A non-Bolshevik and former member of the SR party, he was visiting Smolny. He entered a room.

> The room was rather large. In one corner the Secretary of the Sovnarkom, Comrade N.P.Gorbunov, was working at a small table . . . Farther on, Comrade Menzhinsky, looking very tired, was lounging on a sofa . . . over [which] was the sign: 'The People's Commissariat of Finance'.
> I sat down near Menzhinsky and began to talk with him. In the most innocent way he started to question me about my earlier career and became curious in regard to my past studies.

I answered . . . that I had worked at the University of London, where, among other subjects, I had studied finance.

Menzhinsky suddenly arose, fixed his eyes upon me, and categorically declared: In that case we shall make you the director of the State Bank.

I was frightened and answered . . . that I had no desire to hold this position, since it was entirely 'outside my line'. Saying nothing, Menzhinsky asked me to wait, and left the room.

He was gone for some time, and then returned with a paper signed by Ilyich [Lenin] on which it was stated that I was the director of the State Bank.

I became even more dumbfounded, and began to beg Menzhinsky to revoke the appointment, but he remained inflexible on this point.[18]

And what were the qualifications of Menzhinsky himself to be People's Commissar of Finance? It seems 'he had once been a clerk in a French bank.'[19]

The qualifications of the Secretary of the Council of People's Commissars were also questionable. N.P.Gorbunov, a young man of 25, describes how one day he was called by V.D.Bonch-Bruevich, Lenin's secretary.

I went to him and, without any explanation, he dragged me upstairs to the third floor into the small corner room where Vladimir Ilyich worked in those first days . . . I saw Vladimir Ilyich who greeted me and to my astonishment, said, 'You will be the secretary of the Sovnarkom'. I received no instructions from him at that time. I knew absolutely nothing about my job or about secretarial duties in general. Somewhere I commandeered a typewriter on which, for quite a long time, I had to bang out documents with two fingers; no typist could be found.

The office furniture consisted of one desk. Lenin called him into the first cabinet meeting to take the minutes even though he knew no shorthand and his spelling was imperfect.[20]

One result of the rush to issue decrees and proclamations was that formalities were abandoned. As Iu.Larin, a member of VTsIK and chief of the Bureau of Legislation of Sovnarkom, remembers:

Of the first fifteen decrees which are found in No.1 of the Collection of Laws (*Sobranie Uzakonenii i Rasporiazhenii Rabochego i Kristianskogo Pravitelstva*) only two were actually

considered by the Sovnarkom . . . I remember Lenin's astonish
ment when he first saw . . . the decree No.12, under his signature, which conferred legislative powers on the Sovnarkom
(the Congress of Soviets granted only executive powers).[21]

The Decree on Peace

The first decree drafted by Lenin, which was issued the day
after the insurrection by the newly formed government, was the
decree on peace. The new workers' and peasants' government

> calls upon all the belligerent peoples and their governments to
> start immediate negotiations for a just, democratic peace.
> . . . by such a peace the government means an immediate
> peace without annexations (i.e. without the seizure of foreign
> lands, without the forcible incorporation of foreign nations)
> and without indemnities . . .
> The government considers it the greatest of crimes against
> humanity to continue this war over the issue of how to divide
> among the strong and rich nations the weak nationalities they
> have conquered, and solemnly announces its determination
> immediately to sign terms of peace to stop this war on the
> terms indicated, which are equally just for all nationalities
> without exception . . .
> The government abolishes secret diplomacy, and, for its part,
> announces its firm intention to conduct all negotiations quite
> openly in full view of the whole people. It will proceed imme-
> diately with the full publication of the secret treaties endorsed
> or concluded by the government of landowners and capitalists
> from February to 25 October 1917. The government proclaims
> the unconditional and immediate annulment of everything con-
> tained in those secret treaties insofar as it is aimed, as is mostly
> the case, at securing advantages and privileges for the Russian
> landowners and capitalists and at the retention, or extension, of
> the annexations made by the Great Russians.[22]

The Decree on Land

Another decree of world historical importance, that on
land, was issued on the same day as the decree on peace. This was
also drafted by Lenin.

> *Private ownership of land shall be abolished for ever*; land shall
> not be sold, purchased, leased, mortgaged, or otherwise alien-
> ated.

All land, whether *state, crown, monastery, church, factory, entailed, private, public, peasant, etc., shall be confiscated without compensation* and become the property of the whole people, and pass into the use of all those who cultivate it . . .

Lands on which *high-level scientific* farming is practised – orchards, plantations, seed plots, nurseries, hothouses, etc. – *shall not be divided up, but shall be converted into model farms,* to be turned over for exclusive use *to the state or to the communes,* depending on the size and importance of such lands . . .

The right to use the land shall be accorded to all citizens of the Russian state (without distinction of sex) desiring to cultivate it by their own labour, with the help of their families, or in partnership, but only as long as they are able to cultivate it. The employment of hired labour is not permitted . . .

Land tenure shall be on an equality basis, i.e. the land shall be distributed among the working people in conformity with a labour standard or a subsistence standard, depending on local conditions.[23]

Lenin's tactical adaptability shows itself at its best in the Decree on Land Reform. Unashamedly he adopted the SR programme:

The Socialist Revolutionaries fumed and raved [Lenin wrote], protested and howled that 'the Bolsheviks had stolen their programme', but they were only laughed at for that; a fine party, indeed, which had to be defeated and driven from the government in order that everything in its programme that was revolutionary and of benefit to the working people could be carried out![24]

The Right of the Peoples of Russia to Self-Determination

Another long-standing element in the programme of Bolshevism was the right of oppressed nations to freedom. On 2 (15) November, Sovnarkom issued a decree, to this effect, including the following principles:

1. Equality and sovereignty of the peoples of Russia.
2. The right of the peoples of Russia to free self-determination, up to secession and formation of an independent state.
3. Abolition of all and any national and national-religious privileges and restrictions.
4. Free development of national minorities and ethnic groups inhabitating Russia.[25]

The Decree on Workers' Control

A decree on workers' control was drafted by Lenin and issued by Sovnarkom on 14 (27) November:

> In order to provide planned regulation of the national economy, workers' control over the manufacture, purchase, sale and storage of produce and raw materials and over the financial activity of enterprises is introduced in all industrial, commercial, banking, agricultural, cooperative and other enterprises which employ hired labour or give work to be done at home.
>
> Workers' control is exercised by all the workers of the given enterprise through their elected bodies, such as factory committees, shop stewards' councils, etc., whose members include representatives of the office employees and the technical personnel.
>
> In every city, *guberniia* and industrial district a local workers' control council is set up which, being an agency of the Soviet of Workers', Soldiers' and Peasants' deputies, is composed of representatives of trade unions, factory and office workers' committees, and workers' cooperatives ...
>
> Decisions of workers' control bodies are binding upon the owners of enterprises and may be revoked only by higher workers' control bodies ...
>
> The All-Russia Workers' Control Council works out general plans of workers' control, issues instructions and ordinances, regulates relationships between district workers' control councils, and serves as the highest instance for all matters pertaining to workers' control.[26]

Many, Many Other Decrees

On 21 November (4 December) a decree on the right of recall, also drafted by Lenin, was issued by Sovnarkom:

> No elective institution or representative assembly can be regarded as being truly democratic and really representative of the people's will unless the electors' right to recall those elected is accepted and exercised. This fundamental principle of true democracy applies to all representative assemblies without exception.[27]

On 22 November (5 December) Sovnarkom issued a decree on the judiciary. The old judges were removed from office and replaced by new ones who were to be elected either by the Soviets or by popular vote. Former laws were to be valid 'only inasmuch as they are not abolished by the revolution and do not contradict revolutionary consciousness and a revolutionary sense of right'. This statement was supplemented by a provision to the effect that all laws that conflicted with decrees of the Soviet government and with the minimum programme of the Bolshevik and Socialist Revolutionary Party should be considered invalid.

Two decrees dated 16 (29) and 18 (31) December swept aside the marriage and divorce laws. According to these decrees only civil marriage was to be recognized by the state; children born out of wedlock were to be given the same rights as the offspring of marriage; divorce was to be had for the asking by either spouse. The new laws emphasized the full equality of men and women.[28]

The complete separation of church from state and school from church was decreed by a law promulgated on 2 February 1918. Under this law every Soviet citizen was free to profess any or no religion; no religious ceremonies were to be performed in connection with any state function; religious teaching was forbidden in schools; churches and religious societies were denied the right to own property.[29]

Alongside decrees on subjects of major importance, one finds Lenin dealing with a vast quantity of regulations affecting details of local administration, such as the uniting of some suburbs with the town of Bogorodsk, the assignment of 450,000 rubles (a negligible sum at the time) for the needs of the population of Kremenchug County in Ukraine which had suffered a flood, and the appointment and dismissal of individual officials.[30]

He involved himself with the most trivial affairs. Thus in March 1918 he asks why the clerks in the Moscow post office are required to work such long hours.[31] Then comes a string of complaints at the arbitrary requisitioning of property. In July 1918, as the war clouds gather in the east, he writes to one Ivanov, in a village between Kazan and the Urals: 'It is alleged that you have requisitioned some writing materials, including a table, belonging to the stationmaster. Return these objects at once. Telegraph your explanations.'

History, unfortunately, does not record the fate of the stationmaster's table, nor that of the bicycle belonging to the pharmacist at Zhlobin, which calls for two letters from the solicitous

Lenin.[32] At the time Lenin had at his disposal only the most rudimentary secretarial organization, and his communications system was likewise primitive; he was forever complaining about his malfunctioning telephone.

The Soviet Government Fighting for Survival

The stream of legislation was a product of the immediate struggle of the new regime for survival. There is no doubt that the decrees on peace and land won the new government mass popularity. However, the pen of the legislator had to be accompanied by the sword of the soldier, and for days, weeks, months, even years, the fate of the new regime hung in the balance.

During the week following the seizure of power the Bolsheviks had to face an uprising of the cadets at the military school in Petrograd, and to defend the capital against the movement of troops which Kerensky was trying to organize, which got under way while the Second Congress of Soviets was still in session.

On 26 October (8 November) General P.N.Krasnov, Commander of the Third Cavalry Corps, which had participated in Kornilov's luckless adventure, started to march on Petrograd on Kerensky's orders. Next day his forces occupied Gatchina, 27 miles from Petrograd. The day after, early in the morning, Krasnov advanced on Tsarskoe Selo, 15 miles from the capital.

On 30 October (12 November) Krasnov's Cossacks met strong resistance from a Bolshevik-led unit of sailors on the Pulkovo Heights, just outside the city limits. The Bolsheviks achieved the first military victory in the civil war, and Krasnov was forced to retreat to Gatchina.

On 2 (15) November Bolshevik troops stormed Gatchina. Krasnov was arrested and brought to Smolny under guard. The revolution was still a mild one at this stage. Krasnov was soon released, after giving his word not to take arms against the government again. (He broke his promise, and made his way to the Don where the following spring he became leader of the Cossack White Army movement.)

But even with military victory assured in Petrograd, Bolshevik rule was still limited to a tiny area of Russia – taking power in Moscow was much more difficult. After the Bolshevik victory in

Petrograd on 25 October, it took another eight long days to achieve power in Moscow, by means of a very bloody battle. Before October, for various reasons, Moscow was more difficult to win over to Bolshevism than Petrograd. It was more isolated from the front, it did not have Petrograd's rebellious soldiers and sailors, it suffered much less from food shortages. The Moscow proletariat was dispersed among smaller factories compared with the huge plants in Petrograd.[88] In the years when Bolshevism became a mass workers' party (1912-1914) Moscow lagged far behind Petrograd. As late as October 1917, the Socialist Revolutionaries had a large following among the workers of Moscow, while their influence among the workers of Petrograd was practically non-existent.

The most brilliant Bolshevik leaders, including Lenin and Trotsky, were in Petrograd. The Moscow leadership was split (as indeed was that of Petrograd). Bukharin took the same line as Lenin and Trotsky, while Nogin and Rykov hesitated and vacillated. It was only on 25 October (7 November) that a Military Revolutionary Committee was established in Moscow, and this consisted at first of 4 Bolsheviks, 2 Mensheviks and 1 United Internationalist. The Mensheviks openly declared that they were joining the Military Revolutionary Committee in order to obstruct its work. (They soon withdrew from it.) Only on 26 October (8 November) did a conference of representatives of the garrison convene. Hesitations and delays cost the Moscow proletariat dear. While only five people died in Petrograd during the insurrection, many hundreds of soldiers and workers lost their lives in the struggle in the ancient capital of Moscow.

Moscow was the only place in central and northern Russia where the Bolshevik seizure of power met persistent and violent resistance. Elsewhere the course of the transfer of power to the Soviets varied from place to place depending on such factors as the proportion of industrial workers in the population, the mood of the local garrison and the strength of the local Bolshevik Party organization.

In the central industrial region and the Urals the Bolsheviks took control quickly and easily straight after the October insurrection in Petrograd. Thus in Ivanovo-Voznesensk, 'the Russian Manchester', the Bolsheviks achieved their objectives 'in the most painless manner ... without firing a single shot or shedding a single drop of blood'. The news of the Petrograd coup was announced to an enthusiastic meeting of the town's municipal council and the revolutionary council was established.[34]

At Cheliabinsk and Ekaterinburg and other cities the Bolsheviks took over almost without meeting any resistance.[35] In such middle and lower Volga towns as Nizhni Novgorod, Samara and Saratov, as well as those on the Trans-Siberian railway (Krasnoiarsk, Irkutsk), 'the October days ... took the form of a brief confrontation'.[36] In the north west, in White Russia, the troops were solidly Bolshevik and the transfer of power was very smooth indeed.

In non-industrial provincial centres, such as Penza and Simbirsk, the setting up of an unambiguously Bolshevik regime took place slowly and was only completed in December.

In the industrialized eastern and south eastern regions of the Ukraine, where the Russian population was quite large and Ukrainian nationalism had few roots, the Bolsheviks seized power quite easily. On 31 November (7 December), the Soviet of Kharkov, the largest city in eastern Ukraine, passed a resolution demanding an All-Ukrainian Congress of Soviets to be the repository of power. In the western part of the Ukraine, whose capital was Kiev, and where the industrial working class and Bolshevik organization were relatively weak and nationalism strong, power remained in the hands of the petty bourgeoisie of the Rada.

When at the Third Congress of Soviets (8 (21)-18 (31) January 1918) the Bolsheviks proclaimed the establishment of the Russian Federated Soviet Republic (RSFSR) they were actually in control of only a fragment, albeit a substantial fragment, of the former empire. They held the two capitals, the central and northern part of European Russia, and, more precariously, a few towns in Siberia and central Asia.

In the west the armies of the Central Powers occupied a vast area stretching from the Dniester to beyond the Gulf of Riga. Further north, in Finland, a bourgeois government was waging a bloody civil war against the revolt of the Social Democrats, who were aided by the Bolsheviks. In the south a newly formed nationalist bourgeois government of the Caucasus and the Trans-Volga regions was fighting the extension of Bolshevik power with varying degrees of success. In the south east the first White Guards, under the command of Kornilov, Kaledin, Alekseev and Denikin, moved into action on the Don; and the Cossacks of Orenburg rose under Ataman Dutov.

Fighting Sabotage

While the Bolsheviks had to deal with the external threat of General Krasnov's march on Petrograd, those inside the capital had to deal with another enemy no less dangerous – the saboteurs within. On 27 October (9 November) a general strike of all state employees was called in Petrograd, and almost all the officials and clerks of public institutions came out.

The employees of the Ministries of Agriculture, Labour, Posts and Telegraphs, Food, Finance and Foreign Affairs went on strike. So did the teachers. By 15 (28) December, more than 30,000 Petrograd teachers were on strike. They were joined by the workers in the public libraries and the People's Houses and by 50,000 bank clerks. These strikes confronted the new rulers with grave difficulties.

The telegraphists and telephonists also stopped work. Telegraphy was the only quick means of communication across the huge distances of Russia. These workers were very much under the influence of the Mensheviks and Socialist Revolutionaries. Most of the telegraphists refused to work for the Bolshevik intruders, so it was left to a group of sailors from Kronstadt to struggle with the apparatus in an attempt to inform the country about Lenin's first decrees on peace and land. They soon found that they could not cope with the tasks: some of the machinery and the supply of current had been sabotaged.

The Bolsheviks put up a large placard outside the telegraph office, explaining what had happened and asking for assistance. Eventually, after angry Bolshevik sympathizers from the factories had arrived and intimated the telegraphists, some of them returned to their posts.[87]

Similar difficulties were encountered at the telephone offices. According to John Reed, 'Smolny was cut off, and the Duma and the Committee for Salvation were in constant communication with all the *yunker* schools and with Kerensky at Tsarskee.[188] The Bolsheviks found it was very difficult to operate the telephone system.

> Only half a dozen trained operators were available. Volunteers were called for; a hundred responded, sailors, soldiers, workers. The six girls scurried backwards and forwards, instructing, helping, scolding . . . So, crippled, halting, but *going*, the wires began to hum. The first thing was to connect Smolny with the barracks and the factories; the second, to cut off the Duma and the *junker* schools.[39]

Another group of workers who threatened to sabotage Bolshevik rule was the one million railwaymen. The social composition of the railway employees was complex and hierarchical. At the top of the hierarchy were the civil service employees in the administrative headquarters of the railway networks, and the owners and managers of the private companies. Next came the engineers, planners, statisticians and the less important office workers. These two groups represented between 16 and 17 per cent of all those employed on the railways.[40]

The group which ran the railway union was the Vikzhel. Its composition was: 12 senior administrative staff, 10 engineers and technicians, 3 lawyers, 2 doctors, 3 office workers, 2 engine crew and 8 clerical staff and workers.

Thus Vikzhel's support came chiefly from the middle and higher ranks of the railway employees, who were influenced by the two main moderate socialist parties, the SRs and the Mensheviks. The Bolsheviks were an insignficant minority. The members included 2 Bolsheviks, 14 Socialist Revolutionaries, 7 Mensheviks, 3 Socialist-Populists and 11 non-party representatives, many of whom supported the Cadets.[41]*

The railwaymen, who had played a central role in crushing the Kornilov coup, now, after the October insurrection, presented the Bolsheviks with an ultimatum: unless they entered a coalition

---

* The main group of railwaymen supporting the Bolsheviks were those working in railway workshops and depots – who made up 35 per cent of all railwaymen – but they had opted out of the All-Russian Union by joining the more radical trade unions of the metal workers and joiners.[42]

with the Socialist Revolutionaries and Mensheviks the Vikzhel would launch a general strike, whose consequences could have been very grave indeed (as we shall see later).

It was only after 78 days (on 13 (26) January 1918) that the strike of public employees in Petrograd came to end. In Moscow the strike of the 16,000 municipal employees was to last four months.

The Beginning of Red Terror

The military cadets whom the Bolsheviks had released on parole from the Winter Palace on 26 October (8 November) betrayed their trust two days later and staged an uprising. Similarly mild treatment was shown to General Krasnov, which he also repaid with treason.

Lenin wrote on 5 (18) November:

> We are accused of resorting to terrorism, but we have not resorted, and I hope will not resort, to the terrorism of the French revolutionaries who guillotined unarmed men. I hope we shall not resort to it, because we have strength on our side. When we arrested anyone we told him we would let him go if he gave us a written promise not to engage in sabotage. Such written promises have been given.[43]

Victor Serge, in his *Year One of the Russian Revolution* wrote of the events in Moscow:

> The Whites surrendered at 4 p.m. on 2 [15] November. 'The Committee of Public Safety is dissolved. The White Guard surrenders its arms and is disbanded. The officers may keep the sidearms that distinguish their rank. Only such weapons as are necessary for practice may be kept in the military academies ... The MRC [Military Revolutionary Committee] guarantees the liberty and inviolability of all.' Such were the principal clauses of the armistice signed between Reds and Whites. The fighters of the counter-revolution, butchers of the Kremlin, who in victory would have shown no quarter whatever to the Reds – we have seen proof – went free.

And Serge comments:

> Foolish clemency! These very Junkers, these officers, these students, these socialists of counter-revolution, dispersed themselves throughout the length and breadth of Russia, and there organ-

ized the civil war. The revolution was to meet them again, at Iaroslavl, on the Don, at Kazan, in the Crimea, in Siberia and in every conspiracy nearer home.[44]

These were the early days of revolutionary innocence. But Lenin was not a pacifist. The morning after the October insurrection, on Kamenev's initiative and in Lenin's absence, the death penalty was abolished. When he learned about this first piece of legislation, Lenin was very angry. 'How can one make a revolution without firing squads? Do you think you will be able to deal with all your enemies by laying down your arms? What other means of repression do you have? Imprisonment? No one attaches any importance to this during a civil war when each side hopes to win.'

'It is a mistake,' he went on, 'an inadmissible weakness, a pacifist illusion', and much more. 'Do you really think that we shall come out victorious without any revolutionary terror?'[45]

At the Fifth Congress of Soviets (July 1918) he repeated the point: 'a revolutionary who does not want to be a hypocrite cannot renounce capital punishment. There has never been a revolution or a period of civil war without shootings.'[46]

To organize the struggle against counter-revolution, on 7 (20) December 1917 Sovnarkom established the Cheka, the All-Russian Extraordinary Commission to fight Counter-revolution and Sabotage. At first its staff was small, its resources very limited, and the few death sentences it passed were on common criminals. M.I.Latsis, member of the Cheka in 1918, states that during the first six months of its existence, the Cheka had 22 people shot.[47]

The revolutionary terror in Russia, like its predecessor in France during *its* great revolution, was a reaction to foreign invasion and the immensity of the threat to the revolution. The Paris terror of 2 September 1793 followed the Duke of Brunswick's proclamation threatening foreign invasion and ruthless repression of the revolution.

It was foreign invasion, starting with the victories of the Czechoslovak troops over the Red Army in June 1918, that threatened the greatest danger to the Soviet republic. On 20 June the popular Bolshevik orator, Volodarsky, was assassinated by counter-revolutionaries. On 30 August an attempt was made on Lenin's life. He was badly wounded and for a few days was in a critical condition. Another Bolshevik leader, Uritsky, the President of the Petrograd Cheka, was murdered. The Red terror was unleashed in retaliation. On 2 September 500 hostages were shot in Petrograd. Whereas between September 1917 and June 1918 the Cheka had executed 22 people, in the second half of 1918 more than 6,000 executions took place.[48] September 1918, writes E. H. Carr, 'marked the turning-point after which the terror, hitherto sporadic and unorganized, became a deliberate instrument of policy.'[49]

Compared with the White terror, however, the Red terror was mild. Thus in Finland alone, in April 1918 between 10 and 20,000 workers were slaughtered by the counter-revolutionaries.[50] With complete justification Lenin told the Seventh Congress of Soviets on 5 December 1919:

> The terror was forced on us by the terror of the Entente, the terror of mighty world capitalism which has been throttling the workers and peasants, and is condemning them to death by starvation because they are fighting for their country's freedom.[51]

One should not exaggerate the effectiveness of the Cheka and the Red terror during the civil war. The following incident illustrates this. On 19 January 1919, Lenin was in a car with his sister Maria, driven by his chauffeur, S.K.Gil, who tells the story. The car was moving slowly through the snow, when they heard a shout, 'Stop'. Gil accelerated. A few blocks further on, several men were standing in the middle of the road with revolvers in their hands, and shouted, 'Halt!' Gil, seeing this was not a patrol, drove straight at them. 'Stop, or we shoot,' one of the men yelled. Gil wanted to speed past, but Lenin told him to stop.

'Halt! Stop the car!' the men ordered.

Lenin opened the door and said, 'What's the matter?'

'Get out, shut up,' came the reply.

He grabbed Lenin by his sleeve and pulled him out. Lenin showed his pass, with photograph and name and said, 'What's the matter comrades? Who are you?'

One of the armed men searched Lenin's pocket and took his wallet and a small Browning. Maria exclaimed, 'What right have you to search him? Why, he is Comrade Lenin. Show your papers!'

'We don't need papers,' somebody replied, 'We can do anything.'

Gil, who had remained at the wheel, with his revolver cocked, did not dare use it.

The hold-up group now asked Gil to leave the car. When he obeyed, they all got in and drove off.

Nearby stood the building of the Sokolniky Soviet. They walked over to phone the Kremlin for a car. But the watchman would not let them in. He asked Lenin for his pass.

'I am Lenin,' Lenin said, 'but I cannot prove it. I have just been robbed of my pass.'

The watchman looked sceptical. Gil showed his identification, which served for all of them. Inside they found nobody. In a small room they awakened a sleeping telephone operator, who rang the Kremlin. A car came.[52]

Relying on the Initiative of the Masses

The enormous legislative activity associated with the urgent task of self-defence against counter-revolution, and the creation of effective armed forces and an organ of revolutionary terror in the midst of total chaos, were possible only because Lenin and the Bolshevik leaders knew that their actions merged completely with those of the masses in shaping a new historical epoch.

'Miracles of proletarian organization must be achieved.' This idea of Lenin's was central to the actions of the Government, the party and the proletariat. The initiative of the masses was the most important factor. Lenin wrote:

> One of the most important tasks today, if not the most important, is to develop this independent initiative of the workers, and of all the working and exploited people generally, develop it as widely as possibly in creative *organizational* work . . . There is a great deal of talent among the people. It is merely suppressed. It must be given an opportunity to display itself. It *and it alone*, with the support of the people, can save Russia and save the cause of socialism.[53]

'We must be guided by experience; we must allow complete freedom to the creative faculties of the masses', Lenin declared to the Second Congress of the Soviets the day after the October revolution.[54] 'Creative activity at the grass roots is the basic factor of the new public life . . . living, creative socialism is the product of the masses themselves.'[55] One should not worry at all about mistakes. The mistakes of the masses were in themselves creative. 'Let there be mistakes—they would be the mistakes of a new class creating a new way of life . . . There was not and could not be a definite plan for the organization of economic life. Nobody could provide one. But it could be done from below, by the masses, through their experience.'[56] The building of a new society, Lenin declared at the Third Congress of Soviets on 11 (24) January 1918,

> will entail many difficulties, sacrifices and mistakes; it is something new, unprecedented in history and cannot be studied from books. It goes without saying that this is the greatest and most difficult transition that has ever occurred in history.[57]
> . . . socialism . . . for the first time creates the opportunity for employing it on a really *wide* and on a really *mass* scale, for actually drawing the majority of working people into a field of labour in which they can display their abilities, develop the capacities, and reveal those talents, so abundant among the people whom capitalism crushed, suppressed and strangled in thousands and millions.[58]

Above all Lenin made it clear that the strength of a workers' state is rooted in the strength of the proletariat. 'Our idea is that a state is strong when the people are politically conscious. It is strong when the people know everything, can form an opinion of everything and do everything consciously,' Lenin said to the Second Congress of Soviets, summing up the debate on the Decree on Peace.

The Close Relationship of the Leaders and the Mass of Workers

The closeness of the relationship between the masses and the leadership is well conveyed in a scene described by John Reed. Trotsky was reporting to the Petrograd Soviet on the progress of the fighting:

> 'The cruisers, *Oleg*, *Avrora* and *Respublika* are anchored in the Neva, their guns trained on the approaches to the city . . .'

'Why aren't you out there with the Red Guards?' shouted a rough voice.
'I'm going now!' answered Trotsky, and left the platform.[59]

Another scene illustrates how the leaders had to accommodate the feelings of the masses: V.A.Antonov-Ovsenko, Joint People's Commissar of War and Navy, needed a car to go and inspect the revolutionary front on 28 October (10 November) 1917.

Antonov stood in the middle of the street and signalled a passing machine, driven by a soldier.
'I want that machine,' said Antonov.
'You won't get it,' responded the soldier.
'Do you know who I am?' Antonov produced a paper upon which was written that he had been appointed Commander-in-Chief of all the armies of the Russian Republic, and that everyone should obey him without question.
'I don't care if you're the devil himself,' said the soldier, hotly. 'This machine belongs to the First Machine-Gun Regiment, and we're carrying ammunition in it, and you can't have it.'[60]

2
The Consolidation of Power

At the Congress of Soviets on 29 October (11 November), the representative of the All-Russian Executive Committee of the Union of Railway Workers (Vikzhel), which contained a majority of Mensheviks and Socialist Revolutionaries, declared its opposition to the seizure of power by the Bolsheviks; he demanded a government composed of all socialist parties; declared Vikzhel's intention to keep control of the railways, and threatened that if a coalition government were not constituted it would call a general strike throughout the country.

At this critical moment a number of leading comrades in his own party ranged themselves against Lenin, demanding that the Bolsheviks should relinquish power to a coalition of all socialist parties. Before the October insurrection, the leaders of the right wing of Bolshevism (Zinoviev, Kamenev, Rykov, Nogin, Lunacharsky) had argued that the uprising was premature and would meet defeat. After the victorious insurrection they argued that the Bolsheviks would not be able to retain power unless they entered a coalition with the Mensheviks and Socialist Revolutionaries.

At the insistence of the Right Bolsheviks, negotiations were begun with these parties immediately after the insurrection. The parties overthrown by the October insurrection demanded a majority for themselves, and the exclusion from power of Lenin and Trotsky, as those responsible for the October 'adventure'. These conditions amounted to a demand for the Bolsheviks to declare the October revolution null and void, and to excommunicate the inspirer and the organizer of the insurrection. The Right Bolshevik leaders were inclined to accept these demands.

Lenin did not oppose the negotiations with the Mensheviks and Socialist Revolutionaries, on condition that the Bolsheviks were assured a stable majority, and that these parties recognized the Soviet state, the peace decree, the land decree, and so on. He was convinced that nothing would come of the negotiations, and that they could serve as an important lesson for those who had illusions about the soft option of a coalition government.

At a meeting of the Central Committee of the Bolsheviks, from which Lenin and Trotsky were absent, it was decided unanimously 'that the base of the government has to be widened and that some changes in its composition are possible'.

The question of whether to accept the Vikzhel's ultimatum – including the exclusion of Lenin and Trotsky from the government – was put to the vote. Four voted for: Kamenev, Miliutin, Rykov and Sokolnikov; and seven against: Ioffe, Dzerzhinsky, Vinter, A.Kollontai, Ia.Sverdlov, A.Bubnov, M.Uritsky.[1] The Committee then elected a delegation to attend the conference called by Vikzhel; significantly this consisted of three right-wing Bolsheviks: Kamenev, Sokolnikov and Riazanov.

On 1 (14) November the Bolshevik representative at the negotiations reported that the negotiations were going to a conference of the Central Committee, the Petrograd Committee and representatives of the military organization and the trade unions. Kamenev reported the demand of the Mensheviks, Socialist Revolutionaries and Vikzhel that the Central Executive Committee of the Soviets (TsIK) should be enlarged by the addition of a strong contingent of bourgeois representatives (the municipal councils [dumas] of Petrograd and Moscow), a demand which called into question the Soviet character of the new regime. The other condition, noted above, was the exclusion of Lenin and Trotsky from membership of the government.

> The Central Committee split wide open. Trotsky declared:
> 'One thing is clear from the report, and that is that the parties which took no part in the insurrection want to grab power from the people who overthrew them. There was no point in organizing the insurrection if we do not get the majority; if the others do not want that, it is obvious they do not want our programme. We must have 75 per cent. It is clear that we cannot give a right of objection, just as we cannot yield on Lenin's chairmanship; such a concession is completely unacceptable.'

Dzerzhinsky asserted that 'the delegates did not observe the CC's instructions. The CC definitely decided that the government must be responsible to the TsIK . . . We also stated definitely that we would not allow objections to Lenin and Trotsky. None of this was implemented and I propose an expression of no confidence in the delegation and that they be recalled and others sent.' The same hard line was taken by Uritsky. He considered that 'the CC has taken a firm stand on the position of all power to the Soviets and that means there can be no question of supplementation.'

He objected:

> to representation from the Dumas and considers that a majority of Bolsheviks in the TsIK is obligatory. This must be established conclusively. The same for ministerial posts; we must have a solid majority . . . there is no doubt that we must not yield on either Lenin or Trotsky, for in a certain sense this would be renunciation of our programme; there is no need to insist on the others.

Lenin then stated:

> it is time to make an end of vacillation. It is clear that Vikzhel is on the side of the Kaledins and the Kornilovs. There can be no wavering. The majority of the workers, peasants and army are for us. No one here has proved that the rank and file are against us; choose between Kaledin's agents and the rank and file. We must rely on the masses, and send agitators into the villages.

The right-wingers on the Central Committee, however, were unyielding in their fight for a coalition. Rykov declared: '... there is a gap between us ... If we break off [the negotiations] we will lose the groups which are supporting us as well and we will be in no position to keep power. Kamenev conducted the talks absolutely correctly.'

Miliutin raised 'the question of whether we are going to insist on keeping power exclusively in our own hands ... if we do not get carried away ... it will become clear to us that we cannot sustain a long civil war.' Riazanov stated that he

> went in to these talks as a way out of the position we involuntarily find ourselves in. Even in Peter, power is not in our hands but in the hands of the Soviet, and this has to be faced. If we abandon this course, we will be utterly and hopelessly alone. We made a mistake when we headed the government and insisted on names; if we had not done this, the middle levels of the bureaucracy would have supported us ... If we reject agreement today, we will be without the Left SRs, without anything ... an agreement is unavoidable.

After heated discussion the question, whether to break off the talks or not, was put to the vote. The result was: for breaking off 4; against 10. The intransigent Lenin, Trotsky and Sverdlov found themselves in a minority,[2] and the Bolshevik delegates continued their efforts to form a coalition government.

On the same day as this debate in the enlarged Central Committee meeting, a debate on the same subject took place in the Petersburg Committee of the party. Here again Lenin did not mince his words:

> now, at such a moment, when we are in power, we are faced with a split. Zinoviev and Kamenev say that we will not seize power [in the country as a whole]. I am in no mood to listen to this calmly. I view this as treason ... Zinoviev says that we are

not the Soviet power. We are, if you please, only the Bolsheviks, left alone since the departure of the Socialist Revolutionaries and the Mensheviks, and so forth and so on. But we are not responsible for that. We have been elected by the Congress of the Soviets . . .

As for conciliation, I cannot even speak about that seriously, Trotsky long ago said that unification is impossible. Trotsky understood this, and from that time on there has been no better Bolshevik.

They [Zinoviev, Kamenev and co.] say that we will be unable to maintain our power alone, and so on. But we are not alone. The whole of Europe is before us. We must make the beginning.

Lenin went on to say, 'Our present slogan is: No compromise, i.e. for a homogeneous Bolshevik government.' He did not hesitate to use the threat, which he meant seriously, to 'appeal to the sailors': 'If you get the majority, take power in the Central Executive Committee and carry on. But we will go to the sailors.'

Opposing Lenin's views, Lunacharsky argued that a coalition government was a necessity. He pointed to the sabotage caried out by technical personnel as proof of the need for the Bolsheviks to join a coalition. 'We cannot manage with our own forces. Famine will break out.'

Similar arguments were used by Nogin. 'The Socialist Revolutionaries left the Soviets after the revolution; the Mensheviks did likewise. But this means that the Soviets will fall apart. Such a state of affairs in the face of complete chaos in the country will end with the shipwreck of our party in a very brief interval.'

Trotsky came out strongly in support of Lenin's point of view: against conciliation, against a coalition government with the Mensheviks and Socialist Revolutionaries.

We have had rather profound differences in our party prior to the insurrection, within the Central Committee as well as in the broad party circles. The same things were said, the same expressions used then as now in arguing against the insurrection as hopeless. The old arguments are now being repeated after the victorious insurrection, this time in favour of a coalition. There will be no technical apparatus, mind you. You lay the colours on thick in order to frighten, in order to hinder the proletariat from utilizing its victory . . .

The bourgeoisie is aligned against us by virtue of all its class interests. And what will we achieve against that by taking to the road of conciliation with Vikzhel? . . . We are confronted with armed violence which can be overcome only by means of violence on our own part . . .

The sum total of what the Chernovs can contribute to our work is: vacillation. But vacillation in the struggle against our enemies will destroy our authority among the masses. What does conciliation with Chernov mean? . . . It means an alignment with Chernov. This would be treason.[3]

The Right Bolshevik leaders displayed their differences with Lenin to the outside world. In the Central Executive Committee of the Soviets, Kamenev, the chairman of this body, proposed that the Council of People's Commissars should resign and be replaced by a coalition government. He was supported by Nogin, a member of the Central Committee of the party and People's Commissar for Industry and Commerce; Rykov, also a member of the Central Committee and People's Commissar for Internal Affairs; Miliutin, Member of the Central Committee and People's Commissar for Agriculture; and Teodorovich, People's Commissar for Food, as well as by Zinoviev. The Bolshevik conciliators, together with non-Bolshevik members of VTsIK, voted against their own party. This produced a serious crisis in both government and party. The rule that party members in office should follow party instructions was openly flouted.

Lenin was so angry that next day, on 2 (15) November, he moved a resolution at the Central Committee decisively denouncing a coalition government. He achieved a majority for his position only after a long and bitter debate. His resolution was put to the vote a number of times. In the first vote there were 6 for Lenin's motion and 6 against; the second gave 7 for and 7 against; in a third Lenin emerged as the victor by one vote: 8 for, 7 against.[4]

The next day he got the majority of the Central Committee to issue an ultimatum to the Rightists: 'we demand a categorical reply in writing to the question: does the minority undertake to submit to party discipline . . . If the reply to this question is in the negative or is indeterminate, we will make an immediate appeal to the Moscow Committee, the Bolshevik group in the TsIK, the Petrograd City Conference and to a special party congress.'

If the opposition were not ready to abide by majority decision, let them leave the party. 'A split would be a very regrettable fact, of course. But an honest and open split now is incomparably better than internal sabotage, the blocking of our own decisions, disorganization and prostration.'

Unrepentant, the opposition reiterated its stand, and declared its decision to resign from the Central Committee. On 4 (17) November a statement by Kamenev, Rykov, Zinoviev and Nogin declared:

> We consider that a government [of all Socialist parties] has to be created to avoid further bloodshed and impending starvation, to prevent Kaledin's men destroying the revolution . . . We cannot take responsibility for [the] fatal policy of the CC, pursued contrary to the will of a vast proportion of the proletariat and soldiers, who gave a speedy end to the bloodshed between the different sections of the democracy.
>
> For that reason we relinquish the title of members of the CC so that we can have the right to state our view frankly to the masses of the workers and soldiers and appeal to them to support our call.[5]

The same day four People's Commissars – Nogin, Rykov, Miliutin and Teodorovich – resigned from the government, and Shliapnikov, People's Commissar for Labour, declared his political solidarity with them, but did not resign.

However, when it became clear that Lenin and his close colleagues would not vacillate, the opposition collapsed. On 7 (20) November, Zinoviev capitulated and asked to be taken back on to the party's Central Committee. In words foreshadowing his future more tragic surrenders, Zinoviev appealed to his friends:

> we remain attached to the party, we prefer to make mistakes together with millions of workers and soldiers and to die together with them than to step to one side at this decisive, historic moment.[6]

Three weeks later, on 30 November (12 December) similar statements were issued by Rykov, Kamenev, Miliutin and Nogin. Thus a very threatening split in the party at a critical moment of history was averted.

The logic of the class struggle was far too strong to be

blocked by the conciliatory attitude of the right-wing Bolsheviks. Not only did Lenin oppose them, but the Menshevik and Socialist Revolutionary leaders pulled the carpet from beneath them, by putting forward demands more appropriate for victors rather than for the vanquished. On 29 October (11 November),

> the SRs and Mensheviks had amplified their position by demanding, (1) that the Red or Workers' Guard be disarmed, (2) that the garrison be placed under orders of the city council, and (3) that an armistice be declared, offering for their part to secure a pledge that the troops of Kerensky on entering the city would not fire a shot or engage in search and seizure. A socialist government would then be constituted, but without Bolshevik participation.[7]

At the Vikzhel conference on 1 (14) November,

> The Mensheviks said that one should talk to the Bolsheviks with guns . . . and the Central Committee of the Socialist-Revolutionaries was against an agreement with the Bolsheviks.[8]

One positive outcome of the negotiations was that the Left Socialist Revolutionaries, resentful of the attitude of the Mensheviks and Right Socialist Revolutionaries, decided to join Lenin's party in the government.

3
The Dissolution of the Constituent Assembly

After resolving the crisis in the Bolshevik leadership over coalition with the Mensheviks and the Right Socialist Revolutionaries, the regime had to face a new problem. The Bolsheviks had to decide whether elections to a Constituent Assembly should be allowed. If the result of such elections was to create a body whose composition was radically different from that of the Soviet, what could be done about it?

The demand for the convocation of a Constituent Assembly had been one of the main planks of the programme of the Russian Social Democratic Labour Party since its foundation. Since 1905 Lenin had repeatedly referred to this demand as 'one of the three pillars of Bolshevism'. (The other two were the nationalization of land and the 8-hour day.) This slogan was put forward even more immediately and urgently between the February and October revolutions. The Bolsheviks pressed constantly for a Constituent Assembly to be called and the delay in doing so was one of the many charges they laid at the door of the provisional government. Again and again between April and October Lenin reiterated that the Bolsheviks, and only the Bolsheviks, would ensure its convocation without delay. They were fighting at the time simultaneously for power for the Soviets and the convening of the Constituent Assembly. They asserted that unless the Soviets took power the Constituent Assembly would not be convened.

In early April 1917 Lenin set out the Bolshevik attitude to the question of whether the Constituent Assembly should be convened. 'Yes,' he said, 'as soon as possible. But there is only one way to assure its convocation and success, and that is by increasing the number and *strength* of the Soviets and organizing and *arming* the working-class masses. That is the only guarantee.'[1]

On 12-14 (25-27) September he wrote: 'Our party alone, on taking power, can secure the Constituent Assembly's convocation; it will then accuse the other parties of procrastination and will be able to substantiate its accusations.'[2]

On 24 September (7 October) the Bolshevik daily *Rabochii Put* accused the Cadets of 'secret postponement and sabotage of the Constituent Assembly'.[3]

For many months the Bolsheviks had posed the question not of Soviets *or* Constituent Assembly, but of Soviets *and* Constituent Assembly. In a fiery speech at the Kerensky-convened State Council on 7 (20) October Trotsky, leading the Bolshevik fraction out of the meeting, said in conclusion: 'Long live an immediate, honest, democratic peace. All power to the Soviets. All land to the people. Long live the Constituent Assembly.'[4]

On 29 November (12 December) Bukharin, using precedents from English and French history, proposed that once the Constituent Assembly was convoked the Cadets should be expelled from it, and that the Assembly should declare itself a revolutionary convention. Bukharin hoped that in the Assembly the Bolsheviks and Left Socialist Revolutionaries would command an overwhelming majority, which would give the truncated Assembly legitimacy. Trotsky supported Bukharin's plan of action. Stalin argued that Bukharin's tactic would not work. No-one suggested the dispersal of the Constituent Assembly.

The fact is that the Bolsheviks, who campaigned strongly for the convocation of the Constituent Assembly, were completely unprepared for a conflict between the Assembly and the Soviets. At the same time they were quite clear that the future masters of Russia would be the Soviets, the revolutionary organizations of the proletariat and peasantry. If they did not consider the possibility of conflict between the Constituent Assembly and the Soviet, it was because then it was the provisional government which stood in opposition to both the Soviets and the Constituent Assembly.

Immediately after the October insurrection, Lenin was clearly worried about the results of elections to the Constituent Assembly and wanted them to be postponed, the voting age to be lowered to 18 years, the electoral list revised, and the Cadets and Kornilov supporters outlawed. Other Bolshevik leaders said that postponement was unacceptable, especially since the Bolsheviks had often reproached the provisional government with this very crime.

> 'Nonsense!' objected Lenin. 'Deeds are important, not words. In relation to the provisional government the Constituent Assembly represented, or might have represented, progress; in relation to the regime of the Soviets, and with the existing electoral lists, it will inevitably mean retrogression. Why is it inconvenient to postpone it? Will it be convenient if the Constituent Assembly turns out to be composed of a Cadet-Menshevik-Socialist Revolutionary alliance? . . .
> Sverdlov, who more than others was connected with the provinces, protested vehemently against the adjournment.
> Lenin stood alone. He kept on shaking his head, dissatisfied, and went on repeating:

'You are wrong; it's clearly a mistake which can prove very costly. Let us hope that the revolution will not have to pay for it with its life.'[5]

In the event, the Bolsheviks permitted the election to be held.

The Results of the Elections

The elections took place over a period of a few weeks. One study gives the following results:

The vote by parties for the whole country

Socialist Revolutionaries	15,848,004
Ukrainian Socialist Revolutionaries	1,286,157
Mensheviks	1,364,826
Cadets	1,986,601
Bolsheviks	9,844,637
Others	11,356,651
Total	41,686,876[6]

For the seats in the Constituent Assembly, the archives of the October Revolution have assembled a list of 707 deputies, divided into the following groupings:

Socialist Revolutionaries	370
Left Socialist Revolutionaries	40
Bolsheviks	175
Mensheviks	16
Popular Socialists	2
Cadets	17
National groups	86
Unknown	1[7]

The Socialist Revolutionaries achieved a clear majority, both of the popular vote and of the seats in the Assembly. While the Bolshevik vote was about a quarter of the total, in some key areas they predominated. In the two capitals, the Bolshevik vote was four times larger than that of the Socialist Revolutionaries, and nearly 16 times larger than that of the Mensheviks.

What about the troops?

If the districts were remote from the metropolitan centers, and specifically from the influence of the Petrograd Soviet and the Bolshevik party organization, the SRs carried the day, and the farther removed the district was, the greater their degree of success; but on the Northern and Western Fronts the old-line agrarian appeal of the Socialist Revolutionary Party had been overbalanced by intensive propaganda in favour of immediate peace and immediate seizure of the estates, so that here the SRs sustained a crushing defeat and Lenin's party won a great victory. The contrast is seen in the accompanying tabulation:

	Western Front	Rumanian Front
Bolsheviks	653,430	167,000
Socialist Revolutionaries	180,582	679,471
Mensheviks	8,000	33,858
Ukrainian Socialist Bloc	85,062	180,576
Cadets	16,750	21,438
Residue	32,176	46,257
Total	976,000	1,128,600[8]

If we take the northern and western fronts, the vote polled by the Bolsheviks amounted to over a million, compared with 420,000 votes polled by the Socialist Revolutionaries. However, the strength of Bolshevism waned steadily as the influence of the metropolitan centres receded. Not only the Socialist Revolutionaries, but also the Mensheviks, were helped by distance: thus on the western front Menshevism was already virtually extinct by the time of the election, whereas on the Rumanian front it still retained a following, albeit a modest one.[9]*

'The conclusion is inescapable, that only time was needed to make the more remote fronts resemble the Petersburg garrison,' writes Radkey, historian of the Socialist Revolutionary Party.[10]

Summing up the general position in the country, Radkey writes:

The Bolsheviks had the center of the country – the big cities, the industrial towns, and the garrisons of the rear; they controlled those sections of the navy most strategically located with reference to Moscow and Petrograd; they even commanded a strong following among the peasants of the central, White Russian, and northwestern regions. The Socialist Revolutionaries had

---

* The same is true of the navy. The Bolsheviks overwhelmed the Socialist Revolutionaries three to one in the Baltic fleet, only to succumb by a margin of two to one in the Black Sea fleet.

the black-earth zone, the valley of the Volga, and Siberia; in general they were still the peasants' party, though serious defections had taken place. Particularist or separatist movements had strength in the Ukraine, along the Baltic, between the Volga and the Urals, and in the Transcaucasus; of these movements by all odds the most robust was Ukrainian nationalism. Menshevism was a spent force everywhere save in the Transcaucasus, where it was entwined with Georgian nationalism.[11]

The Bolsheviks Decide
to Disperse the Constituent Assembly

So, contrary to Bolshevik expectations, the Right Socialist Revolutionaries dominated the Constituent Assembly. Lenin used a number of arguments to explain this. First, the elections were held under an obsolete law that gave undue weight to the Rights among the Socialist Revolutionary candidates:

> as is well known, the party which from May to October had the largest number of followers among the people, and especially among the peasants – the Socialist Revolutionary Party – produced united election lists for the Constituent Assembly in the middle of October 1917, but split in November 1917, after the elections and before the Assembly met.
>
> For this reason, there is not, nor can there be, even a formal correspondence between the will of the mass of the electors and the composition of the elected Constituent Assembly.[12]

Radkey, who was far from being partial to the Bolsheviks, confirms this evaluation of Lenin's.[13]

However, the main reason for the conflict between the Assembly and the Soviets was more fundamental. The catchment area covered by the Constituent Assembly was far wider than that of the Soviet. While the Second Congress of Soviets represented about twenty million people, the number of votes for the Constituent Assembly was more than forty million. The Bolsheviks, together with the Left Socialist Revolutionaries, represented the overwhelming majority of the urban proletariat, the peasantry in the neighbourhood of the industrial centres, and the troops in the north and northwest. These were the most energetic and enlightened elements of the masses, on whose active support the revolution depended for survival. The Socialist Revolutionaries who dominated the Constituent Assembly represented the political confusion and indecision of the petty bourgeoisie in the towns and the millions of peasants relatively distant from the capital and the industrial centres.

To consider the Constituent Assembly in isolation from the class struggle was impossible. The interests of the revolution had to take precedence over the formal rights of the Constituent Assembly. At the Second Congress of Russian Social Democracy, Plekhanov had already answered in the affirmative the question he himself posed: whether the proletariat, on coming to power, would be justified in suppressing democratic rights.[14]

The Constituent Assembly met on 5 (18) January 1918. Sverdlov, in the name of VTsIK read a 'Declaration of the Rights of the Toiling and Exploited People' written by Lenin. It summed up the main decrees of the Soviet government: all power to the Soviets, the decree on land, the decree on peace, workers' control over production. Sverdlov's proposal that the Assembly should endorse the declaration was rejected by 237 votes to 136. This sealed the fate of the Assembly. After one day of existence it was dissolved.

Unlike the disagreement among the Bolshevik leadership on the question of coalition government, the decision to dissolve the Constituent Assembly led to little dissension in the party. There were, however, some difficulties.

On 13 (26) December, *Pravda* published Lenin's 'Theses on the Constituent Assembly', in which final form was given to the Bolshevik tactics. Starting from the principle that 'revolutionary Social Democracy has repeatedly emphasized, ever since the beginning of the Revolution of 1917, that a republic of Soviets is a higher form of democracy than the usual bourgeois republic with a Constituent Assembly', Lenin argued that the election returns did not correspond with the actual will of the people. Since the October revolution the masses had moved further to the left, a change not reflected in the Assembly. The civil war then beginning had 'finally brought the class struggle to a head, and destroyed every chance of settling in a formally democratic way the very acute problems with which history has confronted the people of Russia'. If therefore, the Constituent Assembly would not declare that 'it unreservedly recognizes Soviet power, the

Soviet revolution, and its policy on the question of peace, the land and workers' control', then 'the crisis in connection with the Constituent Assembly can be settled only in a revolutionary way, by Soviet power adopting the most energetic, speedy, firm and determined revolutionary measures.'[15]

Lenin used two arguments to justify the dispersal of the Constituent Assembly. The basic one was that the Constituent Assembly was a bourgeois parliament and had become the rallying point for the forces of counter-revolution; the second, that for a number of contingent reasons (the split within the SRs, the timing of the elections, etc.) the composition of the Constituent Assembly did not adequately reflect the actual balance of forces within the country.

Ballots and Bullets

In our times there is not a single issue which can be decided by ballots. In the decisive class battles bullets will prevail. The capitalists count the machine guns, the bayonets, the grenades at their disposal, and so does the proletariat. Lenin expressed this very clearly in his article 'The Constituent Assembly Elections and the Dictatorship of the Proletariat'. While in terms of voting power the countryside outweighed the towns, in real social, political power, the towns were far superior. 'The country cannot be equal to the town under the historical conditions of this epoch. The town inevitably *leads* the country. The country inevitably *follows the town*.' Controlling the capitals gave the Bolsheviks a great 'striking power':

> An overwhelming superiority of forces at the decisive point at the decisive moment – this 'law' of military success is also the law of political success, especially in that fierce, seething class war which is called revolution. Capitals, or, in general, big commercial and industrial centres (here in Russia the two coincided, but they do not everywhere coincide), to a considerable degree decide the political fate of a nation, provided, of course, the centres are supported by sufficient local, rural forces, even if that support does not come immediately.[16]

The Bolsheviks had '(1) an overwhelming majority among the proletariat; (2) almost half of the armed forces; (3) an overwhelming superiority of forces at the decisive moment at the decisive points, namely: in Petrograd and Moscow and on the war fronts near the centre.'

Not only could elections not replace force in achieving the dictatorship of the proletariat, but this dictatorship itself must be 'an instrument for winning the masses from the bourgeoisie and from the petty bourgeois parties'.[17]

Lenin poured ridicule on the reformist leaders who argued

> the proletariat must first win a majority by means of universal suffrage, then obtain state power, by the vote of that majority, and only after that, on the basis of 'consistent' (some call it 'pure') democracy, organize socialism. But we say on the basis of the teachings of Marx and the experience of the Russian revolution:
> the proletariat must first overthrow the bourgeoisie and win *for itself* state power, and then use that state power, that is, the dictatorship of the proletariat, as an instrument of its class for the purpose of winning the sympathy of the majority of the working people.[18]

> The petty-bourgeois democrats . . . are suffering from illusions when they imagine that the working people are capable, under capitalism, of acquiring the high degree of class-consciousness, firmness of character, perception and wide political outlook that will enable them to decide, *merely by* voting, or at all events, to *decide in advance*, without long experience of struggle, that they will follow a particular class, or a particular party . . .
> Capitalism would not be capitalism if it did not, on the one hand, condemn the *masses* to a downtrodden, crushed and terrified state of existence, to disunity (the countryside!) and ignorance, and if it (capitalism) did not, on the other hand, place in the hands of the bourgeoisie a gigantic apparatus of falsehood and deception to hoodwink the masses of workers and peasants, to stultify their minds, and so forth.[19]

From Constituent Assembly to Civil War

Under the banner of the Constituent Assembly reaction assembled its forces. Long before, Engels had explained the role of 'pure democracy' in a letter to Bebel (11 December 1884) on 'pure democracy'.

pure democracy . . . when the moment of revolution comes, acquires a temporary importance . . . as the final sheet-anchor of the whole bourgeois and even feudal economy . . . Thus between March and September 1848 the whole feudal-bureaucratic mass strengthened the liberals in order to hold down the revolutionary masses . . . In any case our sole adversary on the day of the crisis and on the day after the crisis will be the whole of the reaction which will group around pure democracy, and this, I think, should not be lost sight of.[20]

And Marx elaborated: 'from the first moment of victory, and after it, the distrust of the workers must not be directed any more against the conquered reactionary party, but against the previous ally, the petty bourgeois democrats, who desire to exploit the common victory only for themselves.'[21]

Throughout the years of the civil war in Russia (1918-1920), the slogan of the Constituent Assembly served as a screen for the dictatorship of the landowners and capitalists. Admiral Kolchak's banner was that of the Constituent Assembly, carried for him by the Socialist Revolutionaries (until he suppressed them). The South-eastern Committee of the Members of the Constituent Assembly, overwhelmingly Socialist Revolutionary in composition, called for recruits to the Volunteer Army of Generals Denikin and Alekseev. At Archangel, in Siberia, on the Volga, Socialist Revolutionary leaders raised the banner of the Constituent Assembly, under which recruits could be mobilized for the White Armies.

4

The Peace of Brest-Litovsk

One of the first problems for the newly established Bolshevik Government was the issue of war or peace with Germany.

For a number of years Lenin argued that if the proletariat came to power in Russia it would have to launch a revolutionary war against the imperialist powers. Thus in an article published on 13 (26) October 1915, he wrote that, if the revolution put the proletariat in power in Russia, it would immediately offer peace to all the belligerents on condition that all oppressed nations be freed. Of course no capitalist government would accept these terms. 'In that case, we would have to prepare for and wage a revolutionary war.' And, 'We would raise up the socialist proletariat of Europe for an insurrection against their governments . . . There is no doubt that a victory of the proletariat in Russia would create extraordinarily favourable conditions for the development of the revolution in both Asia and Europe.'¹ He used similar arguments a number of times after the February revolution.

On 3 (16) December armistice negotiations were opened with representatives of the Germans and the Austro-Hungarian empire, which led to the signing of an armistice. On 9 (22) December peace negotiations began at Brest-Litovsk. The leader of the Bolshevik delegation was Trotsky. He was accompanied by Karl Radek, who had just arrived in Russia and was the editor of the German paper *Die Fackel* (The Torch), which was distributed in the German trenches. On arriving at Brest-Litovsk Radek, under the eyes of the officers and diplomats assembled on the platform to greet the Soviet delegation, began to distribute revolutionary pamphlets among the German soldiers.

On 14-15 (27-28) December the German representative read out the draft of a harsh annexationist peace treaty. Trotsky broke off negotiations and left for Petrograd.

In critical situations Lenin was in the habit of expressing his views in the condensed form of a thesis. Now, facing an utterly new situation, demanding in his view a radical change of strategy, he did the same. On 7 (20) January 1918 he wrote 'Theses on the Question of the Immediate Conclusion of a Separate and Annexionist Peace':

> That the socialist revolution in Europe must come, and will come, is beyond doubt. All our hopes for the *final* victory of socialism are founded on this certainty and on this scientific

prognosis. Our propaganda activities in general, and the organization of fraternization in particular, must be intensified and extended. It would be a mistake, however, to base the tactics of the Russian socialist government on attempts to determine whether or not the European, and especially the German, socialist revolution will take place in the next six months (or some such brief period). Inasmuch as it is quite impossible to determine this, all such attempts, objectively speaking, would be nothing but a blind gamble.

One cannot make war without an army, and Russia had no army to speak of. 'There can be no doubt that our army is absolutely in no condition at the present moment to beat back a German offensive successfully.'

> The socialist government of Russia is faced with the question – a question whose solution brooks no delay – of whether to accept this peace with annexations now, or to immediately wage a revolutionary war. In fact, no middle course is possible.

One should not derive the necessary tactics directly from a general principle. Some people would argue:

> 'such a peace would mean a complete break with the fundamental principles of proletarian internationalism.'
> This argument, however, is obviously incorrect. Workers who lose a strike and sign terms for the resumption of work which are unfavourable to them and favourable to the capitalists, do not betray socialism.

Would a peace policy harm the German revolution, asked Lenin. And answered:

> The German revolution will by no means be made more difficult of accomplishment as far as its objective premises are concerned, if we conclude a separate peace . . .
> A socialist Soviet Republic in Russia will stand as a living example to the peoples of all countries, and the propaganda and revolutionizing effect of this example will be immense.

He disdainfully rejected a 'heroic' attitude to the solution of life and death questions facing the proletariat.

> Summing up the arguments in favour of an immediate revolutionary war, we have to conclude that such a policy might perhaps answer the human yearning for the beautiful, dramatic and striking, but that it would totally disregard the objective

balance of class forces and material factors at the present stage of the socialist revolution now under way.[2]

Lenin unfortunately met with very tough resistance in the party ranks. His supporters of the October days were by and large surprised and shocked by his stand. On the whole the Right that opposed him in the days of October now came to his support. The most extreme enthusiast for immediate peace was Zinoviev, while the Left, which had supported Lenin during the revolution, was practically unanimous in opposing his peace policy.

The first formal discussion of Lenin's Thesis took place at the Central Committee meeting of 8 (21) January, with a number of lesser party leaders also present.

Wide sections of the party, including the great majority of the Petersburg Committee and of the Moscow Region Bureau, were in favour of a revolutionary war. The views of many of the rank and file could be summed up in the phrase used by Osinsky (Obolensky), a member of the Moscow Regional Bureau: 'I stand for Lenin's old position.' Even Trotsky did not support Lenin.

At this meeting Trotsky reported on his mission to Brest-Litovsk and presented his conclusion: 'Neither war nor peace.' Lenin argued for the acceptance of the German terms. Bukharin spoke for 'a revolutionary war'. The vote brought striking success to Bukharin. Lenin's motion received only 15 votes. Trotsky's position obtained 16 votes. 32 votes were cast for Bukharin's stand.[3]

Shortly after the meeting Lenin wrote:

> The state of affairs now obtaining in the party reminds me very strongly of the situation in the summer of 1907 when the overwhelming majority of the Bolsheviks favoured the boycott of the Third Duma and I stood side by side with Dan in favour of participation and was subjected to furious attacks for my opportunism. Objectively, the present issue is a complete analogy; as then, the majority of the party functionaries, proceeding from the very best revolutionary motives and the best party traditions, allow themselves to be carried away by a 'flash' slogan and *do not grasp the new* socio-economic and political situation, do not take into consideration *the change in the conditions* that demands a speedy and abrupt change in tactics.[4]

At the next session of the Central Committee, on 11 (24) January, Dzerzhinsky reproached Lenin with timidity, with surrendering the whole programme of the revolution: 'Lenin is doing in a disguised form what Zinoviev and Kamenev did in October.'

To accept the Kaiser's *diktat*, Bukharin argued, would be to stab the German and Austrian proletariat in the back. In Uritsky's view Lenin approached the problem 'from Russia's angle, and not from an international point of view'. Lomov argued that 'by concluding peace we capitulate to German imperialism'. On behalf of the Petrograd organization Kosior harshly condemned Lenin's position.

The most determined advocates of peace were Zinoviev, Kamenev, Sverdlov, Stalin and Sokolnikov. Stalin said: 'There is no revolutionary movement in the west, nothing existing, only a potential, and we cannot count on a potential.' As in October, Zinoviev saw no ground for expecting revolution in the west. No matter, he said, that the peace treaty will weaken the revolutionary movement in the west: 'of course . . . peace will strengthen chauvinism in Germany, and for a time weaken the movement everywhere in the west'.

Lenin hastened to repudiate these two clumsy supporters. 'Can't take into account?' Lenin exclaimed on Stalin's position. It was true the revolution in the west had not yet begun. However, 'if we were to change our tactics on the strength of that . . . then we would be betraying international socialism'. Against Zinoviev he declared that it was wrong to say

> that concluding a peace will weaken the movement in the west for a time. If we believe that the German movement can immediately develop if the peace negotiations are broken off, then we must sacrifice ourselves, for the power of the German revolution will be much greater than ours.[5]

Lenin did not for a moment forget the revolutionary potential in the west.

> Those who advocate a revolutionary war point out that this will involve us in a civil war with German imperialism and in this way we will awaken revolution in Germany. But Germany is only just pregnant with revolution and we have already given birth to a completely healthy child, a socialist republic which we may kill if we start a war.[6]

However, he was willing to let Trotsky try playing for time. Against Zinoviev's solitary vote, the Central Committee decided to 'do everything to drag out the signing of a peace'.[7]

On 2 (15) January a group of Central Committee members and People's Commissars issued a statement demanding an immediate convocation of a party conference, declaring: 'in the event of a peace treaty being *signed . . . without such a conference having been called*, the undersigned find it necessary whatever happens to leave such posts of responsibility in the Party and governmental organs as they may hold.' The signatories were: 'Member of the CC RSDLP G.Oppokov (A.Lomov); People's Commissar V.Obolensky (N.Osinsky); V.Iakovleva, Sheverdin, N.Krestinsky, V.Smirnov, M.Vasilev, M.Savelev; Commissar of the State Bank Georgii Piatakov; Member of the CC RSDLP and ed. *Pravda* N.Bukharin; Member of the Urals Regional Committee and the TsIK Preobrazhensky.'

On the same day the Executive Commission of the Petersburg Committee of the party issued a denunciation of Lenin's peace policy, describing it as

> the abdication of our positions in full view of the coming international revolution and the sure death of our party as the vanguard of the revolution . . . If the peace policy is continued . . . it threatens to split our party. With all this in mind, the Executive Commission demands, in the name of the Petersburg organization, that a special party conference be convened immediately.[8]

On 11 (24) January the Moscow Committee of the party unanimously passed a resolution sharply condemning Lenin's peace policy.

> Acceptance of the conditions dictated by the German imperialists goes contrary to our whole policy of revolutionary socialism, would objectively involve renouncing a consistent line of international socialism in both foreign and internal policy and could lead to opportunism of the worst kind.[9]

For six weeks a sharp internal debate took place in the Bolshevik party and, as in previous crises, nearly split it. On 21 January (3 February) the Special Conference took place. It came to no clear conclusion. When the decisive question was put:

'Should the peace be signed if a German ultimatum were received?' the great majority abstained.[10]

With the party leadership in disarray, Trotsky continued with his policy of procrastination. On 29 January (10 February) he broke off negotiations with the Central Powers, declaring that while Russia refused to sign the annexationist peace, it also simultaneously declared the war to be at an end.

On 13 February Trotsky gave a detailed account of the negotiations at Brest and explained the reasons for his policy at a meeting of the Central Committee. In conclusion he said:

> I do not want to say that a further advance of the Germans against us is out of the question. Such a statement would be too risky, considering the power of the German Imperialist party. But I think that by the position we have taken up on the question we have made any advance a very embarrassing affair for the German militarists.

Sverdlov proposed a resolution which was passed unanimously, approving 'the action of its representatives at Brest-Litovsk.'[11]

On 18 February the Germans resumed their military offensive. The Central Committee met again. This time Lenin's proposal to offer peace immediately was defeated by 7 votes to 6. Trotsky voted against.[12] On the evening of the same day the Central Committee met again. Now the mood changed. The news had come that the Germans had captured Minsk and were advancing in the Ukraine, and apparently meeting with no resistance. The Central Committee passed a resolution to 'send the German Government an offer straight away to conclude peace immediately'; 7 (Lenin, Smilga, Stalin, Sverdlov, Sokolnikov, Zinoviev and Trotsky), voted for this resolution, and 5 (Uritsky, Ioffe, Lomov, Bukharin, Krestinsky) against; there was 1 abstention (Stasova).[13]

To add to the disarray in the leadership's ranks, a new factor intervened. On 22 February Trotsky reported to the Central Committee an offer by France and Britain to give military aid to Russia in a war against Germany. The majority of the 'Left Communists' were opposed in principle to accepting aid from such imperialist quarters. Trotsky came out clearly in favour of accepting aid, from whatever source. 'The "Left Communists" arguments do not stand up to criticism. The state is forced to do what the party would not do. Of course the imperialists want to take advantage of us and if we are weak, they will do so; if we are strong, we will not allow it.'

As the party of the socialist proletariat which is in power and conducting a war against Germany, we mobilize every means through state institutions to arm and supply our revolutionary army in the best way possible with all necessary resources and, for that purpose, we obtain them where we can, including therefore from capitalist governments. In doing this, the Russian Social-Democratic Labour Party retains full independence in its external policy, gives no political undertakings to capitalist governments and examines their proposals in each separate case according to what is expedient.

Lenin, who had not been present at the meeting of the Central Committee, added the following statement to the minutes of the session: 'Please add my vote *in favour* of taking potatoes and weapons from the Anglo-French imperialist robbers.'[14]

To explain his readiness to use the conflict between the imperialist powers in the interests of the proletariat in power, Lenin wrote, on 22 February, an article entitled 'The Itch'.

Let us suppose Kaliaev,* in order to kill a tyrant and monster, acquires a revolver from an absolute villain, a scoundrel and robber, by promising him bread, money and vodka for the service rendered.

Can one condemn Kaliaev for 'dealing with a robber' for the sake of obtaining a deadly weapon? Every sensible person will answer 'no'. If there is nowhere else for Kaliaev to get a revolver, and if his intention is really an honourable one (the killing of a tyrant, not killing for plunder), then he should not be reproached but commended for acquiring a revolver in this way. But if a robber, in order to commit murder for the sake of plunder, acquires a revolver from another robber in return for money, vodka or bread, can one compare (not to speak of identifying) *such* a 'deal with a robber' with the deal made by Kaliaev?[15]

---

* A member of the combat group of the Socialist Revolutionary Party, who took part in a number of terrorist acts. On 4 (17) February 1905 he assassinated the Governor General of Moscow, the Grand Duke S.A.Romanov, uncle of Nicholas II. He was executed at Schlüsselburg on 10 (23) May.

In a postscript to the article, Lenin added:

The North Americans in their war of liberation against England at the end of the eighteenth century got help from Spain and France, who were her competitors and just as much colonial robbers as England. It is said that there were 'Left Bolsheviks' to be found who contemplated writing a 'learned work' on the 'dirty deal' of these Americans.[16]

In the end, however, nothing came of the offer of aid from Britain and France.

On 22 February, the German reply to the Russian peace offer was received. It was followed by a revolt in the Bolshevik Party. When the severe German terms became known, both the Petersburg Committee and the Moscow Regional Bureau combined to oppose Lenin's peace policy, in even more extreme terms than hitherto. On the same day Bukharin decided to resign from the Central Committee and from his post as editor of *Pravda*. The following jointly offered their resignation from all responsible posts held by them, and reserved their rights to 'freely agitate both within the Party and outside it': Lomov, Uritsky, Bukharin and Bubnov (members of the Central Committee); V.M.Smirnov, Iakoleva, Piatakov, Stukov and Pokrovsky of the Moscow Regional Bureau; and Spunde of Petrograd. The declaration accompanying the resignation was a harsh condemnation of Lenin's policy:

the advance contingent of the international proletariat has capitulated to the international bourgeosie. By demonstrating to the whole world the weakness of the dictatorship of the proletariat in Russia, it strikes a blow at the cause of the international proletariat . . .
The surrender of the proletariat's positions abroad inevitably prepares the way for surrender internally, too.[17]

On 21 February Lenin launched a public campaign in the press for his peace policy, with an article in *Pravda* called 'The Revolutionary Phrase'. He was relentless in his criticism of the Left Communists:

the revolutionary phrase about a revolutionary war might ruin our revolution. By revolutionary phrase-making we mean the repetition of revolutionary slogans irrespective of objective circumstances at a given turn in events.

The Bolsheviks must face the fact that 'The old army does not exist. The new army is only just being born.'[18]

It was empty talk to suggest helping the German revolution by sacrificing Soviet power in Russia.

> It is one thing to be certain that the German revolution is maturing and to do your part towards helping it mature, to serve it as far as possible by *work*, agitation and fraternization, anything you like, but help the maturing of the revolution by *work*. That is what revolutionary proletarian internationalism means.
> It is another thing to declare, directly or indirectly, openly or covertly, that the German revolution is *already mature* (although it obviously is not) and to base your tactics on it.[19]

> We must fight against the revolutionary phrase, we have to fight it, we absolutely must fight it, so that at some future time people will not say of us the bitter truth that 'a revolutionary phrase about revolutionary war ruined the revolution'.[20]

Lenin was frequently forced to reiterate the basic Marxist tenet that one cannot identify the specific with the general, that the concrete is not the same as the abstract. As he wrote in his *Pravda* article of 25 February, 'A Painful But Necessary Lesson':

> It is indisputable that 'every strike conceals the hydra of the social revolution'. But it is nonsense to think that we can stride directly from a strike to the revolution. If we 'bank on the victory of socialism in Europe' in the sense that we guarantee to the people that the European revolution will break out and is certain to be victorious within the next few weeks, certainly before the Germans have time to reach Petrograd, Moscow or Kiev, before they have time to 'finish off' our railway transport, we shall be acting, not as serious internationalist revolutionaries, but as adventurers.[21]

On 16 February Germany declared that as from noon of 18 February it considered itself at war with Russia. At the time announced, German forces went on the offensive along the whole front, and met no resistance at all.

On 23 February the Central Committee discussed the new German terms. According to these, Soviet Russia was to lose all the Baltic territory, and part of Belorussia; it was also proposed that the towns of Marz, Batum and Ardagan be surrendered to Turkey. Under the conditions of the ultimatum, Russia would have to completely demobilize the army immediately, withdraw forces from Finland and the Ukraine and conclude peace with the Ukrainian People's Republic, i.e. with the bourgeois-nationalist Central Rada. The German government demanded that the terms it had set out be adopted within 48 hours, that plenipotentiaries be dispatched immediately to Brest-Litovsk and that a peace be signed in three days.

Lenin insisted that the terms must be accepted, and to drive the point home he threatened to resign from all his positions in government and party. The members of the Central Committee reacted in various ways. Lomov was unmoved. 'If Lenin threatens resignation, there is no reason to be frightened. We have to take power without V.I. [Lenin]. We have to go to the front and do everything we can.' However, other members, above all Trotsky, gave way under Lenin's pressure. Although not convinced by his arguments, Trotsky declared he was not ready to oppose Lenin's policy any more.

> We cannot fight a revolutionary war when the Party is split . . . The arguments of V.I. [Lenin] are far from convincing: if we had all been of the same mind, we could have tackled the task of organizing defence and we could have managed it. Our role would not have been a bad one even if we had been forced to surrender Peter and Moscow. We would have held the whole world in tension. If we sign the German ultimatum today, we may have a new ultimatum tomorrow. Everything is formulated in such a way as to leave an opportunity for further ultimatums. We may sign a peace; and lose support among the advanced elements of the proletariat, in any case demoralize them.

A similar attitude of abstention was taken by Krestinsky, Ioffe and Dzerzhinsky.*

---

* It is interesting to note that vacillation did not leave the pro-peace camp in the Central Committee untouched. Thus Stalin, at just this moment, found it possible to state: 'It is possible not to sign but to start peace negotiations.' And Lenin had to come down sharply against the vacillation of his own supporters: 'Stalin is wrong when he says it is possible not to sign. These terms must be signed. If you do not sign them, you will be signing the death sentence of Soviet power in three weeks.'

The outcome was that Lenin just got his way. There were 7 votes for his position (Lenin, Stasova, Zinoviev, Sverdlov, Stalin, Sokolnikov and Smilga), 4 against (Bubnov, Uritsky, Bukharin and Lomov) and 4 abstentions (Trotsky, Krestinsky, Dzerzhinsky and Ioffe).

Immediately after this session Bukharin, Uritsky, Lomov, Bubnov, Iakovleva, Piatakov and Smirnov declared they were 'resigning from all responsible party and Soviet posts and retaining complete freedom to campaign both within the party and outside it for what we consider to be the only correct positions'. Stalin raised 'the issue of whether leaving a post does not in practice mean leaving the party'. Lenin hastened to avoid bloodletting. He indicated that 'resigning from the CC does not mean leaving the party'.[22]

On 24 February the Moscow Regional Bureau unanimously adopted a resolution of no confidence in the Central Committee. In explanation it stated:

> The Moscow Regional Bureau considers a split in the party in the very near future hardly avoidable, and it sets itself the aim of helping to unite all consistent revolutionary communists who equally oppose both the advocates of the conclusion of a separate peace and all moderate opportunists in the party. *In the interests of the world revolution, we consider it expedient to accept the possibility of losing Soviet power, which is now becoming purely formal.*

The Bureau made it clear that it was not going to abide by the discipline of the Central Committee.

Lenin's reaction was most patient and tolerant. The party was still deeply democratic.

> In all this there is not only nothing appalling, but also nothing strange. It is completely natural for comrades who differ sharply with the Central Committee on the issue of a separate peace to reprimand the Central Committee sharply and express their conviction on the inevitability of a split. All this is the legal right of members of the party, and this is fully understandable.[23]

On 24 February a Soviet peace delegation left for Brest-Litovsk. Peace negotiations were resumed on 1 March, and on 3 March the treaty was signed. The Soviet delegates made it quite clear that they were signing it under duress. Thus, before signing, the Russian delegation issued a statement saying:

> Under the circumstances Russia has no freedom of choice . . . The German proletariat is as yet not strong enough to stop the attack [of German imperialism]. We have no doubt that the triumph of imperialism and militarism over the international proletarian revolution will prove to be temporary and ephemeral. Meanwhile the Soviet government . . . unable to resist the armed offensive of German imperialism, is forced to accept the peace terms so as to save revolutionary Russia.[24]

The Harsh Terms of the Peace Treaty

It was estimated that by this treaty Russia lost territories and resources approximately as follows: 1,267,000 square miles, with over 62,000,000 population, or one-fourth of her territory and 44 per cent of her population; one-third of her crops and 27 per cent of her state income; 80 per cent of her sugar factories; 73 per cent of her iron and 75 per cent of her coal. Of the total of 16,000 industrial undertakings, 9,000 were situated in the lost territories.[25]

Opposition to Lenin's peace policy now spread widely among the masses. In February a referendum of the views of 200 Soviets was held. Of these a majority – 105 – voted for war against Germany. In the industrial city Soviets the majority in favour of war was overwhelming. Only two large Soviets – Petrograd and Sebastopol – went on record as being in favour of peace. On the other hand several of the big centres (such as Moscow, Krondstadt, Ekaterinburg, Kharkov, Ekaterinoslav, Ivanovo-Voznessensk), voted against Lenin's policy with overwhelming majorities. Of the Soviets of 42 provincial cities that were consulted, 6 opted for peace, 20 for war; 88 county towns and villages opted for peace, 85 for war.[26]

However, the debate in the party came to an end with a specially convened Seventh Congress on 6-8 March. The day before it opened, a new daily, *Kommunist*, 'Organ of the St Petersburg Committee and the St Petersburg Area Committee of the RSDLP' appeared. It was edited by Bukharin, Radek and Uritsky, with the collaboration of a number of prominent Party leaders:

Bubnov, Lomov, Pokrovsky, Preobrazhensky, Piatakov, Kollontai, Inessa Armand and others. The list of names gives some idea of the strength and quality of *Kommunist*.

After a bitter debate, the Seventh Congress resolved to support Lenin's policy by 30 votes to 12, with four abstentions. Local party organizations followed this line, either immediately or after a time.

By 7 March a Petrograd Party Conference had adopted a resolution condemning the Left Communists and calling upon them to stop their 'independent organizational existence'. As a result of this resolution *Kommunist* was soon forced to cease publication in Petrograd and was transferred to Moscow, where it reappeared in April under the auspices of the Moscow Regional Bureau. On 15 May Lenin was able to win the stronghold of the Left Communists, the Moscow region; after a debate with Lomov at a party conference his line was adopted by 42 votes to 9.

In some places the Left Communists continued to prevail. Thus in Ivanovo-Voznessensk, a district party conference held on 10 May, having heard a report by Bukharin, voted 12 to 9 with 4 abstentions for Bukharin's policy.[27]

The final ratification of the treaty took place at the Fourth Congress of Soviets on 15 March, 1918, by a vote of 748 to 261 with 115 abstentions. Among the latter were 64 Left Communists.

From then on the Left Communists lapsed into silence regarding the war question (although, as we shall see later, they continued to oppose Lenin's policy in a different sphere – that of economic affairs). But the Left Socialist Revolutionaries voiced their opposition to the peace policy all the more loudly and impatiently. Immediately after the ratification of the peace they withdrew from the Council of People's Commissars.

Trotsky's Position

As Stalinist historiography exaggerates beyond recognition the differences between Lenin and Trotsky regarding the Brest-Litovsk negotiations, it is important to elaborate somewhat on Trotsky's position.

Throughout the debate on Brest-Litovsk there was not the slightest disagreement between Lenin and Trotsky about the *im-*

possibility of a revolutionary war. Thus, for instance, in a speech on 8 (21) January Trotsky said: 'It is clear as day that if we wage revolutionary war, we shall be overthrown.'[28] He explains his position at the time thus:

> It was obvious that going on with the war was impossible. On this point, there was not even a shadow of disagreement between Lenin and me. We were both equally bewildered at Bukharin and the other apostles of a 'revolutionary war'. But there was another question, quite as important. How far could the Hohenzollern government go in their struggle against us? . . . Could Hohenzollern send his troops against revolutionaries who wanted peace? How had the February revolution, and, later on, the October revolution, affected the German army? How soon would any effect show itself? To these questions, no answer could as yet be given. We had to try to find it in the course of the negotiations. Accordingly we had to delay the negotiations as long as we could. It was necessary to give the European workers time to absorb properly the very fact of the Soviet revolution, including its policy of peace.[29]

Lenin's suggested tactics for the peace negotiations in Brest-Litovsk proved to be correct in practice. This, however, does not mean to say that Trotsky's position must inevitably have been wrong. Possibly the tactic he suggested of 'neither war nor peace' would have worked. From the memoirs of Ludendorff and various statements made by German representatives at Brest-Litovsk, it is clear that the Austrian and German leaders hesitated before launching their offensive against Russia.

The Austrian monarchy especially was almost desperate. On 4 (17) January the Foreign Minister of Austria, Czernin, got a mesage from the Austrian Emperor which stated:

> I must once more earnestly impress upon you that the whole fate of the monarchy and of the dynasty depends on peace being concluded at Brest-Litovsk as soon as possible . . . If peace be not made at Brest, there will be revolution.[30]

While Trotsky was on his way to Brest-Litovsk on 15 (28) January a wave of strikes and outbreaks spread through Germany and Austria. Soviets were formed in Berlin and Vienna. Hamburg, Bremen, Leipzig, Essen and Munich took up the cry. 'All Power to the Soviets' was heard in the streets of Greater Berlin, where half a million workers downed tools. In the forefront of the demands were the speedy conclusion of peace without annexations or indemnities, on the basis of the self-determination of peoples in accordance with the principles formulated by the Russian People's Commissars at Brest-Litovsk, and the participation of workers' delegates from all countries in the peace negotiations.[81]

The Austrians were supported in their attempts to achieve unconditional peace by the Bulgarians and the Turks, and, even more important, by the German Foreign Minister, Baron Von Kühlmann, and Prime Minister, von Hertling.

Ludendorff's and Kühlmann's memoirs make it clear that for days there was a balance between the war party, headed by the German general staff (Hindenburg, Ludendorff, Hoffmann), and the peace party, headed by von Kühlmann and von Hertling. The latter argued repeatedly that the situation on the home front did not permit a military offensive against the Russians. But the German supreme command remained adamant and in the end, with the Kaiser's backing, won the day.

Thus Trotsky's position during the Brest negotiations was based not on sheer idealism, but also on a great deal of realism. When events proved that Lenin was right, Trotsky was generous in acknowledging this. On 3 October 1918, at a session of the Central Executive Committee, he declared:

> I feel it my duty to say, in this authoritative assembly, that when many of us, including myself, were doubtful as to whether it was admissible for us to sign the Brest-Litovsk peace, only Comrade Lenin maintained stubbornly, with amazing foresight, and against our opposition, that we had to go through with it, to tide us over until the revolution of the world proletariat. We must now admit that we were wrong.[82]

Realism and Principled Politics

Lenin's strength in the fateful days of war and peace was his strictly uncompromising adherence to principles, combined with his readiness to adapt his tactics to the changing objective circumstances.

With full recognition of the need to retreat in the face of the imperialist pressure, he insisted on the necessity of adhering to the internationalist principle of subordinating everything, including the fate of Russia, to the needs of the world revolution. While arguing at the Seventh Party Congress for immediate ratification of the peace treaty, he did not for a moment lower the international sights of the revolution.

> Regarded from the world-historical point of view, there would doubtlessly be no hope of the ultimate victory of our revolution if it were to remain alone, if there were no revolutionary movements in other countries. When the Bolshevik Party tackled the job alone, it did so in the firm conviction that the revolution was maturing in all countries.[33]

> it is the absolute truth that without a German revolution we are doomed.[34]

Despite the harshness of the steps he had to take, Lenin did not for a moment try to pull the wool over the eyes of the workers. On the contrary, the truth had to be told to them, however unappetizing it might be. He always stuck to the rule that any manoeuvring that replaces the *real* struggle may destroy the revolutionary morale of the masses. In all the changes of direction imposed on revolutionary leaders, they must never hide the basic truth from the workers. As Trotsky put it:

> The essence of the matter is that Lenin approached the Brest-Litovsk capitulation with the same inexhaustible revolutionary energy which secured the party's victory in October. Precisely this intrinsic, and as if organic, combination of October and Brest-Litovsk, of the gigantic sweep with intrepidity and circumspection, of both boldness and foresight, gives a measure of Lenin's method and of his power.[35]

Principled politics combined with ruthlessly clear realism were the decisive traits of Lenin's behaviour during the Brest affair. He emerged with enormous moral credit from the controversy. Having the courage of his convictions enabled him to defy the prevailing mood in the party. His extraordinary powers of persuasion enabled him finally to change party opinion.

5
The Transition from Capitalism to Socialism

Lenin hoped for a breathing space after the signing of the Brest-Litovsk peace treaty. In a speech to the Moscow Soviet on 23 April 1918 he said:

> We can say with confidence that in the main the civil war is at an end. There will be some skirmishes, of course, and in some towns street fighting will flare up here or there, due to isolated attempts by the reactionaries to overthrow the strength of the revolution – the Soviet system – but there is no doubt that on the internal front reaction has been irretrievably smashed by the efforts of the insurgent people.[1]

Lenin's writings during this period all demonstrate his belief that the destructive phase of the revolution was largely over, and that the main task now was to learn how to operate industry, how to advance a measure of economic construction. However, the revolution was to be denied a breathing space of any appreciable length. Less than three months elapsed between the signing of the Brest treaty and the outbreak of a fierce civil war.

The Marxist Heritage

Lenin always looked to his teachers, Marx and Engels, to help him find his way forward. He used the international experience of the workers' revolutionary movement from 1848 to 1871 and onwards, as analysed by Marx and Engels, to prepare himself for 1905 and 1917. What did he learn from these masters about the transition from capitalism to socialism, after taking power?

In *The Civil War In France* Marx explained that the workers had 'no ready-made Utopias', that they had 'no ideals to realize', but 'to set free the elements of the new society with which the old collapsing bourgeois society itself is pregnant.' The workers well know that 'they will have to pass through long struggles, through a series of historic processes, transforming circumstances and men'.[2]

Marx referred with contempt to the imposition on the proletariat of schemes independent of its own experience. To offer a theoretical analysis of a future economic order before experience provided the material for it would be daydreaming. 'In Marx,' observed Lenin in *State and Revolution*, 'there is no trace of any attempt to construct Utopias, to guess in the void about what cannot be known.'

But the few general remarks by Marx and Engels scattered through *Capital*, *The German Ideology*, *The Critique of the Gotha Programme* and their correspondence could not be readily and directly applied to the Russian revolution. Marx and Engels assumed that the overthrow of capitalism would begin in the most advanced capitalist countries, where powerful industry and a massive and cultured working class existed, and would take place in several key countries at once. Instead the revolution broke out in only one country, and that a very backward one. In such conditions socialist tasks are bound to be outweighed by pre-socialist tasks, and the implementation of both complicated by the pressures and interference of encircling imperialism.

Lenin was hard put to it to find guidelines for the building of a new society. Could he draw any lessons for the construction of socialism from the rise of capitalism? Unfortunately, there are radical differences between the way capitalism developed and the way socialism will arise.

Firstly, while the political revolution – the coming of the proletariat to power – precedes the economic and cultural evolution of socialism, the economic and cultural development of the capitalist system preceded the bourgeois revolution.

Capitalism developed from simple commodity production in the cracks and crannies of the feudal economy. Important elements of capitalism were created in the womb of the old society. Only after hundreds of years of growth did capitalism become the predominant economic form, and place its imprint on the whole of society, delineating the general trend of development.

> They [the bourgeoisie] did not build capitalism, it built itself [Bukharin wrote]. The proletariat will build socialism as an organized system, as an organized collective subject. While the process of the creation of capitalism was spontaneous, the pro-

cess of building communism is to a significant degree a conscious, i.e. organized process.[3]

The Communist Manifesto made it clear that the act of bringing the proletariat to power was an act of revolution. But once the proletariat was in power, its programme of action was a transitional one, which would *gradually* lead to socialism. The social–political revolution would open the door to a prolonged process of reform whose final result would be fully-fledged socialism (or communism). Before the revolution, the communist uses reforms to develop the self-confidence, consciousness and organization of the proletariat, so as to prepare it for the revolution, i.e. breaking the capitalist framework of political, economic and social power. After the revolution, on the foundation of a new class rule, socialist reforms are called for.

Once the dictatorship of the proletariat is established, a programme of economic transformation is to be implemented:

> The proletariat will use its political supremacy in order, by degrees, to wrest all capital from the bourgeoisie, to centralize all the means of production into the hands of the state (this meaning the proletariat organized as ruling class), and, as rapidly as possible, to increase the total mass of productive forces.

The Communist Manifesto goes on to spell out ten measures that the proletariat should take on coming to power, to transform the economy and society. None of these measures abolishes capitalism straight away; each constitutes a partial intervention by the state in the economic mechanism of capitalism, and only in the *totality*, and *over time*, are they deemed to undermine capitalism completely. Thus, for instance, the measure 'a vigorously graduated income tax' assumes that under the dictatorship of the proletariat there would still be marked differences in incomes – that the capitalist would not be expropriated at a stroke. 'During the revolution, the gigantic increase in the scope of taxation may serve as an attack on private ownership; yet even in such a case taxation must be a stepping stone to fresh revolutionary measures, otherwise there will be a return to the erstwhile bourgeois conditions.'[4]

Again, the measure 'abolition of the right of inheritance' assumes the existence of private property in the means of production, and so forth. The measures suggested make it clear that Marx and Engels regarded the transition from capitalism to socialism not as a single step, but as a process spread over a more or less lengthy historical period.

It must be emphasized that there is a *fundamental* difference between the way Marx and Engels posed partial demands and the way reformists put them. 'Inroads upon the rights of property' caried out by a workers' government are radically different from reforms under a bourgeois government. In the first case the partial demands will be outstripped, leading to further encroachment upon the rights of property. In the second they are mere adjustments to capitalism and are containable within it. For Marx and Engels transitional demands were such that each constituted an essential structural change in its own right, and all together added up to the transformation of capitalism into socialism.

Changing 'Human Nature'

For Marx, the agent for the transition from capitalism to socialism, a transition that must take not years but a whole historical epoch, was the active and conscious working class. While capitalism developed spontaneously over centuries in the heart of feudal society, socialism *does not* grow within capitalism; however, the proletariat, which is potentially able to create socialism, does. The clear implication is that capitalism as such does not create socialism, but that the revolutionary struggles of the proletariat to overthrow capitalism produces men with the will and ability to construct socialist society. This ability is developed in the struggle against capitalism, and is the *only* foundation of the new society. The centrality of the human element was made clear by Marx when he pointed out the differences between the propaganda of his group in the German Communist League and that of an opposing minority group:

> What we say to the workers is: 'You will have 15, 20, 50 years of civil war and national struggle and this not merely to bring about a change in society but also to change yourselves and prepare yourselves for the exercise of political power.' Whereas you say on the contrary: 'Either we seize power at once, or else we might as well just take to our beds.' While we are at pains to show the German worker how rudimentary the development of the German proletariat is, you appeal to the patriotic

feelings and the class prejudice of the German artisan, flattering him in the grossest way possible, and this is a more popular method, of course.[5]

It is essential for the creation of a socialist society that the proletariat should not only change social relations, but also change itself, so as to be able to carry out this historical task. To emphasize this, Marx wrote elsewhere: 'The tradition of all the dead generations weighs like a nightmare on the brain of the living.' The working class is an essential part of capitalism, and *potentially* the victor over it. Hence the concluding sentences of the first section of *The Communist Manifesto*: 'What the bourgeoisie therefore produces, above all, are its own gravediggers. Its fall, and the victory of the proletariat, are equally inevitable.'

The key to becoming the builder of a new society from being the subordinate class under capitalism is the proletariat's revolutionary prowess. The changes in social human relations necessary for this transformation are dialectically united by revolutionary practice. As Marx put it in the *Theses on Feuerbach*:

> The materialistic doctrine that men are products of circumstances and upbringing, and that therefore changed men are the product of other circumstances and changed upbringing, forgets that it is men who change circumstances and that the educator must himself be educated . . . The coincidence of the changing of circumstances and human activity can be conceived and rationally understood only as *revolutionizing practice*.

The difficulties of a proletarian government will be not so much in the domain of property, but rather in that of production, and of overcoming human nature as shaped by the old society. The field in which the difficulties will be most acute will be that of work discipline. The workers work because of the discipline of hunger and the threat of the sack. Of course in an advanced stage of socialist society, where working hours will be reduced to a reasonable limit and the unpleasant aspects of the process of labour eliminated, where the workplace will be hygienic and attractive, where the monotony of labour will largely be done away with, where the material inducement will be lavish, workers will work from force of habit and from the desire to serve the needs of fellow human beings. But it will take a whole historical period to change labour from a burden to a joy. How will labour discipline, so necessary for the continuation of production, be established immediately after the social revolution, with the proletariat still affected by the customs of capitalism?

Lenin on the Eve of the October Revolution

Lenin, like Marx and Engels, believed that the conquest of state power by the proletariat would have to be followed by a whole series of reforms taking place over a long period.

On the eve of the October revolution, he drew up a detailed plan for the measures to be put into effect by a Bolshevik government if it came to power in the near future. He wrote in *The Impending Catastrophe and How to Combat it*:

> These principal measures are:
> 1. Amalgamation of all banks into a single bank, and state control over its operations, or nationalization of the banks.
> 2. Nationalization of the syndicates, i.e. the largest, monopolistic capitalist associations (sugar, oil, coal, iron and steel, and other syndicates).
> 3. Abolition of commercial secrecy.
> 4. Compulsory syndication (i.e. compulsory amalgamation into associations) of industrialists, merchants and employers generally.
> 5. Compulsory organization of the population into consumers' societies, or encouragement of such organization, and the exercise of control over it.[6]

These measures are designed to achieve not the once-for-all destruction of capitalist property relations, but to start off a more or less lengthy process for their gradual undermining.

The nationalization of the banks is not to be confused with their expropriation.

> nationalization of the banks . . . would not deprive any 'owner' of a single kopek . . . If nationalization of the banks is so often confused with the confiscation of private property, it is the bourgeois press, which has an interest in deceiving the public, that is to blame for this widespread confusion . . .
> Whoever owned fifteen rubles on a savings account would continue to be the owner of fifteen rubles after the nationalization of the banks; and whoever had fifteen million rubles would con-

tinue after the nationalization of the banks to have fifteen million rubles in the form of shares, bonds, bills, commercial certificates and so on . . .

Only by nationalizing the banks *can* the state *put itself in a position* to know where and how, whence and when, millions and billions of rubles flow. And only control over the banks, over the centre, over the pivot and chief mechanism of capitalist circulation, would make it possible to organize real and not fictitious control over all economic life.[7]

The nationalization of the banks will be a serious invasion of capitalist property relations and will meet tough resistance from the capitalists.

As to the state, it would for the first time be in a position first to *review* all the chief monetary operations, which would be unconcealed, then to *control* them, then to *regulate* economic life, and finally to *obtain* millions and billions for major state transactions, without paying the capitalist gentlemen sky-high 'commissions' for their 'services'. That is the reason – and the only reason – why all the capitalists . . . are prepared to fight tooth and nail against nationalization of the banks.

The nationalization of the syndicates (point 2 of Lenin's programme) would also help 'the regulation of economic activity'. No blanket expropriation is suggested, only encroachment on the wealth of the syndicates by fining heavily those which sabotage the national measures: 'war must be declared on the oil barons and shareholders, the confiscation of their property and punishment by imprisonment must be decreed for delaying nationalization of the oil business, for concealing incomes or accounts, for sabotaging production, and for failing to take steps to increase production'.[8]

Point 3 – abolition of commercial secrecy – is another encroachment on capitalist property relations, but it does not abolish them. The abolition of commercial secrecy will mean

compelling contractors and merchants to render accounts public, forbidding them to abandon their field of activity without the permission of the authorities, imposing the penalty of confiscation of property and shooting for concealment and for deceiving the people, organizing verification and control *from below*, democratically, by the people themselves, by unions of workers and other employees, consumers, etc.

The establishment of workers' control will increase the power of the proletariat as against that of the bourgeoisie, while in no way at a stroke liquidating the latter as a class.

> In point of fact, the whole question of control boils down to who controls whom, i.e. which class is in control and which is being controlled . . . We must resolutely and irrevocably, not fearing to break with the old, not fearing boldly to build the new, pass to control *over* the landowners and capitalists *by* the workers and peasants.

Point 4, 'compulsory syndication (i.e. compulsory amalgamation into associations) of industrialists, merchants and employers generally', again does not abolish capitalist property relations. 'A law of this kind does not directly, i.e. in itself, affect property relations in any way; it does not deprive any owner of a single kopek.'[9]

The spirit of the transitional programme elaborated by Lenin in *The Impending Catastrophe and How to Combat It* is the same as that of the *Communist Manifesto*. Once workers' power has been established, the transition from capitalism to socialism, the 'leap', is seen as a more or less prolonged process of evolution. Capitalism, which grew up over centuries, is going to be replaced by socialism, which is going to be *built* over a much shorter period, but still not at a stroke.

A Long and Complicated Transition Period

In a speech on 11 (24) January 1918 Lenin declared:

> We know very little about socialism . . . We are not in a position to give a description of socialism . . . The bricks of which socialism will be composed have not yet been made. We cannot say anything further.[10]

Socialism will have to be built by people who have been shaped by capitalism. As Lenin said in a speech on 27 November 1918:

> Things would not be so bad if we did not have to build socialism with people inherited from capitalism. But that is the whole trouble with socialist construction – we have to build socialism with people who have been thoroughly spoiled by capitalism. That is the whole trouble with the transition.[11]

Again, on 20 January 1919, in a speech to the Second Trade Union Congress, he said:

> The workers were never separated by a Great Wall of China from the old society. And they have preserved a good deal of the traditional mentality of capitalist society. The workers are building a new society without themselves having become new people, or cleansed of the filth of the old world; they are still standing up to their knees in that filth. We can only dream of clearing the filth away. It would be utterly Utopian to think this could be done all at once. It would be so Utopian that in practice it would only postpone socialism to kingdom come.[12]

Again, he wrote on 17 April 1919:

> The old Utopian socialists imagined that socialism could be built by men of a new type, that first they would train good, pure and splendidly educated people, and these would build socialism. We always laughed at this and said that this was playing with puppets, that it was socialism as an amusement for young ladies, but not serious politics.
> We want to build socialism with the aid of those men and women who grew up under capitalism, were depraved and corrupted by capitalism, but steeled for the struggle by capitalism. There are proletarians who have been so hardened that they can stand a thousand times more hardship than any army. There are tens of millions of oppressed peasants, ignorant and scattered, but capable of uniting around the proletariat in the struggle, if the proletariat adopts skilful tactics.[13]

The proletariat will have to change itself radically if it wants to lead in the establishment of a new society:

> The science which we, at best, possess, is the science of the agitator and propagandist, or the man who has been steeled by the hellishly hard lot of the factory worker, or starving peasant, a science which teaches us how to hold out for a long time and to persevere in the struggle, and this has saved us up to now. All this is necessary, but it is not enough. With this alone we cannot triumph. In order that our victory may be complete and final we must take all that is valuable from capitalism, take all its science and culture.[14]

The going will be very hard:

> we know perfectly well from our own experience that there is a difference between solving a problem theoretically and put-

ting the solution into practice ... Thanks to a whole century of development, we know on which class we are relying. But we also know that the practical experience of that class is extremely inadequate.[15]

We were never Utopians and never imagined that we would build communist society with the immaculate hands of immaculate communists, born and educated in an immaculately communist society. That is a fairy-tale. We have to build communism out of the debris of capitalism, and only the class which has been steeled in the struggle against capitalism can do that. The proletariat, as you are very well aware, is not free from the shortcomings and weaknesses of capitalist society. It is fighting for socialism, but at the same time it is fighting against its own shortcomings.[16]

Though facing up to harsh reality, Lenin does not cease to be a revolutionary optimist: he sees salvation in the creative activity of the masses.

When the masses of the people themselves, with all their virgin primitiveness and simple, rough determination begin to make history, begin to put 'principles and theories' immediately and directly into practice, the bourgeois is terrified and howls that 'intellect is retreating into the background'. (Is not the contrary the case, heroes of philistinism? Is it not the intellect of the masses, and not of individuals, that invades the sphere of history at such moments? Does not mass intellect at such a time become a virile, effective, and not an armchair force?)

In the midst of the greatest hardships and tribulations – in October 1920 – Lenin quotes what he wrote in March 1906, long before the revolution.

The thing is that it is just the revolutionary periods which are distinguished by wider, richer, more deliberate, more methodical, more systematic, more courageous and more vivid making of history than periods of philistine, Cadet, reformist progress. But the Blanks turn the truth inside out! They palm off paltriness as magnificent making of history. They regard the inactivity of the oppressed or downtrodden masses as the triumph of 'system' in the work of bureaucrats and bourgeois. They shout about the disappearance of intellect and reason when, instead of the picking of draft laws to pieces by petty bureaucrats and liberal *penny-a-liner* journalists, there begins a period of direct political activity of the 'common people', who simply set to work without more ado to smash all the instruments for oppressing the people, seize power and take what was regarded as belonging to all kinds of robbers of the people – in short, when the intellect and reason of millions of downtrodden people awaken not only to read books, but for action, vital human action, to make history.[17]

With his usual realism, Lenin explains that the road ahead is not only difficult but bound to be very twisted and uneven, demanding continual adaptation and changes of gear.

The most difficult task in the sharp turns and changes of social life is that of taking due account of the peculiar features of each transition. How socialists should fight within a capitalist society is not a difficult problem and has long since been settled. Nor is it difficult to visualize advanced socialist society. This problem has also been settled. But the most difficult task of all is how, in practice, to effect the transition from the old, customary, familiar capitalism to the new socialism, as yet unborn and without any firm foundations. At best this transition will take many years, in the course of which our policy will be divided into a number of even smaller stages. And the whole difficulty of the task which falls to our lot, the whole difficulty of politics and the art of politics, lies in the ability to take into account the specific tasks of each of these transitions.[18]

We are bound to make many mistakes. What does it matter! This is the price which has to be paid for the advance of socialism.

For every hundred mistakes we commit, and which the bourgeoisie and their lackeys (including our own Mensheviks and Right Socialist-Revolutionaries) shout about to the whole world, 10,000 great and heroic deeds are performed, greater and more heroic because they are simple and inconspicuous amidst the everyday life of a factory district or a remote village, performed by people who are not accustomed (and have no opportunity) to shout to the whole world about their successes.
But even if the contrary were true – although I know such an assumption is wrong – even if we committed 10,000 mistakes for every 100 correct actions we performed, even in that case our revolution would be great and invincible, and *so it will be in the eyes of world history*, because, *for the first time*, not the minority, not the rich alone, and the educated alone, but the real people, the vast majority of the working people, are *themselves* building a new life, are *by their own experience* solving the most difficult problems of socialist organization.

Every mistake committed in the course of such work, in the course of this most conscientious and earnest work of tens of millions of simple workers and peasants in reorganizing their whole life, every such mistake is worth thousands and millions of 'flawless' successes achieved by the exploiting minority – successes in swindling and duping the working people. For only *through* such mistakes will the workers and peasants *learn* to build the new life, learn to do *without* capitalists; only in this way will they hack a path for themselves – through thousands of obstacles – to victorious socialism.[19]

Lenin had no illusions about the fact that the construction of socialism would take a very long time indeed. 'We know that we cannot establish a socialist order now – God grant that it may be established in our country in our children's time, or perhaps in our grandchildren's time.'[20] However, with courage and perseverance, the proletariat is bound to win.

Perseverance, persistence, willingness, determination and ability to test things a hundred times, to correct them a hundred times, but to achieve the goal come what may – these are qualities which the proletariat acquired in the course of the ten, fifteen or twenty years that preceded the October Revolution, and which it has acquired in the two years that have passed since this revolution, years of unprecedented privation, hunger, ruin and destitution. These qualities of the proletariat are a guarantee that the proletariat will conquer.[21]

6

'We Need State Capitalism'

In his mistaken expectation of a peaceful period after the Brest-Litovsk peace treaty, Lenin turned to the task of developing an economic strategy leading on from where his *The Threatening Catastrophe*, written six months earlier, left off. During the months of March-June 1918 he devoted himself to seeking ways of managing industry and achieving some measure of economic reconstruction.

The Chaotic Economic Situation

The whole of Russia was in a state of turmoil. A vivid description of the economic breakdown is given by an English observer, a reporter for the *Manchester Guardian*, travelling in Russia during 1917 and 1918:

> It is no exaggeration to say that during November, December, and the greater part of January something approaching anarchy reigned in the industries of Northern Russia . . . There was no common industrial plan. Factory Committees had no higher authority to which to look for direction. They acted entirely on their own and tried to solve those problems of production and distribution which seemed most pressing for the immediate future and for the locality. Machinery was sometimes sold in order to buy raw materials. The factories became like anarchistic Communes . . . anarcho-syndicalist tendencies began to run riot.[1]

War-damaged industry continued to run down. 'The bony hand of hunger', with which the capitalist Riabushinsky had threatened the revolution, gripped the whole population in the spring of 1918. Powerful evidence of the gravity of the situation was provided by a telegram which Lenin and the food Commissar, Tsiurupa, dispatched to all provincial Soviets and food committees on 11 May 1918:

> Petrograd is in an unprecedentedly catastrophic condition. There is no bread. The population is given the remaining potato flour and crusts. The Red capital is on the verge of perishing from famine. Counter-revolution is raising its head, directing the dissatisfaction of the hungry masses against the Soviet Government. In the name of the Soviet Socialist Republic, I demand immediate help for Petrograd. Telegraph to the Food Commissariat about the measures you have taken.[2]

Bread riots were widespread throughout the country.

The famine was so acute [wrote Victor Serge] that at Tsarkoe Selo, not far from Petrograd, the people's bread ration was only 100 grams per day. Rioting results. Cries of 'Long live the Constituent Assembly!' and even 'Long live Nicholas II!' were heard (this on 6-7 April). On 19 April there were 'hunger riots' . . . at

Smolensk . . . In this period [writes one worker-militant] hardly any horses were to be seen in Petrograd; they were either dead, or eaten or requisitioned, or sent off into the countryside. Dogs and cats were no more visible either . . . People lived on tea and potato-cakes made with linseed oil. As a member of the EC of the Vyborg Soviet [in Petrograd] I know that there were *whole weeks* in which no issues of bread or potatoes were made to the workers; all they got was sunflower seeds and some nuts . . . Soviet power seemed to be in a desperate situation.[3]

Speaking in Moscow before a popular meeting, Trotsky displayed a sheaf of telegrams: 'Viksi, Nizhni-Novgorod province: the shops are empty, work is going badly, shortage of 30 per cent of the workers through starvation. Men collapsing with hunger at their benches.' From Serglev-Posada the telegram says: 'Bread, or we are finished!' From Bryansk, 30 May: 'Terrible mortality, especially of children, around the factories of Maltsov and Bryansk; typhus is raging.' From Klin, near Moscow: 'The town has had no bread for two weeks.' From Paslov-Posada: 'The population is hungry, no possibility of finding corn.' From Dorogobuzh: 'Famine, epidemics . . .'[4]

One of the causes of the famine was the breakdown of transport. The number of disabled locomotives increased from 5,100 on 1 January 1917 to 10,000 on 1 January 1918; so that by the latter date 48 per cent of the total were out of commission.[5]

Industry was in a state of complete collapse. Not only was there no food to feed the factory workers; there was no raw material or fuel for industry. The oilfields of the Baku, Grozny and Emba regions came to a standstill. The situation was the same in the coalfields. The production of raw materials was in no better a state. The cultivation of cotton in Turkestan fell to 10-15 per cent of the 1917 level.

The collapse of industry meant unemployment for the workers. In Petrograd 18,000 workers from the 'Treugolnik' plant were thrown out of work, when the establishment was closed because of lack of fuel. The Petrograd tube works were transferred to Penza: 20,000 Petrograd workers lost their jobs. At the works of Siemens and Halske, the numbers of men fell from 1,200 to 700, and later to 300. The Nevsky shipbuilding works also closed, 10,000 men being dismissed. The Obukhov works were shut down, due to lack of coal. Altogether, 14,000 men were dismissed. The same thing happened at the Putilov works, where more than 30,000 men were laid off.[8]

A similar collapse of industry and mass sackings of workers took place in other towns. Drastic measures had to be taken. And Lenin was not one to shirk responsibility, however unpleasant the task.

'We Need State Capitalism'

Lenin had earlier, in *The Threatening Catastrophe*, developed and elaborated the transitional programme of reforms which had been put forward by Marx and Engels in the *Communist Manifesto* to follow the proletarian conquest of power. Now, in March/April 1918, he produced an entirely new formulation: between capitalism and socialism one must have 'state capitalism', which for him was synonymous with the state regulation of private industry. The defence of state capitalism constituted the essence of his economic policy for this period. By it he meant an extended period of joint management with privately owned industry. He thought that future economic development would proceed chiefly by way of mixed companies, state and private, the attraction of foreign capital, the granting of concessions, etc., i.e. capitalist and semi-capitalist forms of production controlled and directed by the proletarian state. Under these conditions the cooperative organizations would take part in the distribution of goods produced by state capitalist industry, and consequently would become a constituent part of the state capitalist economic apparatus linking industry with the peasantry.*

---

* It should be noted that Lenin uses the term 'state capitalism' in a completely different context from that of many later Marxists, including the present writer,[7] when they describe Stalin's Russia as state capitalist. For Lenin state capitalism meant private capitalism under state control (whether the state were a capitalist or a proletarian state). When Stalin's Russia is called state capitalist, this means a regime under which the state is the repository of the means of production, and in which the proletariat is deprived of all political and economic power, while the bureaucracy carries out the functions of capitalism – the extortion of surplus value from the workers and the accumulation of capital.

State capitalism, of course, is not what we are aiming to achieve: 'We ... must tell the workers: Yes, it is a step back, but we have to help ourselves to find a remedy.'[8]

Lenin did not stop at a declaration of intent. He took active steps towards achieving a partnership between private capital and the state. Accordingly negotiations were opened with Meshchersky, a prominent iron and steel magnate whose group owned the principal locomotive and wagon-building works in the country. In March 1918 Meshchersky put forward an ingenious proposal by which his group would hold half the shares in a new metallurgical trust, and the state the other half, the group undertaking the management of the trust on behalf of the partnership. By a narrow majority VSNKh, the Supreme Council of National Economy, decided to negotiate on this basis. About the same time Stakhaev, another industrialist, proposed a trust for the iron and steel industry of the Urals, 200 million rubles of the share capital to be subscribed by his group, 200 million by the state, and 100 million by unnamed American capitalists. An alternative proposal was for the state to put up all the capital, and for the Stakhaev group to manage the trust on behalf of the state.

Another group of financiers advanced a scheme for the formation of international trading companies – Russo-French, Russo-American, Russo-Japanese – to develop foreign trade on the basis of an exchange of goods. About this time a memorandum was prepared on Russian–American commercial relations, in which American capital was to be invited to participate in the exploitation of the fishing, mining, construction and agricultural resources of Siberia and northern Russia.[9]

In industry generally, Lenin tried to achieve a working compromise between the ruling proletariat and the still property-owning capitalists. Thus the decree on workers' control of 14(27) November gave the factory committees 'the right to supervise the management' and 'to determine a minimum of production' and the right of access to all correspondence and accounts; at the same time the general instructions appended to the decree expressly reserved to the proprietor the exclusive right of giving orders about the conduct of the enterprise, and forbade the factory committees to interfere in this or to countermand such orders.

Article 9 forbade committees 'to take possession of the enterprise or direct it', except with the sanction of the higher authorities.

Lenin was adamant on the need to make the compromise between the dictatorship of the proletariat and the capitalists.

> the present task could not be defined by the simple formula: continue the offensive against capital. Although we have certainly not finished off capital and although it is certainly necessary to continue the offensive against this enemy of the working people, such a formula would be inexact, would not be concrete, would not take into account the *peculiarity* of the present situation in which, in order to go on advancing successfully *in the future*, we must 'suspend' our offensive *now*.
>
> This can be explained by comparing our position in the war against capital with the position of a victorious army that has captured, say, a half or two-thirds of the enemy's territory and is compelled to halt in order to muster its forces, to replenish its supplies of munitions, repair and reinforce the lines of communication, build new storehouses, bring up new reserves, etc. To suspend the offensive of a victorious army under such conditions is necessary precisely in order to gain the rest of the enemy's territory, i.e. in order to achieve complete victory. Those who have failed to understand that the objective state of affairs at the present moment dictates to us precisely such a 'suspension' of the offensive against capital have failed to understand anything at all about the present political situation.[10]

'We Need the Bourgeois Specialists'

Lenin stated unambiguously that economic collapse could not be stopped without the correct use of the bourgeois technicians, the specialists. 'It is now an immediate, ripe and essential task to draw the bourgeois intelligentsia into our work.'[11]

> Without the guidance of experts in the various fields of knowledge, technology and experience, the transition to socialism will be impossible, because socialism calls for a conscious mass advance to greater productivity of labour compared with capitalism, and on the basis achieved by capitalism.

Lenin goes on to discuss the question in the most practical way.

> Let us assume that the Russian Soviet Republic requires one thousand first-class scientists and experts . . . Let us assume also that we shall have to pay these 'stars of the first magnitude' . . .

25,000 rubles per annum each. Let us assume that this sum (25,000,000 rubles) will have to be doubled (assuming that we have to pay bonuses for particularly successful and rapid fulfilment of the most important organization and technical tasks), or even quadrupled (assuming that we have to enlist several hundred foreign specialists, who are more demanding). The question is, would the annual expenditure of fifty or a hundred million rubles by the Soviet Republic for the purpose of reorganizing the labour of the people on modern scientific and technological lines be excessive or too heavy? Of course not. The overwhelming majority of the class-conscious workers and peasants will approve of this expenditure because they know from practical experience that our backwardness causes us to lose thousands of millions . . . The corrupting influence of high salaries – both upon the Soviet authorities . . . and upon the mass of the workers – is indisputable. Every thinking and honest worker and poor peasant, however, will agree with us, will admit, that we cannot immediately rid ourselves of the evil legacy of capitalism.[12]

The proletariat has no alternative. Having achieved power, it must turn to the experience gained under capitalism.

Only those are worthy of the name of communists who understand that it is *impossible* to create or introduce socialism *without learning* from the organizers of the trusts. For socialism is not a figment of the imagination, but the assimilation and application by the protelarian vanguard, which has seized power, of what has been created by the trusts. We, the party of the proletariat, have *no other way* of acquiring the ability to organize large-scale production on trust lines, as trusts are organized, except by acquiring it from first-class capitalist experts.

But Lenin does not hide the harsh truth: giving privileges to specialists is a violation of communist principles.

Now we have to resort to the old bourgeois method and to agree to pay a very high price for the 'services' of the top bourgeois experts . . . Clearly, this measure is a compromise, a departure from the principles of the Paris Commune and of every proletarian power, which calls for the reduction of all salaries to the level of the wages of the average worker, which urge that careerism be fought not merely in words, but in deeds.

Moreover, it is clear that this measure not only implies the cessation – in a certain field and to a certain degree – of the offensive against capital (for capital is not a sum of money, but a definite social relation); it is also *a step backward* on the part of our socialist Soviet state power, which from the very outset proclaimed and pursued the policy of reducing high salaries to the level of the wages of the average worker.

Marxists never hide the truth from the working class. To conceal from the people the fact that the enlistment of bourgeois experts by means of extremely high salaries is a retreat from the principles of the Paris Commune would be sinking to the level of bourgeois politicians and deceiving the people.[13]

One-Man Management

There were more difficult decisions to be accepted. To save industry from complete collapse, Lenin argued for the need to impose one-man management.

Given ideal class-consciousness and discipline on the part of those participating in the common work, this subordination would be something like the mild leadership of a conductor of an orchestra. It may assume the sharp forms of a dictatorship if ideal discipline and class-consciousness are lacking. But be that as it may, *unquestioning subordination* to a single will is absolutely necessary for the success of processes organized on the pattern of large-scale machine industry.[14]

The specialist-manager must, at the same time, be subjected to pressure both from below, i.e. from the workers, and from above, i.e. from the workers' government and workers' organizations – the Soviet and trade unions.

The masses must have the right to choose responsible leaders for themselves. They must have the right to replace them, the right to know and check each smallest step of their activity.[15]

when putting 'management' in the hands of capitalists Soviet power appoints workers' Commissars or workers' committees who watch the manager's every step, who learn from his management experience and who not only have the right to appeal against his orders, but can secure his removal through the organs of Soviet power . . . 'management' is entrusted to capitalists only for executive functions while at work, the conditions of which are determined by the Soviet power, by which they may be abolished or revised.[16]

One must learn to combine workers' democracy with one-man management.

We must learn to combine the 'public meeting' democracy of the working people – turbulent, surging, overflowing its banks like a spring flood – with *iron* discipline while at work, with *unquestioning obedience* to the will of a single person, the Soviet leader, while at work.
We have not yet learned to do this.
We shall learn it.[17]

Undoubtedly, the opinion is very widely held . . . that one-man dictatorial authority is incompatible with democracy, the Soviet type of state and collective management. Nothing could be more mistaken than this opinion.[18]

Lenin also grasped another nettle: the need to impose strict discipline in the factories. Breaking management discipline was a central motive of proletarian action during the weeks and months prior to the October revolution. Now the proletariat in power has to impose a new discipline, a proletarian kind of discipline. To start with, in a speech on 13 (26) January 1918, Lenin defined the necessary work discipline based on the collective will of the proletariat, as *radically* different from the discipline imposed under capitalism: 'The socialist revolution is on, and everything now depends on the establishment of a discipline of equals, the discipline of the working masses themselves, which must take the place of capitalist barrack-room discipline.'[19]

On 23 April 1918, Lenin repeated this point:

the most difficult, the gravest phase in the life of our revolution has now begun . . . only iron endurance and labour discipline will enable the revolutionary Russian proletariat, as yet so solitary in its gigantic revolutionary work, to hold out till the time of deliverance when the international proletariat will come to our aid.[20]

Again, on 5 July 1918, he said:

We say that every new social order demands new relations between man and man, a new discipline. There was a time when economic life was impossible without feudal discipline, when there was only one kind of discipline – the discipline of the lash; and there was a time of the rule of the capitalists, when the disciplinary force was starvation. But now, with the Soviet revolution, with the beginning of the socialist revolution, discipline must be built on entirely new principles; it must be a discipline of faith in the organizing power of the workers and poor peasants, a discipline of comradeship, a discipline of the utmost mutual respect, a discipline of independence and initiative in the struggle.[21]

To impose discipline, Lenin calls for the application of the methods of capitalism itself. With implacable logic he demands the utilization of methods developed in order to intensify the exploitation of the workers, in order to raise productivity.

We must raise the question of piece-work and apply and test it in practice; we must raise the question of applying much of what is scientific and progressive in the Taylor system;* we must make wages correspond to the total amount of goods turned out, or to the amount of work done by the railways, the water transport system, etc., etc. . . . The task that the Soviet government must set the people in all its scope is – learn to work. The Taylor system, the last word of capitalism in this respect, like all capitalist progress, is a combination of the refined brutality of bourgeois exploitation and a number of the greatest scientific achievements in the field of analysing mechanical motions during work, the elimination of superfluous and awkward motions, the elaboration of correct methods of work, the introduction of the best system of accounting and control, etc. The Soviet Republic must at all costs adopt all that is valuable in the achievements of science and technology in this field. The possibility of building socialism depends exactly upon our success in combining the Soviet power and the Soviet organization of administration with the up-to-date achievements of capitalism. We must organize in Russia the study and teaching of the Taylor system and systematically try it out and adapt it to our own ends.[22]

Lenin does not in any way disguise the nature of Taylorism as a method of increasing the intensity of labour. He had, after all, in 1914 described Taylorism as 'man's enslavement by the machine'.[23]

---

* F. W. Taylor, the American industrial expert (author of *Principles of Scientific Management*, 1911), pioneered the use of the stop-watch in industry as a means of extracting intensified labour from workers.

The Petty Bourgeois Threat

All the capitalist measures Lenin argued for – state capitalism, the employment of bourgeois specialists, one-man management, Taylorism, etc. – were necessary, in his view, because of the enormous threat facing the proletarian dictatorship in the form of the mass petty bourgeois peasantry. The island of industry in the hands of the proletariat might be engulfed by the vast seas of the backward peasantry.

He enumerated the socio-economic elements co-existing in the country as follows:

> 1. patriarchal, i.e. to a considerable extent natural, peasant farming;
> 2. small commodity production (this includes the majority of those peasants who sell their grain);
> 3. private capitalism;
> 4. state capitalism;
> 5. socialism.
>
> Russia is so vast and so varied that all these different types of socio-economic structures are intermingled. This is what constitutes the specific feature of the situation.[24]

> The greatest threat to workers' power are the first two elements: in the transition from capitalism to socialism our chief enemy is the petty bourgeoisie, its habits and customs, its economic position. The petty proprietor . . . has only one desire – to grab, to get as much as possible for himself.[25]

> Either we subordinate the petty bourgeoisie to *our* control and accounting . . . or they will overthrow our workers' power as surely and as inevitably as the revolution was overthrown by the Napoleons and Cavaignacs who sprang from this very soil of petty proprietorship.[26]

Compared with petty bourgeois production and exchange, state capitalism, Lenin argues, has great positive advantages.

> State capitalism would be a gigantic step forward . . . because victory over disorder, economic ruin and laxity is the most important thing; because the continuation of the anarchy of small ownership is the greatest, the most serious danger, and it will *certainly* be our ruin (unless we overcome it) . . . state capitalism will lead us to socialism by the surest road. When the working class has learned how to defend the state system against the

anarchy of small ownership, when it has learned to organize large-scale production on a national scale, along state capitalist lines, it will hold, if I may use the expression, all the trump cards, and the consolidation of socialism will be assured.

In the first place, *economically*, state capitalism is immeasurably superior to our present economic system.

In the second place, there is nothing terrible in it for Soviet power, for the Soviet state is a state in which the power of the workers and the poor is assured.[27]

State capitalism is the bridge over which the peasantry will go forward to socialism. 'If the petty bourgeois were subordinated to state capitalism, the class-conscious workers would be bound to greet that with open arms, for state capitalism under the Soviet government would be three-quarters of socialism.'[28]

'At present, petty-bourgeois capitalism prevails in Russia, and it is *one and the same road* that leads from it to *both* large-scale state capitalism and to socialism, *through one and the same* intermediary station called "national accounting and control of production and distribution".'[29]

We Have to Learn New Methods of Organizing the Millions

The situation after the revolution demanded a totally new method of organizing the masses, according to Lenin:

We organized thousands under the tsar and hundreds of thousands under Kerensky. That is nothing, it does not count in politics. It was preparatory work, it was a preparatory course. Until the leading workers have learnt to organize tens of millions, they will not be socialists or creators of a socialist society, they will not acquire the necessary knowledge of organization. The road of organization is a long road and the tasks of socialist construction demand stubborn, long-continued work and appropriate knowledge, of which we do not have enough.[30]

The organizing work must also be radically new in qualitative terms. It must be practical and businesslike.

The chief and urgent requirement now is precisely the slogan of practical ability and businesslike methods . . . One can say that no slogan has been less popular among [revolutionaries]. It is quite understandable that as long as the revolutionaries' task consisted in destroying the old capitalist order they were bound to reject and ridicule such a slogan. For at that time this slogan in practice concealed the endeavour in one form or another to come to terms with capitalism, or to weaken the proletariat's attack on the foundations of capitalism, to weaken the revolutionary struggle against capitalism. Quite clearly, things were bound to undergo a radical change after the proletariat had conquered and consolidated its power and work had begun on a wide scale for laying the foundations of a new, i.e. socialist, society.[81]

Strengthening the Dictatorship of the Proletariat

Of course the policy of concessions to capitalism – in the form of state partnership with private industry, the employment and granting of economic privileges to technicians and specialists, who were bourgeois elements inherited from the old regime, one-man management, Taylorism, etc. – put the proletarian regime at risk. Only fools would not see this. And Lenin as always calls a spade a spade: 'the strength of the working class has always been that it looks danger boldly, squarely and openly in the face, that it does not fear to admit danger and soberly weighs the forces in "our" camp and in "the other" camp, the camp of the exploiters'.[82]

To face up to the threats to the proletarian power inherent in state capitalism does not mean to run away. Only cowards, argued Lenin, are paralysed by threats. What was necessary was to compromise with capitalist elements in the economic field, while strengthening the political dictatorship of the proletariat over them.

Of course we should not trust the bourgeois specialists:

the Soviet government has no loyal intelligentsia at its service. The intelligentsia are using their experience and knowledge – the highest human achievement – in the service of the exploiters, and are doing all they can to prevent our gaining victory over the exploiters . . . We have no one to depend upon but the class with which we achieved the revolution and with which we shall overcome the greatest difficulties, cross the very difficult zone that lies ahead of us – and that is the factory workers, the urban and rural proletariat.[83]

Above all, the dictatorship of the proletariat must be strengthened. We must 'ensure that we have a revolutionary authority, which we all recognize in words when speaking of the dictatorship of the proletariat, but instead of which we often see around us something as amorphous as jelly'.[84]

In Conclusion

After coming to power Lenin had to face a very difficult theoretical and practical task: to give flesh and blood to the concept of the *transition period* between capitalism and socialism. Without attempting to evade the reality, Lenin made it clear that this period would be one in which contradictory elements from the past and the future would co-exist while struggling with each other.

Communist and capitalist economic organization have many common characteristics. The workers' state – a transition stage between capitalism and communism – must inevitably include features of the society from whose ruins it rises, and some of the nuclei of the society of the future. These antagonistic elements will, however, be bound together in the transition period, the former being subordinated to the latter, the past to the future.

Workers' power and workers' control over production will immediately become a bridge between mental and manual labour, and the point of departure for their future synthesis, the total abolition of classes.

Technicians constitute a necessary element in the process of production, an important part of the productive forces of society, whether capitalist or communist. Under capitalism they form a level in the hierarchy of production. They come into being as part and parcel of this hierarchy, which socialism will abolish. In the transition period it will continue to exist in one sense, but in another it will be done away with. Insofar as mental labour remains the privilege of the few, hierarchical relations will continue to exist in the factories, railways, etc., even after the proletarian revolution. But as the place of the capitalist in the hierarchy will be taken by the workers' state, i.e. by the workers as a collective, the technicians will be subordinated to the workers, and the mental hierarchy in this sense will be abolished. Workers' control over technicians means the subordination of capitalist elements to socialist ones. The more effective workers' power, and the higher the material and cultural level of the masses, the more will the monopolist position of mental workers be undermined; eventually it will be completely abolished and a full synthesis of mental and manual labour will be achieved.

The founders of marxism pointed out that, because of the dual role of technicians in their relation to workers in the process of production, their subordination to the interests of society as a whole would be one of the most difficult tasks faced by the new society. Thus Engels wrote:

> If . . . a war brings us to power prematurely, the technicians will be our chief enemies; they will deceive and betray us wherever they can and we shall have to use terror against them but shall get cheated all the same.[85]

The imposition of labour discipline would be very difficult. Every form of social production needs the co-ordination of the different people participating in it; in other words, every form of social production needs discipline. Under capitalism this discipline confronts the worker as an external coercive power, as the power which capital has over him. Under socialism discipline will be the result of consciousness, it will become the habit of a free people. In the transition period it has to be the outcome of a combination of the two elements – consciousness and coercion. The proletarian state institutions will constitute the organization of the masses as a conscious factor. Collective ownership of the means of production by the workers, i.e. the ownership by the workers' state of the means of production, will be the basis for the conscious element in labour discipline. At the same time the working class as a collective, through its institutions – soviets, trade unions, etc. – will act as a coercive power in disciplining the individual workers in production.

The technicians, supervisors, etc., have a special place in labour discipline. Under capitalism, the supervisor is the means by which capitalist coercion of the worker is transmitted and exercised. Under communism a supervisor will not fulfil any coercive function. His relations with the workers will be analogous to those between a conductor and his orchestra, as labour discipline will be based on consciousness and habit. In the transition period, whereas the workers will be both a disciplining and a disciplined factor, a subject and an object, the technicians will serve only as a transmission mechanism, this time for the workers' state, even though they formally retain the role of disciplining the workers.[36]

7
War Communism
(1918–1921)

As we saw in the last chapter, in March and April 1918 Lenin developed an economic policy aimed at achieving a long process of reform on the basis of the proletarian revolution. However, the intensification of the class struggle, and the outbreak of civil war in May 1918, totally shattered this policy.

Nationalization of Industry Replacing Workers' Control

The policy of the Bolsheviks after October – workers' control of industry and selective nationalization – was sabotaged initially by the capitalists. Still hoping for restoration of their former power, and unwilling to work under workers' control, they practised large-scale sabotage.

Thus the All-Russian Congress of Employers' Associations declared at the beginning of December 1917 that those 'factories in which the control is exercised by means of active interference in the administration will be closed'.[1]

The Société Internationale des Wagon-Lits and the Sergeev-Ugalenski mines were nationalized because of 'the refusal of the management to continue work in the workshops', and because of 'the refusal of the management to submit to the Decree on Workers' Control'; M.Helferich-Sade's business was nationalized in January because management 'had closed down its factory and abandoned its principal office at Kharkov'. Similarly, the aeroplane works of Andreev Lanski and Company were taken over because of the company's declared intention to dismiss its workers; the Sestronetsk metallurgical works for refusing to continue production; Rostkino dye works for 'the categorical refusal of its owner to continue production in spite of the reserves of material and fuel in stock'.[2]

The workers reacted spontaneously to capitalist sabotage. As Serge put it:

> The liquidation of the political defences of their capitalist exploiters launched a spontaneous movement among the workers to take over the means of production. Since they were perfectly able to take control of the factories and workshops, why should they abstain? If they could, they ought. The employers' sabotage of production entailed expropriation as an act of reprisal.[3]

Of individual firms that had been nationalized before July 1918, only about 100 were nationalized by decree from the centre, while over 400 were nationalized on the initiative of local organizations.[4]

With the outbreak of civil war, not only did the bourgeoisie's attitude to the regime harden, and any previous willingness to cooperate evaporate completely, but for the Soviet government military necessity immediately took precedence over all other considerations. Such big capitalists as had not previously done so packed their bags and passed through the White Army's lines. For the Soviet authorities direct control over production quickly became an urgent necessity, both to combat attempts at sabotage and to ensure priority for military supplies. Hence there was wholesale nationalization. Altogether it was estimated that 70 per cent of all nationalizations in this period took place because the employers refused to accept workers' control or abandoned their enterprises.[5]

Not until 2 May 1918 was a whole industry nationalized – the sugar industry; then on 17 June the petroleum industry; on 28 June a decree was made for the nationalization of the largest undertakings in the mining, metallurgical, textile, electro-technical, pottery, tanning and cement industries. This set off a vast process of confiscation which continued until all the large factories in Soviet territory had been taken over by the state.

In many cases the nationalization of industry was carried out *independently* of the Soviet government. Thus between July and December 1918, of 1,208 enterprises nationalized, only 345 were expropriated by state decree, while the rest – 863 enterprises – were taken over by local soviets, or local national economic councils.[6]

The process continued, until it covered not only large-scale and medium-sized industry, but even small factories. In November 1920 a decree announced the nationalization of all enterprises employing more than five workers where mechanical power was used, and more than ten workers in purely handicraft workshops; by the end of the year as many as 37,000 enterprises were listed as belonging to the state. This figure included many thousands of quite small workshops: 18,000 of the 37,000 enterprises did not use mechanical power, and more than 5,000 of them were employing only one worker.[7]

The Bolsheviks were forced to go far beyond what they thought economically rational, and to expropriate capitalists in industry and trade, large and small. As the distinguished economic historian of the period, Kritzman, put it:

> In the atmosphere of the kindling civil war every joint effort of capital and the proletarian dictatorship (workers' control, mixed joint-stock companies etc.) is seen to be a quickly evaporating Utopia.
>
> The intervention of world capital, which fanned the expiring counter-revolutionary resistance within Russia into a new blaze, forced its consequence onto the proletariat – the inexorable expropriation of large-scale capital and capital generally, the confiscation of the property of the ruling classes, the suppression of the market and the construction of an all-embracing proletarian organization of the political economy, which depended on overcoming the market, and its exploitation.[8]

Thus from June 1918 onwards the imperative measures were general nationalization of industry and confiscations. The economic policy which Lenin drew up, involving an indirect attack on capitalism while making use of the captains of industry and the bourgeois technicians, proved unworkable.

The Collapse of Industrial Production

The wholesale nationalization of industry was accompanied by a catastrophic decline of industrial production. The civil war tore apart the Russian economy. The main industrial regions of northern and central Russia remained under Soviet rule throughout the civil war. But the factories in these regions and the railway system, were dependent on sources of raw materials and fuel which were often cut off for long periods. The engineering industry of Petrograd, Briansk, Tula and other Soviet industrial towns needed coal from the Donets Basin and iron from the Urals and from the Ukraine. The Urals region was lost from the summer of 1918 until the summer of 1919, when Kolchak was driven back into Siberia. The Donets Basin was completely cut off from Russia from the time of the German occupation of the Ukraine in spring 1918 until the retreat of Denikin's army in the latter months of 1919 (with the exception of a brief period early in 1918, when part of it was held by the Soviets). Baku oil was lost from the time the Turks occupied Baku in summer 1918 until the Red Army entered it in spring 1920. The secondary oil source in Grozny in the North Caucasus was cut off by Denikin. The textile mills of Moscow and the ring of factory towns around it depended on cotton from Turkestan, but Turkestan was cut off from Soviet Russia, first as a result of the Czechoslovak troops' onslaught on the Volga in the summer of 1918, and later, until the latter part of 1919, by Kolchak's advance. By that time the peasants of Turkestan had largely given up planting cotton (and substituted crops which would yield something to eat).

Foreign blockade dealt another serious blow to Soviet Russia's industry:

	Import	Export
	(in million pud)*	
1913	936·6	1472·1
1917	178·0	59·6
1918	11·5	1·8
1919	0·5	0·0
1920	5·2	0·7[9]

* pud = 16·38 kg = 36·11 lb.

A shortage of raw materials, fuel and food combined to bring about a disastrous fall in industrial productivity. Starvation, or semi-starvation, gravely affected workers' efficiency. According to approximate calculations, the gross product per head of the Russian worker changed as follows:

	Productivity per worker (in stable rubles)	
1913	100	–
1917	85	100
1918	44	52
1919	22	25
1920	26	30[10]

Absenteeism reached unprecedented levels. It was sometimes as high as 60 per cent, and quite commonly exceeded 30 per cent.[11] The average rate of absenteeism before the war had been about 10 per cent. In 1920 absenteeism in the best 'shock' plants increased threefold. In the Sormovsky plant it reached 36 per cent in July; in August it dropped to 32 per cent. At the Briansk plant it was 40 per cent during the winter months and rose to 48·5 per cent in June and to 50 per cent in August. At the Tver plant it was 44 per cent during July and August.[12]

It is impossible, of course, to evaluate the precise weight of the various factors leading to the decline in labour productivity. However, an attempt at an estimate, which should be taken only as a rough guide, was made by a Soviet economist, S.G.Strumilin. His assessment was that the decline of productivity in industry was caused by the following factors:

	%
Physical exhaustion of workers	44
Slackening of work discipline	22
Move to time-wages	19
Defects in work organization	6
Shortage of raw materials	6
Wear and tear of machines	4

Even if Strumilin's calculation is taken only as an approximation, it still unmistakably underlines the fact that the physical exhaustion of workers, brought about by undernourishment, was the major cause of the decline in labour productivity.[13] Workers were so wretchedly fed that it was not uncommon for them to faint at the bench. It was an act of heroism to work at all. The labour front demanded no less fortitude than the military front.

The catastrophic decline of large-scale industry can be seen from the following (production in 1913 = 100):

for 1917	77
for 1918	35
for 1919	26
for 1920	18[14]

What happened in different branches of industry can be seen from the following table:

Production in 1920 (1913 = 100)

Petroleum	42·7	Electric bulbs	10·1
Tobacco	42·5	Sugar	6·7
Leather	38	Electrical engineering	
Linen yarn	38	machinery and power	
Salt	30	current apparatus	5·4
Wool yarn	27	Cotton yarn goods	5·1
Coal	27	Railway carriage	
Paper and pulp	25	construction	4·2
Hemp spun yarn	23	Vegetable oils	3·0
Locomotive		Cement	3·0
construction	14·8	Pig iron	2·4
Matches	14	Bricks	2·1
Ploughs	13·3	Iron ore	1·7
Accumulators	12·5	Copper	0·0[15]

Railway transport, central to all economic (as well as military) activities, was in a critical state. The picture here was:

Year	% of damaged locomotives
1913	17
1918	41
1919	52
1920	57[16]

The Compulsory Requisition of Grain

The civil war, as well as breaking up the national economy of Russia, also imposed on industry massive demands from the Red Army. In summer 1920 the army was taking the following proportions of the country's centralized supplies:

	%		%
Flour	25	Fats	40
Groats	50	Soap	40
Feedstuffs	40	Tobacco	100
Fish	60	Matches	20
Meat	60	Cotton material	40
Dried fruit	90	Other textiles	70-100
Sugar	60	Footwear	90[17]
Salt	15		

After the army took its share of the shrinking industrial output, very little remained for the peasantry, so that the economic connection between industry and agriculture, between town and country, was broken. The peasant got very few industrial goods in exchange for the grain he delivered, as can be seen from the following table:

	Supply of grain from peasantry (million pud)*	Supply of textiles to peasantry (million arshin)**	Ratio between the two (arshins of textiles per pud of grain)
1919	108	325	1:3.00
1920	212	180	1:0.85[18]

* pud = 16.38 kg = 36.11 lb.
** arshin = 28 inches.

The only way the army and the town population could be guaranteed food was by the compulsory requisitioning of grain from the peasant. The all-powerful Food Commissariat took from industry whatever it produced for distribution among the population, and took from agriculture whatever could be extracted from the peasants, for distribution to the army and the town population, through rationing.

The collapse of industry and the violent suppression of

commercial relations between town and country meant that the exchange of grain and industrial goods which took place was not a real exchange. While the better-off peasantry supplied the majority of the grain, the poor peasantry got the industrial goods. As Kritzman said: 'The state exchange of products was . . . not so much an exchange between industry and agriculture, as an exchange of industrial products against the services that the poor peasants gave in the extraction of products from the farms of the well-to-do layers of the village.'[19]

The attempt at centralized state control of grain supplies was repeatedly undermined by the activity of millions of peasants,* as well as that of hungry townspeople foraging for food. Thus in 1919 out of the 136·6 million pud of cereal which reached the consumers, 40 per cent (i.e. 54·4 million pud) were delivered by the state distribution bodies (the People's Commissariat for food distribution) and 60 per cent (82·2 million pud) by illegal 'free' trade.[20]

Food Rationing

A central characteristic of the economic system at the time of the civil war was distribution of grain by the state according to rigid class criteria.

In September 1918 the Moscow Soviet divided the population into four categories. The first consisted of manual workers engaged in harmful trades; the second, of workers who were obliged to perform heavy physical labour; the third, of workers in light tasks, employees, housewives; the fourth, of professional men and women and people living on unearned income or without employment. Such food supplies as were available were doled out to these four categories in the ratio 4:3:2:1. However, even the most favoured category got very meagre rations indeed. People in the first category in Petrograd during May 1919 received the following allotments: 15½ pounds of bread, one pound of sugar, half a pound of margarine, four pounds of herrings, two pounds of other fish, one pound of salt and a quarter of a pound of mustard.[21]

---

* See Chapter 10 for the peasants' massive resistance to requisitions.

At the worst period the meagre bread ration of 2 oz. for workers was issued on alternate days.[22]

A Soviet author calculates that the food-card system in Moscow gave the population about one-seventh of the calories which the Germans received on ration cards during the war and about one-tenth of the calories which the British obtained. Even if one makes allowance for the fact that the Russians may have been able to purchase extra food on the private market, it is evident that malnutrition and in some cases downright starvation were far more prevalent in Russia than in wartime Germany or Britain.[23]

Hunger, Epidemics and Cold

Hunger stalked the towns. One result was a massive flight of the population to the countryside. The urban population, and particularly the number of industrial workers, declined very sharply between 1917 and 1920. In the autumn of 1920 the population of 40 capitals of provinces had declined since 1917 by 33 per cent, from 6,400,000 to 4,300,000, and the population of 50 other large towns by 16 per cent, from 1,517,000 to 1,271,000. The larger the city, the greater the decline. The population of Petrograd fell from 2,400,000 in 1917 to 574,000 in August 1920.

In the footsteps of hunger came epidemics, above all typhus. The following is the number of typhus victims in European Russia (in thousands):

1914	83	1918	180
1915	90	1919	2105
1916	102	1920	3114
1917	88		

So in two years over *five million* people fell ill with typhus.[24]

Without exaggeration Lenin could declare to the Seventh Congress of Soviets on 5 December 1919:

> A scourge is assailing us, *lice*, and the *typhus* that is mowing down our troops. Comrades, it is impossible to imagine the dreadful situation in the typhus regions, where the population is broken, weakened, without material resources, where all life, all public life ceases. To this we say, 'Comrades, we must con-

centrate everything on this problem. *Either the lice will defeat socialism, or socialism will defeat the lice!*[25]

Deaths from typhus alone in the years 1918-20 numbered 1·6 million, and typhoid, dysentery and cholera caused another 700,000.[26] All told, the number of premature deaths is estimated for the period from 1 January 1918 to 1 July 1920 at *seven million*, i.e. at 7 per cent of the total population.[27]

This estimate does not cover the peripheral areas of Russia such as Siberia and the South East. If these were included the number of premature deaths must have been more than nine million. This far surpasses the number of deaths in combat – estimated at about 350,000.

Cold added to the suffering of the population. As the most essential industries and the transport system were chronically short of fuel, practically nothing was allocated for domestic heating. So abandoned houses were torn down by the people who had strength for such activity, and the wood used for heating.

Suffering was indescribable. Numerous cases of cannibalism occurred. A quarter of Russia's population – 35 million – suffered from continuous acute hunger. Several million orphan waifs roamed roads, railway tracks and city streets, living on charity and crime. The weak suffered most. And nobody was weaker than the children. On 2 April 1920 Gorky wrote to Lenin: 'In Petrograd there are over 6,000 juvenile delinquents aged 9 to 15, all of them recidivists and with no few murderers amongst them. There are 12-year-olds who have as many as three murders to their name.'[28]

Victor Serge described the terrible affliction of children at the time:

Do you know what Tata is doing? She can't sleep with the commissars, not with a broken nose and a voice like an old worn-out shoe. But she found herself a racket. She undresses little kids. 'Here, little boy, come here. I've got something interesting to show you ...'
She takes the kid by the hand, all sweet and nice, and leads him into a hallway. Two slaps across his little face and Tata collects his coat, his hat, his gloves, a good day's work.
'That turns my stomach,' said Katka. 'Poor little kids.'

'They're gonna croak one way or another,' said Manya softly. 'These days.'

'And anyway,' ventures Dunya-the-Snake, 'if they're the kids of the bourgeois, too bad for them.'

'Shut up, you stupid little Agit-Prop. You know that big building they're putting up over on the canal? Well, a whole gang of kids is holed up in there, with Olenka-the-Runaway as their chief. What do you say to that? Ah, now there's a somebody for all her thirteen years. Looks like a little lamb; sweet, well-mannered and all that, but cunning. I'm sure she's the one who killed that little boy by the Oats Market. You know what they thought up? They catch cats, they eat them, and sell the skins to the Chinese . . . They also work poorboxes in the churches and ration cards in the food lines.'[29]

Egalitarianism

Strict egalitarianism was preached and practised by the Bolshevik party. 'Our salaries were linked to the "Communist Maximum",' Serge recalled, 'equal to the average wage of a skilled worker.' He went on to relate how the eldest son of Ionov, Zinoviev's brother-in-law, an executive member of the Soviet and director of the state Library, died of hunger before their very eyes.[30]

> In the Kremlin, he [Lenin] still occupied a small apartment built for a palace servant. In the second winter, he, like everyone else, had had no heating. When he went to the barber's he took his turn, thinking it unseemly for anyone to give way to him.[31]

Lenin was very angry when he found out that he had been paid too much, and on 23 May 1918 he rebuked V.D.Bonch-Bruevich, office manager of the Council of People's Commissars:

> In view of your failure to fulfil my insistent request to point out to me the justification for raising my salary as from 1 March 1918, from 500 to 800 rubles a month, and in view of the obvious illegality of this increase, I give you a severe reprimand.[32]

Krupskaya used to go to the Kremlin restaurant to fetch the family dinner. She was often seen walking along the icy Kremlin pavement with a big chunk of black bread under her arm, and carrying in front of her a pot of soup. But though her trip to the restaurant was timed for Lenin's return home, she rarely found him there. Maria, Lenin's sister, would phone his office. He promised to come right away. After ten or fifteen minutes she would phone again, pleading with him to come home as the food was getting cold. When at last he did come home, as punishment he would have to wait till the food was warmed again.

A high government official in the Kremlin could tell the *Manchester Guardian* correspondent Arthur Ransome:

> Today is the first day for two months that we have been able to warm this building. We have been working here in overcoats and fur hats in a temperature below freezing point . . . Many of my assistants have fallen ill. Two only yesterday had to be taken home in a condition something like that of a fit, the result of prolonged sedentary work in unheated rooms. I have lost the use of my right hand for the same reason.[33]

Super-Centralization of Management

War communism meant extreme centralization of economic management. But this did not mean rational planning of the economy. Disintegration of production, the substitution of compulsion for exchange between town and country, and compulsion in the labour field, did not aid rational calculation and planning. Orders from the centre were also often confused and contradictory, because of the sheer pressure of the civil war conditions and the inexperience of the administration. As Lenin put it: 'such is the sad fate of our decrees: they are signed, and then we ourselves forget about them and fail to carry them out'.[34]

Kritzman called the resultant confusion 'the most complete form of proletarian natural-anarchistic economy'. 'Anarchistic' because of conflicts between administrative departments and because of the lack of any coherent plan. Anarchistic too because of the 'shock' *(udarnii)* campaigning methods, by which the authorities rushed from bottleneck to bottleneck, creating new shortages while seeking feverishly to deal with others.

There was no unified economic plan. The war was given priority and improvisation was substituted for rational planning. As Maurice Dobb, an economic historian of the period, put it:

The administrative chaos and delays which resulted from the passing of so many decisions about matters of detail through a few central bottlenecks had their reaction in what came to be known as the 'shock' system . . . To by-pass the administrative congestion when its economic results became alarming, certain enterprises of special importance, usually from the immediate military point of view, were singled out as 'shock' enterprises. These were given top priority in the supply of fuel and materials and food rations for their workers, and the best organizers available were assigned to their administration. When applied only to a limited range of industry, it was, of course, a reasonable method of applying priorities and its effect was beneficial (for example, in improving the situation in transport). In the situation of civil war it is difficult to see what other method could have been quickly applied. But in the course of time, as soon as it had come to be applied to all widely, it tended in many cases to increase rather than to lessen the economic confusion.[85]

Has the Communist Millennium Arrived?

The desperate measures taken by the Bolsheviks seemed to many at the time to be an unexpectedly rapid realization of the Party programme for achieving Communism. Socialization of industry, the requisitions of food, the payment of wages in kind, the liquidation of money, the state's growing role in the distribution of resources throughout the national economy, the abolition of the market economy which was the breeding ground of capitalism – all looked like the achievement of full communism. After all, according to Marx, the future Communist economy was to be a natural economy in which socialist planned production and distribution would take the place of production for the market. The Bolshevik leaders were therefore naturally inclined to see the essential features of communism embodied in the war economy of the civil war period. The stern egalitarianism which the party preached and practised strengthened this belief.

In March 1919 Lenin wrote: 'In the sphere of distribution, the present task of Soviet power is to continue steadily replacing trade by the planned, organized and nation-wide distribution of goods . . . The Russian Communist Party will strive as speedily as possible to introduce the most radical measures to pave the way for the abolition of money.'[86]

On the second anniversary of the October revolution Lenin could define the economic system prevailing as communist.

In Russia, labour is united communistically insofar as, first, private ownership of the means of production has been abolished, and, secondly, the proletarian state power is organizing large-scale production on state-owned land and in state-owned enterprises on a national scale, is distributing labour-power among the various branches of production and the various enterprises, and is distributing among the working people large quantities of articles of consumption belonging to the state.[87]

However, Lenin sometimes contradicted himself, saying that the prevailing system was very primitive, and far from real communism.

We give the name of communism to the system under which people form the habit of performing their social duties without any special apparatus for coercion, and when unpaid work for the public good becomes a general phenomenon . . . The expropriation of the landowners and capitalists enabled us to organize only the most primitive forms of socialism, and there is not yet anything communist in it. If we take our present-day economy we see that the germs of socialism in it are still very weak and that the old economic forms dominate overwhelmingly; these are expressed either as the domination of petty proprietorship or as wild, uncontrolled profiteering.[88]

The Bolshevik leader who was most enthusiastic about War Communism as real communism was Bukharin. He saw the distribution of rations in kind instead of wages in money as the disappearance of wage labour. He thought that the monetary system, and with it the commodity system in general, would collapse during the period of transition, this being made manifest through the devaluation of the currency.[89]

Marx's concept of communist society, however, was based on highly developed productive forces with a superabundance of goods and services, and rational organization of the economy. Economic inequality was to be abolished by levelling up living standards. War Communism was, on the contrary, the result of the destruction and disintegration of production, of the unparalleled scarcity of goods and services.

As Marx stated repeatedly: 'Law can never be higher than the economic structure and the cultural level conditioned by it.' The Bolsheviks had no doubt that the material heritage they had acquired on taking power was very meagre, not only in comparison with contemporary developed capitalist countries, but even with these same countries at an early stage of their capitalist development.

The most complete and accurate calculation of the national income in different countries at different periods was undertaken by Colin Clark in his book *The Conditions of Economic Progress* (London, 1940). He estimates the real income per occupied person in Russia in 1913 to be 306 International Units (IUs).* As against this the real income per occupied person in some developed countries was:

Great Britain		France		Germany		USA	
Year	I.U.	Year	I.U.	Year	I.U.	Year	I.U.
1688	372	1850-59*	382	1850	420	1850	787
1860-69*	638	1860-69*	469	1877	632	1880	1,032
1904-10*	999	1911	786	1913	881	1900	1,388
1913	1,071					1917	1,562
						1929	1,636

* Annual average

Thus the average income per occupied person in Russia in 1913 was only 80·9 per cent of the corresponding figure for Britain in 1688.[40] The level of literacy in Russia at the time of the revolution was *below* that of France at the time of its revolution, in 1789!

The Utopian hopes of the Bolsheviks in the period of War Communism appear completely inexplicable at first glance. However, they were based on the hope of an early victory of the revolution in the West, which would have made possible a *direct* progression from War Communism to the systematic construction of socialism. In addition, the illusions prevailing were an integral part of the moral courage of the masses and were imposed by the harsh exigencies of the civil war.

---

* Clark defines the 'International Unit' as 'the amount of goods and services which one dollar would purchase in USA over the average of the period 1925-34'.

In Retrospect

After the civil war and the ending of War Communism, Lenin summed up the balance of experience of the period, admitting both the errors of the time, and their inevitability. Thus, in a speech on 17 October 1921, he said:

> Partly owing to the war problems that overwhelmed us and partly owing to the desperate position in which the Republic found itself owing to these circumstances, and a number of others, we made the mistake of deciding to go over directly to communist production and distribution. We thought that under the surplus-food appropriation system the peasants would provide us with the required quantity of grain, which we could distribute among the factories and thus achieve communist production and distribution.
>
> I cannot say that we pictured this plan as definitely and as clearly as that; but we acted approximately on those lines . . .
>
> that line was wrong . . . it ran counter to what we had previously written about the transition from capitalism to socialism . . . Ever since 1917, when the problem of taking power arose . . . our theoretical literature has been definitely stressing the necessity for a prolonged, complex transition, through socialist accounting and control, from capitalist society (and the less developed it is the longer the transition will take) to even one of the approach to communist society.[41]

The mistakes of the party were the result of overenthusiasm and euphoria, according to Lenin.

> Borne along on the crest of the wave of enthusiasm, rousing first the political enthusiasm and then the military enthusiasm of the people, we expected to accomplish economic tasks just as great as the political and military tasks we had accomplished by relying directly on this enthusiasm. We expected – or perhaps it would be truer to say that we presumed without having given it adequate consideration – to be able to organize the state production and the state distribution of products on communist lines in a small-peasant country directly as ordered by the proletarian state. Experience has proved that we were wrong. It appears that a number of transitional stages were necessary – state capitalism and socialism – in order to *prepare* – to prepare by many years of effort – for the transition to communism. Not directly relying on enthusiasm, but aided by the enthusiasm engendered by the great revolution, and on the basis of personal interest, personal incentive and business principles, we must

first set to work in this small-peasant country to build solid gangways to socialism by way of state capitalism.[42]

Nothing can be an excuse for hiding one's own mistakes. 'We are not afraid to admit our mistakes and shall examine them dispassionately in order to learn how to correct them.'[43]

The Soviet government had to probe the strength of the enemy, to gauge its own forces, to determine by experience the path actually open for systematic development of economic life; and these tasks could not have been achieved without resort to the methods of War Communism. As Lenin, looking back at the period, put it:

> To explain my views and to indicate in what sense we can, and in my opinion should, say that our previous economic policy was mistaken, I would like to take for the purpose of analogy an episode from the Russo-Japanese War . . . the capture of Port Arthur by the Japanese General Nogi. The main thing that interests me in this episode is that the capture of Port Arthur was accomplished in two entirely different stages. The first stage was that of furious assaults, which ended in failure and cost the celebrated Japanese commander extraordinarily heavy losses. The second stage was the extremely arduous, extremely difficult and slow method of siege, according to all the rules of the art. Eventually, it was by this method that the problem of capturing the fortress was solved. When we examine these facts we naturally ask in what way was the Japanese general's first mode of operation against the fortress a mistake? . . .
> At first sight, of course, the answer to this question would seem to be a simple one. If a series of assaults on Port Arthur proved to be ineffective – and that was the case – if the losses sustained by the assailants were extremely heavy – and that, too, was undeniably the case – it is evident that the tactics of immediate and direct assault upon the fortress of Port Arthur were mistaken . . . On the other hand, however, it is easy to understand that in solving a problem in which there are very many unknown factors, it is difficult without the necessary practical experience to determine with absolute certainty the mode of operation to be adopted against the enemy fortress, or even to make a fair approximation of it. It was impossible to determine this without ascertaining in practice the strength of the fortress, the strength of its fortifications, the state of its garrison, etc. Without this it was impossible for even the best of commanders, such as General Nogi undoubtedly was, to decide what tactics to

adopt to capture the fortress . . . without . . . the practical attempt to carry the fortress by assault . . . there would have been no grounds for adopting the more prolonged and arduous method of struggle . . . Taking the operations as a whole, we cannot but regard the first stage, consisting of direct assaults and attacks, as having been a necessary and useful stage, because . . . without this experience the Japanese army could not have learnt sufficiently the concrete conditions of the struggle.[44]

The direct, furious assault on capitalism represented by War Communism was similarly a necessary stage in the development of the dictatorship of the proletariat, an inevitable product of the raging civil war.

The capitalist apparatus – the management of the factories, the banks, etc. – was destroyed. There was no possibility of coming to terms economically with the bourgeoisie, even in terms of concessions or restricted workers' control. With the bourgeois apparatus of economic management destroyed, there was no alternative but to create a substitute, however crude. The policy of compulsory grain requisition and centralized direction of labour followed from the collapse of the market and the conditions of siege economy. As Trotsky put it in retrospect:

> This 'communism' was rightly called *War Communism* not only because it replaced economic methods by military ones but also because it served military purposes above all others. It was not a question of assuring a systematic development of economic life under the prevailing conditions, but of securing the indispensable food supply for the army at the fronts and of preventing the working class from dying out altogether. War Communism was the regime of a beleaguered fortress.[45]

In his Report to the Tenth Party Congress in March 1921, introducing the New Economic Policy (NEP) Lenin reiterated that War Communism had been unavoidable.

> There was no other way out in the conditions of the unexampled ruin in which we found ourselves, when after a big war we were obliged to endure a number of civil wars. We must state quite definitely that, in pursuing our policy, we may have made mistakes and gone to extremes in a number of cases. But in the wartime conditions then prevailing, the policy was in the main a correct one. We had no alternative but to resort to wholesale and instant monopoly, including the confiscation of all surplus

stocks, even without compensation. That was the only way we could tackle the task.[46]

And in a pamphlet, 'The Tax in Kind' explaining NEP, written on 21 April 1921, Lenin repeats:

> It was the war and the ruin that forced us into War Communism. It was not, and could not be, a policy that corresponded to the economic tasks of the proletariat. It was a makeshift.[47]

Despite all the criticism of the policy of War Communism, there is no doubt that it was this policy that enabled Soviet Russia to emerge victorious, despite the breakdown of the economy and the excruciating suffering of the workers and peasants. It enabled the Soviet government to mobilize sufficient strength and concentrate the energy and heroism of the revolutionary masses on the most vital immediate task.

8

The Heroic and the Tragic Intertwine

The Wide Sweep of the Revolution

'Miracles of proletarian organization must be achieved.' This idea of Lenin's provides a key to the victory of the working class. In 1917 and the period following, the policy of the Bolsheviks consisted mainly in awakening – and at the same time guiding – the initiative of the masses. In three years of struggle the proletariat, first in the conquest of power, then in its consolidation and defence, showed exceptional collective heroism and self-sacrifice amidst unparalleled tortures of hunger, cold and constant peril. Every time there was a real threat to the regime thousands of proletarians volunteered for the war front and for voluntary labour behind the front. In fact, half of all trade unionists volunteered for the Red Army, and scattered along a front stretching for thousands of miles, they died and taught others how to die. The revolutionary idealism of the proletariat was unprecedented. Half-starved people in felt shoes and dirty linen showed supreme heroism in the struggle for freedom. Lenin could justifiably declare in March 1920:

> We overthrew the landowners and capitalists because the men of the Red Army, workers and peasants, knew they were fighting for their own vital interests.
> We won because the best people from the entire working class and from the entire peasantry displayed unparalleled heroism in the war against the exploiters, performed miracles of valour, withstood untold privations, made great sacrifices and got rid of scroungers and cowards.[1]

> The determination of the working class, its inflexible adherence to the watchword 'Death rather than surrender!' is not only a historical factor, it is the decisive, the winning factor.[2]

The victories wrested by the Red Army from armies which were infinitely better equipped were a product of the astonishing heroism displayed by the proletariat and its indomitable will to defend Soviet power. For all their miseries, squalor and cruelty, the years of the civil war were years not only of destruction, but also of a mighty sweep of creation, courage and soaring hope.

In the revolution and the period of consolidation of Soviet power, the party relied above all on the aspirations of the masses. Addressing the Second All-Russian Congress of Soviets, at the very moment of the Bolshevik seizure of power, Lenin declared: 'We must allow complete freedom to the creative faculties of the masses.' A few days later he said: 'Creative activity at the grass roots is the basic factor of the new public life . . . living, creative socialism is the product of the masses themselves.'[3] And in an appeal to the population published in *Pravda* of 6 (19) November 1917, he wrote:

> Comrades, working people! Remember that now *you yourselves* are at the helm of state. No one will help you if you yourselves do not unite and take into *your* hands *all affairs* of the state . . . Get on with the job yourselves; begin right at the bottom, do not wait for anyone.[4]

Never before had the working class become the ruling class of a great country, and never had the revolutionary class fought more tenaciously and heroically against a mighty coalition of domestic and foreign enemies. The first workers' republic in world history survived thanks to the most resolute measures carried out by the proletariat and its party. As Lenin stated in retrospect:

> The defence of the workers' and peasants' power was achieved by a miracle, not a divine miracle – it was not something that fell from the skies – but a miracle in the sense that, no matter how oppressed, humiliated, ruined and exhausted the workers and peasants were, precisely because the revolution went along with the workers, it mustered very much more strength than any rich, enlightened and advanced state could have mustered.[5]

Never before had such radical changes in social structure been carried out in so short a time. Semi-feudal relations of land ownership were swept away far more radically than even the French Revolution had done. Practically all the factories, mines and other valuable natural resources of the country were taken over by the workers' state.

The sweep of the revolution was no less wide in the field of what Marx called 'the ideological superstructure'. Above all, it brought about an insatiable appetite for culture in the mass of the workers. Thus Trotsky wrote: 'The greatest advantage, the greatest conquest that the revolution has offered up to this time . . . has been the awakening of a powerful thirst for culture among the working masses.'[6]

John Reed wrote:

> The thirst for education, so long thwarted, burst with the Revolution into a frenzy of expression. From Smolny Institute alone [during] the first six months, went out every day tons, car-loads, train-loads of literature, saturating the land. Russia absorbed reading matter like hot sand drinks water, insatiable. And it was not fables, falsified history, diluted religion, and the cheap fiction that corrupts – but social and economic theories, philosophy, the works of Tolstoy, Gogol, and Gorky . . .
>
> Then the talk, beside which Carlyle's 'flood of French speech' was a mere trickle. Lectures, debates, speeches – in theatres, circuses, school-houses, clubs, Soviet meeting-rooms, union head-quarters, barracks . . . Meetings in the trenches at the front, in village squares, factories . . . What a marvellous sight to see Puti-

lovsky Zavod [the Putilov factory] pour out its forty thousand to listen to Social Democrats, Socialist Revolutionaries, Anarchists, anybody, whatever they had to say, as long as they would talk! For months in Petrograd, and all over Russia, every street-corner was a public tribune. In railway trains, street-cars, always the spurting up of impromptu debate everywhere.[7]

Serge remembers:

In spite of . . . grotesque misery, a prodigious impulse was given to public education. Such a thirst for knowledge sprang up all over the country that new schools, adult courses, universities and Workers' Faculties were formed everywhere. Innumerable fresh initiatives laid open the teaching of unheard of, totally unexplored domains of learning. Institutes for retarded children were founded; a network of institutions for pre-school infants was created; the Workers' Faculties and the special short courses placed secondary education within the grasp of the workers. Soon afterwards the conquest of the universities was to begin. In this period too, the museums were enriched by the confiscation of private collections – extraordinary honesty and care characterized this expropriation of artistic riches. Not one work of any significance was lost.[8]

New libraries were established; a large cheap edition of the works of the leading Russian classical authors in all fields was initiated; there was an effort to expand the primary school system.[9]

Thousands of workers crowded the theatres.

There is great activity in theatres, now set free from the thraldom of the box-office, and crowded nightly . . . It is the proletariat now, in half-sheepskin and home-spun and birch-bark, that fills the boxes and stalls . . . Moscow's workers feasted their imaginations till they passed out from the brightness and glamour of the theatre into the white night and the dust and the hunger outside.[10]

There was hectic activity on the part of painters and sculptors immediately after the Revolution, and for a time futurists and cubists held the centre of the scene and decorated blank walls, pavements and other available places with their creations. Trotsky wrote:

The popular masses were still quivering in every fibre, and were thinking aloud for the first time in a thousand years. All the best youthful forces of art were touched to the quick. During those first years, rich in hope and daring, there were created not only the most complete models of socialist legislation, but also the best productions of revolutionary literature. To the same times belong, it is worth remarking, the creation of those excellent Soviet films which, in spite of a poverty of technical means, caught the imagination of the whole world with the freshness and vigour of their approach to reality.[11]

Above all, the revolution meant the awakening of the personality of the workers. In 1845 Engels had found the essence of socialism to be to create 'for all *people* such a condition that everyone can freely develop his human nature and live in a human relationship with his neighbours.'[12] In the Russian revolution the souls of the oppressed yearned after a purer, better life. With incisiveness Trotsky defined the revolution thus:

> the revolution is in the first place an awakening of human personality in the masses – who were supposed to possess no personality. In spite of occasional cruelty and the sanguinary relentlessness of its methods, the revolution is, before and above all, the awakening of humanity, its onward march, and is marked with a growing respect for the personal dignity of every individual, with an ever-increasing concern for those who are weak.[13]

> Yesterday the man of the mass was still a nobody, a slave of the Tsar, of the gentry, of the bureaucracy, an appendage to the . . . machine . . . a beast of burden . . . Having freed himself, he is now most acutely aware of his own identity and begins to think of himself as of . . . the centre of the world.[14]

Lenin's Revolutionary Realism

The élan of the mass of the workers indicates the goal they are striving to reach. The legacy – material and cultural – of the old order determines their point of departure on the long march. Lenin, who always combined determined perseverance in fighting for revolutionary ideals with a sense of realism, who had his head in the clouds but his feet firmly on the ground, could not but be very conscious of the sharp contradiction between the grand aspirations of the workers and their actual poverty, material and cultural. Lenin knew well that the fate of the revolution lay in this contradiction and its development. Titanic struggles would decide how the contradiction would be solved.

In the period following the revolution, Lenin achieved the highest synthesis of daring in design and prudence in application. A clear understanding of the objective circumstances made it possible for the party and its leadership to retain their bearings and their confidence through the twists and turns of the struggle.

Lenin again and again repeated that the Bolsheviks were badly prepared to govern. Thus in a pamphlet entitled *The Achievements and Difficulties of the Soviet Government*, written in March-April 1919, he wrote:

> The science which we, at best, possess is the science of the agitator and propagandist, of the man who has been steeled by the hellishly hard lot of the factory worker, or starving peasant, a science which teaches us how to hold out for a long time and to persevere in the struggle, and this has saved us up to now. All this is necessary, but it is not enough. With this alone we cannot triumph.[15]

The Bolsheviks were by no means ready to face the problems of managing the economy. Lenin told the Party Congress on 18 March 1919:

> At first we regarded them in an entirely abstract way, like revolutionary preachers, who had absolutely no idea of how to set to work. There were lots of people, of course, who accused us – and all the socialists and Social-Democrats are accusing us today – of having undertaken this task without knowing how to finish it. But these accusations are ridiculous, made by people who lack the spark of life. As if one can set out to make a great revolution and know beforehand how it is to be completed! Such knowledge cannot be derived from books and our decision could spring only from the experience of the masses. And I say that it is to our credit that amidst incredible difficulties we undertook to solve a problem with which until then we were only half familiar, that we inspired the proletarian masses to display their own initiative.[16]

What was needed above all was perseverance, readiness to admit mistakes and correct them. Lenin and his friends showed these attributes in abundance.

> Perseverence, persistence, willingness, determination and ability to test things a hundred times, to correct them a hundred times,

but to achieve the goal come what may – these . . . qualities of the proletariat are a guarantee that the proletariat will conquer.[17]

What was needed for the inexperienced party leading the government of a large country was to confront reality directly.

It is precisely because we are not afraid to look danger in the face that we make the best use of our forces for the struggle – we weigh the chances more dispassionately, cautiously and prudently.[18]

Our strength lies in complete clarity and the sober consideration of *all* the existing class magnitudes, both Russian and international; and in the. inexhaustible energy, iron resolve and devotion in struggle that arise from this.[19]

Neither the euphoria of optimism nor the morass of pessimism is useful. 'Pessimism or optimism? *Calculation of forces.* Sober approach and fervent dedication,'[20] wrote Lenin in late March-early April 1921.

The Harsh Circumstances
of Proletarian Dictatorship in Russia

The French Revolution took place in a country that had achieved the highest level of economic and cultural development in the world except for England. Russia was one of the most backward countries in Europe. And from the outset the Russian bourgeoisie resorted to harsh counter-revolutionary measures, relying on the support of world capitalism. The pressure of counter-revolution and the civil war forced the Bolsheviks to take the extremely harsh economic measures of War Communism, dealt with in the last chapter.

The proletarian dictatorship was forced, therefore, to direct its weapons not only against the big bourgeoisie, but also against the petty bourgeoisie and the mass of the peasantry. With the proletariat in a minority, especially as there were no sharp divisions between proletariat and peasantry, and with hunger and cold gnawing into the very nerves of the workers, the danger was, of course, that the dictatorship would be directed not only against the big bourgeoisie as well as the petty bourgeoisie and peasantry, but also against the proletariat itself. To run ahead of the story, the Central Committee thesis adopted on 22 January 1920 may be quoted:

> In a society which is in a transitional phase of its development and which is hardened with the inheritance of a distressing past, the passage to a planned organization of socialized labour is inconceivable without compulsory measures being applied to the parasitic elements, to the backward sections of the peasantry, and even to the working class itself.[21]

Thus in its weakness, the proletariat which was ripe for dictatorship over society is found to tolerate a dictatorship over itself. The collective, democratic base of the dictatorship of the proletariat was undermined still further by the fact that, as a result of the collapse of industry, the proletariat itself almost ceased to exist.

For Marx the revolution was a prerequisite for the maturing of the proletariat, for it to change itself so as to be able to change society: the 'revolution is necessary, therefore, not only because the ruling class cannot be overthrown in any other way, but also because the class *overthrowing* it can only in a revolution succeed in ridding itself of all the muck of ages and become fitted to found society anew'.[22]

What would happen if the 'old excrement' were too massive and the proletariat too small, and too much weakened in the process of the revolution, to revolutionize itself?

In the Russian proletariat during the civil war there were both collective heroism and paltriness, backwardness and bestiality intermingled; 'obtuse bestiality and the highest revolutionary idealism' intertwined, were Trotsky's words.[23] Novels and stories of the time reveal this duality everywhere. Isaac Babel's stories reveal this – revolutionary heroism mixed with passion, cruelty, fear and blind violence. In the stories in his collection *The Red Cavalry*, he describes his companions flashing their swords right and left to the war cry of 'All hail to the world revolution'. They die for this slogan, but they also die shouting obscenities, blasphemies or imbecile jokes. The appalling cruelty of the Cossacks is fitted in these stories into a heroic framework. Thus in a story called 'Berestechko' Babel describes how in a devastated village in Belorussia, among corpses of old men and pregnant women with their bellies split open by the retreating Poles, Babel's friend Kudrya, a Red Cossack, cuts the throat of a Jew accused of spying. Anti-semitic obscenities flow from the mouths of heroic soldiers. For instance: 'And what did we see in the town of Maykop? We saw there that the rear was not of the same mind as the front and that everywhere was treachery and full of dirty Yids like under the old regime.' In a story entitled 'Salt', a soldier murders a peasant woman because she deceived him in order to sneak into an overcrowded train. Telling the story he ends: 'So I took my faithful rifle off the wall and washed away that stain from the face of the workers' land and the republic.' These same soldiers turn into heroes ready to give up their lives for comrades and for the cause of the revolution. 'During weekdays . . . the consciousness of the class becomes absorbed and distracted by current cares and concerns; the differences in the interests and views among the various groupings within the working class come to the forefront. But the very next major events completely reveal the profound unity of the working class that has passed through the fiery school of the revolution,' Trotsky writes.[24]

One would not expect the masses emerging from capitalism to be free of the filth of this society, as Lenin said: 'the corpse of bourgeois society cannot be nailed in a coffin and buried. The corpse of capitalism is decaying and disintegrating in our midst, polluting the air and poisoning our lives, enmeshing that which is new, fresh, young and virile in thousands of threads and bonds of that which is old, moribund and decaying.'[25]

One may read the stories of Isaac Babel, the poetry of Demian Bedny, describing the less admirable side of the people, or Trotsky's articles about the need to clean one's boots and not to throw cigarette butts on the floor, or the need to avoid swearing and bad language, and say, 'See how inadequate the revolution was, how dull the masses were!' The reaction should be exactly the opposite: see how magnificently the masses behaved, despite famine and the closeness of death, while they still carried the barbarous inheritance of capitalism, and were emerging from the darkness and destitution of Tsarism without any tradition of commanding or wielding power.'

The heroic and tragic also intertwined in the fate of the

party. The fact that a revolutionary party is vital for the victory of the revolution demonstrated both the bond between the party and the class, and the disparity between the vanguard and the rest of the class in terms of the level of consciousness and organization. By organizing the vanguard, the party increased its weight within the working class as a whole. But the party is not omnipotent, and its power depends directly on the level of activity and strength of the proletariat. The process of decomposition of the proletariat must have a radical influence on the party. There are limits to the force of the will and nerves even of the toughest revolutionaries.

In the agony of terrible hunger, cold and death, with the assault of the international counter-revolutionary forces, with the decline in the size, economic and social weight of the Russian proletariat – what prospects could there be for the development, or even preservation, of proletarian democracy? How would the Soviet institutions, by which workers' freedom was brought about, be affected? What would be the fate of the party? What would happen if the international proletariat was late in coming to the rescue of the Russian revolution?

The great Soviet poet of the Russian revolution, Vladimir Mayakovsky, wrote these lines:

> We shall commit heroic deeds,
> three times harder
> than the deeds of God.
> He bestowed things upon emptiness,
> but we must not merely indulge in reveries,
> but must dynamite that which is old.

But what if the old survived the dynamite? What if the heritage of Tsarist barbarism were too heavy for the small young plant of socialism to bear?

The Dream and the Reality

Lenin was above all a revolutionary realist who combined the greatest vision with the urge to look reality in the face. His hero was neither the down-to-earth, commonsense Sancho Panza, nor the builder of castles in the air, Don Quixote. He knew how to distinguish clearly between the communist end and the immediate revolutionary need. For him, as for Marx, socialism was a classless, stateless, self-governing community based on an abundance of material goods in which 'the free development of each is the condition for the free development of all' *(Communist Manifesto)*. Dictatorship, state planning, economic growth and efficiency, iron discipline – all were means to the end, means from which Lenin did not shrink, but not ends in themselves. Lenin was well aware that the road to socialism would be very rough indeed.

He emphasized that the leap into the realm of freedom would happen only after a whole transitional period – and a very harsh period at that.

> it was not without reason that the teachers of socialism spoke of a whole period of transition from capitalism to socialism and emphasized the 'prolonged birth-pangs' of the new society. And this new society is again an abstraction which can come into being only by passing through a series of varied, imperfect concrete attempts to create this or that socialist state.[26]

He compares the birth of the new socialist society to childbirth.

> Consider the descriptions of childbirth given in literature, when the authors aim at presenting a truthful picture of the severity, pain and horror of the act of travail, as in Emile Zola's *La joie de vivre* (The Joy of Life), for instance, or in Veresayev's *Notes of a Doctor*. Human childbirth is an act which transforms the woman into an almost lifeless, bloodstained heap of flesh, tortured, tormented and driven frantic by pain. But can the 'individual' that sees *only* this in love and its sequel, in the transformation of the woman into a mother, be regarded as a human being? Who would renounce love and procreation for *this* reason?
>
> Travail may be light or severe. Marx and Engels, the founders of scientific socialism, always said that the transition from capitalism to socialism would be inevitably accompanied *by prolonged birth pangs*. Engels outlines simply and clearly the indisputable and obvious fact that a revolution that follows and is connected with a war (and still more – let us add for our part – a revolution which breaks out during a war, and which is obliged to grow and maintain itself in the midst of a world war) is a *particularly severe* case of childbirth.[27]

In Soviet Russia hopes turned into despair. With the proletariat decimated and the state and party largely bureaucratized, the *means* for victory – the dictatorship of the proletariat – negated itself.

Lenin knew, like Marx and Engels before him, that the means cannot perfectly *prefigure* the end, that there must be a contradiction between means and ends, between the dictatorship of the proletariat and fully fledged socialism, or communism. As the revolution is a product of a class society it necessarily bears the traits of this society. It reflects capitalism rather than socialism, the present and the past, not the future. As the proletarian dictatorship has to fight bourgeois counter-revolution, it inevitably has to be symmetrical with it, in order to inflict blows on it. However, with all the diversion of *means* from *ends*, unless there is a central core connecting them, the means *will not* lead to the supposed end. 'Seeds of wheat must be sown in order to yield an ear of wheat', to use Trotsky's words about the relation between means and ends in his pamphlet *Their Morals and Ours*. The plough breaking up the hard soil may help the seed of wheat to germinate and grow, but the plough does not prefigure the wheat; in the same way the Cheka may be necessary to smash capitalist counter-revolution, without this institution in any way prefiguring, having in it even the germ, of future socialism. Unfortunately the plough alone will not produce wheat. The liberation of the working class can be achieved only through the action of the working class. Hence one can have a revolution with more or less violence, with more or less suppression of civil rights of the bourgeoisie and its hangers-on, with more or less political freedom, but one *cannot* have a revolution, as the history of Russia conclusively demonstrates, without workers' democracy – even if restricted and distorted. Socialist advance must be gauged by workers' freedom, by their power to shape their own destiny, and by the material and cultural well-being achieved by the masses. Without workers' democracy the immediate means leads to a very different end, to an end that is prefigured in these same means.

In Part II of Goethe's *Faust*, Faust decides to reclaim a strip of land from the sea in order to settle it with 'many millions' of people of 'free toil', thus would 'a free people stand on a free soil'. But during the construction itself Faust deals with the builders as though they were dull-witted slaves.

> To speed the greatest enterprises
> One mind for thousand hands suffices.

With both carrot and stick, the workers are driven on to accomplish the mightiest achievements. Mephistopheles, the foreman, is encouraged by Faust:

> Workmen throng on throng address
> Thyself to get. Put forth all vigour.
> Now with indulgence, now with rigour
> Encourage. Pay, entice, impress!
> Let every day bring news of our successes,
> How this new trench, this mighty groove progresses.

Thus the future community of 'free people' is the Faustian aim, while the serfdom of the toilers is the Mephistophelean means. The link between them is Faust's belief in enlightened despotism: 'One mind for thousand hands suffices.' Will the means not swallow up the aim, the 'groove' become a 'grave'?

Lenin certainly did not call for a dictatorship of the party over the proletariat, even less for that of a bureaucratized party over a decimated proletariat. But fate – the desperate condition of a revolution in a backward country besieged by world capitalism – led to precisely this.

The question of means and ends – not in abstract form, but in all its reality – tortured Lenin repeatedly in the last few months of his life, when after each further stroke he came back as if from the dead to watch over what he was going to leave behind him. In the statements, speeches and notes he made in his last active period, expressions such as 'the fault is mine', 'I must correct another mistake of mine', 'I am to blame',[28] occur repeatedly until they culminate in the statement of 30 December 1922 – the last notes he dictated to his secretary – 'I suppose I have been very remiss with respect to the workers of Russia.'[29]

The machine of state and party was moving in a direction which Lenin certainly did not wish or expect, as he told the 11th Party Congress, in March 1922, the last congress he attended:

The machine refused to obey the hand that guided it. It was like a car that was going not in the direction the driver desired, but in the direction someone else desired; as if it were being driven by some mysterious, lawless hand, God knows whose . . . Be that as it may, the car is not going quite in the direction the man at the wheel imagines, and often it goes in an altogether different direction.[30]

Lenin never shirked looking reality in the face. At the end of the civil war he stated: 'Russia emerged from the war in a state that can most of all be likened to that of a man beaten to within an inch of his life; the beating had gone on for seven years, and it's a mercy she can hobble about on crutches! That is the situation we are in.'[31]

He saw the collapse of the economy, the decomposition of the proletariat, the changes in state institutions and the party, but he could not be certain until the end whether the climax would be a fatal catastrophe in the tradition of Greek tragedies, or whether, as with Goethe, vision and hope would avert disaster and triumph would be achieved over all the odds by the timely arrival of the international working class army to the rescue. The international revolution, was however, very belated. Towards the end of his life we find Lenin facing tragic disappointments

That keep the word of promise to our ear,
And break it to our hope.[32]

9
The Proletariat
Under War Communism

The Proletariat Burns Itself Out in the Struggle

The collapse of industry led to a drastic reduction in the number of workers. This was severely accentuated by the massacre of the civil war, the exodus to the countryside from the towns, and the fact that many of the politically most advanced took up positions in the new state administration, the Soviets, the army, the Cheka and other public bodies, or in industrial management. The number of industrial workers fell from 3,024,000 in 1917 to 1,243,000 in 1921-2, a decrease of 58·7 per cent.[1]

The drop in the number of industrial workers was particularly sharp in Petrograd. While at the time of the October revolution there were 400,000 factory workers there, this fell to 120,495 on 1 April 1918; of these 48,910 were unemployed. So the total number of workers employed in industry was only 71,575.[2]

This shattering decline alarmed the Bolshevik leaders. A warning note was sounded by Y.E.Rudzutak, the leading Bolshevik trade unionist, at the Second All-Russian Congress of Trade Unions in January 1919: 'We observe that in many industrial centres the workers, thanks to the curtailment of production in the factories, are being dissolved into the peasant mass, and instead of a population of workers, we are getting a semi-peasant or sometimes purely peasant population.'[3]

Similarly Lenin, with heavy heart, said to the Eighth Congress of the party on 18 March 1919: 'The top layer of workers who actually administered Russia during the past year, who bore the brunt of the work in carrying out our policy, and who were our mainstay – this layer in Russia is an extremely thin one.'[4] And some time after the end of the civil war he said, in retrospect: 'The creation of a military and state machine capable of successfully withstanding the trials of 1917-21 was a great effort, which engaged, absorbed and exhausted real "forces of the working class".'[5]

The decline of the proletariat was not only quantitative, but also qualitative. The number of industrial workers, as we have said, declined from some 3 million to 1¼ million, but the number of people who stopped being industrial workers was far larger than 1¾ million, for, as Lenin explained, 'Since the war, the industrial workers of Russia have become much less proletarian than they were before, because during the war all those who desired to evade military service went into the factories. This is common knowledge.'[6] Thus many of the workers of 1921-2 were actually former students, shopkeepers and their children, etc. The group that was most reduced was the metal workers, the mainstay of the Bolsheviks in 1917.

Members of the working class were forced by the scarcity of food to act like small individualistic traders, rather than as a collective, or a united class. It has been calculated that in 1919-20 the state supplied only 42 per cent of the grain consumed by the towns, and an even smaller percentage of other foodstuffs, all the rest being bought on the black market.[7] Workers' wages were not enough to pay for the miserable food they and their families had to live on. Thus, while in 1917 an unskilled worker earned 26.75 rubles per month and spent, with his family, 11.57 rubles on food, in 1918 his earnings were 280 rubles per month, but food alone cost him 902.25 rubles per month.[8]

In March-April 1919, 75 per cent of the Petrograd workers bought bread on the black market.[9] It was common for workers to stay away from work in order to forage in the countryside.

During the civil war factories paid part of wages in kind. The workers used a portion themselves and sold the rest on the black market. A speaker at the First All-Russian Congress of Councils of National Economy in May 1918 drew attention to this practice, which acquired the nickname 'piece-selling'.

'Bagging [foraging for food by townspeople] is a terrible evil, piece-selling is a terrible evil; but it is an even greater evil when you begin to pay the workers in kind, in their own products . . . and when they themselves turn piece-sellers.'[10] But the practice persisted, and the Second All-Russian Congress of Councils of National Economy in December 1918 had little option but to turn a blind eye to the practice, passing yet another resolution in favour of payment of wages to factory workers in kind. Two years later the scandal had grown much worse.

At the Fourth Congress of Trade Unions in May 1921 the disorganization of industry and the demoralization of the proletariat were illustrated by a statement that workers in factories were stealing 50 per cent of the goods produced and that the average worker's wage covered only one-fifth of his cost of living, so that he was compelled to earn the rest by illicit trading.[11]

Many workers took to petty thieving and peddling (which,

according to one prominent Soviet economist, brought in up to two-fifths of their income at the time).[12] Under these circumstances they inevitably became middlemen, parasitic on the economy and increasingly inclined to look after their own interests.

On 24 August 1919 Lenin wrote: 'industry is at a standstill. There is no food, no fuel, no industry.'[13] And he summed up the disintegration of the proletariat in these words:

> The industrial proletariat . . . owing to the war and to the desperate poverty and ruin, has become declassed, i.e. dislodged from its class groove, and has ceased to exist as a proletariat. The proletariat is the class which is engaged in the production of material values in large-scale capitalist industry. Since large-scale capitalist industry has been destroyed, since the factories are at a standstill, the proletariat has disappeared. It has sometimes figured in statistics, but it has not been held together economically.[14]

> our proletariat has been largely declassed; the terrible crises and the closing down of the factories have compelled people to flee from starvation. The workers have simply abandoned their factories; they have had to settle down in the country and have ceased to be workers . . . the disruption of proper relations between town and country and the cessation of grain deliveries have given rise to a trade in small articles made at the big factories – such as cigarette lighters – which are exchanged for cereals, because the workers are starving, and no grain is being delivered . . . That is the economic source of the proletariat's declassing and . . . bourgeois, anarchist trends.[15]

> Owing to our present deplorable conditions, proletarians are obliged to earn a living by methods which are not proletarian and are not connected with large-scale industry. They are obliged to procure goods by petty-bourgeois profiteering methods, either by stealing, or by making them for themselves in a publicly-owned factory, in order to barter them for agricultural produce . . .[16] And the proletariat is declassed, i.e. dislodged from its class groove. The factories and mills are idle – the proletariat is weak, scattered, enfeebled.[17]

Workers' Control Over Production

With an enfeebled proletariat, how could the Bolshevik slogan of workers' control over production in fact be applied? Would not the weakness of the agent of control lead inevitably to its distortion, or even its demise? These questions had to be answered by harsh reality.

In Bolshevik propaganda before October the concept of workers' control was that of a half-way house, a *limitation* by workers of management power, the surveillance and even the obstruction by workers of the decisions taken by the capitalist management, which still retained ultimate sovereignty. The situation in which workers themselves possessed sovereignty and collectively initiated all decisions in respect of production was called 'workers' management'. Now, after October, the question was posed sharply: would workers' control remain as such, or would it develop into workers' management?

As we have seen in Chapter 7, the capitalists for their part did all they could to sabotage workers' control. They destroyed the capitalist apparatus of economic management. As this happened on a national scale, as well as in each individual enterprise, the Bolsheviks had to create a substitute apparatus.

Could workers' control be replaced by workers' management of industry? Unfortunately, the weakness of the proletariat, given that workers had not been trained by capitalism to manage, and that the economic collapse strengthened centrifugal tendencies among them, undermined not only workers' control, but also the possibility of workers' management.

Centrifugal forces split the working class. Workers in different factories took over individual enterprises, as if they were their own property. The journal of the People's Commissariat of Labour described the situation thus:

> the factory committees often, and even in the majority of cases, adhered to the narrow interests of a particular enterprise. For the committee it was important that its factory functioned normally, that it was supplied with orders and funds. Individual members often acted in the capacity of expediters to satisfy these needs of the enterprise . . . The factory committees adhering to their 'factory interests' developed their own parochial patriotism and local pride . . . A competition began among the workers of individual factories to assure 'their own factories' of deliveries of coal or metal. The factory committees delegated their emissaries to the provinces, for example, to the Donets Basin, where they exerted pressure to obtain coal or steel, trying

to assure 'their own' factories of it. For example, the Obukhov-skii factory . . . delegated about 50 worker-expediters who tried to obtain coal for their own factory.[18]

One Soviet historian summed up the situation thus: 'Competition and the effort to guarantee for themselves scarce raw materials needed for production led the factory committees to oppose each other; the factories were converted into autonomous federations of a semi-anarchist character.'[19]

An article in *Izvestiia* asked:

What has workers' control given us up to the present? We must have the courage to admit that its results are not always satisfactory. Often – it may be observed in many enterprises – in place of the former owner of the business, another proprietor came who was just as individualistic and anti-social as the previous one. The name of this proprietor is the 'Control Commission'.[20]

Workers' control on the railways was described in stark words by Shliapnikov, People's Commissar of Labour, in his speech to VTsIK on 20 March 1918:

What is happening on the railways can only be described as complete disorganization which is getting worse every day . . . The trains are often operating without lights, there is no signalling, the cars are never cleaned, etc. The usual excuse is that no kerosene or candles are available. However, I found out that both these items were available but were being pilfered in the most shameless manner.

Train crews, being not at all interested in the exploitation of the railways, frequently refuse to take charge of the trains. Because of this, both cars and locomotives may be available, but there are no engineers and no conductors. They either pretend illness or simply refuse to go. It sometimes happens that on certain trains which require a certain number of persons, a substitute has to be found [for someone] who is really ill, but the station-master is unable to exercise his authority, for as soon as he puts someone in place of the sick man the substitute tells him that he will not go without the consent of the Committee. Since it is impossible to get the Committee together on the spot, the train cannot be dispatched . . .

By present-day rules the workers are guaranteed their pay. The worker turns up at his job and spends some time at his bench. Whether he does anything or not, no one can say anything to him because the shop committee is powerless. If the shop committee attempts to control the shops, it is immediately disbanded and another committee is elected. In a word, things are in the hands of a crowd that, due to its ignorance and lack of interest in production, is literally putting a brake on all work.[21]

It was this chaos which led the Soviet government to abolish workers' control in industry, starting with the railways on 26 March 1918. Towards the end of 1918 workers' control councils were abolished in a number of leading branches of industry, such as machine and metal-working plants (18 October 1918) and leather and shoe factories (13 November 1918).[22]

Factory Committees, the Trade Unions and the State

With the drastic weakening of the industrial proletariat, and with the anarchic centrifugal forces pulling it apart, Lenin and the Bolsheviks had no alternative but to put an end to the autonomy of the factory committees which had played such a central role in October. One of the first problems they faced after the revolution was that of the relationship between the factory committees and the trade unions.

At the first All-Russian Conference of Factory Committees, which was held a few days before the October revolution, the Bolshevik Schmidt, the future Commissar of Labour, stated: 'At the moment when the factory committees were formed the trade unions actually did not yet exist, and the factory committees filled the vacuum.'[23] The trade unions that arose in 1917 were Menshevik-dominated and their efforts to bring the factory committees under their control were naturally rebuffed. But now, after the revolution, at the First All-Russian Congress of Trade Unions in January 1918 the Bolsheviks found themselves the dominant force in the trade unions, as they had already been for some time in the factory committees. At the Congress, out of 428 delegates with voting rights, 281 were Bolsheviks, 67 Mensheviks, 32 non-party, 21 Left Socialist Revolutionaries, 10 Right Socialist Revolutionaries, 6 Maximalists and 6 Anarcho-Syndicalists.

The main report on the subject of the relations between the factory committees and the trade unions was given by the Bolshevik Riazanov, who was chairman of the Petrograd Council of Trade Unions, a member of the All-Russian Central Council of

Trade Unions, and on its executive committee. The workers' government, he argued, should exert control over the factory committees.

> Before us . . . stands the question of control by the workers' government, by the whole working class over the workers in individual factory enterprises . . . Without such control on the part of all the working class, on the part of the proletariat – and for this we need a whole network of organs which control the activity of each such individual cell in each factory, in each enterprise – without such a network of organs we will have only a pillage of the people's economy, a pillage of the economy which we want to socialize and organize into a whole out of many parts. We will have a mass of atomized cells.[24]

The Bolshevik Veinberg stated : 'the trade unions – or, more correctly, the industrial unions – espouse the point of view not of the individual factory, not even of the workers of a particular city, but the point of view of the working class of all industry. [Therefore] the factory committees must be subordinated to the trade unions.'[25] By an overwhelming majority the Congress decided that the factory committees should be incorporated into the unions.

In order that workers' control may produce the maximum benefit for the proletariat, it is necessary to reject completely any idea of undermining that control by giving the workers of an individual enterprise the right to make final decisions on questions affecting the very existence of the enterprise.

> The workers of every enterprise and their elected organization – factory-shop committees – will be in a better position to carry on the work [of control] if they operate on the basis of a general plan formulated by the higher organs of workers' control and the regulatory organs of the economy.
> In this colossal work which the organs of workers' control have assumed, the trade unions should take the most active part by championing the interests of the workers as a whole as opposed to the sectional and group interests of the workers of a given trade or enterprise.
> The trade unions which are organized by industries should take part in the local and central organs of workers' control and should assume the role of ideological and organizational leadership.

The trade unions must go over each decree of the factory committees in the sphere of control, explain through their delegates at the factories and shops that control over production does not mean the transfer of the enterprise into the hands of the workers of a given enterprise, that workers' control does not equal the socialization of production and exchange but is only a preparatory step towards it.[26]

Factory and workshop committees should become local organs of the corresponding trade unions.[27]

The factory committees, as well as the trade unions, also had to relate to another newly established institution. On 2 (15) December 1917 the VSNKh was established. The relevant decree described its function thus:

The task of the Supreme Economic Council is organization of the national economy and state finance. With this aim in view the Supreme Economic Council works out guidelines and plans for regulating the country's economy; coordinates and unifies the activity of central and local regulating institutions (conferences on fuel, metal, transport, the Central Food Committee, etc.), the corresponding people's commissariats (of trade and industry, food supplies, agriculture, finance, army and navy, etc.), the All-Russia Workers' Control Council, as well as the relevant activity of working-class organizations.[28]

The VSNKh was to be the central planning and directing organ of the economic life of the country. Its close relationship with the trade unions is clear from the weight granted to their representatives in its composition:

The All-Russian Central Executive Committee – 10 representatives.
The All-Russian Council of Trade Unions – 30 representatives.
The Regional Councils of National Economy – 20 representatives.
The All-Russian Council of Workers' Cooperatives – 2 representatives.
The People's Commissariat of Food – 2 representatives.
The People's Commissariat of Ways and Communication – 1 representative.
The People's Commissariat of Labour – 1 representative.
The People's Commissariat of Agriculture – 1 representative.
The People's Commissariat of Finance – 1 representative.
The People's Commissariat of Commerce – 1 representative.
The People's Commissariat of the Interior – 1 representative.[29]

In the administration of individual branches of the economy the trade unions and VSNKh again worked very closely together. While accepting complete subordination to VSNKh in administrative measures, the trade unions insisted on having a majority of representatives (two thirds) on the administrative bodies. And so at the First All-Russian Congress of the Councils of the National Economy in May 1918, Tomsky, appearing as a delegate of the All-Russian Central Council of Trade Unions, could declare: 'VSNKh and the trade unions are organizations so completely akin, so closely interwoven with each other, that independent tactics on the part of these two organizations are impossible.'[30]

The trade unions also obtained significant powers in relation to the People's Commissariat of Labour. At the Fourth Conference of Trade Unions (12-17 March 1918), the Bolshevik resolution on the relations between the trade unions and the People's Commissariat of Labour stated:

> all decisions of principle of the higher organs of the trade unions (congresses, conferences, etc.) are binding upon the Commissariat of Labour. All legislative proposals and special binding decisions concerning the conditions of labour and production, must be preliminarily approved by the appropriate organs of the trade unions (i.e. the All-Russian and local Soviets of Trade Unions).[31]

The People's Commissar of Labour, V.Schmidt, was proposed for the post by the trade unions, and was himself an active trade unionist. Most of the officials of the People's Commissariat of Labour as well as its regional and local representatives, were from now on nominated by the trade unions. The Commissariat of Labour was to be bound by the principal decisions of the higher bodies of the trade unions, and the unions had to give prior approval to all decisions of the Commissariat.

The Trade Unions and the State

The experience of the first months of the Bolshevik government showed that conflicts were bound to arise between the factory committees, the trade unions and the state.

The factory committees, by definition, had centrifugal tendencies. The trade unions, as mass organizations, consisted of diverse elements with varying levels of class consciousness, and were therefore divided by sectional interests, with various groups of workers trying to further their own interests, at times possibly *against* the interests of the working class as a whole. According to Lenin, it was only the revolutionary party, the vanguard of the class, that represented the total, historical, interests of the proletariat, to which sectional and temporary interests were subordinated. The Soviet government, composed as it was of Bolsheviks, was bound to come into conflict with the trade unions, which represented sectional interests.

Of course the party had to persuade the working class to make the revolution. It had to convince the majority of the proletariat to prepare and organize for it. After the revolution it still had to fight in order to lead the proletariat in the factory committees, in the trade unions, in the Soviet.

But this could not be done *mechanically*, by imposition of the party will. Only through a long struggle to overcome the vacillation of the masses could the party win this leadership. It had to battle again and again to win the confidence of the proletariat, above all of that section of it which was organized in the trade unions.

If the trade unions were autonomous, i.e. self-administering, the revolutionaries could win their confidence only by persuasion. They could not impose a line of conduct with which the majority of the union members did not agree.

The process of conflict and the development of unity between party, state, trade unions and factory committees would have taken a long time to achieve the Marxist goal of the withering away of the state and complete merging of state and trade unions. For this to take place, a situation of increasing economic plenty would be needed, which would also result in the withering away of the trade unions. For if the standard of living of the workers is high and rising, their need to defend it becomes less and less imperative, until a stage is reached when every person 'gets according to his needs' and trade unions as organs for the defence of workers' interests become superfluous. At the same time, incentives for higher production and the use of the unions as a means of urging the workers to greater effort would become unnecessary. The tension in society would decrease and so the state, as well as the unions, would begin to wither away.

Until the complete achievement of communism, the trade unions must be able to defend the workers against their employers, even if this is the state. At the same time as workers' organizations, the unions have to defend the workers' state. They should be both independent of the state and symbiotic with it.

After the revolution in Russia, under the harsh conditions of the civil war, these relationships could not exist: the trade unions could not be independent of the state. Industry was turned into a supply organization for the Red Army, and industrial policy became a branch of military strategy. As industry relied on the state to supply necessary products to the workers, the trade unions were in fact part of the state administration of industry and distribution.

In particular, the trade unions' participation in fixing wage rates lost all significance, since payment in kind to all intents and purposes replaced money wages.*

The Trade Unions, the Military Front and the Labour Front

With the outbreak of civil war, thousands of trade union members went into the army. It was mainly through the unions that the government mobilized men both for the Red Army and for industry. As the civil war dragged on, the trade unions called up 50 per cent of their members into the Red Army. At the same time there was an enormous increase in the number of union members, mainly made up of workers in the new civil service:

	(thousands)
Mid 1917	693
Mid 1918	1,946
Mid 1919	3,707
Mid 1920	5,222[82]

---

* The fact that the proportion of wages in kind was very large, made the difference between price rises and wage rises, referred to above, far less significant. If workers' wages had not been largely paid in kind, their lives, harsh as they were, would have been completely unbearable.

The Bolsheviks quickly came to the conclusion that the unions must play a central role in mobilizing workers on the labour front as well. Accordingly the newly adopted party programme (March 1919) stated:

> it is essential to utilize to the utmost all the labour power at the disposal of the state. Its correct assignment and reassignment as between the various territorial areas and as between the various branches of economic life is the main task of the economic policy of the Soviet power. It can be fulfilled in no other way than by an intimate association between the Soviet power and the trade unions. The general mobilization by the Soviet power of all members of the population who are physically and mentally fit for work (a mobilization to be effected through the instrumentality of the trade unions), for the discharge of definite social duties, must be achieved far more widely and systematically than has hitherto been the case.[33]

And the government imposed a very strict control over the labour of every citizen. For instance, on 7 April 1919, a decree forbade any miner to leave his job.[34] On 12 April another decree prohibited all persons employed in a Soviet institution from transferring on their own initiative to another institution.[35]

In addition compulsory mobilization of labour took place. In 1920 some twenty mobilization orders were decreed, affecting the most important trades:

Former railway workers	30 January
Skilled railway personnel	15 March
Sugar industry workers	24 March
Water transport workers	7 April
Miners	16 April
Skilled water transport personnel	27 April
Construction workers	5 May
Statistical workers	25 June
Medical personnel	14 July
Workers formerly employed in fish industries	6 August
Workers in shipbuilding	8 August
Wool industry workers	13 August
Former metal workers	20 August
Tanning industry workers	15 September
Electro-technical workers	8 October
Former aviation industry workers	20 October

Women for sewing underwear for Red Army	30 October
Tailors and shoemakers who worked in Great	
Britain and the United States	October[36]

Labour Armies

It was a short step from the mobilization of workers to building labour armies. In January 1920 a decree on general labour service provided for: (a) call-up of the entire able-bodied population (men between 16 and 50, women between 16 and 40) for occasional or regular work, to be performed in addition to normal employment; (b) the use of unoccupied army and navy units for civilian work; (c) the transfer of skilled workers engaged in the forces or in agriculture to state enterprises; (d) the distribution of labour according to the needs of the country's economy. On 15 January 1920 a decree of the Workers' and Peasants' Council of Defence, at the suggestion of the leading army personnel, authorized the temporary use for civil work of the Third Army Corps operating in the Urals. When fighting there ceased, practically all the combatant units were sent to the southern and western fronts; but an enormous administrative apparatus was left behind, which it was not thought advisable to demobilize, and which was therefore used for industrial reconstruction work. This unit adopted the name of First Revolutionary Labour Army Corps and was used chiefly for the repair of railway lines and procurement of timber and coal.

With the further temporary easing of the military situation, a second labour army corps was created in March 1920 in the area of the Donbas and parts of the Caucasus. A third was formed in Petrograd, but the war with Poland soon forced both to revert to military duties. A Ukrainian labour army corps was formed in January 1920 in the area of the south-western front. At that time, too, the Workers' and Peasants' Council of Defence decreed the use of the 'Reserve Army of the Republic for the reconstruction of the Moscow–Kazan railway line and the repair of its rolling stock'.[37]

Stalinist legend has it that Trotsky was chiefly responsible for the militarization of labour. Nothing could be further from the truth. It was true that Trotsky was enthusiastic about the policy.

But so was Lenin. Thus, for instance, Lenin told the Third All-Russian Congress of Economic Councils on 27 January 1920:

> in order to utilize our apparatus with the greatest possible dispatch, we must create a labour army . . . In launching this slogan we declare that we must strain all the live forces of the workers and peasants to the utmost and demand that they give us every help in this matter. And then, by creating a labour army, by the harnessing all the forces of the workers and peasants, we shall accomplish our main task.[88]

In a speech on 2 February 1920 he reiterated:

> we must at all costs create labour armies, organize ourselves like an army, reduce, even close down a whole number of institutions . . . in the next few months . . . When the All-Russia Central Executive Committee endorses all the measures connected with labour conscription and the labour armies, when it has succeeded in instilling these ideas in the broad mass of the population and demands that they be put into practice by local officials – we are absolutely convinced that then we shall be able to cope with [the] most difficult of tasks.[89]

Thus we see that for Lenin, during the civil war, and especially in the latter part of it, the mobilization of labour and, in general, the incorporation of the trade unions, their subordination to the state, were of vital and immediate importance.

Under the conditions of civil war the factory committees, which played a crucial role in winning the proletariat to Bolshevism in 1917, completely lost their autonomy, becoming local organs of the trade unions. The trade unions lost their power to dictate wages and conditions and became integrated into the state as organs for mobilizing on the military and labour fronts.*

Subbotniks

The merging of state and unions under War Communism did not preclude the emergence of a new phenomenon, *subbotniks*, i.e. unpaid voluntary Saturday labour. The fact that enthusiastically supported unpaid voluntary labour could exist side by side with state compulsion in the form of the militarization of labour,

---

* On relations between trade unions and the state, see further Chapter 23.

resulted from the prevailing egalitarianism and the deep devotion of the proletariat to the revolution. These blurred the boundaries between compulsion and voluntarism.

On 10 May 1919 the first *subbotnik* was carried out by the Moscow railway workers. It was argued for and led by party members. The resolution of the General Council of Communists of the *Subraion* of the Moscow–Kazan Railway, introducing *subbotniks*, stated that

> in order to overcome the class enemy . . . the communists and their sympathizers again must spur themselves on and extract from their time off still another hour of work, i.e. they must increase their working day by an hour, add it up and on Saturday devote six hours at a stretch to physical labour thereby producing immediately a real value. Considering that communists should not spare their health and lives for the victory of the revolution, the work is conducted without pay.[40]

Lenin was full of praise for the whole concept of the *subbotnik*. On 28 June 1919, in a pamphlet entitled *A Great Beginning*, he wrote:

> Communist *subbotniks* are of . . . enormous significance precisely because they demonstrate the conscious and voluntary initiative of the workers in developing the productivity of labour, in adopting a new labour discipline, in creating socialist conditions of economy and life . . . The communist *subbotnik* organized by the workers of the Moscow–Kazan Railway is one of the cells of the new, socialist society . . . these starving workers . . . are organizing 'communist *subbotniks*', working overtime *without any pay*, and achieving *an enormous increase in the productivity of labour* in spite of the fact that they are weary, tormented and exhausted by malnutrition. Is this not supreme heroism? Is this not the beginning of a change of momentous significance?[41]

In Petrograd the first *subbotnik* on a mass scale took place in August 1919. Again during the fuel crisis of November and December there seems to have been an upsurge of revolutionary élan. Yet it appears from the material available the movement did not reach its short-lived apogee until the spring of 1920. On 11 April 1920 a one-day issue of a newspaper called *Kommunisticheskii Subbotnik* was published, itself a *subbotnik* achievement of the staff of three Moscow papers and the printers of VTsIK publishing house. It contained an article by Lenin on the practical value and moral significance of this voluntary effort.

By decision of the Ninth Party Congress of March-April 1920, May Day, which happened to fall on a Saturday, was to be a gigantic all-Russian *subbotnik*. In Moscow alone 425,000 workers were said to have taken part in it.[42]

The Decomposition of the Proletariat and the Dictatorship of the Proletariat

Paradoxically, the proletariat was economically the most deprived class under the dictatorship of the proletariat. As Lenin put it in a speech to the First All-Russian Congress of Mineworkers in April 1920: 'the dictatorship entailed the greatest sacrifice and starvation on the part of the workers who were exercising it.'

> Nobody during these two years went as hungry as the workers of Petrograd, Moscow and Ivanovo-Voznessensk. It has now been computed that during these two years they received not more than seven pud of bread a year, whereas the peasants of the grain-producing guberniias consumed no less than seventeen pud. The workers have made great sacrifices, they have suffered epidemics, and mortality among them has increased.[43]

There was a dictatorship of the proletariat, even though the proletariat had disintegrated. As Lenin put it to the Tenth Conference of the Party, on 26 May 1921: 'even though the proletariat has to go through a period when it is declassed . . . it can nevertheless fulfil its task of winning and holding political power'.[44]

With some cynicism, Shliapnikov, spokesman of the newly formed Workers' Opposition, could say to the Eleventh Party Congress: 'Vladimir Ilyich said yesterday that the proletariat as a class, in the Marxian sense, did not exist. Permit me to congratulate you on being the vanguard of a non-existing class.'[45]

Of course, to a vulgar materialist it sounds impossible to have a dictatorship of the proletariat without the proletariat, like the smile of the Cheshire cat without the cat itself. But one must remember that the ideological as well as the political superstructure never reflect the material base *directly and immediately*. Ideas have their own momentum. Usually in 'normal' times they are a source of conservatism: long after people's material circumstances change, they are still dominated by old ideas. This interrelation of the ideological superstructure with the economic base became a source of strength to Bolshevism during the civil war. As Lenin put it in a speech of 3 November 1920:

> the habits, usages and convictions acquired by the working class in the course of many decades of struggle for political liberty – the sum total of these habits, usages and ideas – should serve as an instrument for the education of all working people . . . The dictatorship of the proletariat would have been out of the question if, in the struggle against the bourgeoisie, the proletariat had not developed a keen class-consciousness, strict discipline and profound devotion, in other words, all the qualities required to assure the proletariat's complete victory over its old eemy.[46]

Marx has taught us that the class in itself and the class for itself are not one and the same, i.e. that the class can be powerful in its position in production and yet not be conscious of this. The other side of the same coin is that the class which loses three-quarters of its economic power can still maintain its political dominance through its experience, its traditional position in society and the state.

But in the long run, the enfeeblement of the proletariat must in practice lead to a catastrophic decline in morale and consciousness of the people who are supposed to form the ruling class of the new state.

10
War Communism and the Peasantry

Collectivism and Individualism
The October revolution was a fusion of two revolutions – that of the proletariat, and that of the peasantry. We have seen

that the civil war led to a catastrophic decline in the relative weight of the proletariat. What was the impact of the revolution on that of the peasantry?

As has been pointed out earlier, Lenin always insisted that the peasantry was fundamentally different from the proletariat. Throughout the development of the party's agrarian policy there are two central points in Lenin's thinking: (i) the working class must lead the peasantry; (ii) the workers' party has to maintain its independence and clearly distinguish itself from the peasantry.[1]

'We stand by the peasant movement to the end,' Lenin said, 'but we have to remember that it is the movement of another class, *not the one* which can and will bring about the socialist revolution.'[2]

Now, after the revolution, Lenin again emphasized the clear distinction between the proletariat and the peasantry.

> Marx and Engels sharply challenged those who tended to forget class distinctions and spoke about producers, the people, or working people in general . . . There are no working people or workers in general; there are either small proprietors who own the means of production, and whose mentality and habits are capitalistic – and they cannot be anything else – or wage-workers with an altogether different cast of mind, wage-workers in large-scale industry, who stand in antagonistic contradiction to the capitalists and are ranged in struggle against them . . .[3]

> our aim is to abolish classes. As long as workers and peasants remain, socialism has not been achieved . . .[4]

> Their social conditions, production, living and economic conditions make the peasant half worker and half huckster . . .[5]

> We have one extremely dangerous secret enemy, more dangerous than many open counter-revolutionaries; this enemy is the anarchy of the petty proprietor . . . whose life is guided by one thought: 'I grab all I can – the rest can go hang.' This enemy is more powerful than all the Kornilovs, Dutovs and Kaledins put together.[6]

To fight against the anarchy of the petty proprietor in the countryside, Lenin in his *April Theses* suggested two measures: (1) forming large model farms, and (2) organizing the rural poor in Soviets of their own:

The weight of emphasis in the agrarian programme to be shifted to the Soviets of Agricultural Labourers' Deputies.

Confiscation of all landed estates.

Nationalization of *all* lands in the country, the land to be disposed of by the local Soviets of Agricultural Labourers' and Peasants' Deputies. The organization of separate Soviets of Deputies of Poor Peasants. The setting up of a model farm on each of the large estates (ranging in size from 100 to 300 *desiatins*,* according to local and other conditions, and to the decisions of the local bodies) under the control of the Soviets of Agricultural Labourers' Deputies and for the public account.[7]

The April Conference of the Bolsheviks again advised the 'proletarians and semi-proletarians of the countryside' to seek 'the formation out of every landlord's estate of a sufficiently large model farm which would be run for the public account by Soviets of Deputies of agricultural workers'.[8]

As it turned out, the agrarian revolution following the Bolshevik seizure of power in no way aided the formation of large model farms. It is estimated that of all the land confiscated throughout Russia, 93.7 per cent was distributed to the peasants, 1.7 per cent was turned over to collective farms, and only 4.6 per cent remained in the hands of the state.[9]

Lenin did not stop urging collectivization of agriculture. In a speech at a meeting of delegates from the Poor Peasants' Committees of the Central *gubernias* on 8 November 1918, he argued: 'Division of the land was all very well as a beginning. Its purpose was to show that the land was being taken from the landowners and handed over to the peasants. But that is not enough. The solution lies only in socialized farming.' He announced:

> The Soviet government has decided to assign one thousand million rubles to a special fund for improving farming. All existing and newly formed communes will receive monetary and technical assistance . . . the transition to the new form of agriculture may perhaps proceed slowly, but the beginnings of communal farming must be carried into practice unswervingly.[10]

In a speech on 11 December 1918 to the First All-Russian Congress of Land Departments, Poor Peasants' Committees and

---

* *Desiatin* = 1.09 hectares = 2.7 acres.

Communes, Lenin's theme was the coming of socialism in the countryside. What was now necessary was 'the transition from small individual peasant farms to the socialized working of the land'. But of course this was a very arduous task.

> We fully realize that such tremendous changes in the lives of tens of millions of people as the transition from small individual peasant farming to collective farming, affecting as they do the most deep-going roots of the peasants' way of life and their mores, can only be accomplished by long effort, and only when necessity compels people to reshape their lives.[11]

Following Lenin's report, the Congress passed a resolution that the chief aim of agrarian policy must be 'the consistent and unswerving pursuit of the organization of agricultural communes, Soviet communist farms and the socialized working of the land'.

On 14 February 1919 VTsIK issued a new decree on collectivization of agriculture. It proclaimed 'the transition from individual to collective forms of the utilization of land', and declared that 'all forms of individual utilization of land could be regarded as transitory and obsolete'. Its 138 clauses included elaborate provisions for the constitution, prerogatives and obligations of Soviet farms and agricultural communes.[12]

In practice very little came of the mountains of formulations, decrees and resolutions. It is estimated that by the end of 1918 there may have been nearly 3,000 agricultural cooperatives of all types, embracing some 0.15 per cent of the rural population.[13]

In 1920 the total population of the kolkhozes was 717,545, and their land area 700,464 *desiatins*.[14]

The sovkhozes, the state farms, covered a slightly larger area – 1,918,214 *desiatins* in 1919.[15] Altogether less than 1 per cent of all the cultivated land in 1920 was on state, collective and commune farms.

The Agricultural Proletariat

In 1905, in his *Two Tasks of Social-Democracy in the Democratic Revolution*, Lenin argued that while in the first stage of the revolution the proletariat has to march with the peasantry as a whole against the landlord, in the second stage the proletariat would split the peasantry in two, and march with the 'semi-proletarian' poor peasants against the rich peasants.

In May 1918 he again emphasized that the petty bourgeois elements in the countryside could be held in check only 'if we organize the poor, that is, the majority of the population or semi-proletarians, around the politically conscious proletarian vanguard'.[16]

However, the Bolshevik policy of splitting the peasantry and relying on the proletarian elements in the villages could not succeed. First of all the Bolsheviks were very weak in the countryside. At the end of 1917 the party's rural cadres numbered a mere 2,400, grouped in 203 organizations; a year later the figures were 97,000 and 7,370 respectively.[17] At the end of 1919 the number of Bolsheviks in village cells was no more than 60,000.[18] Many of the members were not peasants, but workers and officials living in rural areas. The weakness of the party showed in the fact that as late as 1922 the communists made up only 6·1 per cent of the rural Soviets.[19]

But more important than this, the agrarian revolution weakened, instead of strengthening, the agricultural proletariat. It weakened the class differentiation of the peasantry, leading to a striking equalization of the size of farms. The following table shows this:

(per cent of farms)

Year	No arable land	Arable land up to 2 desiatins	2–4 desiatins	4–10 desiatins	10 desiatins and over
1917	10·6	30·4	30·1	25·2	3·7
1920	4·7	47·9	31·6	15·3	0·5

	No horse	1 horse	2 horses	3 horses	4 horses	5 horses and over
1917	29·0	49·2	17·0	3·4	0·9	0·5
1920	27·6	63·6	7·9	0·7	0·2	— [20]

According to one Soviet statistician, the number of agricultural workers in European Russia fell from 2,100,000 in 1917 to a mere 34,000 in 1919.[21]

Looking back, Lenin said on 27 March 1921:

You know that there has been a levelling off in the Russian countryside in this period. The number of peasants with large areas under crop and without any at all has decreased, while the number of medium farms has increased. The countryside has become more petty bourgeois.[22]

Again on 21 April he wrote: 'In a very large number of cases the peasant "poor" (proletarians and semi-proletarians) have become middle peasants. This has caused an increase in the small-proprietor, petty-bourgeois "element".'[23]

Poor Peasants' Committees

In May 1918 the Bolsheviks decided to organize committees of poor peasants, *Kombedy*. This policy was forced on them by the imperative need to get food for the townspeople and the new-born Red Army.

At a conference of the Petrograd Soviet with delegates from the food supply organizations on (14) 27 January 1918, Lenin advocated the following:

All soldiers and workers must be recruited to form several thousand groups (consisting of 10-15 men, and possibly more) who shall be bound to devote a certain number of hours (say, 3-4) daily to the food supply service.[24]

The most reliable and best armed groups of the mass of revolutionary contingents organized to take extreme measures to overcome the famine shall be detailed for despatch to all stations and *uezds* [counties] of the principal grain supplying guberniias. These groups, with the participation of railwaymen delegated by local railway committees, shall be authorized, firstly, to control the movement of grain freights; secondly, take charge of the collection and storage of grain; thirdly, adopt the most extreme revolutionary measures to fight speculators and to requisition grain stocks.[25]

Under the threat of impending famine, Lenin looked for a way of obtaining support in the villages for the food requisitioning detachments. On 9 May VTsIK issued a 'decree to confer on the People's Commissariat of Supply extraordinary powers for the struggle with the rural bourgeoisie which conceals grain stocks and speculates in them'.

To reaffirm its stand in favour of the grain monopoly and fixed prices, as well as to recognize the necessity of continuing a merciless fight against the bread speculators and bagmen and of compelling every possessor of surplus grain to declare within a week from the promulgation of this resolution in the *volost* [small rural district] that he is ready to hand over all in excess of what he needs . . .

To call on all the toilers and propertyless peasants to unite at once and begin a merciless fight against the kulaks . . .

To confiscate without compensation any surplus grain which has not been reported in accordance with Article 1. One half of the value of the confiscated grain, determined on the basis of fixed prices and after it has actually reached the railway station, shall go to the person who gave the information about the concealed surplus; the other half shall go to the village community. Information about concealed surpluses shall be given to the local food organizations.

The decree did not disguise the fact that only force would achieve what was proposed. Anyone hoarding surplus grain

shall be handed over to the Revolutionary Court to be sentenced to prison for a term of not less than ten years, and shall be expelled for ever from their communes and suffer confiscation of their property . . .

To use armed force in cases of resistance to the requisition of grain and other food products.[26]

This decree was christened by its opponents the 'Food Dictatorship Decree' and was later commonly referred to by this name. To aid the implementation of the decrees, VTsIK issued a resolution on 20 May calling for the organization of the rural poor.

The All-Russian Central Executive Committee, having discussed the question of the tasks of the soviets in the village, considers it imperative to point out the urgent necessity of uniting the toiling peasantry against the village bourgeoisie. Local Soviets must undertake immediately the task of explaining to the poor that their interests are opposed to those of the kulaks, and of arming the poor with the purpose of establishing their dictatorship in the village.[27]

Two days later Lenin wrote a long open letter to the workers of Petrograd entitled 'On the Famine', in which he called on them to join the food detachments organized by the Commissariat of Supply in thousands.

We need a mass 'crusade' of the advanced workers to every centre of production of grain and fuel, to every important centre of supply and distribution – a mass 'crusade' to increase the intensity of work tenfold, to assist the local organs of Soviet power in the matter of accounting and control, and to eradicate profiteering, graft, and slovenliness by armed force.[28]

On 4 June 1918, at a meeting of VTsIK, Lenin declared that what was needed was unity of the workers . . . for the purpose of carrying on agitation in the villages and of waging a war for grain against the kulaks . . . A new form of struggle against the kulaks is emerging, namely, an alliance of the poor peasants . . . We are willing to make . . . awards to the poor peasants, and we have already begun to do so . . . We shall encourage and give every possible inducement to the poor peasants and shall help them if they help us to organize the collection of grain, to secure grain from the kulaks.[29]

On 11 June VTsIK formulated a decree about Committees of Poor Peasants. These were to be instruments for the 'requisitioning of surplus grain from the kulaks and the rich', for the distribution of food and articles of necessity, and in general for the execution on the spot of the agricultural policies of the government. The poor peasants were to be rewarded for their services by obtaining allocations of grain from the quantities seized, free till 15 July, at a discount of 50 per cent on the fixed prices till 15 August, and thereafter at 20 per cent discount.[30]

The organizing of the food detachments took an almost military form. According to an ordinance of the Commissariat of Food of 20 August 1918, 'Every food detachment is to consist of not less than twenty-five men and two or three machine guns.' They were assisted by a Food Army Administration.

Lenin saw in the organization of the Poor Peasants' Committees the transition from the bourgeois revolution to the socialist revolution in the countryside. In a report to the Eighth Party Congress on 18 March 1918 he said:

In a country where the proletariat could only assume power with the aid of the peasantry, where the proletariat had to serve as the agent of a petty-bourgeois revolution, our revolution was largely a *bourgeois* revolution until the Poor Peasants' Committees were set up, i.e. until the summer and even the autumn of 1918 . . . only when the October Revolution began to spread to the rural districts and was consummated, in the summer of 1918, did we acquire a real proletarian base; only then did our revolution *become a proletarian revolution in fact,* and not merely in our proclamations, promises and declarations.[81]

Thus the impact of hunger and civil war pushed the Soviet regime along a path of expediency which also seemed to be the path of socialism. But if a socialist agricultural policy means a policy directed towards collective farming, there was nothing socialist in the food requisition policy of the *Kombedy*. Furthermore, experience proved: (1) that the poor peasants were less numerous than the Bolshevik leaders assumed, and (2) that they were less independent of the middle peasants, and even the kulaks.

So quite early, on 2 December 1918, VTsIK issued a decree disbanding the Poor Peasants' Committees. The party had to come to terms with the fact that, in Lenin's words, the poor peasants 'have become middle peasants'.

Peasant Resistance to Compulsory Requisitions

The mass of the peasantry quite naturally resisted the requisitioning of food. They began by concealing their harvests. It was estimated that in 1920 more than a third of the total harvest was successfully hidden from the government's collection teams.[32] The peasants also began to till only enough land to meet their own needs, so that by the end of 1920 the acreage sown in European Russia was only three-fifths of the 1913 area.[33]

Grain output in 1920 was less than 35 million metric tons, compared with an annual output of 72.5 million in the period 1909-13; the peasants' own consumption was less than 17 million metric tons, a catastrophic reduction of about 40 per cent compared with pre-war levels.[34]

However, the peasants' attitude to the Bolshevik government during the civil war was not one of simple antagonism. While resenting the food requisitions, they did welcome the protection the Bolsheviks gave them against the threat of the landlords returning in the wake of the White Armies.

The ambivalent attitude of the peasantry to the new rulers,

a combination of submissiveness and hatred, was well described by Boris Pilnyak in his story 'Mother Earth'. The Communist Nikulev says: if you ask the fisherman Vassil Ivanov Starkov

> 'How many Communists have we in Viazovy?' he will answer, 'We don't have many Communists, what we have around here is mostly common folk, there's only two families of the Communists.' And if you press him further as to who exactly these common folk are, he will say, 'Common folk, like everyone knows, is common folk. Common folk is something like what you might call Bolsheviks.'[35]

It seemed that the Bolsheviks were acceptable – the party which gave the land to the peasants in 1917 was called Bolshevik; but the communists were few in number and very unpopular: the party changed its name to 'Communist' in 1918, and it was the communists who carried out the grain requisitions. The ambivalent attitude of the peasants, according to Lenin, expressed itself in the slogan: 'For Soviet power. For the Bolsheviks. Down with the *communia*.'[36]

An even clearer expression of the double-edged attitude to Bolshevism was given by a village delegate to the Third All-Russian Congress of Soviets: 'The land belongs to us: the bread to you: the water to us: the fish to you: the forest to us: the timber to you.'[37]

It had been one thing for the peasant to support a government which distributed land, but it was quite another matter when the same government began to requisition his produce to feed the hungry populations of the cities. This dual attitude towards Soviet power was expressed in either passive resistance or open rebellion.

Yet so long as the White Armies were threatening to bring about the return of the landlords, peasant opposition to Soviet state requisitions was limited.

The Peasants' Resistance Shapes the State
There was a close similarity between the attitude of the French peasantry to the state under Robespierre and that of the Russian peasantry to the state under Lenin. In both France and

Russia, at the time of their revolutions, the peasantry made up an overwhelming majority of the population, and the attitude of the peasantry to the state very largely shaped its physiognomy.

The attitude of the French peasantry to the Jacobin government was described by Engels as follows:

> In the first French revolution the peasants acted in a revolutionary manner just so long as was required by their most immediate, most tangible private interests; until they had secured the right of ownership to their land which had hitherto been farmed on a feudal basis, until feudal relations were irrevocably abolished and the foreign armies ejected from their district. Once this was achieved, they turned with all the fury of blind avarice against the movement of the big towns which they failed to understand, and especially against the movement in Paris. Countless proclamations by the Committee of Public Safety, countless decrees by the Convention, above all those concerning the maximum and the profiteers, mobile columns and travelling guillotines had to be directed against the obdurate peasants. And yet no class benefited more from the Terror which drove out the foreign armies and put down the civil war than these same peasants.[38]

One of the best descriptions of the Russian experience, which was so similar to the French, is in a report written by Antonov Ovseenko, head of the Cheka of Tambov province. This report was sent to Lenin on 20 July 1921, and a copy of it was found in Trotsky's archives in Harvard. The report is some 40 pages long, and we shall have to restrict ourselves to excerpts.

It starts by describing a mass protest rising in Tambov province. In this province of 3½ million people, tens of thousands of peasants were actively involved in the rising.

> By the middle of January the organization of the uprising had taken on definite shape:
> In five *uezds* as many as 900 village committees had been set up, elected by meetings and interlinked by *volost* and then *reion* [district], *uezd* and, finally, *guberniia* committees . . .
> In February the fighting men numbered as many as 40,000 . . .
> Besides the 'field' troops there were also internal guard units, some 10,000 in number, in operation.
> The availability of organized collaboration from the local population made the bands less vulnerable, exceptionally mobile and,

so to speak, ubiquitous. Their tactics were confined to sudden attacks on our small, careless units by means of wide, complete encirclements with dense lines of cavalry . . . The Soviet authorities from the villages in five of the *uezds* had almost entirely fled into the towns; the party organization in the countryside had been destroyed; it had not been able systematically and in good time to carry out the concentration and withdrawal of its forces from the villages that had risen up in arms, and up to a thousand communists were slaughtered.

The Red Army and the Cheka took extremely harsh measures against the peasant rebels. For instance:

pro-bandit villages are singled out, and in relation to these massive terrorism is applied: a special 'sentence' is pronounced on these villages, in which their crimes against the labouring people are enumerated, the entire male population is declared to be committed for trial before a Revolutionary Military Tribunal, all the families of bandits are removed to a concentration camp as *hostages* in respect of that member of the family who is a participant in a band, a term of two weeks is given for the bandit to give himself up, at the end of which the family is deported from the *guberniia* and its property (which earlier had been conditionally sequestrated) is confiscated for good. Simultaneously house-to-house searches are carried out, and, in the event of the discovery of weapons, the senior working member of the household is liable to shooting on the spot . . .

As a model of the correct execution of these orders [one can point to] the example of the 1st Sector, where the stubbornly pro-bandit Parevskaia *volost* was crushed by the firm application of the hostage system and the public shooting of them in batches until this secured the surrender of arms and of active members of bands. The effective conduct of this campaign was helped by the successes of our Cheka and of our military . . .

Of the 21,000 fighting men established by our intelligence as serving in the ranks of the gangs at the beginning of May only a few hundred remained by the middle of July; the remainder either had fallen casualty (up to 2,000 bandits were killed in June and July) or had given themselves up or been captured, or had fled . . .

According to reports from the Political Commissions for the period 1 June till 2 July, 1,748 bandits have been taken and 2,452 deserters; 1,449 bandits have surrendered voluntarily . . . and so have 6,672 deserters. In all 12,301 have been accounted for. 3,430 individual hostages have been taken and 913 families. 157

holdings have been confiscated and 85 houses have been burnt down or pulled down. During the last week the number of bandit deserters taken has risen to 16,000, of families to 1,500, of holdings confiscated to 500 and of houses burnt down or pulled down to 250. More than 300 bandit families were allowed to go free after the bandits had given themselves up . . . the harshest measures were applied in the Belomestnaia and Dvoinia *volosts*, where those peasants who had persisted in concealing arms and bandits gave in only after the shooting of two batches of kulak hostages. In all 154 bandit hostages were shot here. 227 families of bandits were taken, 17 houses were burnt down and 24 pulled down, and 22 houses handed over to the village poor. In the Estalsk *volost* 75 hostages and bandits were shot, 12 houses were burnt down and 21 pulled down; in both *volosts* the peasants denounced up to 300 bandits, some of whom they brought in, and handed in 118 rifles, 25 sawn-off shotguns, 10 revolvers, etc. . . .

In the village of Krivopoliane, after the shooting of 13 hostages, a store of spare parts for machine-guns was pointed out; several bandits were denounced and the refuge of the remnants of Selianskyi's band was pointed out. Altogether in the Tambov *uezd*, from 1 June up to 10 July, 59 bandits voluntarily gave themselves up with their arms and 906 without, and 1,445 deserters; 1,455 bandits and 1,504 deserters were eliminated. 549 families were taken as hostages; 295 outright confiscations of property were carried out; 80 houses were pulled down and 60 burnt down; 591 bandits and 70 hostages were shot and two persons for giving them shelter . . .

About 5,000 hostages have been accumulated in the concentration camps.

Why did the mass of peasants take up arms against the regime? The Cheka report candidly explains:

The peasant uprisings develop because of widespread *dissatisfaction, on the part of small property-owners in the countryside with the dictatorship of the proletariat, which directs at them its cutting edge of implacable compulsion, which cares little for the economic peculiarities of the peasantry* and does the countryside no service that is at all perceptible . . .

In general the Soviet regime was, in the eyes of the majority of the peasants, identified with flying visits by commissars or plenipotentiaries who were valiant at giving orders to the *volost* Executive Committees and village Soviets and went around imprisoning the representatives of these local organs of authority for the non fulfilment of frequently quite absurd requirements. It was identified also with the food-requisitioning units . . . The peasantry, in their majority, have become accustomed to regarding the Soviet regime as something extraneous in relation to themselves, something that issues only commands, that gives orders most zealously but quite improvidently.

The Soviet regime had the restrictiveness characteristic of a military administration.

In conclusion the report states:

in the countryside the Soviet regime is still predominantly military-administrative rather than economic in character; it is a force which issues instructions from the outside and not the acknowledged guide of the peasant farmer; in the eyes of the peasants it is tyrannical and not a system that, before all else, organizes and ministers to the countryside itself.[39]

The massive, stubborn opposition of the peasantry to the state inevitably distorted it away from the norm, the ideal, of the proletarian dictatorship as visualized by Lenin in *State and Revolution*. Following Marx and Engels, he argued there that the workers' state would impose a dictatorship on the minority – the bourgeoisie – while it represented total democracy for the majority. But the exigencies of a civil war in a backward country with its economy in ruins, and the international revolution belated, brought about impositions on the peasantry by the state so harsh as to make democracy for the majority – in this case the peasantry – impossible.

There was another factor which deformed the state even further. The peasantry inevitably influenced the mood of the young proletariat, who had only recently left the countryside. Thus the report of the Cheka in Tambov has this to say about the railwaymen of the province:

The railway-men continue to serve as a pivot for the counterrevolutionary organization . . .
For the protection of the railways a system of taking hostages from the adjacent settlements was applied as early as the end of April; in June this system was extended to the protection of the telegraph network and of the bridges on country roads; in July it was decided not to take hostages in these cases but to leave them in their villages, merely announcing that certain

families would be the first to answer for the destruction of rail-ways, etc.

Even the party was not immune from the mood of the peasantry in the province:

> the party organization was going through a grave crisis in the winter of 1920-1921: discipline fell, demoralizing influences gained strength ... and about half its members left
> The party organization has become weakened and overstrained; among the workers a mood of opposition is increasing ... The party organization numbers up to 5,000 members, instead of the 14,000 of last year.[40]

Thus the peasants' attitude to Communism was one of the main influences that shaped the state, giving it a Jacobin character, i.e. an extremely centralistic dictatorship by a revolutionary minority imposing its will on the great majority.

In Conclusion

We saw in the last chapter that the relative weight of the industrial proletariat declined. In this chapter we have seen that the weight of the agricultural proletariat was also reduced. In contrast, that of the petty bourgeois peasantry continued to rise. One graphic expression of the change in the relative power of the two classes is the change in their size. While the number of industrial workers, as we have seen, fell from 3,000,000 in 1917 to 1,240,000 in 1921-22 (a decline of 58.7 per cent), and the number of agricultural workers from 2,100,000 in 1917 to 34,000 in 1919 (a decline of 98.5 per cent), the number of peasant house-holds rose from 16.5 million on 1 January 1918 to over 24 million by 1920, an increase of about 50 per cent.[41]*

In an article entitled 'Economics and Politics in the Era of the Dictatorship of the Proletariat', published in *Pravda* on the third anniversary of the October revolution, Lenin quite rightly stated: 'it was the peasantry as a whole who were the first to gain, who gained most, and gained immediately from the dictatorship of the proletariat.'[42]

---

* Note that the figure for industrial workers gives the number of individuals, not households, i.e. the number of industrial workers' households was much smaller.

The situation and attitudes of the peasantry affected the whole structure of political organization – the state, the soviets, the state officialdom, the party – during the civil war, and even more after it.*

11

The Withering Away of the State?

During the civil war the Bolshevik government found itself under siege not only from world imperialism, but also among its own people, who were often indifferent, sometimes clearly hostile. These circumstances inevitably affected the functioning of the state.

The Dream

Let us deal first with the expectation. In his book *State and Revolution*, Lenin made it clear that the withering away of the state would begin immediately after the establishment of the dictatorship of the proletariat: 'according to Marx, the proletariat needs only a state which is withering away, i.e. a state so con-

---

*The class conflct between proletariat and peasantry explains why the Soviet electoral law under Lenin did not give even formal equality to the two: the All-Russian Congress of Soviets was made up of one deputy for every 25,000 city electors as against 125,000 rural inhabitants. (Since 51 per cent of the population were adults over 20, the urban population was overrepresented by something like 2·5 : 1 compared with the rural population.)
Lenin explained: 'Yes, we have violated equality between the workers and peasants . . . The vote of one worker is equal to several peasant votes. Is that unfair?
'No, in the period when it is necessary to overthrow capital it is quite fair'.[43]

stituted that it begins to wither away immediately, and cannot but wither away'.[1] However long the process, Lenin expected it to be progressive and continuing.

The state would have to be strong and ruthless in crushing the bourgeoisie. At the same time it would have to be democratic, as it would be a dictatorship exercised by a majority over a minority. This would give it a clearly democratic character, and enormously simplify its working. The period after the overthrow of capitalist rule

> is a period of unprecedented violent class struggle in unprecedented acute forms, and, consequently, during this period the state must inevitably be a state that is democratic *in a new way* (for the proletariat and the propertyless in general) and dictatorial *in a new way* (against the bourgeoisie) . . .
> the suppression of the minority of exploiters by the majority of the wage slaves of *yesterday* is comparatively so easy, simple and natural a task that it will entail far less bloodshed than the suppression of the risings of slaves, serfs or wage-labourers, and it will cost mankind far less. And it is compatible with the extension of democracy to such an overwhelming majority of the population that the need for a *special machine* of suppression will begin to disappear. Naturally, the exploiters are unable to suppress the people without a complex machine for performing this task, but *the people* can suppress the exploiters even with a very simple 'machine', almost without a 'machine', without a special apparatus, by the simple *organization of the armed people* (such as the Soviets of Workers' and Soldiers' Deputies).[2]

Lenin invokes the example of ancient democracy where the citizens themselves were administrators.

> Under socialism much of 'primitive' democracy will inevitably be revived, since, for the first time in the history of civilized society, the *mass* of the population will rise to taking an *independent* part . . . in the everyday administration of the state.[3]

The proletariat will be able

> to crush, smash to atoms, wipe off the face of the earth the bourgeois, even the republican-bourgeois, state machine, the standing army, the police and the bureaucracy and to substitute for them a *more* democratic state machine, but a state machine nevertheless, in the shape of armed workers who proceed to form a militia involving the entire population.[4]

And so 'the armed proletariat itself' will 'become the government'.[5]

The proletarian state will be a centralist one, but democratic, based on local autonomy of the communes, and the *voluntary* joining together : 'the proletariat and the poor peasants [will] take state power into their own hands, organize themselves quite freely in communes'.[6] And Lenin quotes approvingly the words of Engels: 'Complete self-government for the provinces (*guberniias* and regions), districts and communes through officials elected by universal suffrage. The abolition of all local and provincial authorities appointed by the state.'[7]

The first decrees and laws issued after the October revolution were full of repetitions of the word 'democracy': a 'democratic peace', 'democratization of the army'. 'As a democratic government', said Lenin introducing the land decree, 'we cannot evade the decision of the popular masses, even if we were not in agreement with it.' Tens and hundreds of similar statements were made. However, faced with the sullen opposition of the peasants, and with the proletariat a small and declining minority, the dictatorship of the proletariat in Russia was not to be that of the 'vast majority' but of a determined minority.

Let us now turn from the ideal to the reality, and see what deviations the situation made necessary from the norm described by Lenin on the eve of the October revolution.

State Administration

The first constitution of the Russian Socialist Federated Soviet (RSFSR), adopted by the Fifth All-Russian Congress of Soviets on 10 July 1918, declared: 'The All-Russian Congress of Soviets is the supreme authority of the Russian Socialist Federated Soviet Republic.'[8]

To start with the Congress of Soviets met frequently. Thus in the seven months between 7 November 1917, when power was declared to be in the hands of the Soviet, and the adoption of the constitution of 10 July 1918, there were four congresses. This frequency fell with the onset of the civil war. The constitution stated that the Congress of Soviets would convene 'at least twice a year'. This was changed to once a year in 1921.[9]

In fact the Congress met only annually during the period November 1918 to December 1922. A simple reason for the declining frequency of the Congresses of Soviets was the massive size of the assembly, which was not at all appropriate for the conditions of civil war: the number of delegates rose from 649 in November 1917 to 1,296 a year later and 2,214 in December 1922.[10]

The power of the Congress of Soviets shifted to its Central Executive Committee (VTsIK). In the constitution VTsIK was subordinate to the Congress. Article 29 states: 'The All-Russia Central Executive Committee is fully accountable to the All-Russia Congress of Soviets.' Nevertheless, the VTsIK was to be a powerful body. The constitution stated:

> In the intervals between Congresses the All-Russia Central Executive Committee is the supreme authority of the Republic.
> The All-Russia Central Executive Committee is the highest legislative, administrative and supervisory body of the Russian Socialist Federative Soviet Republic.
> The All-Russia Central Executive Committee gives general directives for the activity of the workers' and peasants' government and all organs of Soviet power in the country . . .
> The All-Russia Central Executive Committee examines and approves draft decrees and other proposals submitted by the Council of People's Commissars or by separate departments, and issues its own decrees and ordinances.
> The All-Russia Central Executive Committee convenes the All-Russia Congress of Soviets, to which it submits an account of its activity and reports on general policy and particular matters.
> The All-Russia Central Executive Committee appoints the Council of People's Commissars and . . . People's Commissariats.
> The All-Russia Central Executive Committee has the right to cancel or suspend any order or decision of the Council of People's Commissars.[11]

Thus VTsIK, according to the constitution, was a higher and more powerful body than the Council of People's Commissars, the Sovnarkom.

In practice, however, the power of VTsIK was whittled away by its own presidium (and by Sovnarkom). One reason, as in the case of the Congress of Soviets, was the sheer size of VTsIK, which in practice made it inflexible as an administrative leadership. The constitution called for a VTsIK of not more than 200 members. But this provision was altered to allow for an increase to 300 and later to 386 members by the Eighth (December 1920) and Ninth (December 1921) Congresses of Soviets.

The VTsIK met less and less frequently. At first it was required to meet at least once every two months. This was reduced to 'not less than three times a year' by provision of the Ninth Congress of Soviets.

At the Seventh Congress of Soviets (December 1919), Lenin justified the infrequency of the meetings of VTsIK by the requirements of the war against the Whites. 'It is said that the Soviets meet rarely and are not re-elected often enough.' The representative of the Bund complained, 'it is really a terrible crime if your Central Executive Committee has not met'. Lenin, quoting these words, replied:

> We are fighting against Kolchak, Denikin and the others . . . We are conducting a difficult and victorious war. You know that with every invasion we had to send all the members of the Central Executive Committee to the front . . . workers who have been tempered by several years of struggle and who have acquired the necessary experience to be able to lead are fewer in our country than in any other.[12]

The VTsIK was replaced, in practice, by its presidium. There was no such presidium in the system of organs originally established on 7 November 1917. An unofficial body, a presidium of 7 or 8 people was soon set up by VTsIK, however, to prepare material for the sessions, and provide continuous supervision over the existing VTsIK departments. In the succeeding months, it became the practice for VTsIK to entrust certain work to this presidium. But the first Soviet constitution still did not include the presidium among the organs of power.

Official recognition of the existing gap in the formal structure of power came a year and a half later, when the Seventh Congress of Soviets adopted the following specific decisions concerning the presidium of VTsIK on 9 December 1919:

> The presidium of VTsIK conducts the sessions of VTsIK.
> Prepares the materials for the sessions of VTsIK.

Introduces drafts of decrees for examination by the plenum of VTsIK.

Supervises the observance of decisions of VTsIK ...

Has the right, between sessions of VTsIK, to confirm decisions of Sovnarkom, as well as to suspend decisions of the latter, transferring them to the nearest plenum of VTsIK for decision.[18]

The expected frequency of the sessions of the presidium is not indicated. However, in a report on its activity between 19 March and 30 May 1921, Kalinin stated that during that period there were 19 meetings of the presidium. This would make an average of more than 3 meetings a week.[14]

In practice, however, neither the Congress of Soviets, nor VTsIK, nor even its presidium, retained any real power over the Council of People's Commissars, the Sovnarkom. With Sovnarkom staffed with the highest party members, it very early became clear that its subordination to the Congress of Soviets or VTsIK was only formal. The outstanding development of the years of the civil war was the concentration of central authority in the hands of Sovnarkom at the expense of the All-Russian Congress of Soviets and VTsIK.

The provisions of the constitution of 1918 that 'urgent measures can be taken by the Council of People's Commissars directly' was used more and more during the period of civil war and national emergency. Under such conditions, indeed, all decisions are likely to be measures of extreme urgency.

Sovnarkom not only enjoyed full executive authority, but also unlimited power of legislation by decree. In its first year it passed 480 decrees, of which only 68 were submitted to VTsIK for confirmation. Between 1917 and 1921 Sovnarkom issued 1,615 decrees, VTsIK only 375.[15]

Decline of the Power of Local Soviets

After the October revolution the People's Commissariat of Internal Affairs defined the role of local soviets thus:

Locally the Soviets are the organs of administration, the organs of local power: they must bring under their control all institutions of an administrative, economic, financial and cultural-educational character ...

Each of these organizations, down to the smallest, is fully autonomous in questions of a local character, but makes its activity conform to the general decrees and resolutions of the central power and to the resolutions of the larger Soviet organizations into the composition of which it enters.[16]

At the same time as the All-Russian Congress of Soviets was being deprived of its power by Sovnarkom, a process of concentration of authority at the centre at the expense of local soviets was taking place.

The civil war undermined the operation of the local soviets. The borough soviets in major cities disappeared. The administration of numerous city soviets was combined with those of the provinces and districts, while the regional organizations established by the constitution ceased to exist altogether. A major role at this time was played by the so-called Revkoms or Revolutionary Committees. These were set up in regions affected by the war, by a decree of Sovnarkom of 24 October 1919, and all local soviet organizations were instructed to obey them.[17] The Revkoms were frequently identical with the Bolshevik party committee.

At the Seventh All-Russian Soviet Congress in December 1919, Kamenev painted the following dark picture of the soviets during the civil war:

> We know that because of the war the best workers were withdrawn in large numbers from the cities, and that therefore at times it becomes difficult in one or another provincial or district capital to form a soviet and make it function . . . The soviet plenary sessions as political organizations often waste away, the people busy themselves with purely mechanical chores . . . General soviet sessions are seldom called, and when the deputies meet, it is only to accept a report, listen to a speech and the like.[18]

Much of the influence of the local soviets was taken over by the party. One reason was that the local soviet administrations were backward and corrupt. In reporting on the collapse of the eastern front in December 1918, Stalin argued that the local soviets bore the decisive responsibility for the defeat. He had found that most of the staff of this institution had been active in the Zemstva, the old Tsarist local government institutions, e.g. in Viatka 4,467 out of a total of 4,766 of the staff of the soviet authorities.[19] For this reason he called for a strengthening of the local party organization, in order to be able to supervise the unreliable soviets.

The Role of the Cheka

Another important development undermining the soviet, and directly associated with the harsh conditions of the civil war, was the rise of the secret police, the Cheka. Elsewhere we have referred to the rise of the Red Terror, and its instrument, the Cheka, as a response to the White Terror.* To start with the Cheka had a very small staff. But it expanded very quickly. In February 1918 the central Cheka had 120 employees. By the end of the year the entire organization was said by Latsis to have a staff of no less than 31,000.[20]

During the civil war the Cheka invaded every department of state administration, central and local. By August 1918 it had formed sub-committees in 38 *guberniias* and 365 districts, which in practice covered the whole of Russia under Soviet rule at the time. In an instruction from the Central Cheka to the local commissions of 28 August 1918 it was pointed out that in no circumstances should the Cheka be subordinated to any division or soviet executive committee, but that it had on the contrary to exercise the function of leadership.

One historian described the position of the Cheka at the time thus:

> The power of the Cheka was unlimited and nothing could be done without its local commissions in autumn 1918 in the field of supply and military defence, when Soviet Russia was under dire threat from the civil war and foreign intervention. The Cheka had its eyes everywhere. If the constant changing of the fronts caused the collapse of some Soviets, the Cheka, which disposed its own troops, represented the state authority in the areas affected by the war.[21]

At the end of November 1918 the Cheka was given the task of forming subdivisions for railways, water navigation, posts and telegraph. It also took over from the armed units of the Commissariat of Supply.

Since the Cheka had succeeded in building a chain of auth-

---

* See pp. 17-19.

ority right up to the district administration, by setting up local Extraordinary Commissions, and thus in principle represented a genuine central organ, it was not surprising that it came into conflict with the People's Commissariat of the Interior.

When in March 1918 the Cheka began to build up its local branches, the Commissariat for the Interior assumed that these commissions would become part of the soviet organizations and not interfere with the uniformity of the system. But, in fact, the subordination of the Extraordinary Commissions to the local soviets was not put into effect. In the following months the representatives of the soviets and the leaders of the security organs arrested each other from time to time in the fight for domination.[22]

A member of the People's Commissariat of the Interior complained that the slogan 'All power to the Cheka' would supersede the old slogan 'All power to the soviets'.

The tensions between local soviets and Extraordinary Commissions were made clear in an inquiry published by the Commissariat of the Interior on 20 November 1918. According to this, 119 soviets were in favour of the subordination of the Cheka to the Executive Committees of the soviets, 99 wanted to incorporate them into the 'administration divisions' of the soviets, and only 19 advocated an independent position.[23]

The threat that the Cheka might rise above the party was clear. At the turn of the year 1918-19 a press campaign was launched against the Cheka in *Pravda* and *Izvestiia*. Under the pressure of such great mistrust the Extraordinary Commissions were dissolved at district level by VTsIK on 24 January 1919.[24]

However, at the height of Kolchak's and Denikin's offensive in summer and autumn 1919, when the Soviet Republic for a time resembled a beleaguered fortress in an area with a radius of 600 km round Moscow, all criticism of the Cheka, as well as other extraordinary organs, was suppressed.

Although the Cheka was necessary for victory in the civil war, Lenin was aware of the danger that it could develop into a completely independent instrument. At the first opportunity which arose – immediately after the end of the civil war – he moved to curb the power of the Cheka.

In a speech on 23 December 1921 – one of the last speeches of his life – to the Ninth Congress of the Soviets, Lenin stated: 'It is essential to reform the Cheka, define its functions and powers, and limit its work to political problems . . . [It is essential] to put forward the firm slogan of greater revolutionary legality.'[25]

Accordingly the Ninth Congress of Soviets resolved:

> The Congress considers that the present strengthening of soviet power within and without makes it possible to narrow the extent of the activity of the Cheka and its organs, reserving for the judicial organs the struggle against violations of the laws of the soviet republics.
>
> Therefore the Congress of Soviets charges the presidium of VTsIK to review at the earliest date the statute of the Cheka and its organs in the sense of reorganizing them, of restricting their competence and of strengthening the principles of revolutionary legality.[26]

The Red Army

The main arm of the state is the army. In Lenin's words, the state 'consists of special bodies of armed men, having prisons, etc. at their command'.[27]

A few days after coming to power, he wrote: 'The wholesale arming of the people and the abolition of the regular army is a task which we must not lose sight of for a single minute.'[28]

In April 1917, Lenin posed the question: 'Should officers be elected by the soldiers?' And he answered unequivocally: 'Not only must they be elected, but every step of every officer and general must be supervised by persons especially elected for the purpose by the soldiers.'

Then he asked: 'Is it desirable for the soldiers, on their own decision, to displace their superiors?' And answered: 'It is desirable and essential in every way. The soldiers will obey and respect only elected authority.'[29]

Initially, the Bolshevik government introduced extreme measures of democratization for the army. Thus, on 16 (29) December 1917, Sovnarkom issued a decree stating:

> The full power within any army unit or combination of units is to be in the hands of its soldiers' committees and Soviets . . .
> The [soldiers'] committees are to exercise control over those

spheres of [the army's] activity which the committees do not handle directly.

The elective principle for army officers is hereby introduced. All commanders up to the regimental commander are to be elected by a general vote of the [different units] . . . Commanders higher than regimental commanders and including the supreme commander-in-chief are to be elected by a congress . . . of committees of the army units [for which the commander is being elected] . . .

Positions of a technical nature which require special training . . . such as physicians, engineers, aviators . . are to be appointed by the committees . . . from among persons having the required special knowledge.

Chiefs of staff are elected . . . from among persons with special training.

Next day Sovnarkom decided by decree

1. To do away with all ranks and titles from the rank of corporal to that of general, inclusive. The army of the Russian Republic is henceforth to be composed of free and equal citizens bearing the honorable title of 'soldier of the revolutionary army';
2. To do away with all privileges and the external marks formerly connected with the different ranks and titles;
3. To do away with saluting;
4. To do away with all decorations and other signs of distinction;
5. To do away with all officers' organizations . . .
6. To abolish the institution of orderlies in the army.[80]

However, the Bolsheviks were very quickly forced to retreat from the ideal of a democratically structured army. On 13 March 1918 Trotsky was appointed People's Commissar of War and President of the Supreme War Council. And he set about organizing the armed forces of the Republic.

The first soldiers of the revolution consisted of Red Guards. Any attempt to carry out conscription in the first months of the revolution would have been condemned to failure. The country was sick of war, and the main appeal of Bolshevism had been its search for peace. So it was decided to create Red forces of volunteers. More than 100,000 volunteers joined the Red Army up to April 1918.

But the exigencies of the civil war made it impossible for the Soviet government to rely on volunteers alone. With 16 armies defending a front of 8,000 kilometres, conscription had to be undertaken to raise the Red Army first to one, then two, then three and eventually to five million.

Trotsky started to build the Red Army by calling for volunteers from among the proletariat. Only when the proletarian core of the army had been firmly established did he begin to conscript the peasants, first the poor and then the middle peasants. These often deserted en masse, their morale oscillating violently with the ups and downs of the civil war.

It was estimated that the number of such deserters in the period from 1 January 1919 to 1 January 1920 was 2,846,000 in round figures. During the year 1919, 1,753,000 deserters were brought back to the army.

By February 1919 there were about a million men in the Red Army. The number rose by 1 January 1920 to about three million.[81] Over 90 per cent of the deserters were men who failed to comply with call-up orders. The total number of deserters for the second half of 1919 was about 1,500,000. The counter-measures ranged from threats of dire punishment to promises of pardon to those who reported for duty immediately. A Central Commission for Combating Desertion, with regional branches, was set up in December 1918 and reorganized in May 1919 with a wider network of local branches. Nearly one million deserters reported for duty voluntarily during the second half of 1919. At times there were new formations consisting almost entirely of this category of deserters.[82]

The combat efficiency of the soldiers had a great deal to do with their class origin. An article analysing the percentage of workers in the Red Army in 1920 stated:

In the divisions that had distinguished themselves in action, the percentage of workers ranged from 26·4 (8th Red Cavalry Division) to 19·6 (28th Rifle Division). In Budenny's famous First Cavalry Army the percentage of workers was 21·7. On the other hand, in the 9th Rifle Division, regarded as one of low combat value, the workers were only 10·5 per cent of the total number. In penal detachments, workers were 9·7 per cent of the total, in

the detachments from apprehended deserters, 3.8 per cent. For
the Red Army as a whole the percentage of workers at the time
was 14.9; in the field units at the front it amounted to 16.5,
while in the rear it fell to 11.13.[32]

The role of the Bolsheviks in the Red Army was clearly
formulated by an order in May 1920 from Trotsky to the Commissar and commanding personnel of the western front.

It is necessary that in each platoon, section and squad there
should be a communist, even if a young one – but devoted to
the cause. He should observe the morale of the nearest fellow-
fighters, explain to them the problems and the aims of the war,
and, in case he is himself perplexed, approach the commissar of
his unit or some other responsible political worker for eluci-
dation. Without such internal, unofficial, personal, day-by-day
and hour-by-hour agitation under all conditions of the combat
situation, the official agitation through articles and speeches will
not give the required results ...

The conduct of communists in the Red Army has a decisive significance for the morale and the battle efficacy of units. It is
necessary, therefore, to distribute communists in an organized
way, to guide them attentively and to keep careful check of
their work . . . Revolutionary military councils and political
departments of the armies, commissars and political departments
of divisions, commissars of brigades and regiments should
carefully check up on the behaviour of all communists subordinated to them with respect to combat functions after
each new battle ordeal, ruthlessly casting out those lacking in
decisiveness and meting out stern punishment to cowardly ego-
tists.[34]

The Soviet military historian, F.Nikonov, suggests that during
the civil war Red Army units were classified for combat efficiency
according to the percentage of communists in their ranks. He
estimates that those with less than 4 to 5 per cent of communists
among their personnel were regarded as ineffective. Detachments
with 6 to 8 per cent were looked upon as satisfactory, with an
average combat efficacy. Units with 12 to 15 per cent communists
were considered shock troops.[35]

The mass of communists were fanatically devoted to the
cause. They were well aware that if they fell into the hands of
the Whites and were recognized as party members they would

be tortured and killed. So they fought with desperate courage and instilled something of their spirit into the mass of non-party soldiers.

The greatest obstacles to building the Red Army were moral and political. The whole of their recent vivid experience, including Bolshevik activities, encouraged soldiers to rebel against discipline and against authority. When Trotsky came to the conclusion that soldiers' committees could not lead regiments into battle successfully, and that the army needed centralization and formal discipline, this contradicted everything that the Bolsheviks had previously propagated. The tsar's officers who had been driven out of the army now had to be re-enrolled as specialists in the Red Army. Soldiers' committees, the embodiment of the revolution, were not now to be tolerated. The old discipline was still fresh in the memory when a new discipline had to be introduced.

In matters of defence, Trotsky argued, courage and revolutionary enthusiasm are not enough. 'As industry needs engineers, as farming needs qualified agronomists, so military specialists are indispensable to defence.'[36]

The first general call-up of military specialists took place on 29 July 1918; by the end of the year 36,971 such people had been mobilized, of whom 22,295 were officers.[37] By 15 August 1920, 48,409 former Tsarist officers had been called up, about 30,000 of whom saw active service. (The total number of 'commander' personnel towards the end of the civil war was about 130,000.)[38]

To control the ex-Tsarist officers Trotsky relied on the political commissars, who played a very important role. The commissar was supposed to watch over the political loyalty of the officers, to take charge of party work in the unit, and to carry on political propaganda and education work. According to the rules, the signature of the commissar was necessary on an operations order – to ensure that it did not have any hidden counter-revolutionary significance. Military responsibility for any such order, however, remained with the specialists.

From the beginning Trotsky made it clear that the commissar, who was entrusted with great power, would be severely punished if he neglected his duty. Thus on 14 August 1918 he declared: 'I hereby give warning that if any part of the army retreats of its own will the first to be shot will be the commissar, and the second the commander. The soldiers who show courage will be rewarded and promoted to positions of command. Cowards and traitors will not escape the bullets.'[39]

The commissars were an indispensable instrument of proletarian control. At the Seventh Congress of Soviets in December 1919 Trotsky eulogized the commissars: 'In our commissars . . . we have a new communist order of Samurais, the members of which have enjoyed no caste privileges and could die and teach others to die for the cause of the working class.'[40]

But despite the revolutionary spirit of the proletarian core of the Red Army and the heroic devotion of the communists, the Red Army was undeniably as far from Lenin's ideal of a workers' militia, as described in State and Revolution, as chalk from cheese.

The Bureaucratic Leviathan

There was a massive increase in the number of officials. There were 5,880,000 state officials by the end of 1920 – five times as many as the number of industrial workers.[41]

This state apparatus was mostly composed of people with bourgeois origins. It is true that hundreds of thousands of workers were mobilized by the party to strengthen it, but they were a minority, and their weight was further weakened by the dominance which technical superiority and higher cultural standards gave the old officials. As Lenin said on 12 June 1920: 'The soviet government employs hundreds of thousands of office workers, who are either bourgeois or semi-bour is . . . they have absolutely no confidence in our soviet government.'[42]

A confidential inquiry in the summer of 1922 among 270 engineers and technicians in responsible positions in Moscow, probably a fairly representative sample, confirmed Lenin's opinion. These engineers were divided into two categories, the first comprising those who belonged to the higher ranks of the administration before the revolution, and the second those who had been 'ordinary engineers' under the old regime. Three main questions were put to them: Were they sympathetic to the soviet government? Did they consider their work to be of social value? Did they consider the taking of bribes to be inadmissible? Those in the first group who answered the three questions affirmatively were 9, 30 and 25 per cent respectively; among the second group, 13, 75 and 30 per cent.[43]

If there was one person who was always aware of the danger of bureaucracy, who repeatedly used the strongest expressions to denounce it and demand a struggle against it, it was Lenin. Thus at the 11th session of the Petrograd Soviet on 12 March 1919 he spoke

> about the mouldiness, moss and red tape that has grown in the localities and about the need to fight it . . . We threw out the old bureaucrats, but they have come back . . . they wear a red ribbon in their buttonholes and creep into warm corners. What to do about it? We must fight this scum again and again and if the scum has crawled back we must again and again clean it up, chase it out, keep it under the surveillance of communist workers and peasants whom we have known for more than a month and for more than a year.[44]

At the Eighth Congress of the Party, in March 1919, Lenin said:

> The Tsarist bureaucrats began to join the soviet institutions and practise their bureaucratic methods, they began to assume the colouring of communists and, to succeed better in their careers, to procure membership cards of the Russian Communist Party . . . What makes itself felt here most is the lack of cultured forces.[45]

From 1921 onwards his denunciations of bureaucracy became more and more vehement. In a speech on 17 October 1921 to a conference of representatives of the Political Education Departments, Lenin said:

> At present bribery surrounds us on all sides . . . In my opinion, three chief enemies now confront one, . . . the first is communist conceit; the second – illiteracy, and the third – bribery.[46]

On 23 December 1921 he wrote to P.A.Bogdanov of VSNKh: 'We don't know how to conduct a public trial for rotten bureaucracy: for this all of us, and particularly the People's Commissariat for Justice, should be hung on stinking ropes. And I have not yet lost all hope that one day we shall be hung for this, *and deservedly so.*[47]

On 21 February 1922 Lenin wrote to A.D.Tsiurupa, Deputy Chairman of Public Works Committee: 'The departments are shit; decrees are shit. To find men and check up on their work – that is the whole point.'[48]

With the same frankness and plainness, in his last speech to the Comintern Congress, on 13 November 1922, he indicted the bourgeois-conservative nature of the existing state machine:

> We took over the old machinery of state, and that was our mis-fortune. Very often this machinery operates against us. In 1917, after we seized power, the government officials sabotaged us. This frightened us very much and we pleaded: 'Please come back.' They all came back, but that was our misfortune. We now have a vast army of government employees, but lack sufficiently educated forces to exercise real control over them. In practice it often happens that here at the top, where we exercise political power, the machine functions somehow; but down below govern-ment employees have arbitrary control and they often exercise it in such a way as to counteract our measures. At the top, we have, I don't know how many, but at all events, I think, no more than a few thousand, at the outside several tens of thousands of our own people. Down below, however, there are hundreds of thousands of old officials whom we got from the tsar and from bourgeois society and who, partly deliberately and partly unwit-tingly, work against us.[49]

In Conclusion

The civil war shaped all the state institutions. In the words of Bukharin and Preobrazhensky, 'Today, when a fierce civil war is still raging, all our organizations have to be on a war footing. The instruments of the soviet power have had to be constructed on militarist lines . . . What exists today in Russia is not simply the dictatorship of the proletariat; it is a militarist-proletarian dictatorship.'[50]

The siege of the revolutionary state by foreign and Russian White armies, together with the sullen if not actively hostile attitude of millions of peasants, and the weakness of the industrial proletariat, were at the root of the bureaucratic centralism of all the state institutions.

The message of *State and Revolution*, which elsewhere I have called 'Lenin's real testament', and which was the guide for the first victorious proletarian revolution, was violated again and again during the civil war. But it was also invoked again and again against bureaucratic degeneration.

12

The Establishment of the Bolsheviks' Political Monopoly

Days of Innocence

To start with Lenin spoke of the *proletariat*, the *class* – not the Bolshevik Party – assuming state power. Thus on 11 (24) March 1917, in his *Letters from Afar*, he wrote: 'the proletariat must organize and arm *all* the poor, exploited sections of the population in order that they *themselves* should take the organs of state power directly into their own hands, in order that *they themselves should constitute* these organs of state power'.[1]

He did not visualize one-party rule. In *State and Revolution* the party receives very little attention. There are three references to it, two of which have no direct bearing on the issue of the dictatorship of the proletariat. One of these is an incidental remark concerning the need for the party to engage in the struggle 'against religion which stupefies the people';[2] the second, equally incidental, notes that 'in revising the programme of our party, we must by all means take the advice of Engels and Marx into consideration, in order to come nearer the truth, to restore marxism by ridding it of its distortions, in order to come nearer the truth, guide the struggle of the working class for its emancipation more correctly.'[3] The third and most relevant reference reads:

> By educating the workers' party, Marxism educates the vanguard of the proletariat capable of assuming power and *leading*

the whole people to socialism, of directing and organizing the new system, of being the teacher, the guide, the leader of all the working and exploited people, in organizing their social life without the bourgeoisie and against the bourgeoisie.[4]

It is not entirely clear from this passage whether it is the *proletariat* which is capable of assuming power or the *vanguard* of the proletariat, i.e. the workers' party which is so designated.

In general, Lenin distinguished clearly between the soviet state and the party: the former was the creation of the working class as a whole and involved the class as a whole in its operation: 'Under socialism . . . the *mass* of the population will rise to taking an *independent* part, not only in voting and elections, *but also in the everyday administration of the state.*'[5]

In Lenin's concept, the soviet state is the highest expression of the self-activity of the proletariat; the party is that section of the class which is most conscious of the historical role of this self-activity. Because the party and the state are not *identical*, in the same way as the vanguard and the class are not identical, more than one party can contend for influence and power within the framework of the institution of the workers' state.

All revolutionaries took it for granted before the October revolution that more than one workers' party would exist. Thus Trotsky, on being elected President of the Petrograd Soviet on 9 (22) September 1917, said:

> We are all party people, and we shall have to cross swords more than once. But we shall guide the work of the Petersburg soviet in a spirit of justice and complete independence for all fractions; the hand of the praesidium will never oppress the minority.

Sukhanov, quoting these words a few years later, commented:

> Heavens! What liberal views! What self-mockery! But the point is that about three years later, while exchanging reminiscences with me, Trotsky, thinking back to this moment, exclaimed dreamily:
> 'What a happy time!'
> Yes, wonderful! Perhaps not one person in the world, not excluding himself, will ever recall Trotsky's rule with *such* feelings.[6]

However, under the iron pressure of the civil war the Bolshevik leaders were forced to move, as the price of survival, to *a one-party system.*

The fate of the different parties was closely bound up with the development of the civil war. That the openly capitalist parties, above all the Cadets, would be ready to fight to the end against Bolshevik power was obvious. They wanted an open capitalist class dictatorship. The petty bourgeois parties – the Socialist-Revolutionaries and Mensheviks – were less clear in their position. On the one hand the petty bourgeois leaders rallied again and again to the counter-revolution. On the other they were repulsed by the extremism of the White terror, which did not spare even them. The result was vacillation in the SR and Menshevik camps. This was combined with serious fragmentation within the two parties. In each one section joined the Cadets, another moved cautiously and gradually towards the Bolsheviks, and another remained neutral. The positions of the different sections depended very much on the situation on the civil war front. A few Red Army reverses were enough to push the petty bourgeoisie, perpetually hesitant, in the direction of the right.

In suppressing the extreme right, the Bolshevik government faced a dilemma. What were they to do about the petty bourgeois who protested against the 'suppression of freedom'? This dilemma became increasingly difficult to solve by moderate measures: the Right Socialist Revolutionaries were practically indistinguishable from the 'Left' Cadets, and protested strongly when the latter were suppressed; the Right Mensheviks protested against the suppression of the Right SR; then again there was no clear boundary between the Right SR and the moderate SR, and between these and the Left SR, etc. The gradation was continuous. And as long as the final outcome of the civil war was not certain, i.e. for nearly three years, the level of tolerance of both the Bolsheviks and their opponents was very low. As E.H.Carr put it: 'If it was true that the Bolshevik regime was not prepared after the first few months to tolerate an organized opposition, it was equally true that no opposition was prepared to remain within legal limits. The premise of dictatorship was common to both sides of the argument.'[7]

The Cadets

On 28 November (11 December) 1917, Sovnarkom issued a decree banning the Cadet leaders because of their association with the Kornilov-Kaledin White forces. 'Leaders of the Cadet Party, the party of the enemy of the people, are to be arrested and handed over to the revolutionary tribunal. Local Soviets are ordered to keep a careful watch on the Cadet Party because of its connections with the Kornilov-Kaledin civil war against the revolution.'[8]

At a meeting of VTsIK the Left Socialist Revolutionaries and Menshevik Internationalists protested against this decree.[9]

At first, the measures the Bolshevik government took against the Cadets were seen as merely temporary. Thus, Sovnarkom's decree of 27 October (9 November), banning the Cadet press, stated:

> Those organs of the press will be closed which (a) call for open opposition or disobedience to the Workers' and Peasants' Government;
> (b) sow sedition by a frankly slanderous perversion of facts;
> (c) encourage deeds of a manifestly criminal character...
> The above regulations are of a temporary nature and will be removed by a special decree just as soon as normal conditions are re-established.[10]

The Bolsheviks were even more lenient than the law allowed. Thus, in spite of the decrees, the Cadet newspaper, *Svoboda Rossii*, was still being published in Moscow in the summer of 1918. But this leniency evaporated when the civil war raged more fiercely.

Right Socialist Revolutionaries and Right Mensheviks

There was no clear line of demarcation between the Cadets and the Right SRs. O.H.Radkey, the historian of the SR party, describing its members in the Constituent Assembly, said:

> many of these people had developed a Cadet mentality, and were Cadets in everything but name.[11]
> All of these public welfare people, these functionaries, state employees, agronomists, cooperative officials, and others might, indeed, have contributed to the coming of revolution, but after it came, a few months of observing the people in action sufficed to convert them into one of the most conservative elements in

Russian society; the war did the rest by inflaming their latent nationalism. By any rational test, these right-wing populist intellectuals should have been in one camp with the Constitutional Democrats.

Why were they not? Why did they dissemble their convictions under the flag of Socialist Revolutionism? Sentiment might be one reason . . . If not sentiment, then inertia helped to hold them where they were. Personal interest also may have had some influence. They may have realized that they would never achieve the position of power in the Cadet Party that they held in their own. There they would merely be foot soldiers, whereas here they were generals.[12]

After the October revolution the Right SRs quite naturally joined forces with the Cadets. In March 1918 they set up a common organization with the Mensheviks, called the 'League for Renewal' (*Soiuz Vozrozhdeniia*).

'The "League" ', one of the Socialist Revolutionary leaders wrote, 'entered into regular relations with the representatives of the Allied missions at Moscow and Vologda.'[13]

In Moscow the Oktobrists, who traditionally stood to the right of the Cadets, joined the League for Renewal. The Military Commission of the Socialist Revolutionary Party organized the League's 'combat groups', whose command was entrusted to a general. The local committee of the League in Petrograd was made up of two Popular Socialists, one SR (A.R.Gotz, the leader of the party), one Cadet, Pepeliaev, who was to be one of Kolchak's ministers, and two Mensheviks, Potresov and Rozanov.

Another counter-revolutionary organization was created by the former SR terrorist, Boris Savinkov (one of the key participants in the abortive Kornilov coup) – the Fatherland and Freedom Defence League. Its chief of staff was a monarchist, while the majority of participants were Right SRs. This organization led a number of insurrections in the summer of 1918 in Iaroslav, Rybinsk, Murom, Kazan, Kaluga and Vladimirov.

When the Czechoslovak Legion rose in arms against the Bolsheviks in May 1918, it received the wholehearted support of the Right SR. When the Czechoslovaks occupied Samara, an SR committee of members of the Constituent Assembly proclaimed itself the government of the region, under its protection. A similar government was established at Omsk. At Archangel, under Allied protection, a mixed government of Populist Socialists and SRs was set up, headed by the old Narodnik, Peter Chaikovsky. In the Urals, at the end of July, after its capture by the Czechs and Russian White forces, a coalition government of Cadets, Right SRs, Populist Socialists and Right Mensheviks was formed. In Ufa a coalition government of monarchists, Cadets, Right SRs and Right Mensheviks was established under the leadership of Admiral Kolchak, and with the blessing of the French and British diplomatic representatives. By the spring of 1919 Kolchak had such a strong army as to represent a real threat to the survival of the Soviet regime.

The Soviet government had no alternative but to take severe measures against the Socialist Revolutionaries and Mensheviks. By a decree of 14 June 1918 VTsIK excluded both Right SR and Mensheviks from its ranks, because of their association with the Czech counter-revolutionaries seeking to 'organize armed attacks against the workers and peasants', and recommended all Soviets to exclude them.[14]

On 20 June 1918 the Bolshevik leader Volodarsky was assassinated by a Right SR – the first successful political assassination by the counter-revolution. On 30 August a Right SR, Dora Kaplan, made an attempt on Lenin's life and on the same day another Bolshevik leader, Uritsky, was assassinated by a Right SR.

Although he resorted to harsh measures against the counter-revolutionary acts of the Right SR, Lenin was always looking for a way of relaxing these measures. Thus when a professor of the University of Petrograd, Pitirim Sorokin, a former Right SR deputy to the Constituent Assembly, announced in November 1918, in a brief but sensational letter to the press, that he was giving up politics, this was seen by Lenin as:

> a symptom of a change of front on the part of a whole class, the petty-bourgeois democrats. A split among them is inevitable: one section will come over to our side, another section will remain neutral, while a third will deliberately join forces with the monarchist Constitutional-Democrats, who are selling Russia to Anglo-American capital and seeking to crush the revolution with the aid of foreign bayonets.

This development should be encouraged.

> One of the most urgent tasks of the present day is to take into
> account and make use of the turn among the Menshevik and
> Socialist-Revolutionary democrats from hostility to Bolshevism
> first to neutrality and then to support of Bolshevism . . . A revo-
> lutionary proletarian must know whom to suppress and with
> whom – and when and how – to conclude an agreement . . .
> But it would be . . . foolish and ridiculous . . . to insist only on
> tactics of suppression and terror in relation to the petty-bour-
> geois democrats when the course of events is compelling them
> to turn in our direction.[15]

On 8 February 1919 a conference of the Socialist Revolutionary organization in Petrograd 'decisively rejected any attempt to
overthrow the soviet power by way of armed struggle' and
denounced the Russian bourgeois parties and 'the imperialist
countries of the Entente'. This demonstration of goodwill evoked
a VTsIK resolution on 25 February 1919 legalizing the SR Party.
But the Right SRs were not consistent in this line of benevolent
neutrality towards the soviet government. With changing fortunes
on the battlefields they repeatedly resorted to openly counter-
revolutionary actions.

The Mensheviks

Despite their strong opposition to the Bolshevik government,
for some time – i.e. until the armed uprising of the Czechoslovak
Legion – the Mensheviks were not much hampered in their propaganda work. Thus the Left Menshevik paper, *Novaia Zhizn*, published a series of highly inflammatory articles between October
1917 and its suppression in July 1918, which did not bring down
upon it the heavy hand of the state. Maxim Gorky, in the issue
of 7 (20) November 1917, described the Bolsheviks thus:

> Blind fanatics and dishonest adventurers rushing madly, sup-
> posedly along the road of the 'social revolution'; in reality this
> is the road to anarchy, to the destruction of the proletariat and
> of the revolution. On this road Lenin and his associates consider
> it possible to commit all kinds of crimes, such as . . . the abolition
> of freedom of speech, and senseless arrests – all the abomination
> which Plehve and Stolypin once perpetrated.

Gorky said about Lenin: 'Lenin is not an omnipotent magician but a cold-blooded trickster who spares neither the honour nor the life of the proletariat . . . Lenin's . . . madness . . . his Nechaev and Bakunin brand of anarchism . . .'[16] Three days later he wrote: 'Imagining themselves to be Napoleons of socialism, the Leninists rant and rave, completing the destruction of Russia. The Russian people will pay for this with lakes of blood.'[17] These statements were published in the legal press.

The outbreak of the civil war put the Mensheviks in an embarrassing position, since, for all their hostility to the Bolsheviks, they had still less to hope for from a restoration of the old regime.

A meeting of the Central Committee of the Mensheviks in Moscow on 17-21 October 1918 decided to give support – if critical – to the soviet government.

> The Bolshevik revolution of October 1917 was a historical necessity, since, by breaking the links between the labouring masses and the capitalist classes, it expressed the desire of the labouring masses to subordinate the trend of the revolution wholly to their own interests, without which the deliverance of Russia from the clutches of Allied imperialism, the pursuance of a consistent peace policy, the introduction of radical agrarian reform, and the regulation by the state of the entire economic life in the interests of the masses would have been inconceivable, and since this stage of the revolution has had the tendency to enlarge also the scope of the influence which the Russian revolution had on the course of world developments.[18]

The meeting renounced 'all political cooperation with classes hostile to democracy'; at the same time, while promising 'direct support of the military actions of the soviet government against foreign intervention', it demanded 'the abrogation of the extraordinary organs of police repression and the extraordinary tribunals' and 'the cessation of the political and economic terror'.[19]

This public declaration by the Mensheviks was followed by a very conciliatory speech by Lenin, declaring that no more was asked of the Mensheviks and SRs than 'good neighbourly relations': 'But we shall not forget there are still "activists" in your party, and for them our methods of struggle will remain the same, for they are friends of the Czechs and until the Czechs are driven out of Russia, you are our enemies too. We reserve state power for ourselves, *and for ourselves alone.*'[20]

The compromise with the SRs and Mensheviks could not last. When the military situation worsened in spring 1919, Lenin used much harsher language:

> We shall have to change our line of conduct very often, and this may appear strange and incomprehensible to the casual observer. 'How is that?' he will say. 'Yesterday you were making promises to the petty bourgeoisie, while today Dzerzhinsky announced that the Left Socialist Revolutionaries and the Mensheviks will be stood against the wall. What a contradiction!' Yes, it is a contradiction. But the conduct of the petty-bourgeois democrats themselves is contradictory: they do not know where to sit, and try to sit between two stools, jump from one to the other and fall now to the right and now to the left. We have changed our tactics towards them, and whenever they turn towards us we say 'Welcome' to them . . . we certainly do not want to use force against the petty-bourgeois democrats. We say to them, 'You are not a serious enemy. Our enemy is the bourgeoisie. But if you join forces with them, we shall be obliged to apply the measures of the proletarian dictatorship to you, too.'[21]

The Mensheviks, above all Martov, were searching for a 'third force'. Their (and the SR's) tragedy was that a 'third force' was not possible. As Martov wrote in a pathetic letter to Axelrod on 23 January 1920:

> We found a sympathetic audience but it invariably stood far to the right of us. By a healthy instinct, all who have been crushed down by Bolshevism supported us gladly as the most courageous fighters against it. But from our preaching they took only what they felt in need of, only our criticism and indictment of Bolshevism. As long as we exposed it, they applauded; the moment we began to say that another regime was necessary in order to conduct a successful struggle against Denikin, etc., to carry through the real liquidation of speculation and to assist the victory of the international proletariat over reaction, our audience turned cold and even hostile.[22]

In the spring of 1919 the outbreak of kulak uprisings in a number of provinces, and the successful advance of Kolchak, induced the majority of the SRs and Mensheviks to return to their extreme opposition to Bolshevism. In view of this, the Central Committee of the Bolsheviks in May 1919 issued a directive 'concerning the arrest of all prominent Mensheviks and SRs about whom it was not personally known that they were ready actively to support the soviet government in its struggle against Kolchak'.

The Left SRs

After seizing power, the Bolsheviks invited the Left SRs who supported the October revolution to join the Council of People's Commissars. After some hesitation the Left SR leaders reached an agreement with the Bolsheviks on 18 November (1 December) 1917, as a result of which representatives of the Left SR entered the government. They received seven Commissariats as against eleven for the Bolsheviks. The most important was the People's Commissariat of Agriculture.

For three months the Left SRs remained in the government. However, on 19 March 1918 they resigned in protest against the signing of the Brest-Litovsk Peace Treaty. They wanted to tear up the treaty and resume war with Germany. They also disagreed fundamentally with the agrarian policy of the Bolsheviks. They opposed the setting up of 'Committees of Poor Peasants' and the despatch of workers' detachments into the countryside for the purpose of requisitioning grain. These measures aroused strong opposition not only among the kulaks, but also among the middle peasants who were the main supporters of the Left SRs.

On 6 July the Left SRs assassinated Count Mirbach, the German Ambassador, in the hope of restarting the war between Russia and Germany, and at the same time launched a revolt against their previous allies in the streets of the capital.

The Left SR uprising was ruthlessly suppressed by the Bolsheviks. However, no overall banning of the Left SRs took place. On 15 July VTsIK passed a resolution that permitted as representatives of this body those members of the party who 'categorically renounce their solidarity with the assassination and with the revolt which followed it'. Legally, therefore, those Left SRs, and there were very many, who repudiated the action of their Central Committee were after July still entitled to sit in the soviets. The July revolt of the Left SRs caused a break-up of the party. The majority repudiated von Mirbach's assassination and attempted to preserve peace with the Bolsheviks.[23]*

The Bolshevik Party's Political Monopoly

The severity of civil war conditions, the weakness of the proletariat and the sullen animosity of the peasantry forced Lenin to greater and greater restriction of the freedom of action of the Mensheviks and SRs, of whatever variety. Had it been possible to isolate the Whites as the sole targets for attack, the situation would have been very different. Unfortunately, in order to wrench political support away from Kornilov, Denikin and Kolchak, the Bolsheviks had to suppress the Cadet Party. The majority of the Mensheviks and SRs were of course not prepared to defend the White generals, but they were not indifferent to the suppression of the Cadets. On the whole, Left Mensheviks would not defend the Cadets, but could not ignore the suppression of the Right Mensheviks and Right SRs who sided with the Cadets.

The Bolshevik Party programme adopted in March 1919 made it clear that the restriction of the rights of other parties was only temporary. Thus it stated: 'the forfeiture of political rights, and whatever limitations may be imposed upon freedom, are necessary only as temporary measures'.[25] However, circumstances conspired to demonstrate that sometimes there is nothing more permanent than what is intended to be temporary.

---

* The anarchists faced a dilemma in that they opposed both the dictatorship of the proletariat and Bolshevism, in particular, on the one hand, and the Whites on the other. Paul Avrich, the historian of Russian anarchism, writes:
'Ardent libertarians, the anarchists found the repressive policies of the Soviet government utterly reprehensible; yet the prospect of a White victory seemed even worse. Any opposition to Lenin's regime at this time might tip the balance in favour of the counter-revolutionaries; on the other hand, active support, or even benevolent neutrality, might enable the Bolsheviks to entrench themselves too deeply, to be ousted later.
'The acrimonious debates provoked by this dilemma served to widen the fissures in the anarchist camp . . . In the end, a large majority gave varying degrees of support to the beleaguered regime.'[24]

The need to fight a civil war with a weakened proletariat forced the Bolsheviks to suppress one opposition party after another, from Cadets to SRs to Mensheviks. The Fifth All-Russian Congress of Soviets in July 1918 was the last at which the opposition was present in strength. At the next Congress, held four months later, with 950 delegates, there were 933 Communists, 8 Revolutionary-Communists, 4 SRs, 2 Narodnik Communists, 1 Maximalist, 1 Anarchist and 1 non-party delegate.[26]

The Party and the Soviets

Thus it was about a year after the October revolution before an actual monopoly of political power was held by one party. How did this monopoly affect the working of the soviet and political life in general?

The Eighth Congress of the party in March 1919 defined the relations between the party and the soviet thus:

> The Communist Party poses as its task the conquest of a most decisive influence and complete direction in all the organizations of toilers: trade unions, cooperatives, village communes, etc. The Communist Party seeks especially the realization of its programme by the achievement of its complete dominance in the existing state organizations – the soviets . . . By practical, daily self-sacrificing work in the soviets, by putting forth its most stable and devoted members for all soviet posts, the Russian Communist Party must achieve for itself undivided political dominance in the soviets and actual control over all their work. But the functions of the party fractions must on no account be confused with the functions of the state organs – the soviets. Such confusion would produce fatal results . . . The party must carry out its decision through the soviet organs, *within the framework of the soviet constitution*. The party should endeavour to guide the activity of the soviets, not to supplant them.[27]

Again and again party congresses repeated that the party should not substitute itself for the soviet, but only try to guide it. Thus the Eleventh Party Congress (March 1922) resolved:

> Keeping for itself the general guidance and direction of the entire politics of the soviet state, the party must carry out a much more precise demarcation between its own current work and the work of the soviet organs, between its own apparatus and that of the soviets. Such a systematically executed demar-

cation should secure more systematic consideration and decision of . . . questions by the soviet organs, at the same time raising the responsibility of every soviet official for the work entrusted to him, and on the other hand, making it possible for the party to concentrate properly on the basic party work of general guidance of the work of all State organs.[28]

A most important task now is to establish the correct division of labour between party and soviet institutions and to delineate clearly the rights and duties of the one and the other.[29]

But with the party monopoly of power, the separation of party and state was necessarily only formal, especially as party members were bound by discipline to act as one. Thus, for instance, the Eighth Party Conference of December 1919 passed a statute which included the following:

At the general meeting of the non-party organization in which the fraction is working all fraction members must vote unanimously on matters which have been decided within the fraction. Persons violating this rule are subject to the usual disciplinary procedures.[30]

In fact the party and the soviets became increasingly fused. This fusion permeated all levels of the administration. Data from some 60 per cent of local soviets in the second half of 1919 showed that party members and candidates made up 89 per cent of the membership of executive committees of *guberniia* congresses of soviets, 86 per cent of executive committees of *uezd* congresses of soviets, 93 per cent of executive committees of city soviets in *guberniia* administrative centres and 71 per cent of executive committees of town soviets in *uezd* administrative centres.

'It was only at the lowest levels of the rural administration that party saturation of the government executive hierarchy remained incomplete.'[31] This saturation was greatest in units at the higher levels. In 1921, 42 per cent of the delegates to *uezd* congresses were communists compared with 75 per cent of delegates to *guberniia* conferences. Again, party membership levels were higher in the executive committees than in the congresses of soviets. In 1921, for instance, the respective averages were 72 per cent and 42 per cent at the *uezd* level and 88 per cent and 75 per cent at the *guberniia* level.[32]

The Decline of Democracy in State Institutions

Throughout 1917 and at the beginning of 1918 Lenin spoke of the dictatorship of the proletariat as implemented by the *proletariat*. Thus, to choose one statement out of many, at the Seventh Congress of the party in March 1918 he said: 'It is important for us to draw literally all working people into the government of the state. It is a task of tremendous difficulty . . . It can be implemented only by tens of millions when they have learned to do it themselves.'[33]

'As a democratic government', said Lenin, introducing the decree on land on 26 October (8 November) 1917, 'we cannot ignore the decision of the masses of the people, even though we may disagree with it.'[34]

As a result of changes in state–party relations during the civil war, Lenin now argued very differently. Thus he told the Eighth Congress of the Party in March 1919: 'the soviets, which by virtue of their programme are organs of government *by the working people*, are in fact organs of government *for the working people* by the advanced section of the proletariat but not by the working people as a whole'.[35]

Lenin mocked those who treated 'the dictatorship of one party as a bugbear', and added, 'The dictatorship of the working class is being implemented by the Bolshevik Party, the party which as far back as 1905 and even earlier merged with the entire revolutionary proletariat.'[36]

In a letter of 20 February 1922 to D.I.Kursky, the People's Commissar of Justice, he wrote, 'we conscious workers, we communists – who are the state'.[37]

At the Twelfth Party Congress in April 1923, which Lenin did not attend, Zinoviev poked fun at 'comrades who think that the dictatorship of the party is a thing to be realized in practice but not spoken about', and proceeded to develop the doctrine of the dictatorship of the party as a dictatorship of the Central Committee:

> We need a *single* strong, powerful Central Committee which is leader of everything . . . The Central Committee is the Central Committee because it is the same Central Committee for the soviets, and for the trade unions, and for the cooperatives, and

for the provincial executive committees and for the whole working class. In this consists the role of leadership, in this is expressed the dictatorship of the party.

The congress resolution declared that 'the dictatorship of the working class cannot be assured otherwise than in the form of dictatorship of its leading vanguard, i.e. the Communist Party'.[38]

In March 1921, arguing against the Workers' Opposition, Trotsky went to extremes in defending the rights of the party vis-à-vis the working class.

> The Workers' Opposition came out with dangerous slogans, in that they have made a fetish of democratic principles. They have placed the workers' rights to elect representatives for workers' organizations above the party, as though the party had no right to assert its dictatorship even in cases when that dictatorship clashes temporarily with the passing mood of the workers' democracy.
>
> It is essential that we should become aware of the revolutionary-historical birthright of the party, which is in duty bound to retain its dictatorship, regardless of the temporary vacillations of the amorphous masses, regardless of the temporary vacillations even of the working class.[39]

The almost complete fusion of party and state was clear to everyone. Thus Zinoviev told the Eighth Congress of the Party in March 1919:

> Fundamental questions of policy, international and domestic, must be decided by the Central Committee of our Party, i.e. the Communist Party, which thus carries these decisions through the soviet organs. It carries them, of course, cleverly and tactfully, not in such a way as to tread on the toes of Sovnarkom and other Soviet institutions.[40]

Kamenev told the Ninth Party Congress in 1920: 'The Communist Party is the government of Russia. The country is ruled by the 600,000 party members.'[41]

The same point was emphasized again by Trotsky in a speech to the Second Congress of the Comintern in July 1920:

> Today we have received a proposal from the Polish Government to conclude peace. Who decides such questions? We have the Council of People's Commissars but it too must be subject to certain control. Whose control? The control of the working class as a formless, chaotic mass? No. The Central Committee of the

party is convened in order to discuss the proposal and to decide whether it ought to be answered.[42]

Whether the party took over the state, or vice versa, is immaterial: the process of fusion went ahead and strengthened centralistic tendencies in both.*

Could democracy survive under a one-party monopoly? This question was posed clearly and prophetically by Rosa Luxemburg in her pamphlet *The Russian Revolution*, written during September and October 1918 in Breslau prison. She wrote that the proletarian

> dictatorship must be the work of the *class* and not of a little leading minority in the name of the class – that is, it must proceed step by step out of the active participation of the masses; it must be under their direct influence, subjected to the control of complete public activity; it must arise out of the growing political training of the mass of the people.[43]

What will be the result of limiting freedom to one party, or one trend? asks Rosa Luxemburg.

> Freedom only for the supporters of the government, only for the members of one party – however numerous they may be – is no freedom at all. Freedom is always and exclusively freedom for the one who thinks differently. Not because of any fanatical concept of 'justice' but because all that is instructive, wholesome and purifying in political freedom depends on this essential characteristic, and its effectiveness vanishes when 'freedom' becomes a special privilege.[44]

Rosa Luxemburg goes on to describe the effect on society of one-party monopoly:

> with the repression of political life in the land as a whole, life in the soviets must also become more and more crippled. Without general elections, without unrestricted freedom of press and assembly, without a free struggle of opinion, life dies out in every public institution, becomes a mere semblance of life, in which only the bureaucracy remains as the active element. Public life gradually falls asleep, a few dozen party leaders of inexhaustible energy and boundless experience direct and rule. Among them, in reality only a dozen outstanding heads do the leading and an elite of the working class is invited from time to

---

* On the party, see Chapter 13.

time to meetings where they are to applaud the speeches of the leaders, and to approve proposed resolutions unanimously – at bottom, then, a clique affair – a dictatorship, to be sure, not the dictatorship of the proletariat, however, but only the dictatorship of a handful of politicians, that is a dictatorship in the bourgeois sense, in the sense of the rule of the Jacobins.[45]

One must remember that these words were written by an enthusiastic supporter of the October revolution and the Bolsheviks:

Whatever a party could offer of courage, revolutionary farsightedness and consistency in a historic hour, Lenin, Trotsky and the other comrades have given in good measure. All the revolutionary honour and capacity which western social democracy lacked were represented by the Bolsheviks. Their October uprising was not only the actual salvation of the Russian revolution; it was also the salvation of the honour of international socialism.[46]

She also saw clearly that it was the isolation of the Russian revolution that impelled the Bolsheviks to restrict the democratic rights of the masses. Without international revolutionary support, Rosa Luxemburg wrote, 'even the greatest energy and the greatest sacrifices of the proletariat in a single country must inevitably become tangled in a maze of contradictions and blunders'.[47]

After pointing out the contradictions and blunders in Bolshevik policy, Rosa Luxemburg unearths their causes:

Everything that happens in Russia is comprehensible and represents an inevitable chain of causes and effects, the starting point and end term of which are: the failure of the German proletariat and the occupation of Russia by German imperialism. It would be demanding something superhuman from Lenin and his comrades if we should expect of them that under such circumstances they should conjure forth the finest democracy, the most exemplary dictatorship of the proletariat and a flourishing socialist economy. By their determined revolutionary stand, their exemplary strength in action, and their unbreakable loyalty to international socialism, they have contributed whatever could possibly be contributed under such devilishly hard conditions.[48]

However, to explain the reasons for the Bolsheviks' circumscribing of workers' democracy is not to justify it. Rosa Luxemburg above all criticized the Bolshevik leaders for not admitting openly that their deviation from their original policies of workers' democracy was forced on them: 'The danger begins only when they [the Bolshevik leaders] make a virtue of necessity and want to freeze into a complete theoretical system all the tactics forced upon them by these fatal circumstances.'[49]

Undeniably Lenin, with his 'stick-bending', was inclined to do just this. Although he would deal with a particular situation very *concretely*, he always inclined to generalize too far from the immediate task in hand.

Experience showed Lenin the cul-de-sac which a government got into without workers' democracy. When during the trade union debate* he argued 'We now have a state under which it is the business of the massively organized proletariat to protect itself, while we, for our part, must use these workers' organizations to protect the workers from their state, and to get them to protect our state,'[50] the implications for the question of proletarian democracy were far-reaching. If the unions are to defend themselves against the state, they must have the right freely to discuss views different from those of their employer-state, and to select freely the leaders who are to voice these views. If the leaders of both the state and the trade unions are nominated, in practice, by one and the same central body – the Central Committee of the party, its Politbureau or its Secretariat – then the trade unions cannot defend the workers from the state. With party fractions under the same discipline as the other institutions – soviets, trade unions, etc. – the separation of function between them must be largely formal.

As we shall see, Lenin became more and more alarmed by the merging of state and party. Speaking in 1922 at the Eleventh Party Congress (the last he attended), he said: 'The relations between the party and the soviet government bodies are not what they ought to be'; 'the party machinery must be separated from the soviet government machinery'; 'we must raise the prestige of the Council of People's Commissars',[51] in other words of the state, *vis-à-vis* the party.

---

* See Chapter 23.

The establishment of Bolshevik Party monopoly led to a deterioration of political life in general, and a decline of the soviets in particular, which was summed up by Victor Serge:

> With the disappearance of political debates between parties representing different social interests through the various shades of their opinion, soviet institutions, beginning with the local soviets and ending with the VTsIK and the Council of People's Commissars, manned solely by communists, now function in a vacuum: since all the decisions are taken by the party, all they can do is give them the official rubber-stamp.[52]

In conclusion: to assert that the banning of all parties, except for the Bolshevik Party, must have had deleterious consequences, is one thing. To assert that the Bolsheviks could have acted differently, and could have allowed freedom of parties, is altogether different. In essence the dictatorship of the proletariat *does not* represent a combination of abstract, immutable elements like democracy and centralism, independent of time and place. The actual level of democracy, as well as of centralism, depends on three basic factors: (1) the strength of the proletariat; (2) the material and cultural legacy left to it by the old regime; and (3) the strength of capitalist resistance. The level of democracy feasible must be in direct proportion to the first two factors, and in inverse proportion to the third. The captain of an ocean liner can allow football to be played on his vessel; on a tiny raft in a stormy sea the level of tolerance is far lower.

13
Transformation of the Party

Changes in the Social Composition of the Party

In 1917 the Bolshevik Party was overwhelmingly proletarian in composition. There were hardly any intellectuals in local party committees, or in the party as a whole.[1] During the civil war, further hundreds of thousands of workers joined the party. But the effects of the struggle radically changed it social composition.

With the primary task the need to run the administration, tens of thousands of worker party members became state officials. A substantial proportion of party members went into the Red Army during the civil war; in 1920 it reached about 300,000, i.e. every second communist.[2] Over half a million communists saw service with the Red Army during the civil war, of whom roughly half were sent into the army by civilian party organizations and half recruited by the party while on army service. Some 200,000 communists lost their lives.

Lenin could declare in April 1920:

> every time a difficult situation arose during the war, the party mobilized communists, and it was they who were the first to perish in the front ranks; they perished in thousands on the Iudenich and Kolchak fronts. The finest members of the working class perished; they sacrificed themselves.[3]

One inevitable result was a catastrophic decline in the proportion of party members working at the factory bench. Thus statistics for 1919 show that only 11 per cent of party members were then working in factories; 53 per cent were working as government officials; 8 per cent were party and trade union officials, and 27 per cent were in the army.[4]

At the Tenth Congress in March 1921, Shliapnikov deplored the fact that among the metal workers of Petrograd, who before the revolution were a mainstay of Bolshevism, no more than 2 per cent were party members. The corresponding figure for Moscow was 4 per cent.[5]

At the Eleventh Party Congress in March-April 1922, the secretary of the Moscow committee stated that, while 22 per cent of the communists in the capital were members of factory cells, 'a good half' of these were employed in administrative posts, and that in other industrial centres the proportion of workers at the bench was even lower.[6]

At the same Congress, Zinoviev complained: 'It is a fact that there are big districts, mines, etc., where there are from 10,000 to 12.000 workers, where we have a party nucleus of only six.'[7]

An analysis of party membership in rural districts of Riazan province in 1922 showed that 78 per cent held posts in the local soviets, party or cooperative network. The situation was said to be similar in other provinces.[8] A breakdown of members of peasant cells in 1922 showed that only a quarter were engaged in farming, while two-thirds were employed as officials of state, party or cooperatives.[9]

In the countryside many party members were former officials who had been civil servants under the Tsarist regime. Thus in 1922, 42 per cent of party members on the executive committees of rural soviets had been serving for longer than three years, which meant since before 1919. This seems to confirm the suggestion that they were the old civil servants, Zemstvo employees, who carried on the main business of administration as they had done in earlier years.[10]

In the Red Army the proportion of party members who were highly ranked increased. This process accelerated especially after the end of the civil war, when the army was run down. Then army party cells came to consist overwhelmingly of officers and political staff. At the end of 1921 privates and NCOs constituted 50 per cent of all army communists, but by 1924 they had fallen to 20 per cent.[11]

Preventing Careerists from Joining the Party

The sacrifices associated with party membership during the civil war discouraged careerists from joining. During the civil war, when communists fell into the hands of the Whites, which happened very often, they paid with their lives. As the written report of the Central Committee to the Eighth Party Conference put it: 'a party membership ticket under these circumstances meant something approaching a candidature for Denikin's gallows'.[12]

Hence whenever the military circumstances of the Soviet republic were grim, Lenin proposed opening the doors of the party wider than usual. In the autumn of 1919, when Denikin and Iudenich threatened the downfall of the Soviet regime, and it seemed very probable that Petrograd would be taken by the Whites, the party tried to attract new members, and organized a

'Party Week' in October: 'During Party Week in Moscow, 13,000 people were enrolled in the party.'[13]

The party expanded massively. In numerical terms, 'Party Week' was a striking success. New recruits numbered at least 160,000. This expansion continued in the following months. Membership rose from 430,000 at the beginning of 1920 to over 600,000 by the Ninth Congress in March 1920.[14]

Most of those who took on the risks of party membership when the regime was under such pressure must have been convinced supporters of communism. But Lenin was still worried about careerists managing to join the party. On 16 August 1918 he said: 'We must not accept people who try to join from careerist motives; people like this should be driven out of the party.'[15]

Lenin returned to the same theme again and again, till the end of his life. We have quoted in Chapter 11 his statement to the Petrograd Soviet in March 1919 about the 'old bureaucrats' who called themselves 'commonists' when they could not bring themselves to say the word 'communist', and 'wear a red ribbon in their buttonholes and creep into warm corners . . . the scum has crawled back,' he said.[16] At the Ninth Party Congress, March-April 1919, Lenin spoke about the danger of 'the worst elements, the officials of the old capitalist system . . . creeping into the government party . . . fastening themselves onto it . . . for it is the government party, and as such opens the way to power'.[17]

On 3 April 1919, in a speech to the Moscow soviet, Lenin returned to the same theme: 'And what is going on in the rural districts? There, people who call themselves members of the party are often scoundrels, whose lawlessness is most brazen.'[18] On 21 April 1921, he drew attention to the 'abuses committed by former government officials, landowners, bourgeois and other scum who play up to the communists and who sometimes commit abominable outrages and acts of tyranny against the peasantry'.[19] Lenin proposed making it as difficult as possible for careerists to join the party.

The Eleventh Congress (March-April 1922) established three recruitment categories: (1) workers and Red Army men of worker or peasant origin; (2) peasants and handicraftsmen other than those serving in the army; and (3) others – white collar workers, etc. Category (1) was required to spend six months as candidates, category (2) a year, and category (3) two years.[20]

Lenin was unhappy with these arrangements, doubting whether they would improve the proletarian composition of the party. In two letters addressed to the Central Committee secretary, Molotov, on the eve of the Eleventh Congress, he wrote:

> I consider it extremely important to lengthen the probation period for new members of the party. Zinoviev proposes that the probation period should be six months for workers and twelve months for other categories. I propose a period of six months only for those workers who have actually been employed in large industrial enterprises for not less than ten years. A probation period of eighteen months should be established for all other workers, two years for peasants and Red Army men, and three years for other categories.[21]

To get rid of careerists Lenin supported the proposal that the party should be purged of corrupt elements. The Eighth Party Congress (March 1919) resolved:

> Elements which are not sufficiently communist, or even directly parasitic, are flowing into the party in a broad stream. The Russian Communist Party is in power, and this inevitably attracts to it, together with the better elements, careerist elements as well. A serious purge is indispensable in Soviet and Party organizations.[22]

Following the Congress, between 10 and 15 per cent of the membership in the towns, and a higher proportion in some parts of the countryside, were expelled.[23] Lenin thought that this purge should have been far more radical. Thus, in a pamphlet he wrote in June 1919, he stated,

> it. was absolutely inevitable that adventurers and other pernicious elements should hitch themselves to the ruling party. There never has been, and there never can be, a revolution without that. The whole point is that the ruling party should be able, relying on a sound and strong advanced class, to purge its ranks.

Hence the purge should be very radical. About half the members should be expelled.[24]

In 1921 a large-scale purge was carried out, resulting in the expulsion of 136,386 members, a fifth of the total membership.

31 per cent of those expelled suffered this penalty for 'passivity', 25 per cent for careerism, drunkenness, etc., 9 per cent for bribe taking, extortion, etc.[25]

However, all the obstacles Lenin and the party leadership put in the way of non-workers joining the party, and the repeated purges of corrupt elements, did not stop careerists from climbing onto the bandwagon. With the fusion of party and state, a party card became an asset in the scramble for jobs. This is illustrated by the following passage in Zinoviev's Report to the Eighth Party Congress: 'There have been cases in Moscow where a man turns up at the district committee at 8 p.m. to take out party membership, and when he is told to come back the next day he replies: "Do me a good turn, I am going for a job tomorrow, and I need a party card right away." '[26]

The erosion of the proletarian composition of the party continued, above all because former Bolshevik workers ceased to be workers.

Very Few Old-Timers

To add to the weakness of the party, the proportion of old Bolsheviks in it was extremely small. In October 1919 only 20 per cent of members had been members before the October revolution; and only 8 per cent had joined before February 1917.[27] Zinoviev told the Eleventh Congress that only 2 per cent of the members in 1922 were party members before February 1917.[28]

In a letter Lenin wrote to Molotov on 26 March 1922 he said:

> If we do not close our eyes to reality we must admit that at the present time the proletarian policy of the party is not determined by the character of its membership, but by the enormous undivided prestige enjoyed by the small group which might be called the old guard of the party.

The danger inherent in the situation was very great indeed: 'A slight conflict within this group will be enough, if not to destroy this prestige, at all events to weaken the group to such a degree as to rob it of its power to determine policy.'[29]

Increasing Centralization of Power in the Party

The Central Committee, originally a small compact body

and in actuality the *decision-making body* of the party, came increasingly to ratify rather than to make decisions.

At first it was required to meet twice a month (Resolution of the Eighth Party Congress and the 1919 Party Rules).[30] In 1921 the Tenth Congress modified the requirement to once in two months.[31]

Which body or bodies in practice replaced the Central Committee? Formally the Political Bureau was subordinate to the Central Committee. Its function was to 'take decisions on questions not permitting of delay', and to report to the fortnightly meeting of the Central Committee. But the formal restriction of the competence of the Politburo to urgent questions, like the similar restriction of the power of Sovnarkom *vis-à-vis* the All-Russian Soviet or VTsIK, was in fact unreal. The Central Committee met less and less frequently and the Politbureau became the principal source of policy decisions which were executed by the state machinery.

Immediately after the October revolution, the Central Committee met very frequently. We have the minutes of 17 such meetings for a period of a little over three months;[32] (the minutes of a number of other meetings of this body held in the same period have not survived). Subsequently, during the civil war, meetings became less frequent. There were only six between April and July 1918, and between July and November 1918 the Central Committee did not meet at all. (This was complained of at the Eighth Congress in March 1919.) Later the meetings became more regular: April-October 1919, 6 times; April 1920 to March 1921, 29 times.[33] But they were still far less frequent than those of the Political Bureau (or the Organizing Bureau).

The Central Committee met only six times between March and December 1919, while the Politburo and Orgburo had 29 and 110 meetings respectively. During this period there were also 10 joint Politburo–Orgburo meetings. From December 1919 to September 1920 the Central Committee met only nine times, while the Politburo and Orgburo met 77 and 64 times respectively. Between September 1920 and March 1921 the Central Committee held 24 meetings, almost one a week, while the Orgburo and Politburo had 47 and 26 sessions respectively. Between May and

CENTRALIZATION OF POWER 185

August 1921 the Central Committee held nine meetings and the Orgburo and Politburo 48 and 39 respectively. Between September and December 1921 the Central Committee met only 5 times, while the Orgburo and Politburo met 63 and 44 times respectively.[34]

In practice the Politburo and the Orgburo increasingly usurped the power of the Central Committee. In his report to the Ninth Party Congress, Lenin said:

> The Political Bureau adopted decisions on all questions of foreign and domestic policy . . . During the year under review the current daily work of the Central Committee has been conducted by the two collegiums elected by the plenary meeting of the Central Committee – the Organizing Bureau of the Central Committee and the Political Bureau of the Central Committee . . . In practice it has become the main and proper function of the Organizing Bureau to distribute the forces of the party, and that of the Political Bureau to deal with political questions. It goes without saying that this distinction is to a certain extent artificial; it is obvious that no policy can be carried out in practice without finding expression in appointments and transfers.[35]

Another party institution whose power continued to increase was the secretariat. To achieve coordination between the Politburo and the Orgburo, the secretary to the party was a member of both.

To start with, in March 1919, the secretariat consisted of one responsible secretary and five technical secretaries. A year later it was decided to strengthen it by bringing into it three members of the Central Committee, and 'to transfer to the jurisdiction of the secretariat as thus composed current questions of an organizational and executive nature, while preserving for the Orgburo . . . the general direction of the organizational work of the Central Committee.'[36]

The secretariat was originally defined as a purely 'executive organ of the party'. As Lenin put it to the Eighth Congress:

> It must be emphasized from the very outset, so as to remove all misunderstanding, that only the corporate decisions of the Central Committee adopted in the Organizing Bureau or the Political Bureau, or by a plenary meeting of the Central Committee – only these decisions were carried out by the Secretary of the Central Committee of the party.[37]

In practice the secretariat usurped far more power, especially after Stalin was appointed as General Secretary in May 1922. From 1922 onwards Stalin was the only person who was a member of all four party bodies: the Central Committee, the Politburo, the Orgburo and the secretariat.

The secretariat greatly expanded its staff; from 15 in March 1919 it grew in November 1919 to 80 officials in eight departments (general administration, finance, information, organization, distribution, inspection, peasantry, women's work).[38] In March 1920 its staff rose to 150 and a year later it totalled 602 (besides a military detachment of 140 men to act as guards and messengers).[39]

One of the most important powers controlled by the secretariat was the appointment of personnel. Since 1920 one of the three party secretaries had been in charge of what was called the 'accounts and distribution section' (Uchraspred), which kept account of party manpower and supervised its distribution. In its report to the Tenth Congress (March 1922), it showed that in a period of less than twelve months it had been responsible for transfers and appointments of 42,000 party members.[40] Uchraspred had become a powerful organ of control over state and party institutions.

Zinoviev explained at the Twelfth Party Congress (1923) that the presidents of the executive committees of provincial soviets were appointed by the Central Committee of the party and that this was necessarily so.[41] In fact it was the secretariat that had this power of nomination.

Appointment of Secretaries

There were also widespread appointments in internal party bodies. During the civil war, when local party committees, including those representing quite large territorial units, expressed opposition to the Central Committee in Moscow, they were quite often summarily sacked. In the spring of 1919, for instance, the Central Committee dissolved the elected Central Committee of Ukraine and appointed a new one. Between March 1922 and March 1923 the secretariat appointed 42 secretaries of provincial committees.[42]

Again and again party congresses and conferences emphasized the need to avoid appointments instead of elections to leading party bodies. Thus the Ninth Party Conference of September 1920 resolved:

> While it is admitted in principle that it is necessary in exceptional cases to appoint people to elective positions, the Central Committee is none the less advised, as a general rule, to use recommendations instead of appointments.

It added, as an afterthought, throwing a sharp light on the existing situation:

> Attention is drawn to the fact that it is impermissible that party bodies and individual comrades, in mobilizing comrades, be guided by considerations other than those deriving from the job at hand. Repressions of any sort whatsoever against comrades for the fact that they hold divergent views on certain questions resolved by the party, are impermissible.[43]

Even delegates to party congresses were quite often not elected, but nominated. About 50 delegates from the Samara *guberniia* to the Eleventh Party Congress (27 March-2 April 1922) were selected by the plenum of the *guberniia* committee instead of being elected by the *guberniia* conference. In this case, as the mandate commission report of the Eleventh Congress put it, 'the Central Committee allowed it as a result of those objective conditions in which the Samara *guberniia* found itself' – a rather oblique reference to the fact that Samara was a stronghold of the Workers' Opposition and, had elections been held, the delegations would have been composed of the (by now outlawed) oppositionists. While this practice was permitted at the congress only in this one instance, it was also used elsewhere at the time.[44]

The result, of necessity, was a corrosion of inner-party democracy.

Appointments in the Trade Unions

With the fusion of state and party, and with the increasing substitution of appointments for elections in the party, it is not surprising that there were more and more cases of appointments in other organizations. Such was the case in the trade unions.

Let us look at what happened at the Fourth Trade Union

Congress. On 17 May 1921, just a few hours before the opening of the congress, the party fraction in the congress met. Tomsky, Chairman of the All-Russian Central Council of Trade Unions, introduced the Politburo report, 'On the Role and Tasks of the Trade Unions'. Fraction members, noticing that the section on the election of trade union officers did not contain the term 'normal methods of proletarian democracy', decided to amend the resolution. Under Riazanov's leadership, and against the formal objection of Tomsky, they voted by more than 1,500 to 30 to include in the Politburo's statement a section providing for democratic procedures.[45] The Politburo immediately removed Tomsky from the Central Council for exhibiting weakness. He was not even elected to the Presidium of the congress. (He was subsequently sent away, ostensibly on a 'mission' to Turkestan.)

In the same month of May 1921, the Central Committee of the party also intervened heavily in the affairs of the important metalworkers' trade union. The Central Committee submitted to the communist fraction of the union a list of candidates to be elected to key positions in the union. The list contained new and 'loyal' substitutes for those who had supported the Workers' Opposition. By an overwhelming vote of 120 to 40 the fraction rejected the Central Committee list. Incensed by this infringement of discipline, the Central Committee ignored the vote and appointed people of its own choice. It then proceeded to reorganize the union.[46]

'The Old Crap Revives...'

The party was not immune from the rot of corruption. It is true that during War Communism severe egalitarianism prevailed, as we saw in Chapter 7, but these rules were often evaded. Equality does not accord well with general poverty. As the young Marx put it two years before the *Communist Manifesto*: 'this development of the productive forces . . . is absolutely necessary as a practical premise [of communism], because without it only *want* is made general, and with want the struggle for necessities, and that means that all the old crap must revive'.[47]

Behind the façade of extreme equality, despite the very strong moral pressure of Bolshevism, the 'old crap' did rise again in the midst of War Communism. And this corruption ate into the party. One only needs to read the description of a communist bureaucrat during the civil war in Boris Pilnyak's story 'Riazan Apples':

> near the telephone in his room stood an armchair, and when he talked to his subordinates, he sprawled in the armchair, legs spread wide; when he talked to his equals he sat like an ordinary human being; when he talked to those in authority he jumped to attention and jingled his spurs: these were three distinct voices.[48]

Another example is provided by the Soviet author Iury Libedinsky, in his book *A Week* (1922). This is an account of a single week in a small town in the foothills of the Urals, in the spring of 1921. In it he describes a Soviet official, Matusenko, secretary of the political department, a man who would be a communist under one regime and a devout Orthodox churchman under another, but will get a soft job under either, caring only for his personal welfare.

> Today was Sunday, and the typists and shorthand writers, a merry noisy lot of people, would come to the Politdep only at eleven. But Matusenko always held himself aloof from them, or rather, simply did not notice them, did not consider their existence, just as he did not consider the existence of objects and animals that did not concern him, or that of all the people whom he considered below him in rank, like the Red Army soldiers and the school teachers who came to the Politdep.
> But to make up for that, Matusenko thought a great deal about those who stood above him in the service, beginning with Golovlev, the Chief of the Politdep, and ending with Lenin and Trotsky.[49]

While millions were starving Matusenko had 'yellow, creamy butter', 'white bread' and 'perfumed sweetened tea with cream'.[50]

Another passage in Libedinsky's book describes the starving crowd in the railway station and the elegant, cake-eating commissar:

> At one railway station there was a sort of big staircase, and from top to bottom it was covered with people. Men, women, children lying on the steps, together with their pitiable dirty belongings, and on all their faces thin spider's webs of wrinkles

of care and misery, under a veil of many days' dirt. And close by in the buffet there was a speculator eating cakes while a hungry, homeless little boy watched his mouth greedily, and when he was given something for charity, went down on the floor to count the dirty scraps of paper money to see if he had enough money for cigarettes. And down that terrible staircase, stepping squeamishly . . . squeamishly is the word . . . came some smart commissar or other with a communist star glittering on his breast, and he put down his lacquered boots so carefully among those weary, dirty bodies, and came down and ate cakes with the speculator. And in that crowd there were louse-ridden, starving children.[51]

In another Soviet novel, *Cement*, by Fedor Gladkov, one can read how Badin, chairman of a soviet Executive Committee, sitting on the party purge committee, expelled from the party a woman he himself had raped, using his superior physical strength (and his high office).

During the civil war, when the masses were performing acts of heroism, and the traditions of Bolshevism were still very strong, the privileged and corrupt had to keep their affluence more or less concealed. But the rot had started to attack the foundations of the party, the state and society in general.

The Fight to Defend
Party Democratic Traditions Continues . . .

The undermining of inner party democracy did not take place without vigorous protests from party members. K.K.Iurenev, for example, spoke at the Ninth Congress of the methods used by the Central Committee to suppress criticism, including the virtual exile of the critics: 'One goes to Christiana, another sent to the Urals, a third – to Siberia.'[52] He said that in its attitude toward the party, the Central Committee had become 'not accountable ministry, but unaccountable government'. At the same congress, V.N.Maksimovsky counterposed 'democratic centralism' to the 'bureaucratic centralism' for which the centre was responsible. 'It is said', he commented, 'that fish begin to putrefy from the head. The party begins to suffer at the top from the influence of bureau-cratic centralism.'[53] Iakovlev stated: 'Ukraine has become a place of exile. Comrades unwanted for one reason or another in Moscow are exiled there.'[54] And Sapronov declared: 'However much you talk about electoral rights, about the dictatorship of the proletariat, the striving of the Central Committee for party dictatorship in fact leads to the dictatorship of the party bureaucracy.'[55]

Nevertheless, throughout the civil war the atmosphere of free discussion in party conferences and congresses was maintained. During the debate on the Brest-Litovsk Peace Treaty, the party enjoyed, in the words of E.H.Carr, 'a freedom and publicity of discussion rarely practised by any party on vital issues of public policy'.[56] Bukharin's pamphlet defending 'Left Communism' against Lenin's position was published in May 1918 in one million copies.[57]

In the trade union debate* the democratic traditions of Bolshevism remained clear. As a historian not sympathetic to Bolshevism, Robert V. Daniel, put it: 'The fall of 1920 was the high point of open discussion in the Communist Party, and of free oposition to the leaders' authority.'[58]

Victor Serge wrote of the situation in the party during the civil war:

> The party's old democratic customs now give way to a more authoritarian centralization. This is necessitated by the demands of the struggle and by the influx of new members who have neither a Marxist training nor the personal quality of the pre-1917 militants: the 'old guard' of Bolshevism is justly determined to preserve its own political hegemony.

But the party still retains its democratic traditions.

> The party is truly the 'cohort of steel' . . . All the same, its thinking is still very lively and free. It welcomes the anarchists and Left SRs of yesterday . . .
> Nobody is afraid to contradict Lenin or to criticize him. His authority was so little imposed, the democratic manners of the revolution were still so natural, that it was a matter of course for any revolutionary, no matter how recent a recruit, to express himself frankly in the presence of the man who headed the party and the state. Lenin was more than once criticized unsparingly, in factories or conferences, by totally unknown

---

*See Chapter 23.

people. He listened to his contestants coolly and replied to them in a commonsense manner.[59]

Lenin, the Party and the Proletariat

In Chapter 8 of Volume 2, which has the same title as this section, I wrote about Lenin in 1917:

> Throughout all the zigzags in tactics, Lenin's leitmotif was constant: to raise the level of consciousness and organization of the working class, to explain to the masses their own interests, to give clear political expression to the feelings and thought of the people . . . The proletariat made the party and made Lenin. And Lenin helped to shape the party and the proletariat.
>
> By drawing ever broader masses of workers, soldiers and peasants into the struggle under the banner of the revolution, by increasing the scope of the party's influence, by raising the level of self-activity and consciousness of the masses, by constant self-education of the proletariat, the party and the leadership, Bolshevism led the people to victory in October.[60]

The party was the vanguard of the proletariat, and Lenin was in the vanguard of the party. The party advanced slogans which the masses made their own, and elaborated strategy and tactics that helped the masses to organize themselves, to act for themselves.

Now, at the end of a terrible civil war, the situation was radically different. The proletariat had disintegrated; the party did not feel itself to be the leader of an active class, but mainly an administrator of affairs. Lenin could not 'go to the sailors' in order to sort out the 'committeemen', as he had done again and again in 1917, and before that in 1905. The masses in floodtide, as in 1917, bore up the party and the leadership; in the ebb, the masses, with different moods and objectives, had the opposite effect. The contrast between the dream of 1917, with Lenin's 'absolute confidence in the magnificent potential of the proletariat', and the actuality of the atomized working class and largely non-proletarian party, provided the elements of the human tragedy, demonstrating the impotence of the individual (and individuals) in the face of fate, of social forces far larger than themselves.

The magnificent success of the Bolshevik Party before the revolution, during the revolution and in the heroic years of the civil war did not mean that its organization on Leninist lines was in itself any guarantee for the consolidation of achievements. It was not an organizational key to all the doors of history. The revolutionary party is indispensable, but is not sufficient for revolutionary advance. Lenin's genius was that he was able, again and again, to appeal to the masses, so as to make the party respond to their aspirations and at the same time use the party to raise the level of activity and consciousness of the proletariat. In the final analysis the party remained always subordinated to and dependent on the working class. The party can affect the class only to the extent that its words, its propaganda, produce the desired activity by the class; without working class action the party is impotent.

14
Lenin and the Military Front

In Stalin's time and after his death, official Russian historians eliminated Trotsky from their account of the conduct of the Red Army during the civil war. All the successes of this army were attributed to Lenin (and Stalin). Such hagiography is an insult to Lenin. In this chapter Lenin's secondary role to Trotsky in leading the Red Army will be made clear.

Lenin and the Employment
of Tsarist Officers in the Red Army

Trotsky met with great opposition to his employment of ex-Tsarist officers. Most of the 'left communists' who rejected the Peace of Brest-Litovsk and opposed Lenin's economic policy repudiated Trotsky's policy in the name of 'Old Bolshevism'. They refused to accept a centralized standing army, let alone one commanded by Tsarist officers. Led by Smirnov, Bukharin, Radek and Bubnov, the 'left communists' came out strongly and bitterly against Trotsky. Another opposition element was made up of those who did not oppose centralized authority, but only the ex-Tsarist officers, of whom they were suspicious and jealous. They were leaders of guerrilla groups made up of workers, soldiers and sailors, who in the early days after October managed to establish the Soviet regime in various localities where they met very little armed resistance. This was the so-called 'Tsaritsyn opposition' which had its roots in a plebeian hatred of specialists. The leaders of this opposition were Voroshilov, Commander of the Tenth Army, Ordzhonikidze, Political Commissar of the same army, Gusev and, behind the scenes, Stalin. (The Tsaritsyn group became the nucleus of the Stalinist faction of later times.)

The combination of the two groups opposing Trotsky's policy was all the more formidable because Lenin for a long time reserved judgement on the employment of Tsarist officers.

Trotsky had to appeal to Lenin repeatedly to support him. In August 1918 Lenin asked Trotsky's opinion about a proposal introduced by Larin to replace all officers of the general staff with communists. Trotsky replied sharply in the negative:

> Many of them [ex-Tsarist officers] commit acts of treachery. But on the railways, too, instances of sabotage are in evidence in the routing of troop trains. Yet nobody suggests replacing railway engineers by communists. I consider Larin's proposal as being utterly worthless . . . Those who clamour the loudest against making use of officers are either people infected with panic or those who are remote from the entire work of the military apparatus or such party military figures as are themselves worse than any saboteur – such as are incapable of keeping an eye on anything, behave like satraps, spend their time doing nothing and, when they meet with failure, shuffle off the blame on to the General Staff Officers.[1]

On 24 November 1918 Lenin could still say in a speech to Red Army officers: 'in building our new army now, we must draw our officers solely from among the people. Only Red officers will have any respect among the soldiers and be able to strengthen socialism in our army. Such an army will be invincible.'[2]

Not until the eve of the Eighth Party Congress, in March 1919, did he have a clear idea of the extent to which military specialists were being used. At the beginning of March 1919, Trotsky narrates,

Lenin wrote me a note: 'What if we fire all the specialists and appoint Lashevich as commander-in-chief?' Lashevich was an old Bolshevik who had earned his promotion to the rank of a sergeant in the 'German' war. I replied on the same note: 'Child's play!' Lenin looked slyly at me from under his heavy brows, with a very expressive grimace that seemed to say: 'You are very harsh with me.' But, deep down, he really liked abrupt answers that left no room for doubt. We came together after the meeting. Lenin asked me various things about the front.

'You ask me,' I said, 'if it would not be better to kick out all the old officers? But do you know how many of them we have in the army now?'

'No.'

'Not even approximately?'

'I don't know.'

'Not less than thirty thousand.'

'What?'

'Not less than thirty thousand. For every traitor, there are a hundred who are dependable; for every one who deserts, there are two or three who get killed. How are we to replace them all?'[3]

A few days later, Lenin was making a speech on the problems of constructing the socialist commonwealth. This is what he said:

When Comrade Trotsky informed me recently that the number of officers of the old army employed by our War Department runs into several tens of thousands, I perceived concretely where the secret of using our enemy lay, how to compel those who had opposed communism to build it, how to build communism with the bricks which the capitalists had chosen to hurl against us![4]

The above conversation clearly shows how far Lenin was from influencing the organizational structure of the Red Army, and how he took second place to Trotsky in the field of military affairs.

What about the military strategy of the Red Army?

Disagreement on War Strategy

There were four occasions on which the Central Committee of the party was split by disagreements on strategy. In other words there were as many disagreements as there were military fronts. In one of the cases Lenin was right against Trotsky: in all the others Trotsky was proved right and Lenin wrong.

The first acute disagreement, in the summer of 1919, was about the situation on the eastern front. Trotsky supported the position of Vatzetis, the commander-in-chief of the Red Army, who argued that once Kolchak was pushed to the east of the Urals the Red Army should not pursue him further, but should stay in the mountains for the winter. This would have enabled the Red Army to withdraw a few divisions from the east and switch them to the south where Denikin was becoming very dangerous. This plan, however, met with vigorous opposition from S.S.Kamenev, the commander of the eastern front and colonel of the general staff in the Tsar's army, as well as from two members of the Military Council, both old Bolsheviks – Smilga and Lashevich. They were supported by Lenin. They insisted that Kolchak was so near to being defeated that only a few men were needed to follow him, and that the most important thing was that he be prevented from taking a breathing-spell, because in that case he would recover during the winter and the eastern campaign would have to start all over again in the spring. The entire question hinged, therefore, on a true estimate of the condition of Kolchak's army and rear.

Trotsky goes on to admit that he was wrong: 'it proved to be the command of the eastern front that was right in appraising Kolchak's army . . . The eastern armies released some troops for the southern front and continued, at the same time, their advance on the heels of Kolchak into the heart of Siberia.'[5]

The second disagreement in the Central Committee was over the southern front. In this case Trotsky proved right, against Lenin and the majority of the Central Committee, who supported the plan of S.S.Kamenev, newly appointed commander-in-chief. In the south, the enemy forces were composed of two separate and antagonistic groups: the Cossacks, particularly in the province of Kuban, and the volunteer White Army. Trotsky believed that it was necessary to use the antagonism between the two uneasy partners. Kamenev, however, thought only in logistic terms, without taking into account the socio-political implications, and suggested that as Kuban province was the chief base for the volunteers, it was necessary to deliver the decisive blow at this base from the Volga. The result of Kamenev's strategy was a terrible defeat for the Red Army. Trotsky writes:

Whereas Denikin had failed to persuade the Cossacks to a long marching campaign against the north, he . . . was helped by our striking at the Cossack nests from the south. After this, the Cossacks could no longer defend themselves on their own land; we had ourselves bound up their fate with that of the volunteer army.

In spite of the careful preparation for our operations and the concentration of forces and technical means, we had no success. The Cossacks formed a formidable bulwark in Denikin's rear. They seemed to be rooted to their land, and held on with their claws and teeth. Our offensive put the whole Cossack population on their feet. We were expending our time and energy and managing only to drive all those capable of bearing arms directly into the White Army. In the meantime, Denikin swept the Ukraine, filled his ranks, advanced toward the north.[6]

On 25 June 1919 the volunteer army occupied Kharkov, the chief city of the Ukraine. By the end of the month the Don Cossack army had cleared the Don country of Soviet forces and the Kuban Cossacks had captured Ekaterinoslav on the lower Dnieper. On 30 June Denikin, with the help of British planes and tanks, captured Tsaritsyn. On 31 July Poltava was captured. Kherson and Nikolaev on the Black Sea coast were taken on 18 August, and five days later Odessa fell. On 31 August the volunteer army marched into Kiev. Throughout September Denikin's army continued to advance. On 20 September he occupied Kursk; on 6 October Voronezh; on 13 October Orel, less than 250 miles from Moscow. Carr described those weeks as 'the crucial point at which the continued existence of the regime hung by a thread'.

Now Trotsky's plan, which he had fought for from the beginning, was accepted by the leadership. He

demanded that with our first blow we cut the volunteers off from the Cossacks, and, leaving the Cossacks to themselves, concentrate all our strength against the volunteers. The main direction of the blow, according to this plan, would be not from the Volga toward Kuban, but from Voronezh toward Kharkov and the Donetsk region. In this section of the country which divides the northern Caucasus from the Ukraine, the peasants and workers were wholly on the side of the Red Army. Advancing in this direction, the Red Army would have been moving like a knife through butter. The Cossacks would have remained in their places to guard their borders from strangers, but we would not have touched them . . . In the end, it was this plan that was eventually adopted, but not before Denikin had begun to threaten Tula, whose loss would have been more dangerous than that of Moscow. We wasted several months, suffered many needless losses and lived through some very menacing weeks.'[7]

Trotsky's plan for the campaign against Denikin was, as events proved, brilliant in every respect. He took into account two socio-political factors: first, the pro-Bolshevik stance of the Don proletariat; and secondly, the antagonism between the Kuban Cossacks and the White volunteers of Denikin. In both cases his calculation was based on indisputable facts.

On 14 September the Politbureau changed the orders for the southern front, accepting Trotsky's original plan completely. Denikin's army now started to be pushed back. On 20 October the Red Army captured Orel, and four days later Budenny defeated Denikin's cavalry forces. On 15 November Denikin was defeated at Kastornaia, near Voronezh; on 17 November at Kursk; during December the retreat of his armies continued unabated. On 3 January 1920 Denikin lost Tsaritsyn, on 8 January Rostov. After a closely fought battle round Rostov it fell into Denikin's hands again on 20 January, but was recaptured three days later. The White armies continued to retreat. On 15 March Denikin lost Ekaterinodar; on 4 April he gave up the command of the Whites and left for Britain.

The third dispute Trotsky had with Lenin related to Petrograd. In October 1919, while Denikin was threatening Moscow, Iudenich, backed by the British navy in the Bay of Finland, was advancing rapidly from Estonia towards Petrograd. On 12 October his troops captured Iamburg, 10 miles from Petrograd. By 16 October they had reached Gatchina, more than 60 miles on, and shortly afterwards they were in Tsarskoe Selo, a suburban resort near Petrograd. The White generals were so confident that their operational commander is said to have declined an offer to look at Petrograd through field glasses, saying that next day he would be walking down the Nevsky Prospekt, the central thoroughfare of the city.

On 15 October the Politbureau met. Facing the threat to both capitals, Lenin proposed to abandon Petrograd, and to gather all available strength around Moscow. (He even envisaged the possibility of giving up Moscow and withdrawing to the Urals.) Trotsky disagreed, and after some discussion the Central Committee sided with him. On 16 October Trotsky rushed in his armoured train to Petrograd. He believed that they might have to defend the city street by street.

> Having broken through this gigantic city, the White Guards would get lost in this labyrinth of stone, where every house will present them with an enigma, a threat or a deadly danger. From where should they expect a blow? From a window? From a loft? From a cellar? From behind a corner? From everywhere!
> . . . We can surround some streets with barbed wire, leave others open and transform them into traps. All that is needed is that a few thousand people should be firmly resolved not to surrender . . . Two or three days of such fighting would transform the invaders into a frightened and terrified bunch of cowards, surrendering in groups or individually to unarmed passers-by and women.[8]

All Trostky's driving energy, all his gifts of organization and oratory were put to effect. 'The city which has suffered so much, which has burnt with so strong an inward flame . . . this beautiful Red Petrograd remains what it has been, the torch of the revolution,' he proclaimed to the Petrograd Soviet. On horseback, he personally stopped retreating soldiers and led them back into line. With determination and daring the Red Soldiers routed Iudenich's army.

As it happened, the turning point on the Petrograd front occurred on the same day as that on the southern front: on 20 October the Red Army recaptured Orel.

The fourth disagreement Trotsky had with Lenin over military strategy was about the march on Warsaw. On 25 April 1920 Poland started a military offensive against Soviet Russia. The Ukraine was invaded. The Polish troops advanced rapidly, and on 6 May they entered Kiev, capital of Ukraine, and occupied the whole of the western part of the country. On 26 May the Soviet counter-offensive started. On 5 June Budenny's Red cavalry broke through. On 12 June the Poles evacuated Kiev, and afterwards they were quickly pushed back to the Soviet borders.

Up to this point, so long as the war was defensive, there

were no differences between Lenin and Trotsky regarding its conduct. Now the question was posed: should the Red Army go on to invade and occupy Poland? Lenin said 'Yes', Trotsky 'No'. Other members of the Bolshevik leadership on the whole sided with Lenin. Stalin, who showed no enthusiasm for the war so long as it was not going too well,[9] now, as a result of success, became quite enthusiastic.

The Polish communist leaders were split. Dzerzhinsky, Markhlevsky, and above all Radek, argued against Soviet advance into Poland. Unschlicht, Lensky and Bobinsky took the opposite standpoint. Lenin did not hesitate. Indeed, so long as the Polish war was progressing favourably, his confidence increased. On 17 July he forced the decision to march on to Warsaw on the Politbureau without much difficulty. He overruled Trotsky's advice, proferred on behalf of the Supreme Command, to halt the offensive. He carried the five other members with him.

Lenin's policy turned out to be wrong and very costly. Radek was proved absolutely right when he said that the Red Army would not be welcomed by the workers and peasants of Poland. On 15 August the Soviet troops were beaten at the gates of Warsaw, and were rapidly pushed back 400 kms. or more, out of Polish territory.

There were other factors which played a part in the Soviet defeat. For instance, there was an astonishing absence of coordination between the Soviet western and southwestern commands: despite an order to the southwestern command on 13 August to join the western front, it played no significant part in the battle whatever. Trotsky's explanation for the behaviour of the southwestern command was simple and convincing: the private ambitions and petty jealousies of Stalin, political commissar of the southwestern army. Stalin could not bear either to watch Tukhachevsky's triumph in Warsaw or to be overshadowed by the success of Tukhachevsky's political officer, Smilga. He wanted at all costs to enter Lvov at the same time as Tukhachevsky and Smilga were to enter Warsaw.

> Stalin was waging his own war. When the danger to Tukhachevsky's army became clearly evident and the commander-in-chief ordered the southwestern front to shift its direction sharply

toward Zamostye-Tomashev, in order to strike at the flanks of the Polish troops and Warsaw, the command of the southwestern front, encouraged by Stalin, continued to move to the west: Was it not more important to take possession of Lvov itself than to help 'others' to take Warsaw? For three or four days our general staff could not secure the execution of this order. Only after repeated demands reinforced by threats did the southwestern command change direction, but by then the delay of several days had already played its fatal role. On the 16th of August the Poles took the counter-offensive and forced our troops to roll back. If Stalin and Voroshilov and the illiterate Budenny had not 'had their own war' in Galicia and the Red Cavalry had been at Lublin in time, the Red Army would not have suffered the disaster.[10]

(This is not really the place to discuss whether the march on Warsaw was in any case condemned to failure for logistic reasons, because of the poor communications backing the Red Army, the lack of support services, etc.) The whole concept of the march on Warsaw was a political mistake. After the failure of the march on Warsaw Lenin said: 'Our offensive, our too swift advance almost as far as Warsaw, was undoubtedly a mistake.'[11] The Poles were bound to see in this invasion an attack by their hereditary enemies. And Lenin was not one to hide his mistakes. He told Klara Zetkin:

in the Red Army the Poles saw enemies, not brothers and liberators. The Poles thought, and acted, not in a social, revolutionary way but as nationalists, as imperialists. The revolution in Poland which we counted on did not take place. The workers and peasants, deceived by Pilsudski and Daszynski, defended their class enemy and let our brave Red soldiers starve, ambushed them, and beat them to death . . . Radek predicted how it would turn out. He warned us. I was very angry and accused him of 'defeatism' . . . But he was right in his main contention.[12]

Despite all the tactical differences between Lenin and Trotsky regarding the management of the Red Army, their relations were extremely close. To see this, one has only to read the massive correspondence between the two in those years, which were largely confined to matters relating to the civil war; the innumerable short notes and long telegrams.[13]

Their differences in these civil war episodes – the struggles against Kolchak, Denikin, Iudenich and Pilsudski – were of great practical importance, but they did not involve differences of principle. They were arguments about expediency – the best way of fighting the enemy at a given moment at a given place. No doubt if it had been Trotsky and not Lenin who argued for the evacuation of Petrograd, or for the failed march on Warsaw, the Stalinists would have managed to construct legends about Trotsky's capitulations and adventurism, rather than Lenin's. On the whole Trotsky's strategic judgement in military affairs proved far more reliable than Lenin's. Lenin was too absorbed in the conduct of political and economic affairs to visit the front or take part in the everyday work of the military department. His grasp of military affairs was therefore not so sure. As in the technical organization of the October insurrection, Trotsky had a far better understanding than Lenin of what was needed.[14]

At the same time, Trotsky's success at the head of the Red Army no doubt depended very much on the support of Lenin, as Chairman of the Council of People's Commissars and of the Council of Labour and Defence.

The closeness of Lenin and Trotsky during the civil war was reflected in the hyphenating of their names. The government was usually referred to as the government of Lenin–Trotsky, and so was the party, first in Russia and then throughout the world. One symbol of the confidence Lenin had in Trotsky was the blanket endorsement he gave to any order he might issue. Thus at the bottom of a blank sheet of paper Lenin wrote:

> Comrades! Knowing the strict character of the instructions issued by Comrade Trotsky, I am so convinced, supremely convinced that the instruction issued by Comrade Trotsky is correct, to the point, and essential for the good of the cause, that I wholly support this instruction. V.Ulianov (Lenin).[15]

In military affairs Lenin was always convinced that Trotsky's role was crucial. Gorky reported some remarks made by Lenin about Trotsky in private conversation. 'Show me any other man,' he said, 'capable of organizing an almost model army in one year and moreover of winning the sympathy of professional soldiers. We have that man. We have everything. You will see miracles.'[16]

Trotsky was the father of the Soviet victory. He was the founder of the Soviet army and the artisan of its victories. He undertook to create a massive and powerful army out of practically nothing. He galvanized the huge numbers of workers and peasants in the Red Army, strengthened their will for victory, stiffened their morale and led them to victory.

The symbol of the new army was Trotsky's armoured train. It was a flying apparatus of administration, including a secretariat, a printing press, a telegraph station, a radio station, an electric power station, a library, a garage, a bath. It seems to have covered a distance, during the three years of civil war, some 5½ times the length of the equator.[17]

It was a centre of inspiration, propaganda, organization and revolutionary example which transformed a vacillating, unstable mass into a real fighting army. Trotsky's gifts were a rare combination of organization and improvisation, coupled with a genius for making the soldiers know and love what they were fighting and dying for.

The international nature of the Russian revolution

At the end of the civil war Lenin knew that Bolshevism had stood the acid test and that it had triumphed.

But at what a price! How far different was the social-political regime of 1920 from the ideals the Bolsheviks had put forward in 1917! The *end* of the revolution was the establishment of a socialist society without class obstructions, a society administered by its members as a whole, a society with no bureaucracy. In such a society the well-being of all citizens would from the *beginning* foster the independence, initiative and creative powers of the human personality. Russia of the civil war was a very different kind of society. While the revolution managed to defeat the counter-revolutionary forces by relying on popular support, enthusiasm and sheer will power, it paid for victory with the destruction of the proletariat that had made the revolution, while leaving intact the state apparatus built by it. The socialist state of 1917 had become the single-party state. The soviets that remained had become a front for bureaucratically controlled Bolshevik power. The party itself had changed radically from a working class party to one highly centralist party of officials controlled by the Politburo, the Ogburo and the Secretariat.

Nobody was more aware than Lenin of the contradiction between the ideals of 1917 and the reality of 1920. But he knew that bolshevism had to proceed from the *facts*, however unpleasant they were. The only escape from the impasse was, Lenin believed, in the victory of the international revolution.

Part Two
The Bolsheviks
and World Revolution

15
The Rise of the
Communist International

Since the outbreak of the world war in August 1914, Lenin had been convinced of the need to build a new, revolutionary, workers' international. On 18 October (1 November) 1914, at the start of his wartime exile in Switzerland, he published a manifesto in the name of the Central Committee of the Bolsheviks, which ended as follows:

> The proletarian International has not gone under and will not go under. Notwithstanding all obstacles, the masses of the workers will create a new International . . . Long live the international fraternity of the workers against the chauvinism and patriotism of the bourgeoisie of all countries! Long live a proletarian International, freed from opportunism![1]

The manifesto was followed by an article, in which Lenin made it clear that, while the new International would be radically different from its predecessor, the Second International, it would at the same time be built on the foundation laid down by the former, and would continue its historical role.

> The Second International did its share of useful preparatory work in preliminarily organizing the proletarian masses during the long, 'peaceful' period of the most brutal capitalist slavery and most rapid capitalist progress in the last third of the nineteenth and the beginning of the twentieth centuries. To the Third International falls the task of organizing the proletarian forces for a revolutionary onslaught against the capitalist governments, for civil war against the bourgeoisie of all countries for the capture of political power, for the triumph of socialism![2]

With the aim of building the new International, Lenin participated in the socialist conferences at Zimmerwald (September 1915) and Kienthal (April 1916), and organized the so-called Zimmerwald Left.

Both conferences reflected a situation that was to prevail

until the end of the war: the scattered and weak socialist opposition to the war was split into two main factions – the pacifist majority and the hard, Bolshevik-led revolutionary minority.

At the Zimmerwald Conference Lenin refrained from pressing the demand for a new International. The draft resolution merely referred to the future 'reconstruction of the International'. The Bolshevik proposal at the Kienthal Conference also did not refer to the necessity of forming a Third International.[3]

However, towards the end of 1916 Lenin came to the conclusion that 'the time was ripe for a split on an international scale, that it was necessary to break with the Second International . . . to build a Third International'.[4]

Lenin's *April Theses* stated: 'We must take the initiative in creating a revolutionary International, an International against the *social-chauvinists* and against the "Centre".'

The International Nature of the Russian Revolution

On taking power Lenin made it clear again and again that the Russian revolution was only the beginning of the world revolution, and that the fate of the former would be determined by the development of the latter. He told the Third Congress of Soviets on 11 (24) January 1918:

> The final victory of socialism in a single country is of course impossible. Our contingent of workers and peasants which is upholding Soviet power is one of the contingents of the great world army.[6]

> . . . No matter what difficulties we experienced, no matter what defeats were in store for us, the world socialist revolution would come.[7]

> . . . It is the absolute truth that without a German revolution we are doomed.[8]

He told the Eighth Party Congress on 18 March 1919: 'We are living not merely in a state, but *in a system of states*, and it is inconceivable for the Soviet Republic to exist alongside of the imperialist states for any length of time. One or the other must triumph in the end.'[9]

This basic internationalist faith did not falter even when

the revolution was slow in spreading. On the third anniversary of the October revolution Lenin said:

> We knew at that time that our victory would be a lasting one only when our cause had triumphed the world over, and so when we began working for our cause we counted exclusively on the world revolution . . . we staked our chances on world revolution, and were undoubtedly right in doing so.[10]

In a speech on 6 December 1920, he said:

> While capitalism and socialism exist side by side, they cannot live in peace: one or the other will ultimately triumph – the last obsequies will be observed either for the Soviet Republic or for world capitalism.[11]

ʹThe First Congress of the Communist International

Lenin was, however, too practical a person not to realize that there was all the difference in the world between the wish to set up a new international, and its actual launching. While his plans were bold, he was very cautious in implementing the establishment of a new International.

The pamphlet *Socialism and War*, written by Lenin and Zinoviev in summer 1915, while making clear the need for a new international, argues that revolutionaries would possibly have to remain in the Second International as its extreme opposition until such time as the German revolutionaries, members of the most important section of the international proletariat, were ready to found a new International:

> It is perfectly obvious that to create an *international* Marxist organization, there must be a readiness to form independent Marxist parties in the *various* countries. As a country with the oldest and strongest working-class movement, Germany is of decisive importance. The immediate future will show whether the conditions are mature for the formation of a new and Marxist International. If they are, our party will gladly join such a Third International, purged of opportunism and chauvinism. If they are not, then that will show that a more or less protracted period of evolution is needed for that purging to be effected. Our party will then form the extreme opposition within the old International, pending the time when the conditions in the various countries make possible the formation of

an international workingmen's association standing on the basis of revolutionary Marxism.[12]

On taking power the Bolsheviks started international propaganda on the widest possible front.

> Almost in the very hour of the opening of the Brest-Litovsk peace conference . . . Trotsky announced in Petrograd that 'yesterday a freight car full of propaganda and socialism was dispatched to Germany'. 'Although we are negotiating peace with Germany,' declared the Foreign Commissar, 'we continue to speak our revolutionary tongue.'[13]

A decree of the Council of People's Commissars, issued on 13 December, and published in *Pravda* three days later, announced that the Council

> deems it necessary to come to the assistance of the left International wing of the labour movement of all countries, by all possible means, including funds, whether the said countries are at war with Russia, or allied to Russia, or occupying a neutral position. For this purpose the Council of People's Commissars resolves: that the sum of two million rubles shall be placed at the disposal of the foreign representatives of the Commissariat of Foreign Affairs for the needs of the Revolutionary Internationalist Movement.[14]

An international section under Radek, attached to the Commissariat of Foreign Affairs, was set up immediately after the October revolution. It was composed mainly of national groups of prisoners of war; German, Austrian and Yugoslav groups were created, with their own periodical publications and other propaganda literature. Work among prisoners of war at this time was, as Lenin said later, 'the real foundation of what has been done to create a Third International'.[15] Innumerable pamphlets and leaflets were produced in English and French to be distributed to Allied troops landing on Russian soil.

After the German revolution of November 1918 the Bolshevik leaders decided to take immediate steps to found a new International. On 24 January 1919 Radio Moscow directed a broadcast to revolutionary groups throughout the world inviting them to send representatives to a congress that would set up a new Communist International.

On 2-6 March 1919 the Founding Congress of the Communist International met in Moscow, in an atmosphere of exhilarating optimism. Europe was in the throes of an unprecedented social, economic and political crisis. There had been a wave of mass strikes and revolutionary uprisings, in Germany, Austria, Hungary and Italy. There were 51 delegates at this founding conference: 35 with voting rights representing 19 parties and organizations, and 19 with consultative votes representing 16 organizations. These figures are actually very misleading, as the delegates were far from representative. Of the 35 with voting rights, only 4 were not then residing in Russia: one Norwegian, one Swede (in neither of whose countries a Communist Party existed) and two other specially delegated to the Congress in whose countries a Communist Party did exist: Max Albert (pseudonym of Hugo Eberlein) from Germany and Gruber (pseudonym of Karl Steinhardt) from Austria, representing a tiny communist group. The majority of the delegates represented national communist groups affiliated to the Bolshevik Federation of Foreign Communist Groups. The membership of these groups was very small, ranging from about 10 in the French to 90 (in December 1918) in the Hungarian and 112 in the Yugoslav.[16]

This was the only Congress of the Communist International of which Lenin attended every session, indeed, he presided over all of them. In addition he wrote the resolution on bourgeois democracy and the dictatorship of the proletariat, as well as the article about the founding of the International. He also gave the closing speech.

In the history of the international labour movement there had never previously been a meeting so small and so unrepresentative that actually started a massive and powerful international movement. Nothing was further from Lenin's mind than the intention of giving an assortment of small sects the label of an International. When he founded the Communist International he was relying on what he foresaw was going to happen in Europe: mass communist parties would emerge in the revolutionary struggles ahead. He assumed, correctly, that in the revolutionary situation existing after the war and with the example of victorious Bolshevism in Russia, the communist sects would rise to achieve mass influence.

Lenin's opening speech asserted that civil war had become a fact not only in Russia but also in Germany, that the capitalist world was rapidly approaching its end, and that the main thing was to fight the reformists who formed the bulwark of capitalism. Then he moved the 'Theses and Report on Bourgeois Democracy and the Dictatorship of the Proletariat', denouncing parliamentarism and defending proletarian dictatorship. The conclusion of the theses, in the form of a resolution, was adopted unanimously by the congress.

> the chief task of the communist parties in all countries where soviet government has not been established is as follows:
> 1. to explain to the broad mass of the workers the historic significance and the political and historical necessity of the new, proletarian, democracy which must replace bourgeois democracy and the parliamentary system;
> 2. to extend the organization of Soviets among the workers in all branches of industry, among the soldiers in the army and sailors in the navy and also among farm labourers and poor peasants;
> 3. to build a stable communist majority inside the soviets.[17]

The congress made it clear that the communists had to differentiate themselves not only from the reformists but also from the centrists.

> It is absolutely essential to split the most revolutionary elements off from the 'centre'; this can be done only by the ruthless criticism and exposure of the 'centrist' leaders. The organizational break with the 'centre' is an absolute historical necessity. It is the task of the communists in each country to determine the moment for this break, according to the stage of development which the movement has reached there.[18]

The only discord at the congress came with the discussion of whether to found the Communist International *immediately*. Besides the Bolshevik Party, the most important participating party was the German Communist Party (KPD), whose delegate, Eberlein, could justifiably write five years later: 'I was the only one there able to speak for a communist party, apart from the Russian party.'[19] Eberlein came with a mandate to oppose the creation of a new international as premature. He said at the Congress:

> There are real communist parties in only a few countries; in most others they have been created within the last few weeks, and in several countries communists have as yet no organizations . . . All of western Europe is missing: Belgium and Italy are not represented; the Swiss delegates cannot speak in the name of one party; France, England, Spain and Portugal are missing; and America is also not in a position to say which parties would stand with us.[20]

Eberlein, however, was persuaded to abstain from voting in order not to mar the harmony of the proceedings. On 4 March the assembly transformed itself into the First Congress of the Communist International.

The congress adopted a manifesto written by Trotsky 'to the workers of the world', which reviewed the rise and fall of capitalism and the development of communism in the 72 years since Marx and Engels wrote the Communist Manifesto, and was afterwards described by Zinoviev as 'a second Communist Manifesto'.[21]

Closing the congress, Lenin concluded his speech with the words: 'The victory of the proletarian revolution on a world scale is assured. The founding of our international Soviet republic is on the way.'[22]

In an article entitled 'The Third International and its Place in History', written on 15 April 1919, Lenin wrote:

> The First International (1864-72) laid the foundation of an international organization of the workers for the preparation of their revolutionary attack on capital. The Second International (1889-1914) was an international organization of the proletarian movement whose growth proceeded in *breadth*, at the cost of a temporary drop in the revolutionary level, a temporary strengthening of opportunism, which in the end led to the disgraceful collapse of the International . . .
> The Third International has gathered the fruits of the work of the Second International, discarded its opportunist, social-chauvinist, bourgeois and petty bourgeois dross, and *has begun to implement* the dictatorship of the proletariat.[23]

The Immediacy of World Revolution

In both the revolutionary and the counter-revolutionary camp the feeling prevailed that a general assault on the system was under way and that the victory of world revolution was certain.

Thus on 21 March 1919, just a fortnight after the founding congress of the Comintern, a Soviet Republic was proclaimed in Budapest. Next day the US government representative in Paris, Colonel House, wrote in his diary: 'Bolshevism is gaining ground everywhere. Hungary has just succumbed. We are sitting upon an open powder magazine and some day a spark may ignite it.'[24] At almost the same moment, Lloyd George wrote to Clemenceau:

> The whole of Europe is filled with the spirit of revolution. There is a deep sense not only of discontent but of anger and revolt amongst the workmen against pre-war conditions. The whole existing order in its political, social and economic aspects is questioned by the masses of the population from one end of Europe to the other.[25]

The revolutionaries argued in similar vein. In the article quoted above, 'The Third International and its Place in History', Lenin said:

> The international alliance of the parties which are leading the most revolutionary movement in the world, the movement of the proletariat for the overthrow of the yoke of capital, now rests on an unprecedentedly firm base, in the shape of several *Soviet republics*, which are implementing the dictatorship of the proletariat and are the embodiment of victory over capitalism on an international scale . . . the new, third, 'International Working Men's Association' *has already begun to develop*, to a certain extent, into a *union of Soviet Socialist Republics*.[26]

In July 1919 he wrote: 'Take Germany. Immediately the Treaty of Versailles was signed a big revolutionary movement began.' And he predicted that, 'this July will be the last difficult July, and that next July we shall welcome the victory of the world Soviet republic and that victory will be full and complete'.[27]

Zinoviev, the president of the Communist International, was even more euphoric than Lenin about the immediate prospects of world revolution. The May Day (1919) Manifesto of the Executive Committee of the Comintern, written by Zinoviev, stated:

> As these lines are being written the Third International already has as its main basis three Soviet republics, in Russia, Hungary, and Bavaria. But nobody will be surprised if by the time these lines appear in print we have not three but six or more Soviet republics . . . Now it is abundantly clear that the movement in Europe is going ahead far more quickly than even the greatest optimist at the Moscow congress of the Third International expected. The flames of civil war are blazing throughout Europe. The victory of communism in all Germany is wholly inevitable. There will be a few isolated defeats. Here and there perhaps for a while the black will defeat the red. Nevertheless, it is to the red that final victory will fall. And that in the next few months, perhaps even weeks. The movement is advancing so dizzyingly fast that one can say with certainty in a year's time we will already begin to forget that there was a struggle for communism in Europe, for in a year's time the whole of Europe will be communist. And the struggle will have spread to America, perhaps to Asia too, and the other continents. It may perhaps be that in America capitalism can continue to exist for a couple of years alongside a communist Europe. It may perhaps be that even in England capitalism will continue to exist for a year or two alongside the communism which will have triumphed over the whole European continent. But for any length of time such a symbiosis is impossible . . .
> Before a year has passed the whole of Europe will be Soviet. In every country the workers will have realized that the decisive moment has come . . .
> In 1919 the great Communist International was born. In 1920 the great International Soviet Republic will come to birth.[28]

The Revolutionary Storm

The period after the Comintern Congress continued to be one of exuberant optimism. The wave of revolutionary ferment continued to sweep across the continent. Soviet republics were proclaimed in Budapest on 21 March 1919 and in Munich on 7 April. In Vienna there was a wild surge of excitement among the workers. In mid-February, a few weeks after the fierce suppression of the Spartakus rising in Berlin, there were bloody battles between workers and government troops in central Germany at Gotha, Magdeburg and Brunswick, which dragged on until the beginning of April. In May bitter struggles broke out in Leipzig, Eisenach and Erfurt. A wave of mass strikes swept through the Ruhr, and in mid-March Berlin once more became, for two weeks, the scene of a bloody civil war in which nearly 1,200 people were killed. In mid-April the French Black Sea fleet mutinied; on 1 May in Paris tens of thousands of demonstrators, who had responded to the call of the Socialist Party to appear in the streets, clashed in heavy fighting with police and with infantry and cavalry troops. In June 200,000 engineering workers came out on strike in Paris.[29]

Britain was not immune to the rising revolutionary wave. A massive strike movement started at the beginning of 1919. The signal was given by 70,000 dockers, ship-building workers and miners on Clydeside and in Belfast, who went on unofficial strike at the end of February. Glasgow, the centre of unrest, seemed to be on the verge of civil war. The workers had hoisted the red flag over the town hall. A state of emergency was proclaimed and 10,000 heavily armed troops were called in to occupy strategic points in the city with tanks and machine-gun nests. There followed sporadic strikes in other industrial areas and then a strike threat by several hundred thousand miners and railwaymen.*[30]

The Communist International transformed itself from a collection of small sects (if one excludes the Russian party) in March 1919 into a *mass* organization. In Italy the Socialist Party voted to affiliate to the Comintern at its conference in Bologna in September 1919, adding 300,000 members to the International. In June 1919 the Bulgarian Socialists (*Tesniaki* – 'narrow'), who had consistently held a revolutionary internationalist position very close to Bolshevism since the foundation of their party,

---

* The government's anxiety was revealed in a circular sent out by the War Office at the beginning of 1919 to commanders of army units stationed in Britain. They were asked to sound out whether the troops would obey 'instructions to restore law and order' and to 'break srtikes'.[31]

voted to affiliate to the Comintern. This was a mass party with 35,478 members in 1920. The Yugoslav Socialist Party, also a mass party, also joined. The Czechoslovak Social-Democratic Party split in December 1920, the Communist Left taking over half the membership and establishing a Communist Party of 350,000 members. A separate split in the Social-Democratic Party of the German-speaking minority added further forces, and after their unification the Party claimed 400,000 members. The Norwegian Labour Party joined the Comintern in spring 1919. In Sweden the majority of the Socialist Party, after a split, joined the Comintern, adding another 17,000 members.

In Germany the Independent Social Democratic Party (USPD), with its 800,000 members, which had split from the German Social Democratic Party, (SPD) in April 1917 under pressure from the revolutionary mood among the masses, veered markedly to the left in 1919 and 1920. At the Leipzig Congress in December 1919 it decided by 227 votes to 54 to leave the Second International (but by 169 to 114 not to join the Third International). It suggested that a conference be called of the 'Third International and other Socialist Revolutionary organizations' to discuss the foundation of a comprehensive international to include them all. At its next congress October 1920 in Halle, the USPD decided by 236 to 156 to join the Comintern. Of the USPD's 800,000 members, 300,000 joined the Communist Party at a unification conference in December 1920 (while 300,000 continued under the Hilferding–Kautsky leadership, and 200,000 left the USPD without joining the Communist Party). The United Communist Party of Germany, VKPD, at its foundation in 1920, had some 350,000 members.

The example of the USPD greatly influenced the French Socialist Party. At the party conference in Strasbourg a recommendation for affiliation to the Comintern received 1,600 votes, while 3,000 voted against. The conference decided by 4,330 to 331 to break with the Second International, and adopted a resolution expressing its agreement with the basic principles of the Comintern, especially the principle of the dictatorship of the proletariat. It also sent delegates to the Second Congress of the Comintern, to clear up the question of the affiliation of the

French party. This question came up for final decision at the conference in Tours on 25 December 1920. The motion to join the Comintern received 3,247 votes, against 1,308 for the alternative of rejecting the Comintern conditions but continuing negotiations, and 150 for the extreme right wing, rejecting the Comintern completely. Thus the Comintern captured a mass party with 140,000 members – with only 30,000 members lost by the split.

16

The Proletarian Assault Rebuffed – the Need for a New Policy

The Fall of the Hungarian Soviet Republic

The year 1919 was most critical for the bourgeoisie. A couple of years later Trotsky described the situation then as follows:

> In 1919 the European bourgeoisie was in a state of extreme confusion. Those were the days of panic, the days of a truly insane fear of Bolshevism . . . The war has shattered the economic foundation of bourgeois society. At the same time the war has extraordinarily disorganized, weakened, discredited and paralysed the political organs of bourgeois rule: the state, the army, the police, the parliament, the press, and so on.[1]

But the revolutionary assault on capitalism, beyond the borders of Russia, was beaten back. In Hungary the Soviet regime came to power on 21 March. 133 days later – on 1 August – it was overthrown. (The other Soviet government – that of Bavaria – had an even shorter life – 23 days, from 7 April until May Day.)

The events in Hungary showed the local communist leaders

to be extremely immature and ineffective. They committed a series of gross errors, both of opportunism and of ultra-Leftism.

First, they made compromises with Social Democracy.

When the leaders of the Hungarian Social Democratic Party visited the communist leader, Bela Kun, in gaol, on 21 March, to discuss the sharing of power, one of his conditions was affiliation to the Comintern. The Social Democrats yielded, and the Communist and Socialist Parties were amalgamated. Kun, as Commissar of Foreign Affairs in the new government, as well as leader of the Bolshevik wing of the Socialist Party, made early radio contact with Lenin, and Lenin, in one of his first messages, asked him urgently to state whether he could guarantee that the regime would be communist:

> Please inform us what real guarantees you have that the new Hungarian government will actually be a communist, and not simply a socialist, government, i.e. one of traitor-socialists.
> Have the communists a majority in the government? When will the Congress of Soviets take place? What does the socialists' recognition of the dictatorship of the proletariat really amount to?[2]

Kun's answer apparently allayed Lenin's doubts, and he became satisfied that the Hungarian regime was progressing along communist lines.

The Executive Committee of the Communist International (ECCI) gave its approval to the activities of the Hungarian comrades, declaring in a letter to the congress of the new party: 'The actions of the Hungarian government of soviets and Hungarian Communist Party during the first month of your dictatorship will remain forever a model of proletarian fearlessness and communist foresight and wisdom.'[3]

But, as events were to show, Bela Kun had misled Lenin. When the crisis came, the Social Democratic leaders betrayed the revolution: they negotiated secretly with the Allies, and at the crucial point, when the Soviet republic stood with its back to the wall, they joined the counter-revolution.

Immediately after the defeat of the Hungarian revolution, the lesson to be learned from the amalgamation with the Social Democrats was emphasized by Lenin. He referred repeatedly to the experience of Hungary as proof that affiliation with Social Democrats in a position of power would encourage treason against the revolution. In February 1920, Lenin warned the French communists against those socialist leaders who give

> verbal recognition of the dictatorship of the proletariat and Soviet government, although they actually either remain enemies of the dictatorship of the proletariat, or are unable or unwilling to understand its significance and to carry it into effect.
> The fall of the first Soviet Republic in Hungary . . . shows clearly how vast, how immense is the danger of this evil.[4]

In his essay, 'Left Wing' Communism, an Infantile Disorder, written in April-May 1920, Lenin again attacked the Hungarian Social Democratic leaders who styled themselves communist and presumed to support the dictatorship of the proletariat.

> These gentlemen are absolutely incapable of thinking and reasoning like revolutionaries. They are snivelling philistine democrats, who become a thousand times more dangerous to the proletariat when they claim to be supporters of soviet government and of the dictatorship of the proletariat because, in fact, whenever a difficult and dangerous situation arises they are sure to commit treachery . . . while 'sincerely' believing that they are helping the proletariat! Did not the Hungarian Social Democrats, after rechristening themselves communists, also want to 'help' the proletariat when, because of their cowardice and spinelessness, they considered the position of soviet power in Hungary hopeless and went snivelling to the agents of the Entente capitalists and the Entente hangmen?*[5]

As well as committing opportunist errors in relation to the Social Democrats, Bela Kun also committed disastrous ultra-left blunders in his attitude to the peasantry, which made up a large majority of the population of his country. He refused to distribute the great landlords' estates amongst the rural toilers, because he believed it would harm the collectivization of

---

* Even after the collapse of the Hungarian Soviet Republic, Bela Kun defended the joining of the Communists with the Socialists: 'Why did we unite with the nonrevolutionary Social Democrats at the start of the revolution? One must remember that our party was small, with relatively few members and could never have done the job by itself.'[6]

agriculture. He stated at his party congress on 12 June 1919:
'A happy confluence of circumstances has enabled us to see to
it that socialized production has not remained a figment of
Utopianism in our country, for most of our agricultural land is
already being farmed collectively.' After the fall of the Soviet
regime in Hungary, he still stuck to his guns, declaring on
21 December 1919: 'The peasants as a whole approved the
communist program for land tenure and utilization. One should
note in this connection that in our country, unlike Russia, the
land was not divided up.'[7]

In fact Bella Kun's agrarian policy was, in Lenin's view,
one of the reasons for the collapse of the communist regime:
'the establishment of the proletarian dictatorship hardly changed
anything in the Hungarian countryside . . . the day labourers
saw no changes, and the small peasants got nothing.'[8] After the
collapse of the Soviet regime in Hungary the large landowners
had no difficulty in recovering their estates.

Failure in Germany

Of all the Communist movements outside Russia, by far the
most important was that of Germany. Here the nineteen months
after the fall of the Kaiser were very disappointing. This was of
special significance because the German comrades were by far
the most experienced European communists. However, even the
German Communist Party was very immature.

At its founding congress in December 1918 the KPD showed
itself to be suffering from infantile ultra-leftism. The congress
delegates were not willing to follow the lead offered by its
brilliant leader Rosa Luxemburg.

One of the questions the Congress had to decide was the
attitude communists should take towards elections to the National
Assembly. Rosa Luxemburg argued:

> We are now in the midst of revolution, and the National
> Assembly is a counter-revolutionary fortress erected *against*
> the revolutionary proletariat. Our task is thus to take this
> fortress by storm and raze it to the ground. In order to
> mobilize the masses *against* the National Assembly and to
> appeal to them to wage a very intensive struggle against it,

we must utilize the elections and the platform of the National Assembly itself . . . To denounce mercilessly and loudly all the wily tricks of this worthy Assembly, to expose its counter-revolutionary work step by step to the masses, and to appeal to the masses to intervene and force a decision – these are the tasks of participation in the National Assembly.[9]

But the delegates decided instead to boycott the elections. The mood of the majority was expressed by the former Social Democratic MP, Otto Rühle. He insisted that they did not need to use the Assembly as a tribune. 'We have other tribunes. The street is the great tribune that we have conquered and that we will not abandon, even if they shoot at us.'[10] So, by 62 votes to 23, the Congress voted against participation in elections to the National Assembly that was to create the new Republic.

The same impatience was shown in the discussion on the economic struggle. Lange, who introduced the session for the leadership, did not take a position on whether or not revolutionaries should remain in the old unions. Many other delegates expressed the opinion that to do so was incompatible with being a revolutionary communist. Paul Frölich raised the slogan 'Out of the Unions', calling instead for 'revolutionary workers' unions' which would end once and for all the distinction between the party and the trade unions. He was attacked by Rosa Luxemburg for not putting the stress on building workers' councils. She was not happy with the slogan 'Out of the unions', but went so far as to suggest that the 'liquidation of the unions' was on the order of the day. Only Heckert pointed out that the unions were far from played out, that they were still accepted by vast numbers of workers and that the slogan 'Out of the unions' was extremely dangerous.

The discussion on the trade union question at the KPD conference was another expression of the impatience of the delegates, of their inability to take seriously the task of winning the broadest layers of the masses for the revolution.[11]

Rosa Luxemburg, conscious of the seriousness of her defeat at the congress on the question of elections to the National Assembly, still believed that it was a symptom of the party's youth and inexperience, and that the party would be able to outgrow this immaturity. 'Our defeat,' she wrote to her old friend Clara Zetkin,

> was merely the triumph of a somewhat childish, half-baked, narrow-minded radicalism. In any case, this happened at the beginning of the Conference. Later contact between us [the Executive] and the delegates was established . . . an entirely different atmosphere . . . than at the start . . . *Spartakisten* are a fresh generation, free from the cretinous traditions of the 'good old party' . . . We all decided unanimously not to make the matter [of the boycott] into a cardinal question . . . and not to take it too seriously.[12]

What mattered most for Luxemburg was that the newly founded Communist Party was attracting the best of the younger generation to its ranks. Their inexperience and their 'ultra-leftism' were inseparable from their youth and fighting spirit. However, she underestimated their effect in a party that lacked a reliable experienced cadre. It was to prove fatal in the days that followed, despite the fact that the old leadership was re-elected in its entirety.

The lack of cohesion within the party was aggravated by another consequence of the ultra-left positions adopted at the Congress. The most experienced and influential group of worker militants in Berlin itself, the revolutionary shop stewards from the large factories, had been expected to join the party on its foundation. But discussions between a delegation from the new party, led by Liebknecht, and the leaders of the shop stewards soon ran into trouble. Their most influential leaders mistrusted the impatience of the KPD.

The outcome in the weeks that followed was disastrous. The new Communist Party was to be faced with massive struggles, without some of the best and most influential workers' leaders in Berlin in its ranks. The shop stewards, on the other hand, were to be plunged into a complex and rapidly changing situation without the guidance that figures like Luxemburg, Radek and Jogiches could have given them. As a result they were to fall into the same disastrous 'putschism' that they had denounced in the KPD.

On 5 January 1919 the still tiny Communist Party, with the support of local sections of the USPD, attempted to seize power in Berlin. The rising had not been planned, on the basis of a calculation of the balance of forces. It was the spontaneous reaction of Communists and some USPD militants to the attempt of the government to dismiss Emile Eichhorn, a USPD member who had taken over as chief of the Berlin police during the November revolution. Luxemburg was opposed to the rising. She was overruled and reluctantly put herself at its head. Lacking majority working-class support, even in Berlin, the rising was soon crushed. Ebert, Scheidemann and Noske, the Social Democratic leaders lent 'Socialist' and 'Republican' legality to hastily reconstructed right-wing army units led by former Imperial officers. In the repression that followed, Rosa Luxemburg, Karl Liebknecht and many others were murdered.

The tactics of the KPD were fundamentally wrong. The simple juxtaposition of Soviet and National Assembly, and the boycott of the latter in the name of the former, could only lead to a cul-de-sac. This becomes clear from the composition of the workers' and soldiers' soviets in Germany, as well as from the results of the election to the National Assembly. At the First All-German Workers' and Soldiers' Congress of Soviets, which met on 16 December 1918, of 488 delegates only 10 were KPD supporters; Liebknecht and Luxemburg failed to get elected to this congress. At the election to the National Assembly of 19 January 1919 the SPD won 11,466,000 votes, and the USPD 2,315,000. The KPD boycotted it, but would certainly not have got more than a few tens of thousands of votes. (In the 6 June 1920 Reichstag elections the SPD received 5,614,000 votes, and the USPD 4,895,000, while the KPD got only 441,000; the corresponding figures for Berlin were 187,000, 456,000 and 14,000.)

The ultra-left stance of the KPD in January 1919 ended in catastrophe. The January 1919 rising in Germany was in many ways comparable with the July Days in Russia in 1917. In Petrograd in July 1917 (as in Berlin in 1919), the workers and soldiers felt very powerful; the government staged a provocation. The workers responded by moving rapidly towards revolution.

In Russia, Lenin was firm in his view that the movement was premature and extremely dangerous: 'We must be especially attentive and careful, so as not to be drawn into a provocation . . . One wrong move on our part can wreck everything . . . If we were now able to seize power, it is naive to think that having taken it we should be able to hold it.'[13]

The Bolshevik leaders were not able to hold back the masses. The demonstrations took place despite them. Should they then simply have ordered their own party members not to take part in the demonstration? To have done so would have been fatal. It would have confused and demoralized a vast number of workers who only the day before had broken with the Mensheviks and Social Revolutionaries. They would not have continued to see the Bolsheviks as their party if the Bolsheviks had withdrawn from the battle. They had to be with the masses on the streets, attempting to give the demonstration slogans which would hold the masses together, and express their combative spirit, while avoiding an attempt to seize power. Lenin, as we have seen elsewhere, was adamant that the party should not leave the masses alone to fight it out. 'Had our party refused to support the 3-4 July mass movement which burst out spontaneously despite our attempts to prevent it, we should have actually and completely betrayed the proletariat, since the people were moved to action by their well founded and just anger.'[14] As he wrote a couple of years after the event: 'Mistakes are inevitable when the masses are fighting, but the communists *remain with the masses*, see these mistakes, explain them to the masses, try to get them rectified, and strive perseveringly for the victory of class-consciousness over spontaneity.'[15]

What this meant in practice was that the Bolsheviks, realizing that an attempt to argue against action by the workers and soldiers would be useless, issued their own call for armed demonstrations, which should, however, be 'peaceful and organized demonstrations'.

In contrast, the German Communist Party leaders did not make it clear that they regarded the movement as having only limited objectives. The explanation was that Rosa Luxemburg was afraid to be too hard in her criticism of the newly radicalized workers, because she was trying desperately to build a party out of them. By contrast Lenin had already built a party. Its militants were already so widely respected within the working class that they could afford to adopt views that risked temporary unpopularity among the newly radicalized workers and soldiers – providing, of course, that they participated in the mass action.

There are severe difficulties for someone in Rosa Luxemburg's position, of trying to build a revolutionary party out of next to nothing in the course of revolutionary events.* The tactical helplessness of the KPD was not coincidental. It was the inevitable result of the past experience of Rosa Luxemburg's group. She had never organized a disciplined party, or even a faction in the SPD. Her group was merely a propaganda group. The strict discipline demanded by Lenin aimed above all to achieve unity in action. A group which generally restricted itself to propaganda would have no need of such a stern regime: the free play of ideas would be much more important. Because Rosa Luxemburg's mind was focused on propaganda, the distinction

---

* It was easy after the events to argue that German revolutionaries should have organized independently before the war as Paul Levi said in 1920, or as Radek wrote in 1926 in a letter to Clara Zetkin:
'For the anniversary of the death of Karl and Rosa, I spoke to a meeting of the Young Communist League, in Moscow, at which you also were to speak. I prepared the speech, leafed through some old articles by Rosa, and it was with the deepest conviction that we, the left radicals in Germany, did not open our eyes too early, but too late, that we fought the dangers, not too vigorously but too weakly.'[16]
The fact is that even Lenin never demanded before the war that revolutionaries in Germany should organize independently.[17]
When, in the summer of 1930 *Proletarskaia revoliutsiia*, the leading Russian historical journal, published an article by Slutsky, who suggested that in pre-war days Lenin had underestimated the danger of international centrism, it provoked an angry response from Stalin. In an article 'On Some Questions of the History of Bolshevism', he attacked the editors – which meant primarily M.N.Pokrovsky – for permitting discussion on issues affecting the essence of Bolshevism; Slutsky's ideas were denounced as disguised Trotskyism.

between party members subject to party discipline and supporters or sympathizers – so vital for Lenin – concerned her much less. For Rosa Luxemburg the influence of the party over the proletariat was to be exercised primarily through ideas, rather than through the power of its organization or its own initiation of activities, whereas for Lenin the two elements were much more evenly balanced.

There was a very good reason why Rosa Luxemburg held back from organizing an independent revolutionary organization in Germany. Having a faction would invariably raise the question of a split from the SPD, which she utterly opposed. Possibly she was influenced in this attitude by the fate of the Independent Socialist Party, quite a large group of revolutionaries, who split from the SPD in 1891 accusing it of reformism. This party had a very short life before completely disappearing. As late as January 1917 Rosa Luxemburg was still arguing against a split.[18]

Without a party Rosa Luxemburg's ideas were necessarily reduced to the level of a commentary on revolutionary events, rather than constituting a moulding force behind them. On visiting Berlin in November 1918, Radek commented: 'I still did not feel that I was in the presence of a party.'[19] Luxemburg's most ardent and uncritical supporters, like Frölich, confirm this position of weakness (though Frölich does not recognize its decisively harmful effect on strategy). 'When the revolution came the *Spartakusbund* was only a federation of local groups existing in almost all the larger towns and not yet a political party.'[20]

Heinrich Brandler, a disciple of Rosa Luxemburg and future leader of the German Communist Party, remembered that *Spartakusbund* had only 3,000 members at the end of the war. 'And a good half of them were moral pacifists not Marxists.'[21]

After the debacle of January 1919, Paul Levi, who inherited the leadership of the KPD, did his best to free the party from its ultra-leftism. At the KPD Congress in October 1919 in Heidelberg, he decided to present a programme endorsing participation in parliamentary elections and in the trade unions. He intended to expel all who disagreed. His resolution was passed by 31 votes to 18; the minority left the Congress and later formed the

German Communist Workers' Party (KAPD). The KPD lost nearly half its membership, the heaviest losses being in Berlin and other parts of north Germany.

In the autumn of 1919 the revolutionary wave was ebbing fast throughout Central Europe. Failure in Bavaria and Hungary sapped what was left of the revolutionary faith of the masses. To cap the failure of the KPD came the Kapp putsch.

On 13 March 1920 German generals, leading units of the Reichswehr, invaded Berlin and proclaimed a Right nationalist government led by a Prussian official, named Wolfgang Kapp, as Chancellor. An effective counter-attack came from the trade union leaders, who called a general strike; four days later the Kapp regime fell. At the time the general strike was called Levi was in prison and the other members of the *Zentrale*, i.e. the Berlin members of the Central Committee, refusing to support the Social Democrats, issued a leaflet calling on workers to refuse 'to lift a finger for the democratic republic'. It is true that on the second day of the strike, when it appeared successful, and when it was clear that communists were following the lead of the trade union comrades, KPD headquarters reversed its position and supported the strike. But the damage of ultra-left 'neutrality' was done. The KPD leadership again showed its inexperience. If only they had recalled how Bolshevik sailors had guarded Kerensky's winter palace against Kornilov!

The Need to Teach the Young Communist Parties
In 1918 and 1919 it seemed to Lenin, Trotsky and their friends that the bourgeoisie was so disorganized and disheartened that a direct assault of the proletariat, even led by very young and inexperienced communist parties, could lead to victory. However, despite the readiness of the proletariat in a number of countries of Europe to struggle, and despite its spirit of self-sacrifice and heroism, victory was still out of reach. By the middle of 1920 it became clear that the revolutionary movement was ebbing away in waves of strikes, demonstrations and isolated uprisings which were all crushed. The defeat of the soviet governments of Hungary and Bavaria, and the disastrous errors of the KPD in January 1919 as well as during the Kapp Putsch in March

1920, must have forced Lenin to shed some of his illusions about the possibility of a revolutionary victory to be achieved by the young, inexperienced communist parties of central and western Europe.

The question of training these new parties in tactics and strategy became central. Such training had to be done right in the midst of open mass struggles. The communist parties had to be built up at the same time as the leadership of swiftly developing mass movements was being taken over. Whereas the Bolsheviks had had prolonged training for October – a whole series of offensive struggles followed by retreats, of uprisings followed by defeats, of activities, electoral and trade union – preparations spread over some 14 years – the communist parties of central and western Europe had to go through a short course of tempering for revolutionary victory.

Lenin put a great deal of effort into training the young communist parties in tactics and strategy in the remaining months of political activity left to him. The Second and Third Congresses of the Comintern, in which he participated actively, were by and large schools for strategy and tactics.

17

The Comintern – School for Tactics

The failure of the first post-war revolution everywhere in Europe except Russia made it essential to elaborate on the strategy and tactics necessary for the Comintern: to analyse the role of the communist parties in the revolution, to work out a correct attitude towards social democrats; to take a position towards participation in parliamentary elections; towards the existing trade unions; to the agrarian question and the colonial and national questions. These problems occupied the Second Congress of the Comintern. They were also the themes of a pamphlet Lenin wrote in April-May 1920, called 'Left-Wing' Communism: an Infantile Disorder.

The pamphlet first appeared in Russia in early June, but the Comintern had it translated into German, French and English, and these translations were published in July, ready to be distributed to the delegates attending the Second Congress of the Comintern.

Rarely has such a short work had so powerful and lasting on influence on the international labour movement. Its influence could be compared to that of the Communist Manifesto. It was of enormous importance in creatively developing the strategy and tactics of the revolutionary movement, and it was the last major work which Lenin wrote.

The International Significance of the Bolshevik Experience

Lenin's essay starts from the premise that the Russian revolutionary experience had international significance.

> We now possess quite considerable international experience, which shows very definitely that certain fundamental features of our revolution have a significance that is not local, or peculiarly national, or Russian alone, but international.[1]

> Bolshevism . . . went through fifteen years of practical history (1903-17) unequalled anywhere in the world in its wealth of experience. During those fifteen years, no other country knew anything even approximating to that revolutionary experience, that rapid and varied succession of different forms of the movement – legal and illegal, peaceful and stormy, underground and open, local circles and mass movements, and parliamentary and terrorist forms. In no other country has there been concentrated, in so brief a period, such a wealth of forms, shades, and methods of struggle of all classes of modern society, a struggle which, owing to the backwardness of the country and the severity of the Tsarist yoke, matured with exceptional rapidity, and assimilated most eagerly and successfully the appropriate 'last word' of American and European political experience.[2]

On Compromises

Firstly Lenin dealt directly with the main slogan of the ultra-lefts: opposition to *all* compromises *on principle*. One cannot state simply: on no account are compromises allowed. Lenin used a very simple, telling analogy:

> Imagine that your car is held up by armed bandits. You hand them over your money, passport, revolver and car. In return you are rid of the pleasant company of the bandits. That is unquestionably a compromise. 'Do ut des' (I 'give' you my money, fire-arms and a car 'so that you give' me the opportunity to get away from you with a whole skin). It would, however, be difficult to find a sane man who would declare such a compromise to be 'inadmissible on principle', or who would call the compromiser an accomplice of the bandits (even though the bandits might use the car and the fire-arms for further robberies).[3]*

> The conclusion is clear: to reject compromises 'on principle', to reject the permissibility of compromises in general, no matter of what kind, is childishness, which it is difficult even to consider seriously.[4]

To be able to make the right decision about the tactics necessary, to differentiate between justified and unjustified compromises, one needs a revolutionary leadership tempered in struggle.

> Of course, in politics, where it is sometimes a matter of extremely complex relations – national and international – between classes and parties, very many cases will arise that will be much more difficult than the question of a legitimate 'compromise' in a strike or a treacherous 'compromise' by a strike-breaker, treacherous leader, etc. It would be absurd to formulate a recipe or general rule ('No compromises!') to suit all cases. One must use one's own brains and be able to find one's bearings in each particular instance. It is, in fact, one of the functions of a party organization and of party leaders worthy of the name, to acquire, through the prolonged, persistent, variegated and comprehensive efforts of all thinking

---

* It is possible that this analogy drew on Lenin's own experience, when he was robbed by a gang on 19 January 1919, an incident described elsewhere (see pp. 19-20).

representatives of a given class, the knowledge, experience and – in addition to knowledge and experience – the political flair necessary for the speedy and correct solution of complex political problems.[5]

To accept battle at a time when it is obviously advantageous to the enemy, but not to us, is criminal; political leaders of the revolutionary class are absolutely useless if they are incapable of 'changing tack, or offering conciliation and compromise' in order to take evasive action in a patently disadvantageous battle.[6]

The communists cannot avoid resorting to temporary alliances even with the most unreliable and unstable of allies:

To carry on a war for the overthrow of the international bourgeoisie, a war which is a hundred times more difficult, protracted and complex than the most stubborn of ordinary wars between states, and to renounce in advance any change of tack, or any utilization of a conflict of interests (even if temporary) among one's enemies, or any conciliation or compromise with possible allies (even if they are temporary, unstable, vacillating or conditional allies) – is that not ridiculous in the extreme? It is not like making a difficult ascent of an unexplored and hitherto inaccessible mountain and refusing in advance ever to move in zigzags, ever to retrace one's steps, or ever to abandon a course once selected, and to try others?[7]

Communists and Parliamentary Elections

In 1919, while expectations of a successful, direct revolutionary assault on capitalism were very much alive among communist leaders, including Lenin, he dealt very calmly with the question of whether communists should, or should not, participate in parliamentary elections.

In a letter to the Italian, French and German communists written on 10 October 1919, he argued that differences on this question were not of great significance: such

differences are nothing to worry about, they represent growing pains, not senile decay. Bolshevism, too, has experienced differences of this kind more than once, as well as minor breakaways caused by such differences. But at the decisive moment, at the moment of taking power and establishing the Soviet Republic, Bolshevsim was united.[8]

Again on 28 October 1919 Lenin wrote to the Central Committee of the KPD against the expulsion of the ultra-lefts who opposed participation in trade unions and parliament.[9]

When Sylvia Pankhurst, leader of the Workers' Socialist Federation, wrote to Lenin claiming that the majority of the communists in Britain opposed participation in parliamentary elections, Lenin, in his reply, while holding to the position that communists should participate in such activities, added that this was a 'secondary question'. After expressing the wish that a single party should be created – out of the five organizations in Britain claiming to be communist – he suggested an interesting alternative. If no union could be achieved, because of the controversy over the question of parliamentary activity,

> then I should consider a good step forward to complete unity the immediate formation of *two* communist paries . . . Let one of these parties recognize participation in the bourgeois parliament, and the other reject it; this disagreement is now so immaterial that the most reasonable thing would be not to split over it.[10]

Now, in April-May 1920, after the bourgeois victory over the proletarian revolution in central and western Europe, Lenin began to express a new view. *'Left-Wing' Communism* makes it very clear that communists should stand for parliament and be active there. He wrote that, while declaring oneself an opponent of bourgeois democracy, of parliamentarism, one does not necessarily have to draw the conclusion that one cannot use parliament for the purpose of promoting the revolution. Only reformists would argue that one can achieve socialism through parliament. No. Bourgeois parliaments have to be destroyed, dissolved and replaced by working class bodies, soviets. But one should not conclude that parliament cannot be used as a platform for communist work, so long as the communists are not strong enough to overthrow it. For this, of course, it is necessary that the centre of gravity of party struggle be *outside* parliament, i.e. strikes, demonstrations, etc. and that the activity of communist MPs should be subordinated to this mass work.

Lenin directly tackles the argument of the ultra-lefts that parliamentarism is 'historically obsolete':

That is true in the propaganda sense. However, everybody knows that this is still a far cry from overcoming it in *practice*. Parliamentarism is of course 'historically obsolete' to the communists; but – and that is the whole point – we must *not* regard what is obsolete *to us* as something obsolete to a class, to the masses . . . You must not sink to the level of the masses, to the level of the backward strata of the class. That is incontestable. You must tell them the bitter truth. You are in duty bound to call their bourgeois-democratic and parliamentary prejudices what they are – prejudices. But at the same time you must *soberly* follow the *actual* state of the class-consciousness and preparedness of the entire class (not only of its communist vanguard), and of all the *working people* (not only of their advanced elements).

So long as masses of workers have illusions in parliament,

> participation in parliamentary elections and in the struggle on the parliamentary rostrum is *obligatory* on the party of the revolutionary proletariat, *specifically* for the purpose of educating the backward strata of *its own class*, and for the purpose of awakening and enlightening the undeveloped, downtrodden and ignorant rural *masses*. Whilst you lack the strength to do away with bourgeois parliaments and every other type of reactionary institution you *must* work within them.[11]

The proletarian masses will learn the real nature of bourgeois parliamentarism only by practical experience.

> Propaganda and agitation alone are not enough for an entire class, the broad masses of the working people, those oppressed by capital, to take up such a stand. For that, the masses must have their own political experience.[12]

Lenin goes on to refer to the Bolsheviks' attitude to the election to the constituent assembly after the victory of the October revolution – as proof that one must go through the parliamentary experience with the masses in order to free them from parliamentary illusions:

> did we, the Russian Bolsheviks, not have *more* right than any western communists to consider that parliamentarianism was politically obsolete in Russia? Of course we did, for the point is not whether bourgeois parliaments have existed for a long time or a short time, but how far the masses of the working

people are *prepared* (ideologically, politically and practically) to accept the Soviet system and to dissolve the bourgeois-democratic parliament (or allow it to be dissolved). It is an absolutely incontestable and fully established historical fact that, in September-November 1917, the urban working class and the soldiers and peasants of Russia were, because of a number of special conditions, exceptionally well prepared to accept the Soviet system and to disband the most democratic of bourgeois parliaments. Nevertheless, the Bolsheviks did *not* boycott the Constituent Assembly, but took part in the elections both before *and after* the proletariat conquered political power . . . these elections yielded exceedingly valuable (and to the proletariat, highly useful) political results.

Lenin concludes:

participation in a bourgeois-democratic parliament, even a few weeks before the victory of a Soviet republic and even *after* such a victory, actually helps that proletariat to *prove* to the backward masses why such parliaments deserve to be done away with; it *facilitates* their successful dissolution, and *helps* to make bourgeois parliamentarianism 'politically obsolete'.[13]

Communists and the Trade Unions

Lenin's pamphlet deals with the question of the trade unions. He ridicules the 'childish nonsense' of those who argue that communists should withdraw from the existing trade unions:

To refuse to work in the reactionary trade unions means leaving the insufficiently developed or backward masses of workers under the influence of the reactionary leaders.

Revolutionaries

must absolutely *work wherever the masses are to be found.* You must be capable of any sacrifice, of overcoming the greatest obstacles, in order to carry on agitation and propaganda systematically, perseveringly, persistently and patiently in those institutions, societies and associations – even the most reaction-ary – in which proletarian or semi-proletarian masses are to be found . . . We must be able . . . to make any sacrifice, and even – if need be – to resort to various stratagems, artifices and illegal methods, to evasions and subterfuges, as long as we get into the trade unions, remain in them, and carry on communist work within them at all costs.[14]

Lenin uses the experience of Bolshevism to support his argument:

> Under Tsarism we had no 'legal opportunities' whatsoever until 1905. However, when Zubatov, agent of the secret police, organized Black-Hundred workers' assemblies and workingmens' societies for the purpose of trapping revolutionaries and combating them, we sent members of our party to these assemblies and into these societies.[15]

Communist Leadership must be Tempered

> A revolutionary leadership [I have written elsewhere] needs not only an understanding of the struggle as a whole, but the capacity to put forward the right slogans at every turning point. These do not derive simply from the party programme, but must fit the circumstances, above all the moods and feelings of the masses, so that they can be used to lead the workers forward. Slogans must be appropriate not only to the general direction of the revolutionary movement, but also to the level of consciousness of the masses. Only through the *application* of the general line of the party does its real value become manifest. The organic unity of general theory and particular tactics was at the heart of Lenin's struggle and work style.[16]

Lenin argued that the leadership of the newly created communist parties should be trained, and trained well, in strategy and tactics.

> politics is a science and an art that does not fall from the skies or come gratis, and . . . if it wants to overcome the bourgeoisie, the proletariat must train its *own* proletarian 'class politicians', of a kind in no way inferior to bourgeois politicians.[17]

The communists must be trained in a *general variety* of methods of struggle.

> History, as a whole, and the history of revolutions in particular, is always richer in content, more varied, more multiform, more lively and ingenious than is imagined by even the best parties, the most class-conscious vanguards of the most advanced classes. This can readily be understood, because even the finest of vanguards express the class-consciousness, will, passion and imagination of tens of thousands, whereas at moments of great upsurge and the exertion of all human capacities, revolutions are made by the class-consciousness, will, passion and imagination of tens of millions, spurred on

by a most acute struggle of classes. Two very important practical conclusions follow from this: first, that in order to accomplish its task the revolutionary class must be able to master *all* forms or aspects of social activity without exception . . . second, that the revolutionary class must be prepared for the most rapid and brusque replacement of one form by another.

One will readily agree that any army which does not train to use all the weapons, all the means and methods of warfare that the enemy possesses, or may possess, is behaving in an unwise or even criminal manner. This applies to politics even more than it does to the art of war. In politics it is even harder to know in advance which methods of struggle will be applicable and to our advantage in certain future conditions. Unless we learn to apply all the methods of struggle, we may suffer grave and sometimes even decisive defeat, if changes beyond our control in the position of the other classes bring to the forefront a form of activity in which we are especially weak.[18]

Practical Advice

In looking through Lenin's writings and speeches during 1919 and 1920, one is impressed with how much time and attention he devoted to the problems facing various communist parties, despite the fact that as head of the soviet state and party he was continually faced with the gravest and most urgent political, economic and military problems. He followed closely the fierce arguments about programme and tactics which frequently broke out among the newly formed communist groups outside Russia. He also concerned himself with the minutest details of the revolutionary movement in other countries.

He was anxious not only to give *general* advice to the young communist parties, but to be as concrete, as specific, as he could. As an example, one can quote his message to the Bavarian Soviet Republic of 27 April 1919:

What measures have you taken to fight the bourgeois executioners, the Scheidemanns and co.; have councils of workers and servants been formed in the different sections of the city; have the workers been armed; have the bourgeoisie been disarmed; has use been made of the stocks of clothing and other items for immediate and extensive aid to the workers, and especially to the farm labourers and small peasants; have the capitalist factories and wealth in Munich and the capitalist farms in its environs been confiscated; have mortgage and rent payments by small peasants been cancelled; have the wages of farm labourers and unskilled workers been doubled or trebled; have all paper stocks and all printing-presses been confiscated so as to enable popular leaflets and newspapers to be printed for the masses; has the six-hour working day with two- or three-hour instruction in state administration been introduced; have the bourgeoisie in Munich been made to give up surplus housing so that workers may be immediately moved into comfortable flats; have you taken over all the banks; have you taken hostages from the ranks of the bourgeoisie; have you introduced higher rations for the workers than for the bourgeoisie; have all the workers been mobilized for defence and for ideological propaganda in the neighbouring villages? The most urgent and most extensive implementation of these and similar measures, coupled with the initiative of workers', farm labourers' and – acting apart from them – small peasants' councils, should strengthen your position. An emergency tax must be levied on the bourgeoisie, and an actual improvement effected in the condition of the workers, farmer labourers and small peasants at once at all costs.[19]

What an amazing grasp of tactical details!

The Second Congress of the Comintern

The Second Congress of the Comintern began on 19 July and ended on 7 August 1920. It was a far larger affair than the First Congress, which lasted only five days, and had 217 delegates representing 35 countries. There were delegates from three mass communist parties outside Russia: Italy, Norway and Bulgaria; from the very significant Communist Party of Germany, as well as the small Communist Parties of Austria and Hungary. There was a delegation from the Socialist Left in Czechoslavakia. Representatives of the German USPD and the French Socialists were present for the purpose of negotiations. Delegates representing the supporters of the Comintern in France and the various British and American groups were also present. Finally, the most important Asiatic countries were represented, with the Indian M.N.Roy as the outstanding person among them. It was a world congress, although still weighted heavily in the direction of the European parties.

The Congress faithfully reflected Lenin's concerns in 'Left-Wing' Communism: an Infantile Disorder: parliamentarism, the role of the Communist Party, trade unions, policy towards the (British) Labour Party, were all put on the agenda for debate. The only important issues at the Congress not dealt with in the pamphlet were the agrarian question and the national question.

Throughout the Second Congress Lenin was very active, writing many important documents and participating in many debates, both in committees and at the congress plenum. Trotsky was busy on the military front, and managed to appear at the congress only briefly twice: once to endorse the 21 conditions, and then at the end of the congress to present the manifesto he had written on behalf of the International.

Lenin wrote the original text of the theses of the congress on the national and colonial question, the agrarian question, the basic tasks of the Second Congress, conditions for admission to the International, the world situation and the tasks of the Comintern.

He also delivered many speeches. At the first session on 19 July he presented the report on the world situation and the tasks of the International. On 23 July, at the second session, he gave a speech on the role of the communist parties. On 26 July he delivered the report of the committee on the national and colonial issue. On 30 July he discussed the terms for admission to the International. On 2 August he spoke on the problem of parliament, and on 6 August on whether British communists should join the Labour Party. He participated in all the key commissions that took place before, during and after the congress. He talked with more foreign delegates than on any other occasion in his life.

Revolutionary Ecstasy

The Second Congress of the Comintern met in the excitement of the Red Army advance on Warsaw. The Red Army was carrying with it the hope that a connection would be made with the German revolutionary proletariat which would facilitate the spread of the revolution into central Europe. Confidence in the immediacy of revolutionary victory was a theme throughout the Congress. All eyes were on the Red Army. The USPD delegate, Däuming, said to the Congress: 'Every kilometre which the Red Army covers is a spur to revolution, a step towards the revolution in Germany.'[20]

> Zinoviev, who presided at the Congress, afterwards described the scene. In the Congress hall hung a large map. Every day we marked on it the advance of our armies, and every day the delegates stood with breathless interest examining the map . . . All of them realized that if the military objective of our armies was achieved it would mean an immense acceleration of the international proletarian revolution. All of them understood that on every step forward of our Red Army depended in the literal sense of the word the fate of the international proletarian revolution.[21]

The impact of the march on Warsaw permeated Zinoviev's opening speech to the Congress, in which he declared his conviction that the victory of the European revolution was a matter of a year or so. He said:

> Comrades, in an article which was written immediately after the founding congress of the Communist International and bears the title 'The Prospects of the International revolution', I said with some over-enthusiasm that perhaps only a year would pass before we forgot that in Europe a struggle had been waged about Soviet power, since this struggle would already have ended in Europe and been transferred to the remaining countries. A bourgeois German professor fastened onto this sentence. and . . . remarks maliciously: Well, soon the 2nd Congress will be opened. More than a year has passed. In Europe, as it seems, it has not yet come to the full victory of the Soviet power.
> To this we can easily answer this educated bourgeois; it is indeed really so; it will probably take not one year, but two or three for the whole of Europe to become the Soviet Republic.[22]

> I shall allow myself to express the hope that we will have the Soviet Republic in France by the fiftieth anniversary of the Paris Commune.[23]

The anniversary of the Commune was in March 1921.

Zinoviev was not the only exuberant person at the congress. As one British delegate remembered: 'The congress closed on 7 August 1920, amidst scenes of tremendous enthusiasm . . . There would be another congress in a year's time, and who knew how far the revolution would have swept the world by then?'[24]

A Battle on Two Fronts

The congress was not only an enthusiastic event. It was also a very serious one. It was by far the most important school of strategy and tactics the labour movement had ever had.

While *'Left-Wing' Communism: an Infantile Disorder* directed its attack against the ultra-lefts, the congress had to act on two fronts: not only against the 'Lefts', but even more strongly against the 'Centrists' on the right. With hundreds of thousands becoming members of the Comintern, with whole parties joining *en bloc*, one of the central tasks faced by the leadership was the struggle against centrist leadership.

Centrism by its nature lacks clear definition. It covers a whole variety of tendencies and groupings ranging from reformism to Marxism. One of the main characteristics of centrists is their obscuring of the need for a clear demarcation between the vanguard of the class and the mass. Centrism's main drawback is its historical fatalism. Because it is so indefinite in nature, so lacking in a clear, sharp, character, because it vacillates between Marxism and reformism, centrist groupings do not all move in the same direction. Some move leftwards towards Marxism, some rightwards towards reformism. In addition, lacking consistency as they do, centrists sometimes move first to the left, and later veer to the right.[25]

At the Second Congress Lenin saw as the main danger for the young, inexperienced communist parties the centrist leadership predominant in a number of them. He drew a distinction between the centrism of workers coming from social democracy and the incurable professional centrism of many leaders.

The nature of the leadership of some contemporary

European communist parties may be gathered from a description given by Bukharin at the Second Congress:

> Let's take the Italian party and its parliamentary faction. This party belongs to us and is in the Communist International. It is one of our best parties, and we can maintain: If we were to divide the members of this parliamentary faction into three parts . . . we would get the following figures: 30 per cent of the whole faction belong to the Turati tendency, 55 per cent to the centre and 15 per cent to the left . . . If we look at the French party, we have the following figures: 69 parliamentarians, among them 40 open reformists within the already opportunist party and 26 from the centre – not in our sense of the word, but the word here means the centre of the French party – that is, centre squared. As concerns the communists, well they have perhaps two votes. In the Norwegian party, which is quite a good party, the parliamentary faction has 19 members. Of these about 11 are right, 6 centre and 2 are communists. The Swedish parliamentary faction has quite a number of comrades who should in no way be described as communists.[26]

The Debate on Parliamentarism

In the debate on parliamentarism at the congress Lenin had to tackle both the ultra-lefts, who opposed any participation in parliamentary activities, and the centrists, who suffered from 'opportunist parliamentarism'.

The main vocal opposition came from the left. Thus, for instance, Amadeo Bordiga from Italy declared: 'In the present period of history . . . there is no possible way in which the parliamentary rostrum can be used to advance the revolutionary task of the Communists.'[27]

A similar position was taken by the Swiss: 'The Swiss Communist Party rejects any participation in bourgeois parliaments.'[28] The Communist Party of Austria also came out in favour of boycotting all parliamentary elections, as did the Hungarian leaders, George Lukacs and Bela Kun, who arrived in Vienna after the fall of the Hungarian Soviet republic; also William Gallacher of the British shop stewards' movement, and Souchy, the German syndicalist.

Less vocal at the congress, but far more influential and

dangerous, were the centrists. Hence the main attack of the Theses on Parliamentarism introduced by the ECCI was directed against centrism, and against parliamentary reformism.

After elections, the organization of the parliamentary fraction must be completely in the hands of the central committee of the Communist Party, whether or not the party as a whole is at the time legal or illegal. The chairman and presidium of the communist parliamentary fraction must be confirmed in their office by the Central Committee. The Central Committee must have a permanent representative in the fraction, with the right of veto and, on all important political questions, the fraction must seek in advance guidance from the party Central Committee. The Central Committee has the right and the duty, when the communist fraction in parliament is about to undertake an important step, to appoint or to contest the spokesman for the fraction and to require that the outline of his speech or the speech itself be submitted for approval by the Central Committee, etc. Every communist candidate must officially give a written undertaking that he is ready to resign from parliament at the first request of the party Central Committee, so that in any given situation resignation from parliament can be carried out in unison . . .
A communist member of parliament is obliged, on the decision of the Central Committee, to combine legal with illegal work . . .
Communist deputies must subordinate all their activities in parliament to party action outside parliament. Demonstrative legislative proposals should be regularly submitted on the instructions of the party and its Central Committee, not with the idea that they will be accepted by the bourgeois majority, but for purposes of propaganda, agitation and organization . . .
Every communist member of parliament must bear in mind that he is not a legislator seeking agreement with other legislators, but a party agitator sent into the enemy camp to execute party decisions. The communist deputy is responsible not to the loose mass of the electors, but to his communist party, legal or illegal.
The speeches of communist deputies in parliament must be readily understandable to every ordinary worker, every peasant, every washerwoman, every shepherd, so that the party can issue his speeches as leaflets for distribution in every corner of the country.'[29]

The Trade Union Issue

The question on whether communists should participate in existing trade unions led by reformists was also debated at the Second Congress.

This debate was much sharper than on the question of the attitude of communists to parliamentary activity. After all, there were at the time very few communists in Parliament, while all, or practically all, communist activists were affected by the question of work in the trade unions. The argument was long and vigorous. The delegates from Britain and the United States argued that it was impossible to win the reformist trade unions to communism, and that communists should therefore form new unions. The commission to which the theses were referred held six long sessions, but the conflict was unresolved. When the question came before the congress again, the discussion was ended by a motion of closure proposed by Zinoviev, which was passed by 50 votes to 25. The Theses, following Lenin's arguments in 'Left-Wing' Communism, were carried by 64 votes for, with none against, but 13 abstentions including the British and United States delegates.

The Agrarian Question

The Second Congress adopted theses written by Lenin on the agrarian question and on the national and colonial question. As the overwhelming majority of the population in the colonial countries are peasants, the two are closely connected, the revolutionary potentialities of the one being directly related to the other.

Very early in his political life, Lenin had made a close study of rural life, and in 1900 had elaborated an agrarian programme for Russia. He was also the author of the agrarian programme adopted by the Russian Social Democratic Labour Party in 1903. He thrashed out the agrarian question very thoroughly during the 1905 revolution.[30]

Throughout the development of Bolshevik agrarian policy there were two central points in Lenin's thinking: (1) the working class must lead the peasantry; (2) the workers must be organized separately from the peasants.[31] These were Lenin's guidelines in developing the theses on the agrarian question for the Comintern.

> Only the urban industrial proletariat led by the Communist Party can liberate the working masses of the countryside from the yoke of capital and large landownership . . . On the other hand the industrial workers cannot accomplish their world-historical mission of emancipating humanity from the shackles of capital and war if they shut themselves up within the circle of narrow craft trade unionist interests . . . The proletariat is a genuinely revolutionary class, a class acting in genuinely socialist fashion, only when it comes forward and acts as the vanguard of all working and exploited people, as leader in the struggle for the overthrow of the exploiters. But this cannot be put into effect without the class struggle being carried over on to the land, without rallying the working masses of the countryside, without the Communist Party of the urban proletariat, without the training of the rural by the urban proletariat.

In the countryside the only support for communism came from the agricultural workers and the rural poor. The revolutionary proletariat cannot win the wholehearted support of the middle peasants.

> The revolutionary proletariat cannot undertake, at least in the immediate future and in the early stage of the proletarian dictatorship, to attract this group to its side. Rather it must restrict itself to the job of neutralizing them, that is, preventing them from giving active help to the bourgeoisie in their struggle with the proletariat.

To overcome exploitation in the countryside, agriculture has to be organized in large farms. But one has to be *very sensitive* to peasants' prejudices when one tries to introduce these:

> In the most advanced capitalist countries the Communist International recognizes that it is correct to maintain the majority of large-scale agricultural undertakings and to run them on the lines of the state farms in Russia. It will also be appropriate to encourage the formation of collective undertakings (cooperative estates, communes) . . .
> In countries and regions where large-scale agriculture is of comparatively insignificant proportions, but where there are large

numbers of small peasant proprietors who hope to receive land, the division among them of the land of the large proprietors will be the most certain means of winning the peasantry for the revolution.[32]

Lenin had to fight hard to defend the last part of the theses. The USPD delegate, Crispien, accused the Soviet government of a 'direct relapse into long outworn petty bourgeois ways of thought', and demanded that 'the landed proprietors should be dispossessed and their land handed over to cooperative associations.'[33]

Similar arguments against the theses were used by the Italian centrist leader Serrati.[34] Lenin, using the example of the catastrophic agrarian policy of the Hungarian Soviet government, won the day only after a very heated debate.

The National and Colonial Question

Lenin raised the national and colonial question to a central place in the debate at the congress – a thing that had never happened in the Second International.

> The vast majority of the world's population, over a thousand million, perhaps even 1,250 million people, if we take the total population of the world as 1,750 millions, in other words, about 70 per cent of the world's population, belong to the oppressed nations, which are either in a state of direct colonial dependence or are semi-colonies, as, for example, Persia, Turkey and China.

The national movements in the colonies have to be given full support by the communists in the oppressing countries.

> the Communist International's entire policy on the national and the colonial questions should rest primarily on a closer union of the proletarians and the working masses of all nations and countries for a joint revolutionary struggle to overthrow the landowners and the bourgeoisie. This union alone will guarantee victory over capitalism, without which the abolition of national oppression and inequality is impossible . . .
> all communist parties should render direct aid to the revolutionary movements among the dependent and underprivileged nations (for example Ireland, the American negroes, etc.) and in the colonies.

However, this does not mean seeing the national liberation struggles themselves as socialist struggles. There is

> the need for a determined struggle against attempts to give a communist colouring to bourgeois-democratic liberation trends in the backward countries; the Communist International should support bourgeois-democratic national movements in colonial and backward countries only on condition that, in these countries, the elements of future proletarian parties, which will be communist not only in name, are brought together and trained to understand their special tasks, i.e. those of the struggle against the bourgeois-democratic movements within their own nations. The Communist International must enter into a temporary alliance with bourgeois democracy in the colonial and backward countries, but should not merge with it, and should under all circumstances uphold the independence of the proletarian movement even if it is in its most embryonic form.[35]

And what was the prospect for these countries? The material basis of socialism, developed industry and a high productivity of labour, did not exist in them. The human basis of socialism, a modern working class, was weak or even absent. Must they then follow the path taken by the advanced countries, the path of capitalism? Lenin's answer was a conditional negative.

> If the victorious revolutionary proletariat conducts systematic propaganda among them, and the soviet governments come to their aid with all the means at their disposal – in that event it will be mistaken to assume that the backward peoples must inevitably go through the capitalist stage of development . . . with the aid of the proletariat of the advanced countries, backward countries can go over to the soviet system and, through certain stages of development, to communism, without having to pass through the capitalist stage.*[36]

---

* In his careful, conditional evaluation of revolutionary possibilities in backward countries, Lenin was, by the way, following in the tradition of Karl Marx and Friedrich Engels, who had written in 1882 regarding Russia: 'can the Russian *obshchina* [a form of primitive communal ownership] . . . pass directly to the higher form of communist common ownership? Or, on the contrary, must it first pass through the same process

(continued overleaf)

If Asia, Africa and Latin America were taken in isolation, then capitalism still had the possibility of long development. But the colonies were closely tied to the metropolitan countries, and their fate was intimately linked with the fate of these. In recognition of the importance of the national struggle, Lenin even sanctioned the modification of the *Communist Manifesto's* central exhortation to read 'Workers of all countries and all oppressed peoples, unite!'[38]

The theses on the national and colonial question were approved by the congress with three abstentions.

The 21 Conditions

One characteristic of centrism is its vagueness. Hence centrists cannot tolerate a clear *discipline*. No party which contains a revolutionary wing, a reformist wing and a centrist swamp in between can in practice be a disciplined organization, as each tendency has fundamentally divergent aims. Lenin therefore decided to resort to organizational means in order to fight the centrist leaderships. The result was the 21 conditions for membership of the Comintern.

At the beginning of the congress the Executive Committee of the Communist International published a list of 19 conditions to serve as a basis for discussion. Lenin wrote the draft. The preamble stated:

> Aware that the Second International is beyond hope, the intermediate parties and groups of the 'centre' are trying to find support in the Communist International, which is steadily gaining in strength. At the same time, however, they hope to retain a degree of 'autonomy' that will enable them to pursue their previous opportunist or 'centrist' policies. The Communist International is, to a certain extent, becoming the vogue . . .

---

of dissolution as constitutes the historical evolution of the west?
'The only answer to that possible today is this: If the Russian revolution becomes the signal for a proletarian revolution in the west, so that both complement each other, the present Russia common ownership of land may serve as the starting point for a communist development.'[37]

In certain circumstances, the Communist International may be faced with the danger of dilution by the influx of wavering and irresolute groups that have not as yet broken with their Second International ideology . . .

In view of all this, the Second World Congress deems it necessary to lay down absolutely precise terms for the admission of new parties, and also to set forth the obligations incurred by the parties already affiliated.[39]

The terms of admission may be summed up as follows:

Point 1 demanded that the party press must be edited by reliable communists, must consistently spread the idea of the dictatorship of the proletariat, and must relentlessly expose the bourgeoisie and the reformists.

Point 2 required the removal from office of all 'reformists and centrists' – including the party organization, editorial board, trade unions, parliamentary groups, etc.

Point 3 called for organization of both legal and illegal party work in all countries.

Point 4 Dealt with the need for systematic propaganda work in the army, including the need to organize communist cells in it.

Point 5 called for systematic work in the rural districts of each country.

Point 6 called for an attack on social patriotism and social pacifism, and the need to argue that only 'the revolutionary overthrow of capitalism . . . will save mankind from new imperialist wars'.

Point 7 expanded on 'the need for a complete and absolute break with reformism and centrist policies'.

Point 8 called on communists to support the struggle of colonial peoples against imperialism.

Point 9 declared it the duty of all parties to conduct systematic work in the trade unions, cooperative organizations and other mass organizations.

Point 10 dealt with the need to oppose the Amsterdam (Social-Democratic) Trade Union International and to call for a break with it.

Point 11-14 sought to tighten central party control over all fields of work. The Central Committee of each party must re-examine the composition of its parliamentary group, eliminate unreliable elements and subordinate these groups to its control. The Central Committee must have complete control over all the publications of the party. 'Communist parties in countries where communists can conduct their work legally must carry out periodic membership purges (re-registrations) with the aim of systematically ridding the party of petty-bourgeois elements that inevitably percolate into them.'

Point 15 obliged each party to give every possible aid to any Soviet republic in the struggle against counter-revolution.

Point 16 specified that the communist parties must draw up new programmes, 'in the spirit of communist internationalism', and must submit these programmes for ratification to a future congress of the Comintern or its executive.

Point 17 dealt with the question of how far decisions should be centralized in the International and how far local conditions should be taken into account.

All decisions of the Communist International's congresses and of its Executive Committee are binding on all affiliated parties. Operating in conditions of acute civil war, the Communist International must be far more centralized than the Second International was. It stands to reason, however, that in every aspect of their work the Communist International and its Executive Committee must take into account the diversity of conditions in which the respective parties have to fight and work, and adopt decisions binding on all parties only on matters in which such decisions are possible.

Point 18 required all parties to adopt the name 'Communist' and emphasized that this was not merely a formal point, but necessary to underline the radical abyss between it and Social Democracy.

Point 19 called upon member parties to summon special congresses immediately to approve the work of the Second Congress.[40]

As a result of the debate at the congress, two further points were added:

Point 20 required that all parties must be reorganized so

that 2/3 of each party's Central Committee would be people who had endorsed the Third International before the Second Congress.

Point 21 provided that all who voted against accepting the conditions at future congresses of the communist parties in the various countries should be expelled.[41]

The 21 Conditions were accepted by the congress almost unanimously: there were only two votes against.

Zinoviev, in summing up the work of the Second Congress, said: 'Just as it is not easy for a camel to pass through the eye of a needle, so, I hope, it will not be easy for the adherents of the centre to slip through the 21 conditions.'[42]

As we shall see, this was easier said than done: there were various ways of circumventing these conditions in a number of national parties. The Dutch Wijnkoop was right when he said: 'What is a piece of paper to an opportunist? He will sign it if he has to, and he will still do what he wants to do. He is always two-faced and speaks with two tongues.'[43]

Following the Second Congress, the majority of the USPD in Germany, the French SP, the SP of Czechoslovakia, a minority of the Italian SP, the large Bulgarian, Yugoslav and Norwegian parties and the tiny Dutch, Austrian, Hungarian and other parties, accepted the 21 conditions.

18
Lenin, Bolshevism and the Comintern

In the last chapter we saw how the congresses of the Comintern were schools of strategy and tactics. How effective they were depended not only on the quality of the teachers, but also on the background, the level of preparation and the quality of the pupils. In the Comintern Lenin, Trotsky and other Russian leaders on the whole played the part of teachers, and the leaders of other communist parties were the pupils. The latter brought to the International their own national traits, and their own traditions. How far these facilitated or hindered their assimilation of Bolshevism was crucial to the fate of the International.

Before dealing with the central question of the relationship between Bolshevism and the national characteristics of the newly formed communist parties, we shall have to ask: how well prepared was Lenin for the task of leading the International?

For all his mastery of revolutionary strategy and tactics, his vast experience in teaching and training Russian revolutionaries, Lenin had certain shortcomings when it came to training leaders in western and central Europe. His experience in this field was very small. During his long years of exile before the outbreak of the world war, Lenin never became involved in the local labour movement, whether in England, Switzerland, France or Poland. During the first twenty-five years of his prolific career as a writer, he wrote only a couple of articles for readers outside Russia; and these were to defend the Bolsheviks from criticisms by Russian opponents published in the foreign press. All Lenin's efforts were concentrated on building and leading a revolutionary party in Russia, and this had its disadvantages. Again, the fact that until the outbreak of the 1914 war Lenin had *never* criticized Karl Kautsky or the German Social Democratic Party shows that he did not appreciate the strength of the hold of reformism and opportunism over the labour movement in western and central Europe. The same unawareness is shown by Lenin's overoptimistic expectation in 1918 and 1919 of victory for the proletarian revolution in Europe, even though there were no mass communist parties, and certainly no experienced ones, in existence.

This weakness of Lenin's, however, was relatively insignificant in influencing the fate of the Comintern, compared with a far more fundamental factor: the tradition of the labour movements in western and central Europe. The history of Lenin's Comintern repeatedly demonstrated the correctness of Marx's dictum that 'the tradition of all the dead generations weighs like a mountain on the mind of the living'.

Again and again the observer of the development of the Communist International in its first few years is struck by the cleavage between the strategic and tactical decisions of its congresses – especially the second and third – and the actual policies of its national sections. The experience of the first four years of the Comintern showed that there were many difficulties in combining Bolshevism with the international labour movement.

Direct Experience is Fundamental

Bolshevism was formed during long and bitter years of struggle. Its character was shaped by the experience of the 1905 revolution, the period of reaction that followed it, and the later revolutionary upsurge; by operating illegally and in the Duma, in the heat of numerous industrial and political strikes, offensive and defensive battles, insurrection and civil war. It matured through extended ideological and political struggle, and by an analysis of its own experience, including its mistakes. It had to fight against both the centrist Mensheviks and the ultra-lefts in its own ranks, at the same time as it was struggling with the real problems of life in Russia. In this process an independent, self-reliant leadership was selected, tested and forged.

A party always learns primarily from its *own* experience. Clearly, this does not mean that the experience of other countries or other parties is irrelevant. On the contrary. The Bolsheviks assimilated the experience of the great French revolution, of the 1848 revolution, and of the Paris Commune. But this assimilation meant using the international experience in the struggle of the Russian workers themselves. The experience of the 1905 revolution was fundamental to the genuine assimilation by the Bolsheviks of the international revolutionary experience. The problems of the international labour movement were examined and absorbed in the light of the revolutionary lessons of the struggle of the Russian proletariat itself.

With the founding of the Comintern, many came to believe that revolutionary tactics and strategy, as well as the function and selection of cadres and leaders, could be learned primarily from the experience of others – in this case the Russian party. Of course the International could help the sharing of experience between countries, thus reducing the training costs of any national party. But every party must pay by its own struggle for the lessons learnt.

The Second Congress of the Comintern declared: 'The Communist International must, in fact and indeed, be a single communist party of the entire world. The parties working in the various countries are but its separate sections.'[1] In order to have a really united international party, one must be able to transmit experience effectively from one country to another. The history of the Comintern shows this to be extremely difficult.

An obstacle to the transfer of revolutionary experience from the Russian Bolsheviks, the vanguard of world revolution, to the parties in central and western Europe was the latter's native traditions.

For decades the European working class had been trained in a reformist spirit, in legal parliamentary and trade union activities. Unlike the Russian class, it had not experienced illegal activity, armed conflict and insurrection, or a revolution. The communist parties of central and western Europe were inevitably weighed down by the traditions of their parliamentary and opportunist past. Although they reacted against this past, this did not mean that they were necessarily successful in assimilating the theoretical principles of communism and revolutionary method of struggle. In fact, the pressure of revolutionary feeling among the masses, brought to communism numerous elements imbued with bureaucratic, parliamentary and reformist traditions.

Even the best leaders of the western European communist parties were not absolutely immune to the traditions of gradualism. Thus the great revolutionary, Rosa Luxemburg, did not completely free herself from a fatalistic approach to the fundamental tasks of the revolution, but was influenced by the pressure of German Social Democracy and the trade union bureaucracy. The weakness of Rosa Luxemburg's group, the Spartacists, as Broué wrote, was certainly a reflection of that of Social Democracy as it developed before the 1914-1918 war. Social Democracy was a society within a society, it was perfectly integrated into capitalism, opposing it in principle, but in practice adapted to it. Social Democracy offered experience, responsiblities and jobs, not to those who were capable of making history with the workers, but only those who wished to make politics by using them . . . The communist leaders who had emerged from the ranks of pre-war Social Democracy bore its imprint in their tendency towards passivity and propensity for tailism.'[2]

As the Communist International was recruited from centrist elements which had moved to the left – not only individuals and groups, but also entire parties with their old leadership or parts of it – the influence of bourgeois public opinion on the upper layers of the party, felt through material, social and political links, was substantial. One characteristic of reformist politicians with their roots in bourgeois society has been their capacity for adaptation, and manœuvring. As Rosmer, a very keen observer, wrote about the behaviour of the French Communist leaders at the Second Congress of the Comintern and after:

> The Russian communists had drawn [the 21 conditions for admission to the Comintern] up meticulously . . . These Draconian conditions would form such a formidable barrier that the opportunists would never be able to pass through it. They were soon to see that this was an illusion . . . they didn't and couldn't know the lengths to which these men would go with their skilful manœuvres, for they had received their training in the practices of parliamentary democracy. They could pull more tricks out of the bag than the suspicious Russians could ever imagine. The secretary of the French Communist Party, Frossard, for example, was going to spend two years giving them a lesson in the art of evasion.[3]

Given the adaptability of the old leadership, and the lack of authentic revolutionary experience, the danger that new communist leaders would identify Bolshevism with 'cleverness', with manœuvring, was very great indeed. As Rosmer noted about Lenin's book 'Left-Wing' Communism: an Infantile Disorder, approvingly quoting a Belgian Communist leader:

'What a dangerous book,' he said to me; 'with Lenin there's no risk, because he will always use a manœuvre in favour of the working class, and any compromise he makes will be in its interests. But remember the young communists – and even some who aren't all that young any more – who have no practical experience of workers' struggles . . . They will take only the secondary points out of this manual, because that is what is easiest and most convenient for them. They won't bother with the work and study necessary. Since they don't have a solid socialist base to support manœuvres and compromises, they will tend to see these as the essence of the matter, and find an easy justification for all their actions.'

Rosmer adds: 'We didn't have long to wait to see that this danger was by no means imaginary: the "Zinovievist Bolshevization" undertaken immediately after Lenin's death saw it raising its head in every section of the International, and with Stalin, "communism" itself was reduced to the level of a manœuvre.'[1]

The strength of Bolshevism lay not mainly in its tactical adaptability, but in its rigid, principled nature. Elsewhere I wrote:

> Lenin believed in improvization. But in order for this not to degenerate into simply shifting impressions of the day, it had to be blended into a *general perspective* based on well thought-out theory.[5]

The two basic themes in his theory of the party were: first, adherence to firm principles, involving a willingness to accept for a time the position of being a tiny minority in the working class; and secondly, the closest possible relationship with the mass of the workers by providing a practical, i.e. adaptable, leadership in every struggle involving them. Only one's own struggle enables a person or a party to assimilate both. A revolutionary party must not only be able to translate the ideas of Marx and Lenin into the language of Germany, France or Italy, but must also learn to translate into the language of Marxism the suffering, aspirations and hopes of the German, French or Italian proletariat. This requires a great deal of application and experience.

Economic-Social Obstacles

There were also powerful economic and social impediments to the introduction of Bolshevism in European countries outside Russia. Recalling Engels' comment on the bureaucratization of a section of the British working class due to Britain's industrial and colonial monopoly,[6] Lenin argued:

> The receipt of high monopoly profits by the capitalists in one of the numerous branches of industry, in one of the numerous countries, etc., makes it economically possible for them to bribe certain sections of the workers, and for a time a fairly considerable minority of them, and win them to the side of the bourgeoisie.
>
> This stratum of workers-turned-bourgeois, or the labour aristocracy, who are quite philistine in their mode of life, in the size of their earnings, and in their entire outlook, is the principal prop of the Second International, and in our days, the principal *social . . . prop of the bourgeoisie*. For they are the real *agents of the bourgeoisie in the working-class* movement, the labour lieutenants of the capitalist class.[7]

The conclusion of Lenin's analysis of reformism is that its real support arises only in the thin conservative crust of the proletariat, which conceals the revolutionary urges of the masses of the workers.

But the capitalist economy, including monopoly of the market, works in such a way that its benefits, if any, cannot be confined to a single section of the working class. As I wrote elsewhere:

> The first question one has to ask in tackling Lenin's analysis of this: How did the super-profits of, say, British companies in the colonies, lead to the 'throwing of crumbs' to the 'aristocracy of labour' in Britain? The answer to this question invalidates the whole of Lenin's analysis of reformism . . .
>
> No capitalist says to the workers: 'I have made high profits this year, so I am ready to give you higher wages.'
>
> *Imperialism, and the export of capital, can, of course, greatly affect the wages level in the industrial country by giving employment to many workers who produce the machines, rails, locomotives, etc., which made up the real content of the capital exported. This influence on the level of employment obviously affects the wages level generally. But why should it affect only*

the real wages of an 'infinitesimal minority?' Does the increase of employment possibilities, and decline in unemployment, lead to the rise of a small 'aristocracy of labour' while the condition of the masses of the working class is hardly affected at all? Are conditions of more or less full employment conducive to increasing differentials between skilled and unskilled workers? They are certainly not.

One may argue that the high super-profits of the capitalists on their investments in the colonies led to a rise of wages in another way: that the capitalists do not oppose labour laws defending workers' conditions as strongly as they would do if profits were low. This is so. But these laws cannot be said to lead to an increasing differentiation of living standards between the different layers of the working class . . .

Look at simple examples like the prohibition of child labour or limitations on female labour in certain industries. This does not affect the supply and hence wages, in the skilled labour market more than in the unskilled. The limitation of the workday also does not affect the skilled labour market more than the unskilled. Indeed, everything that raises the standard of living of the mass of the workers, unskilled and semi-skilled, *diminishes* the difference between their standards and those of the skilled workers. The higher the general standard of living, including the educational level, the easier is it for unskilled workers to become semi-skilled or skilled. The financial burden of apprenticeship is more easily borne by better-off workers. And the easier it is for workers to learn a skill, the smaller is the wage differential between skilled and unskilled workers.

Again, one can argue that imperialism throws 'crumbs' to workers through the fact that it gets foodstuffs (and raw materials) extremely cheaply from the backward, colonial, countries. But this factor, again, affects the standard of living not only of a minority of the 'aristocracy of labour' but the whole of the working class of the industrial countries. To this extent, by raising general living standards, it *diminishes* differences between sections of this same working class.[8]

The fact that the economic roots of reformism go much deeper than a small layer of the proletariat means that the effort to establish communist hegemony in the west is bound to meet with much greater difficulties than were encountered in Russia, that it demands a hard and prolonged struggle. And of course no mass party – including a communist party – can be completely immune to the influence of ideas current among the masses.

Lenin and his friends in the Russian Communist Party did achieve amazing results in bringing into existence mass parties in a series of countries in a very short period. The Bolshevik leaders could help in the teaching of revolutionary strategy and tactics. But nothing could replace the actual individual experience of parties in struggle. It was impossible to create real communist leadership overnight, and to do this on the basis of a working class which had for decades been absorbing a reformist spirit moulded in the environment of gradually expanding capitalism, with its by-product of improvements in workers' living conditions. The question of *timing*, of whether enough time would be granted by history and by the Communist International leadership for the leaders of national parties to learn by experience, therefore became crucial.

Russian Hegemony in the International

As the Russian revolution was the first victorious proletarian revolution, Lenin quite rightly took it for granted that it should be seen as a model for subsequent revolutions. Thus he wrote in his pamphlet, *The Proletarian Revolution and the Renegade Kautsky*:

> Bolshevism *has created* the ideological and tactical foundations of a Third International, of a really proletarian and Communist International, which will take into consideration both the gains of the tranquil epoch and the experience of the *epoch of revolutions, which has begun* . . . Bolshevism has indicated the right road of escape from the horrors of war and imperialism . . . Bolshevism *can serve as a model of tactics for all*.[9]

However, Lenin was firmly convinced that the hegemony of Russian communism was only a temporary phenomenon – to continue only so long as the revolution was limited to Russia. In his article 'The Third International and its Place in History', written in April 1919 and published in the first issue of the Comintern journal, Lenin stressed the transitory nature of Russian hegemony in the international labour movement. 'Leadership in the revolutionary proletarian International has passed for a time

– for a short time, it goes without saying – to the Russians, just as at various periods of the nineteenth century it was in the hands of the British, then of the French, then of the Germans.'[10] He hastened to add that one must not copy mechanically from the Russian experience:

> It is now essential that communists in every country should quite consciously take into account . . . the *concrete features* which [the] struggle assumes and must inevitably assume in each country, in conformity with the specific character of its economics, politics, culture, and national composition . . . its colonies, religious divisions, and so on and so forth.[11]

To the extent that the *only* party in the Comintern that had won power and held it was the Russian party, it was natural for it to be regarded as a giant among dwarfs, with unlimited prestige and authority. Having failed to make a revolution themselves, the German, French, Italian and other communist leaders could not help but see extraordinary qualities in the Russians who had succeeded. 'The Russians led the dance, and their superiority was so obvious that this was quite legitimate,' wrote Victor Serge. 'The only figure in Western socialism that was capable of equalling them, or even perhaps of surpassing them so far as intelligence and the spirit of freedom were concerned, was Rosa Luxemburg, and she had been battered to death with a revolver butt in January 1919 by German officers.'[12]

Boris Souvarine, one of the main leaders of French communism, said in March 1923:

> Thank you, Bolshevik Party, for making true revolutionaries of us, for delivering us from democratic prejudice, from humanitarian illusions, from reformist errors, by its example creating other parties in its image in all the countries of the world. We will strive to folow its path, to learn from its teaching, and serve, like it, the revolution. We are proud to belong to the world party. It is our greatest pride to have its trust, our greatest hope to be worthy of this.[13]

Such subservience would have been much more appropriate for a yes-man of Zinoviev, or later of Stalin, than an independent-minded revolutionary leader.

The uncritical attitude of communist parties all over the

world towards the Russian party showed itself in every congress of the International. At the first Congress there was only one real debate – about the proposal to set up the International. At the Second, Third and Fourth Congresses, delegates of individual parties – German, French, Italian, etc. – raised points about their respective countries, hardly touching on the Comintern as such. In all the debates the Russian delegates criticized other parties, while the representatives of those parties did not once criticize the Russians. A remark by J.T.Murphy, a delegate to the Second Congress, was well founded: 'When a general or principal question was under consideration, every delegation approached it from the angle of his or her own particular country. Only the Russians showed any real knowledge and sense of internationalism, though frequently they wore Russian spectacles when looking through the international window.[14]

The British delegate, Jack Tanner, said plaintively at the Second Congress of the Comintern: 'I ask the Russians and other representatives whether they do not also have something to learn from the others, that is, that one has to learn from the economic struggles and the revolutionary movement of the other countries and not just teach them.'[15]

Arthur Crispien, a delegate of the USPD, told the Second Congress: 'Only the Russian communists were not criticized. Not one of the other parties was spared.'[16]

The Russians were far more experienced and far more knowledgeable about the western labour movement than the representatives of the other parties were about the international scene; hence the communist leaders genuinely felt inferior to the Russians. For instance, Serrati declared at the Second Congress of the Comintern: 'I haven't felt myself so weak and powerless in any national congress as is the case here in Moscow. In no congress have I seen so much difference. I am not speaking of the epoch and the culture of the people, but of their power. What am I in comparison to Comrade Lenin? He is the leader of the Russian Revolution. And I represent a very small communist socialist party.'[17]

Even when the Russian leaders spoke complete nonsense, they were not criticized by other communist leaders.

No one even protested when Radek lectured the Chinese comrades at the Fourth Congress of the Comintern in hardly more than warmed-up Menshevism:

> 'In the first instance it is the duty of the Chinese comrades to take into consideration all the possibilities of the Chinese movement. You must understand, comrades, that neither the question of socialism, nor of the Soviet Republic are now on the order of the day. Unfortunately, even the historic questions of national unity and of the united national republic are not yet on the order of the day in China. The present state of China reminds us of the eighteenth century in Europe, and especially in Germany, where capitalist development was too weak to allow the establishment of a united national centre.'[18]

At the same Congress, after the speeches of Lenin, Trotsky, Clara Zetkin and Bela Kun on the first five years of the Russian Revolution, there was not a single speech from the floor, not one word of criticism or advice to the Russian comrades!

Lenin and Trotsky, unlike Zinoviev, and in later years Stalin, never hectored or browbeat the foreign communist leaders. They expected them to speak their minds on the affairs of the Russian party as openly as they themselves did about the conditions of their parties. Lenin and Trotsky were not to blame for the fact that the foreign communists lacked the confidence to express themselves directly.

This uncritical attitude towards the Russian party was dangerous. The latter took charge of the whole policy of the Comintern, being given the credit for successes, and completely exonerated for the failures, which were always someone else's fault.

The main reason for the continued passive submission of the foreign communist parties to Russian leadership was the series of defeats inflicted on the international working-class movement. The Russians alone retained the prestige of success. The communist parties were also slow to learn to avoid mistakes resulting either from centrism or from ultra-leftism, and were thus open to continued criticism from Moscow. As a consequence, they absorbed not the Leninist method of criticism and self-criticism, but only the idea that Moscow was always right.

Obsequiousness towards Moscow was also strengthened by a good deal of deference towards the Soviet state. Deference towards a strong state standing above the people is one of the attitudes inculcated by capitalism. Such a psychological trait certainly does not make for independent, self-reliant, revolutionary leadership.

Democratic Centralism and Bureaucratic Fiat

The Comintern saw itself as a world party, not a conglomeration of national parties. This was the organizational expression of the view that the social order superseding capitalism had to be a world order. Given this standpoint, an internal 'general staff' was indispensable to lead the world movement.

The Comintern stressed that its centralism would be consistently democratic. The Fourth Congress condemned 'centralization in the hands of a party bureaucracy of "power" to dominate the other members or the masses of the revolutionary proletariat outside the party'. 'Centralism in the communist party organization is not formal and mechanical but the centralization of communist activity, that is, the formalism of a strong, militant, and at the same time flexible leadership.'[19]

The successful working of democratic centralism on a national or international scale requires a high level of homogeneity in the party, a high level of consciousness, training and also trust between leaders, as well as between all members and the leadership. If 'staff' and 'troops' are well integrated, discipline follows 99 per cent from conviction, and only 1 per cent from mechanical obedience.

Where such conditions do not exist, bureaucratic fiat will inevitably take over. After all no organizational rule can, in practice, rise much higher than the political base on which it rests.

The extreme comparative backwardness of communist leaders outside Russia explains why in practice administrative fiat did play a crucial role in the working of the Comintern. The authority of Moscow was bolstered by administrative measures.

The most immediately striking organizational difference between the First and Second Internationals on the one hand,

and the Third International, was that the former were loose federations of independent national parties, whereas the latter was intended to be strictly centralized.

Supreme authority was vested in the world congress, which was to meet regularly once a year, but between congresses the International was to be run by its elected Executive Committee, which was given extensive powers. As the Statutes of the Comintern, adopted at the Second Congress, state:

> The Executive Committee conducts the entire work of the Communist International from one congress to the next . . . and issues instructions which are binding on all parties and organizations belonging to the Communist International. The Executive Committee of the Communist International has the right to demand that parties belonging to the International shall expel groups or persons who offend against international discipline, and it also has the right to expel from the Communist International those parties which violate decisions of the world congress.[20]

One kind of pressure which Moscow could exert on the sections of the International was finance. Let us compare its situation with earlier international workers' organizations. Of the First International's finances we have taken this sketch:

> the income of the General Council from individual members' subscriptions for the first six years was: 1865 – £23; 1866 – £9 13s; 1867 – £5 17s; 1868 – £14 14s; 1869 – £30 12s; 1870 – £14 14s. The last financial report submitted by Engels to the Hague Congress for the years 1870-2 showed a deficit of 'more than £25' owed by the General Council to 'members of the General Council and others'. For example, the total income of the General Council for 1869-70 was £51 7s. 1d. Expenditure for the same year amounted to £47 7s. 5d., but there was still £4 0s. 4d. outstanding in arrears of rent.[21]

Even if one multiplied the above figures by more than twenty to obtain present-day sterling equivalents, the amounts would still be derisory.

The poverty of the First International is clear from the fact that its General Council was even evicted from its premises for not paying the rent. It is therefore rather surprising to read

Zinoviev's statement to the Second Congress of the Comintern: 'The First International was a strongly centralized institution.'[22]

Again, let us look at the finances of the Zimmerwald Left during the First World War: In his autobiography Karl Radek wrote:

> The fighting funds of this organization [the Zimmerwald Left] were gathered as follows: Vladimir Ilyich contributed from the Bolsheviks 20 francs, Borchardt from the German leftists 20 francs, and I from Hanecki's pocket in the name of the Polish Social Democrats 10 francs. In this manner the future Communist International had at its disposal for the conquest of the world 50 francs.'[23]

Compare these puny figures with the Comintern's allocation of £16,000 to the Communist Party of Great Britain in 1925! The party paper, *Workers' Weekly*, wrote: 'our ordinary normal weekly income apart from the allocation, is estimated at about £20 a week'. As one historian of the British Communist Party commented:

> This indicates that in 1925 the Communist Party expected to receive £1,000 from its own members and £16,000 from the Comintern. Clearly this meant their complete reliance on the Comintern to finance the organization and activity of the party, in particular to finance the full-time officials, the various subsidiary organizations and their publications. This financial dependence gave great authority to the Comintern representative working with the British party.[24]

Brandler indicated that in 1923 the finances received by the German party from Moscow made it possible to run 27 dailies and pay the wages of 200 full-time workers. With its own resources the KPD could have managed only four papers and paid only 12 people.[25]

The financial bonanza was not altogether beneficial to the recipients. To quote Brandler:

> Without the financial help of the Comintern we would have been developing in a much healthier manner. Before, we were publishing a few newspapers with pennies contributed by workers. We were dependent on workers, we had to be in constant touch with them, and we would not have embarked

on enterprises which were above our real political strength. All this changed from the moment when we received money from the Comintern. Suddenly we owned twenty newspapers; we had not enough editors – we had either workers who could not write, or 'drop-out' students who could write but had very little in common with the worker's movement. Thalheimer employed them in *Die Rote Fahne* and dismissed them after two months at the latest. Our financial means were all the time greater than our political possibilities, and we began to judge our strength and importance according to the length of our purse and not according to the support of the workers. This was bound to lead to disaster.[26]

The trend towards centralization in the Comintern was also encouraged by the people who actually ran the organization. There was a dialectical interaction between the people selected for jobs and the effect of the jobs on the people filling them. A world party needed world leadership. The leadership of the Comintern was vested in its Executive Committee. But the most important national party leaders were not members of the ECCI. It did include some of the great names of the Bolshevik party; but given the conditions ruling in Russia at the time, they had little time to spend on the affairs of the International. Of course it was different during congresses. At the First and Second Congresses Lenin played a central, and crucial role. He was far less active at the Third Congress. At the Fourth he took a very small part indeed. When it came to supervising the day-to-day affairs of the International, Lenin and Trotsky were far too busy, so that the task fell to Zinoviev, Radek and Bukharin.

Zinoviev, as president of the International, relied very much on the idea of 'authority'. At the Second Congress he declared: 'It will be of great benefit for the parties of all countries if they acquire a fear of the Communist International. We should always provide a mirror in which the parties can see themselves.'[27]

Zinoviev had played a lamentable role in opposing the October insurrection. There was no reason to believe that he would do better in the case of the German October or insurrection elsewhere. While a brilliant speaker, he lacked theoretical depth and strength of character, being cowardly, erratic and prone to duplicity and intrigue.

Trotsky's judgement of Zinoviev was devastating:

> The agitator of the revolution lacked revolutionary character. When it was a question of conquering minds and hearts Zinoviev remained a tireless fighter, but he suddenly lost his fighting confidence when he came face to face with the necessity for action . . . then his insinuating, almost feminine voice, losing its conviction, would expose his inner weakness.[28]

Zinoviev, in Lenin's words, was 'an agitator and nothing but an agitator'.[29] And Victor Serge wrote, ' "Zinoviev", we used to say, "is Lenin's biggest mistake".'[30]

Radek did not come to Russia or join the Bolsheviks until after the October revolution. So he had no direct experience of leading the Bolshevik Party during the years of its long, hard struggle. He was brilliant, but very unstable.

Bukharin was an old Bolshevik who was elected to the Central Committee of the Party in August 1917, played an important part in the October revolution, but afterwards took an ultra-left position (on questions of economic and peace policies). His thinking was very angular, non-dialectical, and therefore inclined to swing from one extreme to another. (After Lenin's death he veered to the extreme right of the Russian party and the Comintern.)

The second most important party in the Comintern was the German. The ECCI included a German, Ernst Meyer. 'This choice was significant,' wrote Broué.

> Ernst Meyer, a member of the old Spartakist core, was without doubt a personality representative of the KPD, but he certainly was not one of the most important leaders. Nothing indicated that he was capable of occupying a decisive position in the International leadership. The only German likely to fill such a role was Paul Levi. No-one, least of all he, thought for a moment of making him a permanent member of the International Executive. Everyone thought his presence on the ground was indispensable for the construction of the German party; symbolically he was elected as Meyer's substitute.[31]

The Second Congress of the Comintern also elected a French member, Alfred Rosmer. Rosmer was a fine, honest and courageous revolutionary. However, he did not yet belong to the

Socialist Party which affiliated to the International at Tours, bringing the latter the major part of its French troops.

The daily work of the Executive was in fact undertaken by a small number of full-timers belonging to the Bolshevik Party – the best elements until 1921 being drawn away by the civil war – and the émigrés. There were the Hungarians Bela Kun, Pogany and Rudnianski (who was to disappear, it was said, with 'war treasure'), the Bulgarians Dimitrov, Kabatchiev, Minev and Kolarov, and the Finn Kuusinen. Broué described these men thus:

> Now the experience of these men was limited, if not rudimentary, and leftist tendencies were rife among them. They did not know the workers' movement in western Europe well and were instead permeated by a belief in the superiority of the Russian experience, of which they enjoyed the results . . .
>
> it was therefore a small core of barely tested men, who were in no way destined to be international leaders, who took over the daily business of the executive around Radek, the one-man band, a journalist of great talent, a sincere but unstable militant . . . the International never functioned between congresses as a truly international body with its own existence, [it] was always at the top an appendage of the Bolshevik Party.[32]

To strengthen centralization the Comintern leadership relied not only on the formal structure of relations between the ECCI and the Central Committees of the national parties, but also on a special administrative weapon: the Comintern agent.

These agents were actually more powerful than the national leaderships. Two examples are the ECCI agents at the conference of the Socialist Party of Italy in Livorno (January 1921): the Bulgarian Khristo Kabachiev and the Hungarian Matyas Rakosi.

> While entrusting a Comintern mandate to these two militants who enjoyed no international authority and were completely unknown in the movement in Italy, Zinoviev refused to grant one to Paul Levi, who possessed all the qualities lacked by the other two, for he knew the country and could speak its language, enjoyed great prestige in the international Communist movement and belonged to the Comintern Executive Committee elected at the Second World Congress.[33]

Serrati, General Secretary of the Italian Socialist Party, a member of the ECCI, did not even know that Kabachiev had been in Italy for weeks before the conference. Using his experience with Kabachiev and Rakosi, Levi wrote after the Livorno Conference:

> I refer to these delegates' direct and secret communication with Moscow. To our knowledge, in virtually every country in which such emissaries are at work the dissatisfaction with them is the same . . . They never work with, but always behind the backs of, and quite frequently against, the domestic party's central committee. Moscow listens only to them.[34]

August Guralski, who played an infamous part in the German Märzaktion (see below, pp. 73–5), was sent by Zinoviev to Germany as a watchdog of the ECCI and was duly 'elected' (under the pseudonym Klein) into the Zentrale. Two historians of the Comintern, B.Lazitch and M.M.Drachkovitch, justifiably wrote:

> There was an enormous discrepancy between the decisive role played in 1919 and 1920 by the first Comintern emissaries and the humble roles that they had played until then within the Russian revolutionary movement. In the autumn of 1918, Y.S.Reich (Thomas) was a simple functionary at the Soviet embassy in Bern, in charge of putting out the official bulletin *Russische Nachrichten (Russian News)*. A year later he was head of the Comintern's Secretariat for Western Europe, which kept watch over the German Communist Party, the most important communist party in Europe, and submitted confidential reports about such top-ranking communists as Paul Levi. In the autumn of 1918 Liubarsky, too, was a functionary at the same embassy. A year later, he was playing an influential role in Europe's first mass socialist party to have joined the Comintern, the Italian party, and his reports shaped the attitude of Lenin and Zinoviev in their growing hostility toward Serrati. Abramovich and Degot, low-level Bolshevik militants in 1919-20, emerged in France and Italy as key personalities in the relations between Moscow and the communist leadership of those countries.[35]

Bela Kun, the top agent, a member of the ECCI, member of the Little Bureau of this august body, and of its secretariat, attracted the most scathing epithets from Lenin. As an ex-prisoner of war he was in Russia during the October revolution, where he could have learnt from the Bolsheviks two lessons of primary importance for the future Hungarian revolution: on the questions of agrarian policy and of policy towards the reformists. Kun later went to Hungary and decided: (1) not to give the land to the peasants; and (2) to unite with the Social Democrats. His sorry role in Germany during the catastrophic Märzaktion will be described below. 'Bela Kun was a remarkably odious figure,' writes Victor Serge. 'He was the incarnation of intellectual inadequacy, uncertainty of will, and authoritarian corruption.'[36] He covered himself with the borrowed authority of the Hungarian revolution in spite of the fact that he actually helped to ruin it.

Circumstances and relationships in the international communist movement thus made it possible for a group of grotesque mediocrities – from Zinoviev downwards – to play grand roles. These Comintern leaders bathed in the reflected glory of Bolshevism, while merely caricaturing it.

The Comintern 'Far too Russian'

In his last speech to a Comintern Congress, on 13 November 1922, Lenin made it clear that he felt that the structure of the organization was 'far too Russian'. He said:

> At the Third Congress, in 1921, we adopted a resolution on the organizational structure of the communist parties and on the methods and content of their activities. The resolution is an excellent one, but it is almost entirely Russian, that is to say, everything in it is based on Russian conditions. This is its good point, but it is also its failing. It is its failing because I am sure that no foreigner can read it . . . if by way of exception some foreigner does understand it, he cannot carry it out.[37]

But when it came to suggesting how to overcome the 'too Russian' character of the Comintern, Lenin did not offer any clear advice:

> The resolution is too Russian, it reflects Russian experience. That is why it is quite unintelligible to foreigners, and they cannot be content with hanging it in a corner like an icon and praying to it. Nothing will be achieved that way. They must assimilate part of the Russian experience. Just how that will be done, I do not know.[38]

Lenin had to face the fact that no administrative measures could free the Comintern from its dependence on the actual level of leadership, consciousness and training in the different sections of the organization. The inevitable result was the crucifixion of the International.

Protected by the aura of Bolshevism, the Comintern *aparatchiks* became increasingly high-handed in dealing with foreign communist parties. Instead of letting the leaders of the national sections learn by experience, they simply replaced them at every point of crisis, thus preventing the leaders and cadres from gaining real experience, and learning from their mistakes and successes. Instead, an obedient 'leadership' was gradually selected, with no independence of judgement, self-reliance or capacity for self-criticism. As Trotsky put it:

> In this manner, the organic process of the selection and weld-
> ing together of the revolutionary cadres, on the basis of the
> proletarian struggle under the leadership of the Comintern was
> cut short, altered, distorted, and in part even directly replaced
> by the administrative and bureaucratic sifting from above.
> Quite naturally, those leading communists who were the readiest
> to adopt the ready-made decisions and to counter-sign any and
> all resolutions frequently gained the upper hand over those
> party elements who were imbued with the feeling of revolu-
> tionary responsibility. Instead of a selection of tested and
> unwavering revolutionists, we have frequently had a selection
> of the best adapted bureaucrats.[39]

19

The Grafting of Bolshevism Fails

Both anti-communists and stalinists have spread the story that Moscow was powerful enough to 'manufacture' communist parties in its own image. Nothing was further from the truth. In fact the national traditions of the communist parties of Europe were very resistant to the pressures of Bolshevism.

To demonstrate this we shall use three examples: one from France, where right opportunism persisted in the CP leadership, despite pressures from Moscow; the second from Italy, where ultra-leftism did not respond at all to the admonitions of the Comintern leadership; the third from Germany, where an immature, inexperienced party leadership took the catastrophic road of adventurism, aided and abetted by the Moscow leadership.

Right Opportunism Persists in the French Communist Party

The Comintern leadership failed completely to overcome the national traditions out of which the French Communist Party had developed – persistent right opportunism.

Before the Russian revolution, very few people in France opposed the war, refused to accept the principle of national defence, or called on socialist deputies to vote against the war credits: 'no more than a hundred militants, without any influence on the masses',[1] according to Robert Wohl, a historian of the early years of French communism. 'Except in a few groups on the extreme left . . . the names of Lenin and Trotsky had been unknown until the February revolution.'[2]

After the war, as a result of the clear bankruptcy of French reformism, the victory of the October revolution, and the survival of Bolshevik power, hundreds of thousands of people in France, as elsewhere, moved towards communism.

At the Congress of the French Socialist Party in Tours in December 1920, the overwhelming majority decided to join the Communist International. The result was that of the 179,800 members of the French Socialist Party (SFIO) in December 1920, 110,000 joined the Communist Party, while the dissidents were scarcely able to rally 30,000.[3] But the Socialist-turned-Communist Party was far from being really revolutionary. It was 'a coalition of left-wing and centrist groups . . . and unwieldy and hybrid political formation . . . an unstable compound of conflicting elements'.[4] Its most prominent leaders were out-and-out opportunists.

Take the case of Marcelle Cachin, who remained a leader of the party until his death in 1958. When the 1914 war broke out he was

> a social-patriot of the deepest conviction; in 1915, as an agent for the French government, he had tried to persuade the Italian socialists to enter the war on the side of the Entente. Legend has it that it was Cachin who handed Mussolini the French subsidies that enabled him to start his own newspaper and shift from anti-patriotism to violent nationalism.[5]

In March 1917 Cachin went to Russia as a member of a delegation with the blessing of the French government, in order 'to revive the interest of the Russian socialists in the pursuit of the war'.[6] He went so far as to accuse Lenin of being a German agent.[7]

The General Secretary of the Communist Party, L.O.Frossard, had similar political characteristics. He joined the Comintern simply hoping 'to drape traditional French socialism, which was now in disgrace because of its participation in the sacred union, with the prestige of the Russian revolution and the Bolshevik regime'.[8]

At the Strasbourg Conference of the SFIO in February 1920, Frossard declared:

> No one has the right to say that adopting an attitude [in favour of national defence] is a sufficient ground for expulsion . . . Those who consider it necessary to defend their fatherland even under capitalism will not let themselves be treated as pariahs.[9]

At the Tours Congress Frossard told the right wing who opposed communism, and hence split from the party: 'For my part, tomorrow I will speak of you without bitterness. Tomorrow I will not utter a single wounding word about you. I consider you socialists and I will say so.'[10]

In 1923 Frossard resigned from the French Communist Party. He rejoined the Socialist Party in 1936, held ministerial posts in several Third Republic governments and was a member of Petain's first government in 1940.)

The tradition of the French Socialist movement was that the party, being a parliamentary organization, kept out of industrial disputes. To cite an extreme example: the metal workers and the shipyard workers of Le Havre came out on strike on 19 June 1922, when the management announced that their wages would be cut by 10 per cent. During July and August, tension between the employers and the strikers mounted. In mid-August the port workers and sailors joined the movement, bringing the number of strikers to 40,000. On 25 August, after the arrest of some workers, the local unions called a one-day general strike. The next day there were bloody encounters between the police and the strikers. Three workers were killed, fifteen more wounded. The CGTU – the left-wing General Confederation of Trade Unions – replied by calling a general strike for 29 August. The night the general strike was declared, there was no one at the offices of *L'Humanité*, the CP daily, or at the party headquarters. The leaders of the Left were all on vacation. The next day's edition of *L'Humanité* did not even carry the strike order.[11]

Another clear expression of the far reaching reformism of the French Communist Party was its attitude to the colonial question, a question that should have been central to a party in the metropolis of a great empire.

Thus, for instance, the Algerian branch of the French Communst Party had 'come out clearly against nationalist movesments and nationalist revolts, unanimously and without a single voice being raised to sustain a contrary point of view, without a single native comrade having made the slightest comment'. When the Comintern drafted an appeal for the liberation of Algeria and Tunisia in May 1922, the Algerian section of Sidi Bel Abbès replied with a memorandum requesting that its publication in Algeria be countermanded. Despite their long tradition of leftism, according to the memorandum read, the communists of the Sidi Bel Abbès section could not accept the International's colonial policy. The liberation of Algeria would be reactionary, not progressive, if it preceded a victorious revolution on the mainland. The native population of north Africa was composed mostly of elements hostile to the economic, social, and intellectual development necessary to enable an autonomous state to build communism. The job of the French CP in north Africa was therefore to establish a favourable attitude toward communism. These propositions were accepted unanimously by the Second Communist Interfederal Congress of North Africa, on 7 December 1922. The attitude of the North African communists was that appeals to revolt and communist propaganda among the native population would be not only premature, but dangerous.[12]

Ultra–Leftism Persists
in the Italian Communist Party

Despite all its efforts, the Comintern failed to overcome the ultra-left sectarianism dominating Italian communism. In order to understand the relationship between Italian Communism and Moscow, a number of historical facts need to be taken into account.

First of all, the Italian Communist Party had origins which separated it completely from Bolshevism. D.W.Urquidi, in his excellent study of the origins of Italian Communism, writes:

> The basic doctrines, programmes and political orientation of the various individuals and groups which combined to form the Italian Communist Party evolved for the most part independently of Bolshevik influence.
> The dominant groups in the extreme left alliance which constituted the PCI in early 1921 were the abstentionist faction led by Amadeo Bordiga and the *Ordine Nuovo* group led by Antonio Gramsci. It is not known exactly when either Bordiga or Gramsci first came in contact with Bolshevik doctrine. But it is clear that the doctrines of both young Italians were not derived from Lenin. Bordiga's program, as it evolved in his paper, *Il Soviet*, revealed a decided orientation toward the Dutch [ultra-left] Tribunists rather than the Russian Bolsheviks. Gramsci's emphasis on the formation of factory councils was derived mainly from the writings of the American, Daniel de Leon, and the experience of the IWW and the British shop stewards.[13]

It appears that the initial influence of the Bolsheviks on the Italian movement was based on their successful revolution rather than on their doctrine. The ideas of Lenin and the Bolsheviks were almost completely unknown in Italy before the revolution. Italian representatives had come in contact with

Lenin at the Zimmerwald Conference in 1915 and the Kienthal Conference the following year, but no Bolshevik writings had been published or even translated in Italy during the war. In 1917, following the February revolution, brief items, largely censored, began to appear in the Italian press on Lenin and the Bolsheviks, but it was only in 1918 that Lenin really became known in Italy.[14]

Even then very little was known of Lenin's theoretical works. Anton Pannekoek of the Dutch Tribunists was the foreign writer who appeared most frequently in the columns of *Il Soviet*, the journal of Bordiga, who was destined to be the most powerful communist leader.

> In addition there are several articles by Herman Gorter and Henriette Roland-Holst, also of the Dutch group. What is more striking is that from 1918 to 1921, there is not one article by Lenin. A short extract by Bukharin appeared and another by Alexandra Kollontay, but these were the only Russians to find space in Bordiga's journal.[15]

What were the aims of the Bolshevik leaders regarding the Italian party? There were three:

1. To expel the right wing under Turati and Modigliani;
2. To make the party participate in electoral campaigns;
3. To promote Gramsci's *Ordino Nuovo* in the Italian party.

On all these issues Moscow was defeated by Bordiga. Instead of purging the PSI of its relatively small extreme right wing, Bordiga led a split by the extreme left minority at the party's Livorno conference in January 1921, thus forming the Italian Communist Party (PCI). The ECCI's objectives were obvious – and they were precisely the opposite of Bordiga's. While Bordiga was hoping to provoke a split to the left, the ECCI was still insisting on the expulsion of the right: 'the Comintern leadership and the leadership of the Italian extreme left were pulling in opposite directions'.[16]

The Comintern continued to try to pull Serrati and the PSI into its orbit. At the Third Comintern Congress in 1921, both the PCI and the PSI were invited to send delegates, and serious overtures were made to the Socialist Party. Following the expulsion of Turati and the right wing from the Socialist Party in 1922, the Italian communists were ordered to merge with the PSI and form a united Communist Party. This Comintern decision was vehemently opposed by Bordiga, who procrastinated, and avoided bringing about the fusion. The merger, however, was finally agreed upon at the Fourth Comintern Congress in 1922, despite Bordiga's vociferous objections.

> But the Comintern had won a Pyrrhic victory: the agreement was denounced by a majority of the PSI, under the new leadership of Pietro Nenni, and those in favour of the fusion with the PCI were expelled from the party. In spite of all its manœuvres to undo the effects of the split at Livorno, the Comintern was never able to achieve its original objecting of transforming the PSI into a Communist party by the elimination of the right-wing leaders.[17]

The other policy which Moscow tried to impose on the Italian movement – acceptance of the tactic of electoral participation – was also successfully opposed by Bordiga. 'Not only did the PCI under Bordiga resist the policy of electoral participation, but the party waged a determined and indeed largely successful campaign against the policy of a united front launched by the Comintern in 1922.'[18]

How far Bordiga was from Bolshevism is clear from his reaction to the factory occupations in September 1920: he argued that the movement was in no sense revolutionary. 'We wish to point out that a problem such as this has no real content, that the factory councils and the occupation of the factories are artificial organisms and movements.'[19]

Bordiga's ultra-leftism characteristically also expressed itself in his attitude to the soviets, which he saw in effect as mere extensions of the party.

> While factory councils might be formed before the revolution [Urquidi writes], Bordiga opposed the creation of soviets while the capitalist system existed. Rather, the instrument which would politically represent the workers before the revolution and which would carry out the revolution itself was the Communist Party. And after the revolution, the soviets would be based on the local sections of the Communist Party rather than on factories.[20]

Bordiga's ultra-left and immature attitude is also demonstrated by his reaction to Mussolini's seizure of power. Bordiga defined Fascism as 'liberal and democratic'. At the Fourth Congress of the Comintern, he declared:

> Naturally, I do not say that the present situation is a favourable situation for the proletarian and socialist movement, when I predict that Fascism will be liberal and democratic. Democratic governments have never given the working class anything but proclamations and promises.[21]

Bordiga's understanding of the nature of Fascism was not helped by Zinoviev's statement to the Fourth Congress of the Comintern:

> Our Italian comrades do not agree among themselves as to whether what has recently happened in Italy is a *coup d'état*, or a comedy. It might be both. Historically, it is a comedy; in a few months this will turn to the advantage of the Italian working class, but for the time being it is quite a serious change, an actual counter-revolutionary act.[22]*

The immaturity of the Italian communist movement, its poverty of experience, played into Bordiga's hands. In the final analysis, in Urquidi's words: 'the Comintern obtained a Communist Party which it neither anticipated nor fully accepted'.[24]

The German Märzaktion (March Action)

The March Action of the German Communist Party – the biggest adventurist putsch ever – was the child of both the inexperienced German leadership and the Comintern leadership.

In Italy in the second half of 1920 a genuine mass revolutionary movement leading to the occupation of factories could have brought about the establishment of soviet power; a fundamental shift in the balance of power in Europe was ruined by the spinelessness of Serrati's centrist leadership. In Germany, in

---

* Radek's grasp of the nature of Fascism was much deeper. 'In my opinion the victory of Fascism is something more than a mechanical victory of Fascist arms. I regard it as the greatest defeat which socialism and communism have sustained since the opening of the epoch of the world revolution.'[23]

March 1921, in the absence of a nationwide mass revolutionary movement, the party leadership tried to *force the pace*, to *substitute the party militants for the mass movement.* The result was a severe defeat, which, because of Germany's key position, was to have a profound influence on the international workers' movement.

After the murder of Luxemburg, Liebknecht and Jogiches, the leadership of the KPD was inherited by Paul Levi, a talented disciple and friend of Rosa Luxemburg. In the two years during which Levi led the KPD he was determined to turn it into a mass party. To achieve this he first ousted the ultra-lefts who opposed participation in existing trade unions and parliamentary elections, skilfully engineered a fusion with the left wing of the USPD, and following this, on 7 January 1921, took a new radical step: he published an 'Open Letter' in the *Die Rote Fahne*, the KPD daily, addressed to the other working-class parties and trade unions, in which he called for a united front aimed at achieving certain limited goals. The communists invited their fellow workers to fight for a number of demands, ranging from an improvement in unemployment legislation, and ceilings on food prices, to the dissolution of all bourgeois para-military organizations, the creation of proletarian defence organizations, an amnesty for all political prisoners, and the resumption of economic and diplomatic relations with Soviet Russia. If the Social Democrats agreed, the KPD would have the chance to demonstrate its superiority as defender of the proletariat. If they rejected the proposals, then the blame for any disunity would fall on them. Levi knew that the KPD was still very much a minority party in the German proletariat. He believed that with the aid of a united front policy this could change.

Zinoviev was far from pleased by Levi's independence of spirit. He and Bukharin also opposed Levi's policy for a united front as developed in the 'Open Letter' (although on this issue Levi was supported by Lenin, Trotsky and Radek). The Comintern leadership, in this case including Lenin, were also unhappy about Levi's forecast during the march on Warsaw that the German workers would not rise at the approach of the Red Army.

Zinoviev was assisted in his machinations against Levi by

developments inside the KPD. An ultra-left group arose in opposition to Levi's 'Open Letter', and in complete support of Zinoviev and Bukharin. The leaders of this group were the young intellectuals Ruth Fischer, Arkadi Maslov and Ernst Friesland. They were encouraged by the ECCI representative in Berlin, 'Thomas' (real name Y.S.Reich).

A particular incident played into Zinoviev's hands in his scheming against Levi. Levi, who was present at the Livorno conference of the Italian Socialist Party, analysed its results in the German Communist Party paper, *Die Rote Fahne*. His conclusion was that while a split with the right of the Italian Socialist Party, led by Turati, was inevitable, the loss of the majority of the party was not. As Bordiga was supported by the ECCI delegates to the Livorno conference, Levi's article appeared to be a challenge to the Comintern leadership. So Zinoviev decided to get rid of Levi at whatever cost. He was now supported by the volatile Radek.

Accordingly Rakosi was sent by the ECCI as an emissary to Berlin (from Livorno). He convened a meeting of the KPD *Zentralausschuss* (Central Committee – at the time a periodic conference of the Zentrale with the representatives of all the districts). After a very heated debate, the claims of loyalty to the Comintern were used by Rakosi to win Levi's condemnation (by 28 votes to 23). Levi was ejected from the leadership of the KPD. Five members of the Zentrale, including Clara Zetkin, followed him in resigning from this body. After this victory Rakosi left Berlin for Moscow, followed by three other emissaries of the ECCI. At the end of February 1921 the Hungarians Bela Kun and Josef Popper, alias Pogani, and the Pole August Guralski, alias Klein, came to Berlin. It is not clear exactly what mandate they were given – whether they had received specific instructions, or were given authority to use their own discretion. In any case the three emissaries decided to prod the KPD into an immediate mass revolutionary assault.

Returning to the question of the mandate given Bela Kun and his associates by the Comintern leadership, we shall have to wait for the opening of the Moscow archives before we know the exact nature of the mission Zinoviev gave them. The documents we have do not mention it. Curt Geyer, the KPD representative at the ECCI at the time has insisted that the mission was never raised at the Executive.[25] Ruth Fischer, one of the 'left' leaders of the KPD at the time, writes that: 'the action in Germany . . . had been concocted by a caucus of the Russian party, centring around Zinoviev and Bela Kun'.[26] Trotsky stated that 'the entire ultra-left wing of the Comintern at the time advocated the line of the March 1921 days', and singled out Bukharin, in particular, for having expressed the 'opinion that unless the proletariat in Europe was "galvanized" . . . the Soviet power was threatened with certain destruction'.[27] It appears that Zinoviev, Bukharin and Kun were the main initiators of this line.

The three Comintern delegates, on arriving in Berlin, found the young inexperienced leadership of the KPD ready to fall into line with their prompting. They were eager to prove their mettle, especially after the failure of the party during the Kapp putsch.* The party, Kun urged, must take the offensive even if it had to resort to provocative measures. Once an offensive was launched, two to three million German workers would follow the lead of the communists. Kun made many such optimistic estimates, and his enthusiasm captured the imagination of most members of the Zentrale.

His plan of action received further support from events taking place independently of him. On 16 March Otto Hörsing, the Social Democratic governor of Saxony, announced a police occupation of the Mansfeld district of Prussian Saxony on the grounds that wildcat strikes, looting, robbery, terrorist acts and other expressions of lawlessness had to be stopped. In this part of Saxony the KPD was extremely strong.

Kun persuaded Brandler, who had taken Levi's place in the leadership, to write an article, which appeared in *Die Rote Fahne* on 18 March, whose central theme was a call for the mass arming of workers. Three days later the communist district executive of Mansfeld (in the mining centre of Saxony) issued a call for a general strike. This call was ignored outside the immediate Mansfeld district. When the proclamation of the general strike failed

* See p. 228.

to have the desired effect, Hugo Eberlein, who had recently been put in charge of the party's military-political organization (*MP-Apparat*), was dispatched to central Germany on 22 March.[28] He suggested that trusted comrades should commit acts of violence which could be blamed on the police – in this manner, even the most reluctant of workers would be provoked into action. Eberlein's fertile imagination provided a number of additional suggestions. He wanted to stage a mock kidnapping of the two regional communist leaders, Lemch and Bowitzki, who were nominally in charge of directing the *Aktion*. Other popular leaders should disappear for a day or two, only to re-emerge with stories about how they had been liberated from the reactionaries. Another scheme was to blow up a police ammunition train and to claim in *Klassenkampf*, the Communist newspaper in Halle, that carelessness on the part of the reactionaries had destroyed the homes of numerous workers, and had caused the death of hundreds of victims. Once it became known that the report was false, the paper could print a correction. Two more targets for Eberlein's store of dynamite were an ammunition factory at Seesen, and a workers' producers' co-operative in Halle.

None of these projects was carried out successfully, although several abortive attempts were made to blow up both the ammunition factory and the producers' cooperative. Eberlein's reaction to the initial failure of the dynamiting exercises was an attack on the inefficiency of the local illegal apparatus which, he complained, did not even own a piece of fuse long enough to do a reliable job.

Most of the attempts to extend the scope of the uprising in accordance with Eberlein's unorthodox directives were either bungled, or actually backfired. For example, the repeated dynamiting and derailing of passenger trains alienated railroad personnel, whose support of the insurrection would have been of vital importance for its success.[29]

Undeterred, the KPD leadership issued a call for a nation-wide general strike on 24 March, urging the workers to seize arms, to organize themselves, and to join the struggle against the counter-revolution. It was a desperate step, because all plants closed down in any case from Good Friday (25 March) through to Easter Monday. But the response to the communist appeal was negligible.

In Berlin, the seat of the Zentrale, the strike movement failed completely. Most workers reported to their jobs on 24 March, and only a few factories were idle, despite attempts by the KPD to enforce shutdowns by attempted invasions by the unemployed. These methods aroused sharp criticism even within the party. Ernst Däumig, for instance, sent a furious letter to the Zentrale, in which he protested against the practice of pitting proletarians against proletarians. Equally indignant were the party officials in charge of trade union activities, who complained that the tactics employed by the Zentrale were wrecking their influence within the unions. (The Zentrale obtained slightly more support in the Ruhr region and the Rhineland.)[30]

All in all, the general strike was a complete fiasco: the number of workers participating in it was estimated at 200,000.[31] In his report to the Third Congress of the Comintern Zinoviev spoke of the involvement of 500,000 workers.

The KPD organized demonstrations were also pathetic. In Berlin they attracted less than 4,000, while just a few weeks earlier the party had won 200,000 votes in elections.[32]

On 1 April, even the most stubborn die-hards among the communist leaders had to recognize the futility of the exercise; the Zentrale resolved to end the insurrection by calling off the 'nationwide' general strike. The collapse of the adventure was followed by a massive decline of the KPD: from some 400,000 members to 150,000 or less. Thousands of militants were thrown into prison and tens of thousands lost their jobs.

In Conclusion

The German, Italian and French communist parties were the most important in the Comintern outside Russia. Their characteristics were reflected in one form or another, or in combination, in the other parties of the Comintern.

Lenin aimed to build communist parties welded together by a clear understanding of their historical tasks, parties founded on clear programmes, combined with correct relationships with the masses, i.e. parties of strict principle united by revolutionary realism. Instead, the communist parties outside Russia exhibited opportunist vagueness on the one hand, and sectarian aloofness on the other. They oscillated violently between opportunism and adventurism – the two poles of left centrism.

Of course one could argue that communist parties could not be expected to come into existence fully fledged even in the most acute revolutionary situation, which is true; or, that time would have welded the parties into real, consistent revolutionary organizations. That is possibly also true, but time was the one thing history did not grant.

The oscillations in the policies of the communist parties, as well as the divergences between them – as the fate of all centrist organizations shows – could have led to the disintegration of the Comintern. This was prevented by the fact that the Moscow leadership controlled the Comintern. Unfortunately, however, the autocratic and bureaucratic fiats of the Zinoviev leadership supported centrism in the leadership of the national communist parties.

Developments in the Comintern after Lenin's death show how its left centrism turned into bureaucratic centrism: a specific refraction of the rule of the bureaucracy in Russia.

20
Britain and Bulgaria – Two Antipodes

There is no better guage of the power Lenin and the Bolsheviks leadership held to shape communist policies abroad than a comparison of two Communist Parties that were poles apart: the British and Bulgarian parties.

The Communist Party of Britain was a tiny fledgling created by a merger of small sects. It existed in a highly industrialized country with a massive proletariat which had longstanding autonomous organizations: massive trade unions that had endured for generations, and more recently a shop stewards' movement. The Bulgarian Communist Party had been a mass revolutionary organization for nearly two decades; it claimed to be the first authentic Bolshevism party outside Russia. But it existed in a very backward country – the most backward in Europe excluding Albania – with a tiny proletariat, hardly any trade unions and a very small strike record.

The history of the two parties will show: (1) that the October revolution was central in drawing revolutionaries towards Moscow; (2) that the Comintern leadership played a crucial role in shaping the policies, tactics and organization of the two parties; and (3) that the marriage of Bolshevism with British Communism on the one hand, and Bulgarian Communism on the other, was not very successful. The national traditions that led towards international communism also prevented a successful union. Lenin's magic wand could not obliterate the sectarianism of the British revolutionary left. Nor could it radically change the Bulgarian communists, product of a weak proletarian base, even though they willingly aped Russian Bolshevism.

One Strand in British Communism: the BSP

The small size and slight influence of the British Communist Party compared with many other sections of the Communist International hardly merits a separate chapter for the British party. But as this book is written largely for a British audience, the relationship of Lenin to British communism does warrant attention.

The large communist parties of western and central Europe – of Germany, France, Italy, Czechoslovakia, etc. – were created out of splits in existing mass parties. The British Communist Party was created out of a fusion of small groups; this took more than two years to achieve, and only a part of the original groups did in fact merge. The two main groups were the British Socialist Party (BSP) and the Socialist Labour Party (SLP).

The BSP was the direct descendant of the Social Democratic Federation, the first Marxist organization in Britain.

The British Marxist movement was founded in 1880 by H.M.Hyndman, who formed the Democratic Federation which in 1884 changed its name to Social-Democratic Federation. Marx and Engels did not hold a high opinion of Hyndman and his organization. Above all they criticized the SDF's isolation from the mass movement.

> In a letter to Sorge, Engels accused the SDF of having contrived to reduce the Marxist theory of development to a rigid orthodoxy. This theory is to be forced down the throats of the workers at once and without development as articles of faith, instead of making the workers raise themselves to its level by dint of their own class instinct . . . that is why (it) remains a mere sect.[1]

Hyndman and his friends opposed any active intervention of the party in the industrial struggle. The SDF paper *Justice* described the great dock strike of 1889 as 'a lowering of the flag, a departure from active propaganda, and a waste of energy.'[2]

'We are opposed to strikes altogether,' wrote Hyndman in April 1903. 'They never were a powerful weapon, and now they are quite out of date.' At the time of the threatened railway strike of 1907 Hyndman wrote: 'We of the Social Democratic Party and *Justice* are opposed to strikes on principle . . . Political action is far safer, far better and far less costly.' Even in 1912, the years of the greatest upsurge the working class had ever known, Hyndman repeated: 'Can anything be imagined, more foolish, more harmful, more in the widest sense of the word, unsocial than a strike . . . ? I have never yet advocated a strike . . . I have never known . . . a successful strike.'

In the name of real socialism the SDF leaders scorned the industrial struggle of workers. Once a strike began, however, the Party would give its support in principle. This usually meant a lecture on the impossibility of making real gains while the capitalist system lasted.

Basically SDF policy was determined by its inability to come to terms with the powerful, if ideologically helpless, mass labour movement that existed.

In a country where reformism was deeply entrenched in the workers' movement the SDF's 'purism' had a natural attraction for socialists. Sectarianism was the reverse of reformism. In practice this 'purism' led the SDF to oscillate between ultra-revolutionary formal positions and purely reformist practice. Its work boiled down almost exclusively to parliamentary and local electioneering. To a large extent it was constrained by the fact that it was born at a time when trade unionism in general and the industrial struggle in particular were at an unusually low ebb. Unfortunately when the situation changed at the beginning of the twentieth century, the organization was far too conservative to change with it.

In 1908 the Social-Democratic Federation became the Social-Democratic Party, and in 1911, after fusing with some other small groups, the British Socialist Party. It continued to be quite small, its membership in 1913 amounting to 11,300.

The BSP did not manage to break with the traditional style of the SDF. It continued to focus on the politics of the street – open-air propaganda, organizing the unemployed, etc., and municipal elections. It is true that the 1913 conference of the party tried to change its mode of operation by passing a resolution which declared that 'the proper function of the British Socialist Party is to lead the working class in its economic and political struggle', and instructed the executive 'to organize the trade union members of the British Socialist Party for systematic work and socialist propaganda inside the trade unions'.[3] But little was done to put this resolution into effect among the dwindling active trade union members who were 'voting with their feet', particularly after the party attacked syndicalism and 'direct action' in October 1912.[4]

In practice the BSP continued to maintain an artificial separation between industrial and political action, never really relating to the former. This does not mean that there were not quite prominent workers among its membership. As one historian of the industrial scene in Britain in the years 1900-1914 wrote:

There remained a significant industrial unionist faction within the SDF (and later the British Socialist Party, BSP) right through the pre-war years . . . The syndicalist element in the British

Socialist Party (BSP) had for example been responsible for a 'Manifesto to Railway Workers' published in the wake of the Royal Commission report. This had suggested that the current lack of genuine progress in meeting grievances could only be resolved by joint action between 'miners, transport workers and seamen' in support of each other's claims.[5]

The outbreak of the first world war put the BSP into a very serious crisis: Hyndman and his close friends supported the war enthusiastically; a large section of the Party took a pacifist position, and a small group, led by John Maclean from Glasgow, adopted a revolutionary defeatist line. At the 1916 conference of the BSP, Hyndman and co. were defeated and left the party with a small minority to establish a new organization, with the ill-fated name National Socialist Party.

The BSP now adopted a pacifist position. Even after the March 1917 revolution in Russia it remained on the whole far from Bolshevism. This may adequately be indicated by reference to one of the best leaders of the party, Theodor Rothstein. Early in 1916 Lenin found occasion to attack Rothstein's position on the war as 'Kautskyite' because he supported the Second International and did not see the need to build a Third International.[6]

In a pamphlet, *Essays on War and Peace*, published by the BSP in 1917, Rothstein reveals that he did not advance any further towards a Leninist position: instead of calling for an end of the war through socialist revolution, he wished to see a negotiated peace.

It is instructive to read Rothstein on the situation in Russia during 1917. Writing in *Plebs* (August 1917), he described the Russian revolutionaries as being characterized by 'jealousy, quarrelsomeness, and excessive predilection for theoretical niceties.' He backed the entry of the Mensheviks into the Provincial Government, describing it as 'a great step which marked the official triumph of the revolutionary proletariat.' By contrast, he criticized the 'violent opposition of the Leninites'. 'Rothstein does not seem to have declared for Bolshevism until after the October Revolution.'[7]

At the same time profound changes were taking place in the BSP as a result of the rising industrial struggle during the war and the creation of a shop stewards' movement. That section of the membership actively participating in the industrial struggle was strengthened very much. A number of them played an important role in the shop stewards' movement, from Willie Gallacher, Chairman of the Clyde Workers' Committee, to others in London[8] and Manchester.[9] The main effort of people like William McClaine, the Manchester shop stewards' leader, was to promote a fusion of anti-war politics and the shop stewards' movement. He argued for a fusion between the BSP and the SLP. Speaking at the 1918 BSP conference, he thought that

> 'within the last two or three years . . . the most important factor, as far as Socialist unity was concerned, had been the activity of various SLP and BSP members in industrial districts. In consequence of unity of action on the industrial field, closer unity was now desired in all aspects.'[10]

However, despite the changes taking place in the BSP it did not cease to be a sect: poorly implanted in the mass movement, it continued to be an arena for warring factions, for breakaways and quarrels.

If one had to characterize the BSP at the end of the war, one could not call it a revolutionary party, nor a reformist one. It was, par excellence, a centrist party. Taking this into account, the original invitation to the First World Congress of the Comintern was extended not to the BSP as a whole but only to 'the left elements . . . in particular the group represented by Maclean'.[11]

The SLP

The other important strand in the formation of the Communist Party of Britain was the SLP.

With the rising industrial struggle at the beginning of the century, the SDF's contradictory practices, a combination of sectarianism and opportunism, were more and more criticized by some members of the party. One result was a split of Scottish members in 1903 which led to the founding of the Socialist Labour Party. This tiny group of Marxists tried to implant revolutionary politics in the industrial struggle for the first time in Britain. Contrary to SDF theory were the industrial unionist ideas of the American socialist Daniel De Leon which were developed in Britain by the great Irish revolutionary James Connolly.

The SLP argued that the fragmentation of working class organization – for example, the existence of 225 different unions in the engineering industry – must be ended; instead there should be one union for each industry. In this way maximum class unity would be achieved. It was necessary to oppose the trade union bureaucrats – 'the labour lieutenants of capitalism' – who always sell their members out, by building a strong rank and file organization to control the unions. In the SLP's opinion a policy of militant industrial unionism was not only the means of achieving better wages and working conditions today, but also provided the basis for a new society tomorrow. Socialism would be run democratically, industry by industry, through workers' control.

The SLP suffered from two connected defects that can be summed up in the words syndicalism and sectarianism. Syndicalism emphasized the need for the reorganization of the trade unions rather than the building of a workers' political party as the main agency of the transition to socialism. The clearest theoretical statement to emerge from the shop stewards' movement during the first world war, which shows up the syndicalist weakness of the SLP, is a pamphlet by the well-known engineering militant and SLP leader J.T.Murphy, *The Workers' Committee, an Outline of its Principle and Structure.*[12] In its statement of principles nothing is said of the main political fact of the time, the imperialist war – and this was 1917. Nor is there any reference to the need for a revolutionary political party. The question of the conquest of state power by the working class is not posed.

Within the general syndicalist stream the SLP acted like a small sect, so that during the period when the most massive, most militant struggle of the British working class took place, raising large rank and file movements in opposition to the employers and the trade union bureaucracy, the SLP continued to be a tiny organization. In 1903 it had about 80 members; in 1914, after the years of the greatest industrial struggle – only 300; in 1915, 200.[13] Even in 1918 the membership did not exceed 800.

The circulation of its monthly paper was also small – about 2,000 by 1918. Its membership was overwhelmingly in Scotland, particularly on the Clyde, with some contacts and small branches in Northern England, especially Yorkshire (in particular Sheffield).

The smallness of the SLP and the circulation of its paper are not accidental, but rooted in its sectarianism. It played no role at all in the mass struggles of the miners in 1910 and 1912, nor in the transport workers' strikes of 1911 and 1912, nor the South Wales miners' strike of July 1915.

One of the reasons for this was that the party did not relate to rank and file movements that were not under SLP influence. The best example was the SLP's attitude to Tom Mann's Industrial Syndicalist Education League founded in December 1910. To this movement 'activists (were) drawn from every existing current of syndicalist thought with the notable exception of the sectarian de Leonists', writes the historian Bob Holton.[14]

Not only did the SLP boycott the founding conference, but it kept up a hostile propaganda barrage outside, under placards bearing the slogan 'Tom Mann exposed'.[15]

South Wales miners were heavily represented in the Industrial Syndicalist Education League. Even members of the SDF and the Independent Labour Party were there, but not the SLP. The two conferences the League held in November 1912, one in London, the other in Manchester, attracted 235 delegates representing upwards of 100,000 workers. Participants were drawn from trade union branches, trades councils and rank-and-file amalgamation committees representing workers from a large number of different occupations. They included railwaymen, dockers, carpenters and engineering workers, shop assistants, bricklayers and stonemasons.[16]

Characteristic of the SLP's sectarianism was the expulsion of its former national secretary Neil Maclean of Glasgow, for the crime of supporting the 'palliative' reformist activity of unemployed workers demanding the right to work.[17] The same sectarianism forced James Connolly to break with the SLP.

At the 1912 party conference, a resolution was moved stating that 'to support reforms . . . is inconsistent with the revolutionary character of the SLP'. This just failed to win by

14 votes to 16. In the aftermath of the Conference the majority of the membership resigned from the party on the grounds that it had become reformist.[18] As a consequence the SLP paper of March 1913 could write: 'That the SLP is on its last legs goes without saying.'[19]

Despite its weakness, the SLP undoubtedly played a vital role in the working class, especially during the war. Its significance during the industrial battles of that time was quite out of proportion to its size. It had been the main political force within the rising engineering shop stewards' movement. Unfortunately it always acted as an abstract propaganda group rather than a party in the Bolshevik concept of the term, i.e. an organization that leads the struggle deciding the tactics the members have to follow. Thus, for instance, while the SLP came down firmly in opposition to the war, it never put an anti-war policy on the Clyde Workers' Committee, where it had quite an influence. Its members, and particularly John Muir – who was known to be 'soft' on the war – pushed a line of neutrality. Whatever its members might say as individuals, the Committee itself was neither for nor against the war; it was concerned only to defend the workers against the threats to their organization brought about by the war.[20]*

Again, one finds a leading member of the SLP, Dave Kirkwood, convenor of Parkhead, the largest factory in Glasgow, adopting a line on the vital issue of dilution that was completely opposed to the policy of the Clyde Workers Committee, despite the fact that this policy had been drawn up by a fellow SLP member, John Muir.[22]

Murphy remembers: 'None of us saw a political party as anything other than a propaganda body for the spread of socialist ideas.'[23]

---

* The SLP did not take the attitude of the Bolshevik Party, but called on its members to refuse to serve in the army, and to declare that the only war for which they would enlist was the class war. In practice it meant that the members of the SLP became conscientious objectors on the basis of the class war theory while a considerable section of the BSP and the ILP were conscientious objectors on pacifist grounds.[21]

The Shop Stewards' Movement

Besides the BSP and the SLP a third strand contributed to British communism – the shop stewards' movement. This was the first mass movement in the engineering industry and rose during the first world war.[24]

However massive and militant the Shop Stewards' and Workers' Committee Movement was, involving as it did tens of thousands of workers, it never managed to outgrow many of its limitations.

It never spread outside the engineering industry and hardly beyond the skilled men in this industry. It was a very localized movement with only a very loose national structure. It was never more than a federation of autonomous groups of militants. The mass unofficial engineering strikes on the Clyde in 1915 and 1916 did not spread beyond this region. Even the mass movement of October-November 1915 that had a *national* impact leading to the freezing of rents at pre-war levels through the Rent Restriction Act, did not spread beyond the Clyde.

The largest movement of the war period was the unofficial engineering strike which began in Rochdale in May 1917 and spread rapidly throughout the Manchester area. It involved 200,000 engineering workers over a period of more than three weeks, and 1½ million days were lost. The strike included 15,000 engineers in Sheffield and Rotherham; in Coventry 30,000 engineers came out but most of them returned to work after one day, and the rest a few days later; Birmingham failed to come out at all, and Glasgow and the Tyne neither.[25] Not only was the May 1917 strike movement not *national* in spread; it did not even cover all *sections* of the engineering industry. As the historian James Hinton sums it up:

> The strike movement of May 1917 was a massive battle in defence of craft privilege. In the history of the shop stewards' movement to this point a central paradox has been apparent: the contradiction between the revolutionary aims of its leaders, and the craft motivation of its rank and file. The May strikes served to confirm the latter.[26]

This was not the climax of the Shop Stewards' and Workers' Committee Movement. In August 1917 a national leadership was established in the form of a National Administrative Council. But this did not provide a real centralized leadership. The National Administrative Council, as its name implied, held no executive power and was intended to function as 'little more than a reporting centre for the local committees'. 'No committee shall have executive power, all question of policy and action being referred back to the rank and file, was a principle accepted throughout the movement.[27]

From the autumn of this year a series of wage battles took place. This time skilled and unskilled fought side by side.[28] Then a number of factors led the NAC to go further than hitherto: the impact of the October revolution in Russia; the bloody stalemate on the Western front, and the acute food shortage. The NAC decided to challenge the continuation of the war itself. In January 1918 it called for a national strike to force the government to begin peace negotiations. Despite a big campaign the strike did not materialize, the call going unheeded by the workers. Huge meetings of engineers threatening strike action were to be as near as the movement came to fulfilling its revolutionary potential. At the last moment, quite suddenly, the engineering craftsmen drew back from their political challenge to the state, into the militant but extremely sectional demand for continued exemption of skilled workers from military conscription.[29]

In seeking the cause of failure of the Shop Stewards' and Workers' Committee Movement it would be wrong to exaggerate the subjective failure of leadership. Both the collapse of the May 1917 strike movement and the failure of the strike call of January 1918 were much more deeply rooted in the level of consciousness of the mass of the working class, including its advanced section. As Murphy, writing many years after the events, remembers:

> None of the strikes that took place during the course of the war were anti-war strikes. They were frequently led by men such as myself who wanted to stop the war, but that was not the actual motive. Had the question of stopping the war been put to any strikers' meeting it would have been overwhelmingly defeated. The stoppages had a different origin and a different motive. They arose out of a growing conviction that the

workers at home were the custodians of the conditions of labour for those in the armed forces, as well as themselves . . .[30]

The October revolution was received with great enthusiasm by the Movement. It meant the victory of the Soviets, which was for them an extension and development of what the Workers' Committees were. To use Hinton's words,

> the SLP leaders now found in the local Workers' Committees the embryonic form of a proletarian state power, of the organization of the workers as 'the ruling class'. 'The striking masses have spontaneously created the Workers' Committees, the basis of a workers' state', declared *The Socialist* at the end of January 1919: 'These committees representing every department in every mine, mill, railway, or plant, contain the elements of an organization which can transform capitalism into a Soviet Republic . . . All power to the Workers' Committees.'[31]

> Of course the development of the idea of Soviet power in the British revolutionary movement owed a very great deal, including the word, to the Russian Revolution. But the 'soviet heresy' was not simply an attempt to graft alien experience on to the British labour movement. The enthusiasm with which sections of the left took up and developed the soviet idea in Britain is to be explained not only by understandable elation over the Russian Revolution, but also, and primarily, by the fact that this idea answered to a real theoretical need felt by British revolutionaries as a result of their own domestic experience.[32]

However, October was not only a victory for the Soviets, but also a victory for the Bolshevik party. Alas, the Shop Stewards' and Workers' Committee Movement, including its best leaders, did not grasp the Bolshevik doctrine of the Party. They were far too imbued with syndicalism, whose emphasis was on the spontaneous, economically based organization of the masses, to the exclusion of the *political* role of the vanguard organized in a party. The soviet idea fitted the *positive* experience of the Shop Stewards' Movement; the need for the party could mainly be rooted in its *negative* experience – the failure of the May 1917 strike to spread, the fiasco of the January 1918 call for general strike etc. The crucial role of the party in generalizing workers' struggle, in overcoming the unevenness in the consciousness of the proletariat, was not at all clear to the shop stewards' leaders. With full justification Hinton could write:

> it is very doubtful whether, by the time of the formation of the Communist party in 1920-1, any substantial proportion of its members or leaders had grasped the Bolshevik idea of the party or would have approved of it had they done so. In this sense they carried their syndicalism over into the new party.[33]

Lenin Plays a Central Role in Shaping the Communist Party of Great Britain

The various British revolutionary groups groped towards unity under the banner of communism from the beginning of 1918. The first organization to declare itself Bolshevik was the SLP. Even prior to the October revolution it had declared itself 'the British Bolsheviks'.[34] The BSP turned towards communism a little later. The leaders of the shop stewards' movement were enthusiastic about communism. The urge towards unity of the revolutionary groups got a fillip from the founding congress of the Communist International in March 1918.

Immediately after the Congress the SLP leaders, Tom Bell and Arthur MacManus were contacted by the Russian Communist Party and urged to organize all the separate groups supporting the Russian revolution into a single party.[35]

Following the founding of the Comintern the BSP decided to ballot its branches on whether the BSP should leave the Second International and join the Third. The branches voted by 98 to 4 in favour. The Workers' Socialist Federation led by Sylvia Pankhurst decided to affiliate to the Comintern immediately. The South Wales Socialist Society followed suit. A conference of the Shop Stewards' and Workers' Committee Movement in January 1920 also decided to join the Comintern.

From the beginning of negotiations between the different groups it became clear that the old traditions of the separate sects could not readily be overcome.

Two issues dominated the debate: one, the question whether the future Communist Party should participate in parliamentary elections; and two, whether it should affiliate to the Labour Party. To these two questions the BSP replied affirmatively, the SLP gave an affirmative response to the first but a vehement 'no' to the second. Both the Workers' Socialist Federation and the South Wales Socialist Society answered the two questions in the negative.

Quite early on Lenin took a clear position on the two questions. He argued for participation in parliamentary elections and for the British Communist Party to affiliate to the Labour Party. His stand sharpened with time.

On 28 August 1919 Lenin wrote to Sylvia Pankhurst:

I am personally convinced that to renounce participation in the parliamentary elections is a mistake on the part of the revolutionary workers of Britain, but better to make that mistake than to delay the formation of a big workers' Communist Party in Britain out of all the trends and elements listed by you, which sympathize with Bolshevism and sincerely support the Soviet Republic . . .

What if in a given country those who are Communists by conviction and by their readiness to carry on revolutionary work, sincere partisans of Soviet power (the 'Soviet system', as non-Russians sometimes call it), cannot unite owing to disagreement over participation in Parliament?

I should consider such disagreement immaterial at present, since the struggle for Soviet power is the political struggle of the proletariat in its highest, most class-conscious, most revolutionary form . . . the question of parliamentarism is now a partial, secondary question.[36]

Lenin thus made it clear that while he was for communist participation in parliamentary elections, the issue was of only secondary importance, and disagreement with his views should not hold up the establishment of the Communist Party in Britain.

However, a few months later Lenin took a much stronger stand against the British opponents of participation in parliamentary elections. *Left Wing Communism – An Infantile Disorder*, which he completed on 27 April 1920, was written specially to refute the anti-parliamentary left of the Pankhurst-Gallacher variety; indeed, these two leaders are particularly referred to and argued against for their opposition.

At the second congress of the Comintern Lenin chaired the special committee on the British question, which included a number of well known leaders Bukharin, Zinoviev, Paul Levi and others. It dealt again with the two questions and strongly recommended both participation in parliamentary elections and affiliation to the Labour Party.

In arguing for affiliation Lenin made no concession at all regarding the reactionary nature of the Labour Party. He told the Congress that he disagreed with McLaine, the spokesman of the BSP at the Congress: 'He calls the Labour Party the political organization of the trade-union movement. Later on he repeated this when he said: the Labour Party "is the political expression of the trade-union movement".' In fact,

> The Labour Party is a thoroughly bourgeois party, because, although it consists of workers, it is led by reactionaries, and the worst reactionaries at that, who act fully in the spirit of the bourgeoisie. It is an organization of the bourgeoisie which exists in order with the aid of the British Noskes and Scheidemanns to systematically deceive the workers.[87]

Lenin's reason for affiliation to the Labour Party was in fact to fight it from within. Hence for him the basic condition for communists affiliating to the Labour Party was their complete freedom of propaganda *against* the policy and leadership of the Labour Party. 'We must say frankly that the party of the Communists can join the Labour Party only on condition that it retains complete freedom of criticism and can pursue its own policy.'[38]

Lenin accepted the view of the SLP that the Labour Party was a bourgeois party which would never lead the workers to socialism and had to be replaced by a Communist Party. On the other hand he agreed with the BSP that the Communist Party should take advantage of the unique feature of the Labour Party constitution which permitted the affiliation of socialist parties and societies.*

---

* One should avoid drawing conclusions as regards our time from Lenin's position regarding the Labour Party at that time, as the Labour Party was then very different. The constituency parties (at present largely middle class in composition) were first formed only in 1919; at that time the Labour Party was

The session of the Second Congress devoted to the Labour Party affiliation ended after Lenin spoke, with a vote of 58 to 24 (and 2 abstentions) in favour of the affiliation. (Although the 24 was a minority, it represented the largest vote against the Russian's views at any congress of the Communist International.)

The power of the prestigious leaders of the Comintern was still not great enough quickly or easily to overcome all the traditions of the sects that so bedevilled British Marxists for decades. As a historian of the CPGB, Macfarlane, put it:

> The long and tortuous negotiations for the formation of a united Communist Party would probably never even have begun but for the insistence of the Russian Bolshevik leaders. Once initiated, however, control of the negotiations was in the hands of participants whose prejudices and sectarian tendencies dominated the proceedings.[40]

The leadership of the Comintern spend a lot of time discussing the British communist movement: in 1921-2 the Praesidium of the Comintern discussed Britain 13 times – more often than any country other than France, Italy, Hungary and Germany. But the impact of the Comintern leadership on the actual situation in the British communist movement was not very great.

The Expectations

Lenin expected that quite a large Communist Party would be created as a result of the fusion of the various organizations which claimed to be communist. Thus in his speech to the Second Congress of the Comintern on 6 August 1920 he stated:

---

practically synonymous with the labour movement. This explains a number of phenomena which could not now recur. Could anyone imagine a Labour leader today breaking the law, going to prison in support of the unemployed and being met by a demonstration of 20,000 people outside the jail, as George Lansbury did in 1921? Can one imagine a general election, like that of December 1923 where out of 9 Communist candidates, 7 were adopted as Labour candidates? Can one imagine that it would take the right wing until 1928 to get rid of Communist supporters in the Labour Party by disaffiliating 26 constituency parties with 80,000 members?[39]

The last conference of the British Socialist Party, which took place in London three or four days ago, decided to rename the Party a Communist Party, and adopted a point in its programme providing for participation in parliamentary elections and affiliation to the Labour Party. At the Conference ten thousand organized members were represented.

He added, turning to Gallacher, that many should join the party from Scotland:

it would not be difficult at all for the Scottish comrades to bring into this "Communist Party of Great Britain" more than ten thousand revolutionary workers better versed in the art of working among the masses, and thus to change the old tactics of the British Socialist Party.[41]

Many thousands were also expected to join the Communist Party from the Shop Stewards' Movement. These estimates were not dreamed up by Lenin. The representative of the shop stewards' movement at the Congress, Jack Tanner, had claimed that this movement had 200,000 members.[42] In addition it was expected that many would join from the ILP. In the report which Helen Crawford, secretary of the ILP left wing, gave to the Second Congress it was claimed that Preston, Liverpool, Nelson and Barrow-in-Furness were strictly communist ILP branches. The left wing supporters in these alone were claimed to number 1,000.[43] The *Communist*, weekly of the CPGB, wrote at the beginning of April 1921: 'Twenty per cent of the ILP have come out straight away and joined with us. Some 5,000 or more have thus joined the Party *en bloc*.'[44]

The Results Were Different to Expectations
The little Marxist organizations with their long history of squabbles and sectarianism, spent months and months on negotiations regarding fusion. When it came to the unity conference, only the BSP joined as a unified organization. The SLP withdrew from the talks after a ballot of its members in November-December 1919. As a result a section of the SLP created its own organization and joined the CP. The number amounted to probably a couple of hundred. The Workers' Socialist Federation,

after long and tortuous negotiation, refused to join the CPGB as did the South Wales Socialist Society. John Maclean, the best-known revolutionary in Britain, also refused to join the Party. Maclean, more than any other individual, represented for the Russians the authentic voice of the British revolution. He had been appointed to the Praesidium of the First All-Russian Congress of the Soviets and made Soviet Consul for Scotland in February 1918. Instead of joining the British Communist Party Maclean tried to build a separate Scottish Communist Party. As regards the ILP's claim Macfarlane writes: *The Communist* wildly talked of five thousand ILP members joining the Communist Party *en bloc*. In point of fact, as Tom Bell wrote later, they gained one or two hundred members.[45]

Altogether, according to James Klugman, official historian of the CPGB, the Party started with a membership around 3,000 which dropped to 2,000 by mid-1922.[46]

The bulk of the members came from the BSP while the core of the leadership came from the SLP: Arthur McManus, Tom Bell, William Paul and Jack Murphy.

Not only was the CP very small in size, but the quality of its organization and leadership was far from satisfactory. As Klugman put it:

> Party brainches resembled the traditional branches of the socialist propaganda societies or sects; the Party was not participating in the mass struggle with anything like the effectiveness of which it was capable; its organization remained essentially that of the old type of socialist party; the federally elected geographically-based leadership was not capable of mobilizing the Party nor indeed suitable for a revolutionary Party.[47]

Only in 1922-3 did the CPGB start to work systematically to get rid of its sectarian tradition of propaganda sects and transform itself into a party rooted in industry that leads workers in struggle.

A concatenation of subjective and objective factors paralysed the attempts of Lenin and the Comintern leadership to shape the Communist Party of Britain. One factor was the slowness of the negotiations on fusion of the revolutionary groups, so that when the new Communist Party came to life the high tide of the revolutionary struggle had passed.

By 1920 the shop stewards' movement was completely in ruins, consequent upon a high level of unemployment caused by the run-down of munitions production, the widespread victimization of known militants and the reassertion of control over the trade unions by its leaders. Already in July 1919 J.T.Murphy could state:

> At Vickers, Sheffield, it is questionable whether there is a single, active shop steward or literature seller left in the place. They have practically all been cleared out under the cloak of unemployment. The same applies to many prominent people on the Clyde.[48]

Missing the Tide

Had the CPGB been established at the time of the rising militant struggles of 1918 and 1919 it would have got off to a grand start. Throughout 1919 the industrial and political class struggle had risen to unprecedented heights, with millions of workers fighting for wage increases and shorter hours. The miners fought for the nationalization of their industry. Even the police caught the fever. The head of the Special Branch, Basil Thomson, considered February 1919 'the high water-mark of revolutionary danger'. 'We cannot hope to escape some sort of revolution,' declared Lord Burnham, 'and there will be no passionate resistance from anybody.' Likewise Field Marshal Sir Henry Wilson told the Cabinet that in his opinion 'a Bolshevik rising was likely'.[49]

Government strategy throughout 1919 was to settle wage claims separately so as to prevent solidarity action developing.

In January 1919 a 40-hour strike spread throughout the whole of the Clyde. Over 60,000 men came out on strike in Belfast. Barrow engineers struck work on 5 February. London engineers decided to strike on 6 February. But the movement spread too slowly, and on 11 February it was called off without achieving its aim. The government gave concessions and the trade union leaders managed to reassert control over the local leaderships.

With the miners the government and employers played for time, and by appointing the Sankey Commission to look into miners' grievances while they made some concessions on wages and hours they achieved just that.

Widespread discontent and mutiny gripped the army in the early months of 1919. One thousand five hundred RASC men from Osterley Park seized lorries, drove them to London and demonstrated in Whitehall. Other soldiers demonstrated outside No. 10 Downing Street. Similar acts of mutiny were reported over a wide area of the Home Counties. Before the month was out twenty thousand soldiers refused orders at Calais. General Bying was forced to negotiate with the mutineers. On 7 and 8 February armed soldiers demonstrated on Horse Guards Parade. The War Office thought it necessary to send a 'confidential questionnaire to the commanding officers of all units to ascertain whether or not it was thought that the troops would remain loyal in the case of a revolution in England.' The Guards Division was recalled from Germany as a precautionary measure. In March 1919 five men were killed and twenty-one soldiers wounded in a mutiny at Rhyl.[50]

The Navy did not remain untouched. Aboard HMS *Kilbride* matters got out of control: on 13 January 1919 its seamen hauled the red flag up its masthead, declaring, 'Half the Navy are on strike and the other half soon will be.'[51]

In May a mass strike of policemen took place in London and Liverpool. This was beaten and a mass victimization of police was carried out.

In September a national strike of railwaymen took place and went on for 9 days.

The railway strike was followed by a strike of ironmoulders and coremakers – 65,000 workers were on strike for 105 days. They demanded fifteen shillings per week increase and seven shillings and sixpence increase for apprentices. They secured after the long dispute only five shillings per week increase.[52]

Had the CPGB been established in 1918 or even 1919 it would have taken advantage of the rising tide. But it missed it. In 1920 and 1921 the employers were on the offensive and the working class was on the retreat. After smashing shop-floor organization in 1919 the ruling class turned on the trade unions themselves: by taking them on one at a time it won a series of victories against the engineering workers, the miners, the railwaymen.

The subjective weakness of the British Marxists compounded the disadvantages of the objective situation created by the belated founding of the Communist Party. Naturally the subjective characteristics of the revolutionary groups were largely the by-product of the subjective conditions of the past: the general stability of British capitalism over many decades, the strength of conservatism in the labour movement, the hypertrophy of trade union bureaucratic power, etc. The hopes arising from the marriage of British traditions with the tradition of Bolshevism were not fulfilled. Russian power proved to be unable to convince the British partner quickly and effectively enough.

In conclusion: the notion that the CPGB was the brainchild of Lenin is facile and untrue. The CPGB was shaped by a complex process of the interaction of numerous factors: first the various strands in the British economic and social situation of the British proletariat over a long period. Secondly, the impact of the first world war, with its sharpening of the class struggle which raised the shop stewards' movement and the post-war spring tide of struggle and then its ebb. Thirdly, the Russian revolution and the arrival of Bolshevism on to the international arena in the shape of the Comintern. The intervention of Lenin and the Comintern leadership in the affairs of the British revolutionary movement was vital for the creation of the CPGB. One can say without hesitation that without this intervention a Communist Party would not have come into being. But the ability of the Russians to teach their British comrades to husband Bolshevik principles in British soil met with great obstacles. The British comrades came to Communism in their own way, and there were strengths and weaknesses in this rooted in the native land. The chief weakness was the inertia engendered by small group politics in the most conservative country in the world, which the might pressure of the Comintern leadership and the great prestige of the Bolshevik leadership which had won power was unable to overcome. To merge the small sects and semi-sects into an effective revolutionary party proved more difficult than to bring about a split in the mass centrist parties of Germany and France.

Failure Even in Bulgaria

The perfect antipode to the Communist Party of Britain was the Bulgarian Communist Party (BKP). This was a mass party that for nearly two decades claimed to be a model of Bolshevik revolutionary consistency. Would the disciples here prove able to follow the Russian teachers? For if there was one country outside Russia in which the Communist Party should have done so successfully, it was Bulgaria. History shows that even in this case the *native* traditions caused incompatibility in the relationship of the two Communist Parties.

For a very long period a close relationship had existed between the Russian Bolsheviks and the Bulgarian revolutionaries. Because of language and Slavic sentiment radical Bulgarian intellectuals received their advanced education in Russia during the latter part of the nineteenth century. Kimitar Blagoev, the founding father of the Bulgarian socialist movement and venerated till his death as the grand old man of the Bulgarian Communist Party, finished his education at the University of Petersburg. It was he who had founded the first known Marxist circle in Russian in the winter of 1883-4.[53]

The Bulgarian Social-Democratic Party dated from 1892. It was founded by Blagoev. In 1902 the party split into two factions: the Right led by Yanke Sakazov called itself the 'Broad Socialists' and supported collaboration with the opposition Liberal party, and argued for the political neutrality of the trade unions, as did the Economists in Russia and the followers of Bernstein in Germany. Blagoev led the opposition, called the 'Narrow Socialist Party' (*Tesniaki*).

A bond of sympathy and from time to time practical collaboration united Russian Bolshevism and Bulgarian *Tesniaki*. Both strongly opposed the first world war. When the Comintern was founded, the Bulgarian party joined it as a unit, 'thus bringing into the fold of the Comintern,' as E.H.Carr said, 'it's only mass party, other than the Russian, of indubitably Bolshevik complexion.'[54] Victor Serge recalls hearing the Bulgarian leaders, Kolarov and Kabakchiev at a meeting at the Kremlin 'speaking proudly of their Party, the only Socialist Party in Europe that was, like the Bolsheviks, intransigently loyal to principle.'[55]

Like the Bolsheviks, the *Tesniaki* were a mass party. In 1907 the membership was 1,795.[56] As the population of Bulgaria was less than 5 million, in relative terms the Bulgarian party was even bigger than the Bolshevik party, which had 46,000 members at the time.[57]

Taking a firm internationalist position during the Balkan war of 1912-13, the Bulgarian party increased its influence and membership even further. In 1912 the membership reached 2,923, in 1915, 3,400. When Bulgaria entered the world war in 1915, the BKP's strong anti-war position drew thousands towards it, so that by the spring of 1919 it had a membership of 21,557.[58]

Like the Bolshevik party, the Bulgarian party had a very effective press. By September 1909 the party paper *Rabotnicheski Vestnik* was published three times a week. It had 2,700 subscribers a not inconsiderable figure for such a tiny country. In 1911 it became a daily, by 1914 the circulation rose to 5,000 and by 1918 to 30,000. The party's almanac *Red People's Calendar* was distributed in 15,000 copies.[59]

The party's mass influence showed also through elections. In the 1913 elections they gained 52,777 votes and won 16 seats to parliament.[60] At the general election of August 1919 the party emerged as the second strongest in the country with 47 deputies and 119,000 votes.[61]

The Bulgarian party was not an accommodating, soft organization. It was not by chance that it was Blagoev who translated and published a big portion of Lenin's *What is to be Done?* in 1902 and 1903, commenting very favourably on its intransigence. Nor was it an inexperienced party. The party members had shown a fine readiness to sacrifice. By January 1917, because of their opposition to the war, 1,000 party members were in prison, and another 600 had been sent to the front though they were over the age for conscription.[62] Hundreds of members died in prison after horrifying tortures.

With the Bulgarian party joining the Comintern, it should,

on the face of it, have been easy to graft Bolshevism onto the Bulgarian party. Alas, when it came to the crunch, the party failed tragically.

We shall have to skip a little to show this.

The June 1923 Right–Wing Coup

On 8 June 1923 the government of Alexander Stamboliski, the leader of the Peasant Union, was overthrown by a military coup led by Tsankov. In the previous elections in April 1923 the Peasant Union had won 212 out of a total of 245 seats, the Communists 16 and the Socialists 2. The bourgeois parties, practically outlawed by Stamboliski, got only 16 seats. These parties, relying on the Bulgarian army, on the 20,000 Russian soldiers of Wrangel's White Army, who had escaped to Bulgaria after the end of the civil war in Russia, and on Macedonian units that resented Stamboliski's signing of the peace treaty after the war because it had cut big chunks off Bulgarian territory, joined forces to overthrow the democratically elected government.

The Communist Party's attitude to the coup was astonishing – practically a repetition of the KPD's attitude to the Kapp putsch of March 1920 in Germany. Its leaders simply stood aside. The result was that the incoming regime shortly afterwards decapitated the Communist Party and drove it underground for twenty years; it emerged only after the entry of the Russian army into Bulgaria in September 1944.

On the morning of 9 June 1923, the Central Committee of the BKP issued a proclamation 'To the Workers and Peasants of Bulgaria', which read:

> Last night the government of the Peasant Union was overthrown by a military putsch . . . The government of Stamboliski, which maintained its power . . . by terror and coercion has been overthrown. The government of the peasant bourgeoisie which . . . used its power to defend its class and clique interests has been overthrown. The government of the Peasant Union . . . suppressed the rights of the toiling people and waged a merciless crusade against their only protector, the Communist Party . . . Therefore, the workers and peasants must not today come to the aid of this government . . . The working masses in town and village will not participate in the armed struggle . . .

between the urban and rural bourgeoisie, for by such participation the toilers would be pulling the chestnuts out of the fire for their own exploiters and oppressors.

As the broadsheets bearing this manifesto appeared, Communist agitators, driven through the streets of Sofia on trucks, were calling on the people to remain calm and passive. When the local Communist leaders of Plevna, Plovdiv, Karlovo, Kazanlam, and Tirnovo, unaware of the Central Committee's decision for neutrality, mobilized their comrades to cooperate with the armed peasant Orange Guard in armed resistance to the coup, Todor Lukanov, one of the two secretaries of the Central Committee, telegraphed them orders to desist from this course of action.[63]

A meeting of the BKP's central committee, convened on 11 June, reaffirmed the line. This, they said, was merely a conflict between two bourgeois parties.

> The Communist Party, and the hundreds of thousands of workers and peasants united beneath its flag, are not taking part in the conflict . . . It is a struggle for power between the bourgeoisies of the city and of the village, that is between two wings of the capitalist class.[64]

An appeal to the masses, following the central committee session, stated:

> The armed struggle between the new power and the followers of the agrarian republic overthrown by the military putsch of June 9 is now approaching its end. The toiling masses fighting under the flag of the Bulgarian Communist party side with neither one party nor the other in this armed struggle.[65]

A session of the enlarged ECCI, meeting from 12-23 June, criticized the BKP leadership very sharply:

> Whoever mistakenly thinks that the struggle of the now triumphant white clique against Stambuliski is a struggle between two bourgeois cliques in which the working class can be neutral, will now be taught better by the bloody persecution of the workers' organizations. The putschists are now *the* enemy, and must be defeated. Unite for the fight against the white revolt not only with the broad masses of the peasantry, but with the leaders of the peasant party who are still alive.

Show them what the split between workers and peasants has led to, and summon them to a common struggle for a workers' and peasants' government.[66]

Radek was instructed to make a thorough study of the BKP's policy and present recommendations for its correction. He managed to gather the facts and prepare his report in time for delivery at the last session of the ECCI plenum on 23 June. He was vitriolic. The events of 9 June were 'the greatest defeat ever suffered by a Communist Party.'

The second largest party in Bulgaria, one enjoying the support of one fourth of the voters, had opted for a policy of servile inactivity and spineless surrender when the manifestly correct reaction would have been immediate fighting support for Stamboliski who, though not a Communist, nevertheless represented a genuinely radical, anti-bourgeois social force. In a country where 80 per cent of the population were peasants, the Communist Party's understanding of the peasant movement and appreciation of the peasant temper had been proven completely deficient.[67]

The party council of the BKP met at the beginnning of July and rejected Moscow's criticism.

> The committee of the party, after hearing the report of the Party central (committee) on the attitude of the party to the events of June 9, unanimously passed the following resolution:
> 1. The committee of the party completely approves of the attitude adopted by the party central (committee) to the events of June 9, and declares that the attitude and instructions of the party central (committee) are in complete accord with the resolution passed by the party committee in January and April 1923. The attitude which was taken by the Bulgarian Communist party to the events of June 9 was the only possible one under the circumstances.
> The party committee is of the opinion that the differences of opinion which have arisen with respect to the tactics of the party on the occasion of the coup d'etat between the Executive of the Communist International, on the one hand . . . and the Communist Party of Bulgaria, on the other hand, are to be attributed to the insufficient information of the Executive on the events of 9 June . . . The party committee is convinced that the Executive of the Communist International, once in

receipt of accurate information, will recognize the correctness of the attitude of the Communist Party of Bulgaria.

With respect to the appeal made by the Executive of the Communist International to the working masses, in which these are summoned to join forces with the leaders of the Peasant Union, the party committee is of the opinion that . . . it would be an error for the Communist Party to restore to the agrarian leaders, who have betrayed the interests of the rural working people, their lost influence.[68]

The resolution was adopted by 42 votes to 2.

Swing of the Pendulum

In Germany, after being passive during the Kapp putsch, the KPD initiated the Märzaktion a year later. Now the BKP, after being passive during the Tsankov coup of June 1923, in striving to make good its mistakes, plunged headlong in September three months later, into an insurrection with none of the political and organizational preparation necessary for such an undertaking.

The ECCI had not merely criticized the BKP leadership, but also directly ordered it to overthrow the Tsankov government by an armed uprising, and to set up a workers' and peasants' government. The leadership of the BKP, Khristo Kabakchiev and Todor Lukanov, held mainly responsible for the wrong tactics of 9 June, were replaced by Vasil Kolarov and Georgi Dimitrov.

The BKP leadership planned the armed uprising to take place at the end of October. But the government, finding out through its secret agents of the plan, carried out a pre-emptive coup, and on 12 September arrested nearly 2,000 Communists, including Kabakchiev and many other leaders. The party leadership now chose the night of 22-3 September for the rising.

The main insurrection was staggered in its eruption through about fifty towns and villages, beginning with Stara Zagora on the night of 19-20 September, so that the government, which retained complete control over the communications system, was able to shift its troops in time from one incendiary point to another as each ignited in its turn. The rebels, claimed by Communist sources to have been about 20,000 strong, were poorly armed and easily routed. In no major city did an uprising occur, and only the towns of Ferdinand, where the Supreme Revolutionary Committee had established its headquarters, and its neighbour Berkovitsa, both in the northwest, were captured on September 23 and 24 respectively and held for a few days by the insurgents. Everywhere the rebel columns were overwhelmingly peasant in composition and in most cases the uprising took the form of hopeless charges by scythe-armed villagers upon the towns and their garrisons. Indeed, the Communist Party district committees of the advanced and presumably more sophisticated centres of Russe and Burgas refused to obey the order to revolt. No doubt these local leaders regarded the premature launching of an insufficiently prepared insurrection as suicidal, as indeed it was.[69]

Zinoviev now praised the BKP![70]

Caught by surprise by the events of June and September, leaders of the BKP reacted in two ways: the majority adapted themselves to Moscow's instruction, while the minority rebelled and broke the discipline of the Comintern. An attempt by some of the BKP leaders, including former secretary Todor Lukanov, to condemn the party's policy in September were rebuffed at a special party congress held in the middle of May 1924. When communist M.P. Nikola Sakarov repudiated Moscow intervention and the September failed uprising, and declared that he and the other six communist members of parliament (the eighth member Kabakchiev was in prison) would only employ lawful methods in future, all the seven were expelled from the party.[71]*

Postscript to Adventure

The political bankruptcy of the BKP leadership did not lead to a disintegration of party influence. In the November 1923 elections to parliament, notwithstanding gerrymandering and intimidation, the BKP bloc with the Peasant Union secured 217,607 votes, and 31 Peasant and 8 Communist deputies took their seats in parliament.

---

* Blagoev was too old and ill to prevent the September coup, although it seems he did oppose it.[72]

The BKP and the Comintern came through the catastrophes of 1923. No mass party going back decades and with roots very deep in the people could be annihilated by even such a collection of mistakes, not to say crimes, as committed by the BKP in June and September 1923. Loyalties of masses to a party cannot be easily cast aside unless an alternative political party exists which offers a better chance to advance. The power of conservatism and inertia made it possible for the leadership to turn defeats and martyrdom into assets.

The September insurrection has become the great myth of the Bulgarian Communist Party, the sacred fire in which it was steeled and hardened into a 'truly Bolshevik' party, 'the Bulgarian 1905'. From the morrow of the uprising unending libations of gratitude have been poured by Bulgarian leaders to the deities in Moscow who turned the party from the evil ways of the June neutrality policy and directed it to the straight path of revolutionary activism.[73]

Though it failed, the insurrection had some lasting consequences. Within the Comintern it gave the small Bulgarian Communist Party a prestige second only to that of the Russians and Germans, and the readiness of the Bulgarian leaders to reverse their own policy with robot-like obedience ensured for them the lasting favour of the Russian masters.[74]

Super Adventure

Falling outside the period we cover is an event in the history of the Bulgarian Communist Party which certainly was the by-product of the failed September coup.

On 16 April 1925 a time bomb blew up Sofia's Nedelia Cathedral, where the king, many ministers, officers and deputies were gathered for a funeral ceremony for a general, a leading supporter of the government, who had been assassinated two days earlier. 128 people, including three deputies, fourteen generals, the Chief of Police and the mayor of Sofia were killed and 323 people wounded.

The ECCI immediately issued a statement denying any responsibility for the act by the Comintern or 'any of its sections', because of their opposition on prinicple to acts of individual terror.[75] Stalin at the fourteenth party congress in December 1925 referred to the outrage and repeated, in particularly emphatic terms, that 'communists had not, have not, and cannot have, anything to do with the theory and practice of individual terror'.[76]

Fifteen years after the event, in the course of his political report to the Fifth Congress of the Bulgarian Communist Party, Dimitrov finally confessed that the disaster had been 'an ultra-left deviation, an act of desperation perpetrated by the leadership of the military organization of the party'.[77]

How Can One Explain the Failure of the BKP?

Why did a mass party, that had existed as long as the Bolsheviks, fail so abysmally when put to the test of the struggle for power?

The basic cause was the weakness of the proletarian core of the Bulgarian party. Unlike the Bolshevik party, which was overwhelmingly proletarian, the Bulgarian party, once it became a mass party, was very largely composed of non-proletarian elements.

In its early days, the 'narrow' party was quite proletarian in composition, and became more so over the ensuing few years.

Year	All Members	Proletarian Members	
		Number	%
1903	1,174	480	40·9
1910	2,126	1,519	71·4[78]

However, after the Balkan wars, with a massive expension of the party, its proletarian core declined very much relatively and hardly expanded even absolutely.

In May 1919 the Bugarian Communist Party had 21,577 members, of whom 2,215 (or 10·3 per cent) were industrial workers, while as many as 9,421 (or 43·7 per cent) were from the bourgeoisie.[79]

In 1922 the party had 38,136 members of whom only 1,563 (or 4·1 per cent) were genuine industrial workers.[80]

The trade union base on which the party could rely was

also extremely narrow. Thus the number of members of the trade unions under the control of the 'Narrow Socialists' and later the Communists was as follows:

1908	2,080
1909	3,420
1910	4,600
1911	5,400
1914	6,560
1915	7,590
1919	13,000[81]

The Bolsheviks led strikes of thousands and tens of thousands time and time again. In the years 1895-1904 an average of 431,000 workers went on strike annually in Russia. In 1905 the number of workers on strike rose to 2,863,000.[82] After the massacre of the miners in Lena in 1912 as many as 300,000 workers took part in protest strikes. These merged with the May Day strike, in which 400,000 workers took part. Other political strikes followed.

In the first half of 1914 the number of workers participating in strikes was 1,425,000, of which 1,059,000 were in political strikes. On May Day 1914 250,000 workers went on strike in St Petersburg, and about 50,000 in Moscow. Strikes also took place in a number of provincial towns.[83]

Compare this with the strike record of Bulgaria between 1904 and 1913 the trade unions under the control of the 'Narrow Socialists' led 630 strikes involving altogether 32,519 workers or an average of 52 workers per strike.[84] Bulgaria had no Putilov factories of 30,000 workers. It had no large-scale factories at all.

The peasant backing of the BKP was also very different to that of the Bolsheviks. Lenin's strategy was based on a combination of the industrial proletarian vanguard with the mass of the peasantry rebelling against large landlordism. Bulgaria had no large landlords to speak of. When it achieved its liberation from the Turkish yoke in 1878 the Turkish landlords fled and the Bulgarian peasants took the land. The result was, as Shablin, the representative of the BKP at the Second Congress of the Comintern, stated:

The predominant form of ownership in the countryside in Bulgaria is petty landed property. In Bulgaria there are 495,000 landowners and the average area of each property is 0.9 hectares. But these holdings are shared out in the following way:

1. less than	5 hectares	225,000
2. less than	10 hectares	175,000
3. less than	100 hectares	95,000
4. more than	100 hectares	936[85]

The expropriation of large estates had very little meaning in Bulgaria. The countryside was far more petty bourgeois than Tsarist Russia. In Tsarist Russia about 30,000 large landlords had total land amounting to about 17 million desiatins (1 desiatin = 1.09 hectares), each big landlord owning about 2,300 desiatins. Some ten million peasant households owned equal amounts of land averaging 7 desiatins.[86]

The mass base of the Bolshevik party was completely proletarian. Up to the October revolution there were no Bolshevik branches in the villages, and the Bolshevik press hardly went into the countryside. All the Bolshevik duma deputies were from workers' curias in the cities. As against this the majority support for the BKP was in the countryside. Thus a leading communist estimated that 75 per cent of the Communist votes in the parliamentary elections of April 1923 in Bulgaria were cast by peasants.[87]

Having an independent strong proletarian base, the Bolshevik party could both mistrust the petty bourgeois peasantry and lead it against landlordism. The Bulgarian party was both dependent on the peasantry and showed an extremely sectarian, dogmatic attitude towards peasant movements.[88]

To add to the above weaknesses, and relating to them, Bulgaria did not have its 1905 – its dress rehearsal of a revolution.

Even though Blagoev copied *What is to be Done?* and tried to build his party according to the pattern of Bolshevism, it must not be forgotten that history does not move primarily through the party but through its interrelation with the action of the proletariat. Without active and conscious, independent, proletarian masses, even the best organized party cannot develop really revolutionary practice, cannot train its members, its cadres and its leadership.

When the 'Narrow Socialist Party' changed its name into Bulgarian Communist Party and joined the Comintern it entered a marriage of two ill-assorted partners – a national largely petty bourgeois party, and an international leadership rooted in the Russian proletariat. The Bulgarian national traditions did not disappear by the order of Moscow. The events in Bulgaria show how ridiculous were the assumptions of both Stalinists and anti-Communists that the Comintern was merely the child of Moscow, that the Communist parties abroad were merely the creation of the Russian party in its own image. The bankrupt policy of the BKP in June 1923 was home-grown.*

21
The Great Cover-up

Now we need to go back to the *Märzaktion*.** This was by far the most serious defeat of the communist movement in the first couple of years of the existence of the International. It was, unlike other defeats, not brought about by misdeeds of the local national leadership, but by the adventurist policy imposed on the German party by the leadership of the Comintern.

One of the saddest chapters in the Comintern's history during Lenin's lifetime followed the fiasco of the *Märzaktion*.

---

* This was compounded by the effort to correct the mistake, by the ukase from Moscow. The September 1923 catastrophe was a 'gift' from the ECCI. The Bulgarian party found no easy way to escape from its own history, now compounded by the history of the Russian party and the International.
** See pp. 278-9.

Would the Comintern openly denounce the misdeeds of Zinoviev, Bukharin, Radek, Kun and their associates, or would they be concealed? This question was connected with another: what would happen to Paul Levi, the talented former leader of the KPD, who had been wronged by the central leadership of the Comintern?

Levi's Public Criticism

On 29 March Levi sent a confidential summary of his findings regarding the *Märzaktion* to Lenin. A few days later he also published a pamphlet, *Unsere Weg*, publicly attacking the methods and tactics of the Zentrale and including several oblique references to Bela Kun and his colleagues. Levi's conclusion was:

> An action which merely expresses the political needs of the Communist Party and not the subjective needs of the proletarian mass is bound to fail. It is impossible for the communists, especially as long as they remain such a minority among the proletariat, to engage in an action *in place* of the proletariat, or *without* the proletariat, or in the end even *against* the proletariat . . .[1]

The Märzaktion was 'the greatest Bakuninist putsch in history'.[2]

The Comintern leadership made a mistake in relying on the incompetent delegates it sent out in all directions. Levi wrote:

> We believe that the dissatisfaction about these delegates is more or less the same in all the countries in which they are active . . . They never work with, always behind the back of, and often against the Zentrale of the individual country. They have the confidence of Moscow, others don't. This is a system which must undermine all confidence in mutual endeavours on both sides, on the part of the executive as well as the member parties. These comrades are usually useless or insufficiently trusted to undertake political leadership. The result is a hopeless situation: the absence of political leadership from the centre. The only thing which the executive accomplishes in this respect is to issue appeals which come too late and papal bulls which come too soon . . . The executive operates only as an arm of Russia extended beyond its borders – an impossible situation.[3]

Levi's blast was countered by a complimentary message from the ECCI to the KPD:

The Communist International says to you: You acted rightly! The working class can never win victory by a single blow. You have turned a new page in the history of the German working class.[4]

On 15 April the Zentrale of the KPD expelled Levi from the party for breaking discipline in openly attacking the party leadership.

A Split in the Russian Party

The *Märzaktion* led to a split in the Bolshevik leadership in Russia. Lenin, Trotsky and Kamenev condemned it, while Zinoviev, Bukharin and Radek defended it.[5]

Victor Serge remembers Lenin's severe attack at the ECCI on Bela Kun's stupidity during the *Märzaktion*.

> Lenin spoke in French, briskly and harshly. Ten or more times, he used the phrase 'les betises de Bela Kun': little words that turned his listeners to stone. My wife took down the speech in shorthand, and afterwards we had to edit it somewhat: after all it was out of the question for the symbolic figure of the Hungarian revolution to be called an imbecile ten times over in a written record![6]

On 10 June Lenin wrote to Zinoviev:

> The crux of the matter is that Levi in very many respects is *right politically*. Unfortunately, he is guilty of a number of breaches of discipline for which the party has expelled him.
> Thalheimer and Bela Kun's theses are politically utterly fallacious. Mere phrases and playing at leftism.
> Radek is vacillating, [making] a number of concessions to 'leftist' silliness . . .
> all the shouting about an offensive – and there was any amount of it – was erroneous and absurd;
> . . . it was a tactical *error* to call for a *general* strike once there was provocation on the part of the government, who *wanted* to draw the *small fortress* of communism – into the struggle.
> Premature acceptance of a general battle – that is what the *Märzaktion* really was.

Lenin went on to emphasize that the general line developed by Levi on the united front in the 'Open Letter' of January 1921 was absolutely correct:

The tactics of the Communist International should be based on a steady and systematic drive to win the *majority of the working class*, first and foremost *within the old trade unions* . . . Hence: the tactic of the 'Open Letter' should definitely be applied everywhere. This should be said straight out, clearly and exactly, because waverings in regard to the 'Open Letter' are extremely harmful, extremely shameful and *extremely widespread*. We may as well admit this. All those who have failed to grasp the necessity of the Open Letter tactic should be *expelled* from the Communist International within a month after its Third Congress.[7]

The Third Congress of the Comintern

The *Märzaktion* became a central issue at the Third Congress of the Comintern, which took place from 22 June to 12 July 1921. The record of the heated debates on the subject occupies over half the minutes of the congress.

Zinoviev, who as President of the International presented the report on activity, did not deal directly with the *Märzaktion*. No doubt because he was felt to be too compromised by his connections with Bela Kun and the protection given to the supporters of the offensive, he limited himself to explaining how the executive reached its conclusion on the matter:

it was not an offensive, but simply a defensive battle. The enemy attacked us by surprise . . . Many mistakes were made, many organizational weaknesses revealed. Our comrades at the German Zentrale have not hidden these faults; they want to correct them. The question must be answered: *can we consider these struggles as a step forward, as an episode in the tormented path of the German working class, or must it be seen as a putsch?* The executive thinks that *the March action was not a putsch*. It is ridiculous to speak of a putsch when half a million workers took part in the battle . . . We must clearly expose the mistakes and learn the lessons. We hide nothing, we do not carry out small group politics, nor secret diplomacy. We think that *all in all the German party should not be ashamed of this struggle, quite the contrary*.[8]

Apart from this quite summary reply to Levi's arguments (Zinoviev had the text of a long appeal against Levi's exclusion, which he did not read and whose existence he did not even mention during the congress), the President of the International said nothing on the March action. At the end of the discussion on his report, however, a general resolution, of which one paragraph approved the disciplinary actions taken during the year by the executive, was voted on. This method of dealing with the Levi case without thorough discussion provoked indignant protests from the German minority, and Clara Zetkin inveighed against the procedure.

> In my opinion, the case of Levi is not just a problem of discipline, it is in the first place essentially a political problem. It can only be correctly judged and evaluated in the context of the whole political situation, and this is why I think that it can only be dealt with properly in the framework of our discussion of the tactics of the Communist Party and in particular in the framework of discussion on the March action . . . If Paul Levi must be severely punished for his criticism of the March action and for the mistake he undoubtedly committed at that time, what punishment is merited by those who made the mistakes themselves? The putschism that we denounce did not consist of the masses in struggle . . . It was in the members of the Zentrale who led the masses into struggle in this way.

Nor did she exonerate the ECCI:

> It remains a fact . . . that representatives of the ECCI indeed bear a large share of responsibility for the way in which the *Märzaktion* was conducted, [and] that representatives of the executive are largely responsible for the wrong slogans, the wrong political attitude of the party, or, more correctly, of the Zentrale.

While admitting that Levi had committed an act of indiscipline, she asked how Zinoviev and Kamenev had been dealt with after a similar mistake in 1917.[9] This was an unpleasant illusion for the parties concerned, but doubtless a salutary lesson for the congress, referring as it did to the attitude taken at the time of the October insurrection by the man who, now President of the International, was posing as the champion of discipline against Levi![10]

Radek executed a typically abrupt turn. To avoid exposing the role of the Moscow leadership of the Comintern, he criticized the German Zentrale, which he said had been taken by surprise by Hörsing's offensive, and, worst of all, did not understand the need to organize acts of solidarity with the Mansfeld miners while not disguising from them that they could not win. It had aggravated the situation by irresponsibly calling for a general strike on 24 March which merely revealed the party's weakness. Then, instead of frankly admitting its mistake, the Zentrale had preferred to concoct the theory of the offensive to justify itself. But Radek concluded, like Zinoviev, that it would nevertheless be wrong to characterize the March action as a putsch because it represented 'a step forward'. He did his best to play down the severity of the defeat and to gloss over it by optimistic phrases:

> If the left comrades have made mistakes . . . during the *Märzaktion*, then I say that these mistakes speak in favour of them [as] they demonstrate the will to fight. For this reason we were with them, their mistakes notwithstanding. But it is better to win than merely to prove that one wanted to win. And therefore, comrades, *our tactical line is focused on world revolution*. We see the road toward world revolution in the conquest of the great masses. These masses we want to lead into the great struggles which history has decreed for us . . . We stand at the threshhold of a historical turning point, and there is no power . . . which can save capitalism.[11]

Bela Kun spoke only once, on a point of order, when he ranged himself with the so-called left.[12]

Lenin and Trotsky Attack the Märzaktion

Trotsky launched a powerful attack on the ultra-lefts, who did not understand the mistakes of the 'theory of the offensive':

> The congress must say to the German workers that a mistake was committed, and that the party's attempt to assume the leading role in a great mass movement was not a fortunate one. That is not enough. We must say that this attempt was completely unsuccessful in this sense – that were it repeated, it might actually ruin this splendid party . . .
> It is sometimes forgotten that we must learn strategy, must cold-bloodedly weigh the forces of our enemy as well as our own, must estimate the situation and not plunge into struggle in order to breach a wall of passivity or, as one comrade put it, to 'activate the party' . . .
> It is our duty to say clearly and precisely to the German

workers that we consider this philosophy of the offensive to be the greatest danger. And in its practical application to be the greatest political crime.[13]*

Trotsky was strongly supported by Lenin, but they had a hard job to gain the day. The German, Austrian and Italian delegates came out in support of the theory of the offensive and the *Märzaktion*. Lenin attacked them sharply:

> If the congress is not going to wage a vigorous offensive against such errors, against such 'leftist' stupidities, the whole movement is doomed. That is my deep conviction . . . In Europe, where almost all the proletarians are organized, we must win the majority of the working class and anyone who fails to understand this is lost to the communist movement; he will never learn anything if he has failed to learn that much . . . If it is said that we were victorious in Russia in spite of not having a big party, that only proves that those who say it have not understood the Russian revolution and that they have absolutely no understanding of how to prepare for a revolution . . .
> Comrade Terracini has understood very little of the Russian revolution. In Russia, we were a small party, but we had with us in addition the majority of the Soviets of Workers' and Peasants' Deputies throughout the country . . . Do you have anything of the sort? We had with us almost half the army, which then numbered at least ten million men. Do you really have the majority of the army behind you? Show me such a country! If these views of Comrade Terracini are shared by three other delegations, then something is wrong in the International! Then we must say: 'Stop.' There must be a decisive fight! Otherwise the Communist International is lost.[15]

Lenin Confides in Clara Zetkin

On the eve of the congress Lenin made it clear to Clara Zetkin that he agreed with Levi's criticism of the *Märzaktion*

---

* It is sad, however, to record Trotsky's subsequent words, uttered in the spirit of the collective solidarity of the Russian leadership and the ECCI: 'I am in complete agreement with Comrade Zinoviev and cherish, as he does, the hope that at this congress we shall arrive at a unanimous verdict on the character of our activity.'[14]

and only objected to the methods which he had employed in making them.

> The congress will condemn Paul Levi, will be hard on him . . .
> but his condemnation will be only on account of breach of disci-
> pline, not of his basic political principles. How could it be
> otherwise at the very moment when those principles will be
> recognized as correct?
> The way is open for Paul Levi to find his way back to us, if
> he himself does not block the road. His political future lies in
> his own hands.[16]

He added:

> You know how highly I value Paul Levi . . . Ruthless criticism
> of the March action was necessary, but what did Paul Levi give?
> He tore the party to pieces . . . He gave nothing to which the
> party could usefully turn. He lacks the spirit of solidarity with
> the party, and it was that which has made the rank and file . . .
> deaf and blind to the great deal of truth in Levi's criticism,
> particularly to his correct political principles . . . The 'leftists'
> have to thank Paul Levi that up to the present they have come
> out so well, much too well.[17]

The congress resolutions which Lenin and Trotsky formulated were very much in the spirit of Levi's criticism of the
Märzaktion.

The Congress Resolutions

The Third Congress in practice adopted Levi's united front
policy with the slogan 'To the masses!' but the *Märzaktion* was
characterized as a step forward. This was a compromise, a sorry
compromise to save the face of the Zentrale, and much more
important, that of *Zinoviev* (and Bukharin).

The 'Thesis on the World Situation and the Tasks of the
Comintern', written by Trotsky, (assisted by Varga), stated:

> The first period of the post-war revolutionary movement, dis-
> tinguished by the spontaneous character of its assault, by the
> marked imprecision of its aims and methods, and by the
> extreme panic which it aroused among the ruling class, seems
> in essentials to be over. The self-confidence of the bourgeoisie
> as a class, and the outward stability of their state organs, have

undeniably been strengthened. The panic fear of communism has abated, even if it has not altogether disappeared . . .

It cannot be denied that the open revolutionary struggle of the proletariat for power is at the present moment slackening and slowing down in many countries . . .

The chief task of the communist party in the present crisis is to direct the defensive struggles of the proletariat, to broaden and deepen them, to link them together and, in harmony with the march of events, to transform them into decisive political struggles for the final goal.[18]

The slogan of a united front between communist parties and social democratic parties was essential in order to win the masses of the workers to support communism.

The reaching of this decision to put forward the slogan of the united front was in itself an achievement. If the communist parties were to be organizations of numerically insignificant minorities, the leadership of the masses would remain in the hands of the Social Democratic parties, and the question of a united front would not even arise. Similarly, the problem of the united front does not arise where the communist party has the majority – as in Bulgaria at that time. But wherever the party was already a mass organization, but *not* the majority of the proletariat, there the question of the united front had to be posed in all its acuteness. And where the slogan of the united front was raised, the fight for transitional demands had inevitably to be advanced.

If the Third Congress resolution on the *Märzaktion* was a compromise, and an unsatisfactory one at that, it was partly because of Paul Levi's public attack on the KPD, and also because of his insinuation against the ECCI. But the main reason was the strength of the ultra-lefts in the Comintern and Lenin's and Trotsky's fear of a split in the KPD and the Comintern.

The resolution on the *Märzaktion* was a very dangerous precedent: a cover-up for the highest leaders – Zinoviev, Bukharin and Radek – instead of an honest accounting. The prestige of the leadership was protected at the expense of Marx's watchword: the Communists never hide the truth from the working class. The manœuvres of Zinoviev, the about-turn of Radek and the stupidities of Bela Kun were covered up. The fact that the motions dealing with the *Märzaktion* were adopted unanimously was a bad omen.

An Extremely Serious Defeat

The defeat in Germany coincided with the defeat of the Bolsheviks in Poland, and the retreat forced on them on the home front. As Zinoviev put it in February 1922, at a meeting of the ECCI:

> Had the Red Army in 1920 taken Warsaw, the tactics of the CI today would be other than they are . . . the strategic setback was followed by a political setback for the whole workers' movement – the Russian proletarian party was compelled to make extensive concessions . . . that slowed down the tempo of the proletarian revolution; but the reverse is also true; the setback which the proletariat of the western European countries suffered from 1919 to 1921 influenced the policy of the first proletarian state and slowed down the tempo in Russia.[19]

Altogether, developments in Germany were very disappointing. For the Bolsheviks Germany was the key to the international situation. As the Manifesto of the Second Congress of the Comintern, written by Trotsky, put it: 'A Soviet Germany united with Soviet Russia would have represented a force exceeding from the very start all the capitalist states put together.'[20] But the KPD repeatedly proved itself too immature, too inexperienced to lead the masses.

The defeat of March 1921 did not strengthen the German leadership. On the contrary. Until the *Märzaktion* the German communists had demonstrated a spirit of independence in argument with the Russian leaders – as can be seen from the debates at the congresses of the Comintern. At the Third Congress, the KPD leadership fell prostrate before the Moscow leaders.*

In Conclusion

On the home front Bolshevism came into conflict with the grim reality of traditional peasant conservatism. Lenin and the

---

* That the traumatic experience of the *Märzaktion* was a turning point in the history of the KPD in relation to Moscow is accepted by a number of historians of this party.[21]

Bolsheviks found themselves less and less able to reshape the Russian economy, society, culture and state. Now, on the international front, in one country after another, they were opposed by all the conservative traditions in the labour movement, traditions that resisted the ideas of Bolshevism. Given enough time it would have been possible to raise the international communist movement to the level necessary for proletarian victory. But time was running out.

Between the development of Bolshevism in Russia and the Communist International there were dialectical relations. The dream of a world revolution helped to sustain the morale of the Russian communists in the most difficult hours of the civil war. The October victory made it possible to organize masses of workers in a single world party in a short time – an achievement which in many respects was the highest point of the world Marxist movement so far. The documents, resolutions, theses and debates of the first two years of the Comintern provide the most complete guidance for the application of the developed Leninist theory of the party, 'an invaluable programmatic heritage', in Trotsky's words.

However, when the communist parties outside Russia failed to win victories, the fate of Bolshevism in Russia was seriously affected. The fact that the *Märzaktion* took place at the same time as the Kronstadt uprising and, that the retreat on the international proletarian front coincided with NEP, the retreat on the home front, strengthened the vicious circle of decline. Finally, the greatest defeat of the European proletariat, that of the German revolution in 1923, coincided with the victory of the Stalinist bureaucracy in Russia and Lenin's withdrawal from political activity. One defeat encouraged the others. Russia, now highly bureaucratic, became the rock on which the Communist International foundered. The Comintern became a weapon of the emergent Russian state bureaucracy.*

---

* As early as the Fourth Congress, only a few days before
Lenin left the active political scene, the opportunist strategy of
subordinating communist policy to the foreign interests of the

'It became no longer a question of "making the greatest national sacrifices for the overthrow of international capitalism" [Lenin's words], but of making the greatest international sacrifices for the preservation of Russia's national "Socialism".'[23] But we are running ahead of our story.

22

The Bolshevik Regime in Crisis

Crisis in the Trade Unions

Russia emerged from the civil war in a state of economic collapse 'unparalleled in the history of mankind', as an economic historian of the period writes.[1] As we have seen, industrial production was about a fifth of the pre-war level and the city population had shrunk. Between the end of 1918 and the end of 1920 epidemics, hunger and cold killed nine million Russians. (The world war as a whole had claimed four million victims.)

Towards the end of 1920, with victory at hand, and the

Russian state was formulated in a speech by Bukharin, who told the congress:
It ought . . . to be stated clearly in our programme that the proletarian state should and must be protected not only by the proletariat of this country, but also by the proletariat of all countries . . . The second question is: should the proletarian states, for reasons of the strategy of the proletariat as a whole, conclude any military alliances with the bourgeois states? Here there is no difference in principle between a loan and a military alliance . . . Under this form of national defence, i.e. the military alliance with bourgeois states, it is the duty of the comrades in every country to *aid this alliance to victory* [emphasis added].[22]
Nobody contradicted this statement.

civil war almost over, the system of War Communism reached crisis point. Stresses became particularly intolerable on the labour front. During the civil war the trade unions had stood more or less united behind the state and the party in tightening labour discipline in a way which was not compatible with traditional trade union practices. During the war they had supported industrial mobilization and the militarization of labour. The latter had now lost its justification. The problem of the role of the trade unions once again became the cause of friction, both within the trade unions themselves, and between them and the state apparatus.

The trade unions now reacted against state interference in their affairs, and protested against appointments and dismissals of trade union officials by the party.

As we have seen,* the First Congress of Trade Unions (1918) had argued that the unions ought to become 'organs of state power'; the Eighth Party Congress in the following year had declared that the trade unions 'must proceed to the practical concentration into their own hands of the work of administration of the whole economic life of the country'. In the heat of the civil war these views could be shelved – by state/union subordination of everything to the needs of the front. But once the civil war was over, the question of the relationship between the state and the trade unions was bound to re-emerge.

A very heated debate on the issue broke out at the Fifth Trade Union Conference in Moscow on 2-6 November 1920. The Bolshevik delegates, as usual, met before hand to decide their line at the conference. Trotsky launched a general attack on the trade unions, which he described as in need of a 'shake-up' – similar to the one that he had undertaken in the rail union. He purged the Central Committee of the Union of Workers in Rail and Water Transportation (Tsektran) with the aid of the Chief Political Department of the People's Commissariat for Communications – *Glavpolitput*. It was necessary, as in *Tsektran*, to replace 'irresponsible agitators' by production-minded trade unionists.[2] Tomsky, Chairman of the All-Russian Central Council

---

* See pp. 119-20.

of Trade Unions, openly attacked Trotsky and found an ally in Lenin. At the meeting of the Central Committee of the Party on 9 November, Lenin and Trotsky presented alternative draft resolutions on *Tsektran*. With four votes against (Trotsky, Kresinsky, Andreev and Rykov), a resolution modelled on Lenin's draft was adopted, calling for the democratization of the trade unions, an end to the practice of appointing officials to the trade unions from above, and elections instead. This was a rebuff for Trotsky.

The Central Committee was so divided on the question of the trade unions, that eight separate platforms were advanced. The discussion spread throughout the party. In the four months leading up to the Tenth Party Congress on 8 March 1921 the debate raged in party meetings and in the party press. Throughout January 1921 *Pravda* carried almost daily articles by supporters of one platform or another. Before the congress met the principal documents were published by order of the Central Committee in a volume edited by Zinoviev. The party also published two numbers of a special *Discussion Sheet* in order to provide a forum for a detailed exchange of views. As well as *Pravda* publishing the platform of one of the contenders, the newly formed Workers' Opposition, a separate issue of Kollontai's pamphlet putting the case for the Workers' Opposition was printed in 250,000 copies. Since coming to power the Bolsheviks had never been divided by so sharp a controversy.

In the end three platforms were presented to the congress. On one side were Trotsky, Bukharin, Andreev, Dzerzhinsky, Krestinsky, Preobrazhensky, Rakovsky and Serebriakov – eight members of the Central Committee. On the other was the Workers' Opposition, whose main leaders were Shliapnikov and Kollontai, a well-known Bolshevik feminist. In between was the Platform of the Ten – Lenin, Zinoviev, Tomsky, Radzutak, Kalinin, Kamenev, Lozovsky, Petrovsky, Artem and Stalin.

The Views of Trotsky and Bukharin

Basically the Trotsky–Bukharin group reacted to the economic collapse by arguing that army methods should be transferred from the war front to the factories and trade union organizations in order to tighten discipline. They wanted the complete 'statification' of the trade unions. Trotsky drew the logical conclusion from his statement on labour policy to the Third Congress of Trade Unions: 'the transformation of the trade unions into production unions – not only in name but in content and method of work as well – is the greatest task of our epoch.'[3]

He argued that in practice the statification of the trade unions had already gone quite far, and should be pushed to its conclusion. Secondly, the gradual transference of economic administration to the trade unions, promised by the party programme, presupposed 'the planned transformation of the unions into apparatuses of the workers' state'. This should be implemented consistently. He argued that his policy was only a continuation of the Lenin–Trotsky policy of earlier months and years.

The Workers' Opposition

This group included, besides Kollontai, a considerable number of worker leaders: Shliapnikov, originally an engineer and the first Commissar of Labour, Iv.Kh.Lutovinov and S.Medvedev, leaders of the Metalworkers' Union, were the most prominent.

The Workers' Opposition demanded that the management of industry should be in the hands of the trade unions. The transition to the new system should begin from the lowest industrial unit and extend upwards. At the factory level, the factory committee should regain the dominant position it had had at the beginning of the revolution. An All-Russia Producer Congress should be convened to elect the central management for the entire national economy. National congresses of separate trade unions should similarly elect managements for the various sectors of the economy.

Finally, the Workers' Opposition proposed a radical egalitarian revision of wages policy. Money wages were to be progressively replaced by rewards in kind; the basic food ration was to be made available to workers without payment. The same was to apply to meals in factory canteens, essential travel facilities, and facilities for education and leisure, lodging, lighting, etc.

The Platform of the Ten

Lenin's attitude to the trade unions changed much more quickly than Trotsky's. The end of the civil war meant for him the end of talk about the 'statification' of the trade unions, and about 'militarization of labour'. In a speech on 30 December 1920 he came out strongly against Trotsky's position. The speech was published in a pamphlet with the title 'The Trade Unions, the Present Situation and Trotsky's Mistakes'. In Lenin's view, the trade unions held a unique position. On the one hand, as their members made up the bulk of industrial workers, they were organizations of the ruling class – a class using state compulsion. On the other hand they were not, and should not be, state bodies, organs of compulsion:

> the trade unions, which take in all industrial workers, are an organization of the ruling, dominant, governing class, which has now set up a dictatorship and is exercising coercion through the state. But it is not a state organization; nor is it one designed for coercion, but for education. It is an organization designed to draw in and to train; it is, in fact, a school: a school of administration, a school of economic management, a school of communication . . . we have here a complex arrangement of cogwheels which cannot be a simple one; for the dictatorship of the proletariat cannot be exercised by a mass proletarian organization. It cannot work without a number of 'transmission belts' running from the vanguard to the mass of the advanced class, and from the latter to the mass of the working people. In Russia, this mass is a peasant one.[4]

With the end of the civil war trade union policy had to change radically. Compulsion, justified in wartime, was wrong now.

> Where did Glavpolitput and Tsektran err? Certainly not in their use of coercion; that goes to their credit. Their mistake was that they failed to switch to normal trade union work at the right time and without conflict . . . they failed to adapt themselves to the trade unions and help them by meeting them on an equal footing. Heroism, zeal, etc. are the positive side of military experience; red tape and arrogance are the negative side of the experience of the worst military types. Trotsky's theses, whatever his intentions, do not tend to play up the best, but the worst in military experience.[5]

Trotsky insisted that the militarization of labour was essential for socialist reorganization of the economy. Against this Lenin argued that militarization could not be regarded as a permanent feature of socialist labour policy.

In his speech to the Tenth Congress, he said that it would be a grave mistake to assume an identity between the state – even a workers' state – and the trade unions. The unions have to defend the workers from their own state:

> Trotsky seems to say that in a workers' state it is not the business of the trade unions to stand up for the material and spiritual interests of the working class. That is a mistake. Comrade Trotsky speaks of a 'workers' state'. May I say that this is an abstraction . . . it is . . . a patent error to say: 'Since this is a workers' state without any bourgeoisie, against whom then is the working class to be protected, and for what purpose?' The whole point is that it is not quite a workers' state. For one thing, ours is not actually a workers' state but a workers' and peasants' state. And a lot depends on that. (Bukharin: 'What kind of state? A workers' and peasants' state?')*[6]

> Ours is a workers' state *with a bureaucratic twist to it.*
> We now have a state under which it is the business of the massively organized proletariat to protect itself, while we, for our part, must use these workers' organizations to protect the workers from their state, and to get them to protect our state.[8]

A balance must be struck, Lenin argued, between the role of the unions in production and in consumption. They should

---

* In an article written a couple of weeks after the congress Lenin corrected one aspect of his speech.
I must correct [another] mistake of mine. I said: 'Ours is not actually a workers' state but a workers' and peasants' state.' Comrade Bukharin immediately exclaimed: 'What kind of a state?' . . . I was wrong and Comrade Bukharin was right. What I should have said is: '. . . What we actually have is a workers' state, with this peculiarity, firstly, that it is not the working class but the peasant population that predominates in the country, and secondly, that it is a workers' state with bureaucratic distortions.'[7]

not be turned into appendages of the state. They should retain a measure of autonomy, so as to be able to speak for the workers, if need be against the state.

At the same time as he was fighting Trotsky on one front, Lenin was also fighting, much harder, against the Workers' Opposition. He accused them of syndicalism, differing radically from communism.

> Communism says: The Communist Party, the vanguard of the proletariat, leads the non-party worker masses, educating, preparing, teaching and training the masses ('school' of communism) – first the workers and then the peasants – to enable them eventually to concentrate in their hands the administration of the whole national economy.
>
> Syndicalism hands over to the mass of non-party workers, who are compartmentalized in the industries, the management of their industries . . . thereby making the party superfluous, and failing to carry on a sustained campaign either in training the masses or in *actually* concentrating in *their* hands the management *of the whole national economy.*
>
> The Programme of the Russian Communist Party says: 'The trade unions *should eventually arrive*' (which means that they are not yet there or even on the way) 'at a *de facto* concentration in their hands . . . of the whole administration of the whole national economy, as a single economic entity' (hence, not branches of industry, or even industry as a whole, but industry *plus* agriculture, etc. Are we anywhere near to actually concentrating the management of agriculture in the hands of the trade unions?) . . .
>
> Why have a party, if industrial management is to be appointed . . . by the trade unions nine-tenths of whose members are non-party workers?[9]

Throughout the trade union debate Lenin made it clear that his differences with the Workers' Opposition were far more fundamental than his differences with Trotsky. As he told the Tenth Congress:

> When I had occasion to debate with Comrades Trotsky and Kiselev at the Second Miners' Congress, two points of view were definitely revealed. The Workers' Opposition said: 'Lenin and Trotsky will unite.' Trotsky came out and said: 'Those who fail to understand that it is necessary to unite are against

the party; of course we will unite, because we are men of the party.' I supported him.[10]

The chief defect of the Workers' Opposition programme was that it lacked any concrete proposals for ending the economic impasse. Its declaration of confidence in the proletariat, when the latter was so demoralized, was no substitute for a realistic programme of action. The demand for the immediate satisfaction of workers' needs, for equal wages for all, for free food, clothing, etc., was totally unrealistic in a situation of general economic collapse. With the proletariat demoralized and alienated from the party, it was absurd to suggest that the immediate objective of this heterogeneous group should be the administration of industry. To talk about an All-Russian Congress of Producers, when most of the producers were individualistic peasants, estranged from the dictatorship of the proletariat, was wishful thinking. (The concept of a 'producer' is, in any case, anti-Marxist – it amalgamates proletarian with petty bourgeois elements, thus deviating from a class analysis.) In substance the policy the Workers' Opposition advocated could be summed up in one sentence: the unionization of the state. (Trotsky was advocating the statification of unions.) However, if the proletariat is small and weak, the unionization of the state is a Utopian fancy. In terms of positive policies the Workers' Opposition had very little to offer.

The Conclusion of the Trade Union Debate

The debate on the trade unions ended with an overwhelming victory for the Platform of the Ten at the Tenth Party Congress. This congress was unique in the way its delegates were elected. On 3 January 1921 the Petrograd party organization, led by Zinoviev, issued an appeal to all party organizations. It called for elections to the forthcoming Tenth Congress on the basis of the various platforms on the trade union question. This provoked protests from the Moscow organization and from Trotsky. On 12 January the Central Committee, by 8 votes to 7, approved the election of delegates to the congress by platform – for the first time in the history of Bolshevism. At the Tenth Congress Lenin's motion was accepted by an overwhelming majority; 336 delegates voted for it, against 50 for Trotsky's motion, and only 18 for the Workers' Opposition.

Basically the trade union debate was an expression of the profound unease in the party due to the economic paralysis ruling at the end of War Communism. The economy was in a total impasse. The Bolshevik regime, having emerged triumphantly from the civil war, was losing its support, even among the workers. The Workers' Opposition reflected this popular discontent.

The discussion on the role of the trade unions proved irrelevant in practice to the search for new economic policies. Trotsky predicted at the congress that the victorious resolution would not 'survive to the Eleventh Congress'.[11] He was proved correct. As long as the party and state continued the policy of War Communism there were no matters other than administrative ones to try and get the economy out of the impasse. But these methods – whether the extreme ones advocated by Trotsky or the less stringent ones suggested by Lenin – proved incapable of breaking the vicious circle of war communism.

Even if the discussion on the trade unions proved irrelevant to further development, it nevertheless demonstrated Lenin's sensitivity to the mood of the proletariat. Trotsky admitted his error in the trade union debate a few years later:

> the working masses, who had gone through three years of civil war, were more and more disinclined to submit to the ways of military rule. With his unerring political instinct, Lenin sensed that the critical moment had arrived. Whereas I was trying to get an ever more intensive effort from the trades unions, taking my stand on purely economic considerations on the basis of War Communism, Lenin, guided by political considerations, was moving toward an easing of the military pressure.'[12]

Mass Disaffection

Disaffection was particularly widespread among the peasantry. So long as the civil war continued, the peasants on the whole tolerated the Bolshevik regime as the lesser evil compared with White restoration. However resentful they were of the grain requisitions, they were far more fearful of the return of the former landowners. Armed peasants often confronted the grain collection detachments, but the scale of the opposition was not such as to threaten the regime. Now that the civil war had ended, waves of peasant uprisings swept rural Russia. The most serious outbreaks occurred in Tambov province, the middle Volga area, the Ukraine, northern Caucasus and western Siberia. As Lenin noted in his speech to the Tenth Congress of the party on 8 March 1921:

> We find ourselves involved in a new kind of war, a new form of war, which is summed up in the word 'banditism' – when tens and hundreds of thousands of demobilized soldiers, who are accustomed to the toils of war and regard it almost as their only trade, return, impoverished and ruined, and are unable to find work.[13]

By early 1921 some 2,500,000 men – nearly half the total strength of the Red Army, had been demobilized in a situation of social unrest which threatened the very existence of the state.

In February 1921 alone the Cheka reported 118 separate peasant uprisings in various parts of the country.[14] The fiercest uprising occurred in Tambov province, and was led by A.S.Antonov, a former Socialist Revolutionary. At its height the Antonov movement involved some 50,000 peasants. It took the capable Red commander Mikhail Tukhachevsky more than a year to overpower this rebellion.*

Disaffection spread to the urban proletariat, many of whose members returned to the countryside for good, while others went foraging for food again and again in the villages. The rural disturbances became contagious and led to industrial agitation and military unrest.

In February 1921 an open breach occurred between the Bolshevik regime and its principal mainstay, the working class. Since the onset of winter, unusually severe even by Muscovite standards, cold and hunger, combined with the undiminished

---

* On the Tambov rising, see pp. 138-43.

rigours of War Communism, had produced a highly charged atmosphere in the large towns. This was particularly true of Moscow and Petrograd, where only a spark was needed to set off an explosion. It was provided on 22 January, when the government announced that the already meagre bread ration for the cities was to be cut by one-third. Severe though it was, the reduction was apparently unavoidable. Heavy snows and shortages of fuel had held up food trains from Siberia and the northern Caucasus, where surpluses had been gathered to feed the hungry towns of the centre and the north. During the first ten days of February the disruption of railway links became so great that not a single carload of grain reached the empty warehouses of Moscow.[15] In early February more than 60 of the largest Petrograd factories were forced to close for lack of fuel. Meanwhile, food supplies had all but vanished:[16] 'the Executive Committee of the Petrograd Soviet, chaired by Zinoviev, proclaimed martial law throughout the city. An 11 p.m. curfew was imposed, and gatherings in the streets were forbidden at any time.'[17] Strikes spread through the Petrograd factories. As Serge remembers: 'every day in Smolny the only talk was of factory incidents, strikes, and booing at party agitators. This was in November and December of 1920.'[18]

On 28 February the strike wave reached the giant Putilov metal works with its 6,000 workers, a formidable body even though its size was only a sixth of what it had been during the first world war.[19] Menshevik agitators received a sympathetic hearing at workers' meetings, and their leaflets and manifestoes came into many eager hands.[20]

Initially the resolutions passed at factory meetings dealt overwhelmingly with familiar economic issues: regular distribution of rations, the issue of shoes and warm clothing, removal of roadblocks, permission to make foraging trips into the countryside and to trade freely with the villagers, elimination of privileged rations for special categories of workers, and so on. But political demands came increasingly to the forefront – demands for the restoration of political and civil rights.[21]

This turmoil was accompanied by a flare-up of anti-Semitic feeling. The Jewish inhabitants of Petrograd were apprehensive, and some left the city, fearing a pogrom if the government collapsed and the mobs had the freedom of the streets.[22]

After a week, however, Zinoviev gained control of the situation and checked the unrest. Force and propaganda alone were not enough to restore order in Petrograd. Of equal importance was a series of concessions sufficiently large to take the edge off the opposition movement. As an immediate step, extra rations were distributed to soldiers and factory workers. On 27 February Zinoviev also announced a number of additional concessions to the workers' most pressing demands. Henceforward they would be permitted to leave the city in order to look for food. To facilitate this, he even promised to schedule extra passenger trains into the surrounding countryside. But most important of all, he revealed for the first time that plans were under way to abandon the forcible seizure of grain from the peasants in favour of a tax in kind, that a New Economic Policy was to replace War Communism.

By 2 or 3 March nearly every striking factory was back at work.

Kronstadt Takes Up Arms

These strikes in Petrograd aroused the sailors of neighbouring Kronstadt to armed insurrection.

In July 1917 Krondstadt had earned the accolade from Trotsky of 'the pride and glory of the revolution'. The Krondstadters had changed considerably since then. Being out of the battle area, Krondstadt was emptied of its original sailors, who were mobilized to the most difficult fronts and replaced by a new intake. The bulk of the Krondstadt sailors in 1921 were not those of 1917. By 1921, according to official figures, more than three-quarters of the sailors were of peasant origin, a substantially higher proportion than in 1917, when industrial workers from the Petrograd area made up a sizeable part of the fleet.[23] In addition, three-quarters of the garrison were natives of the Ukraine, some of whom had served with the anti-Bolshevik forces in the south before joining the Soviet navy.[24] This was why they were particularly influenced by the mood of the people in the rural areas.

The widespread unrest affected even party members among the sailors. In January 1921 alone some 5,000 Baltic seamen left the Communist Party. Between August 1920 and March 1921 the Krondstadt party organization lost half its 4,000 members.[25] The main reason was War Communism. The Krondstadters charged the government alone with the responsibility for all the ills afflicting the country. They neglected the effects of the chaos and destruction of the civil war itself, the inescapable ravages of contending armies, the Allied intervention and blockade, the unavoidable scarcity of fuel and raw materials, or the difficulties of feeding the hungry and healing the sick in a situation of famine and epidemic. All the suffering and hardship was laid at the door of the Bolshevik regime:

> Communist rule has reduced all of Russia to unprecedented poverty, hunger, cold, and other privations. The factories and mills are closed, the railways on the verge of breakdown. The countryside has been fleeced to the bone. We have no bread, no cattle, no tools to work the land. We have no clothing, no shoes, no fuel. The workers are hungry and cold. The peasants and townsfolk have lost all hope for an improvement of their lives. Day by day they come closer to death. The communist betrayers have reduced you to all this.[62]

A degree of anti-Semitic feeling was mixed with hatred for the Communist Party. The worst venom was directed at Trotsky and Zinoviev. Prejudice against the Jews was widespread among the Baltic sailors, many of whom came from the Ukraine and the western borderlands, regions of traditionally virulent anti-Semitism in Russia. For men of their peasant and working-class background, the Jews were a customary scapegoat in times of hardship and distress. For instance Vershinin, a member of Krondstadt's Revolutionary Committee, when he came out on the ice on 8 March to parley with a Soviet detachment, appealed: 'Enough of your "hoorahs", and join with us to beat the Jews. It's their cursed domination that we workers and peasants have had to endure.'[27]

The Communist Party almost disintegrated in Krondstadt during the fortnight of the rebellion (1-17 March 1921). Trotsky estimated that 30 per cent of the Krondstadt communists participated actively in the revolt, while 40 per cent took a 'neutral position'.[28] As has been mentioned, party membership in Krondstadt declined from 4,000 in August 1920 to 2,000 in March 1921, and some 500 members and nearly 300 candidates now resigned from the party, while the remained were badly demoralized.[29]

'The Krondstadt events,' Lenin said, were 'Like a flash of lightning which threw more of a glare upon reality than anything else.'[30]

Peasants' Brest

The Tenth Party Congress met on 8 March 1921 in the shadow of the Krondstadt uprising. There was clear evidence that the party was losing its grip on the people. Some idea of the alarm this caused can be seen in the fact that, on receiving the news about Kronstadt, the Congress interrupted its debates and sent most of the delegates off to participate in the storming of the city. At no other time during the civil war had there been comparable panic.[31]

The first lesson the Bolshevik leaders drew from the peasant uprisings, from the disaffection of a broad section of the proletariat even in Petrograd, and above all from Krondstadt, was the need to end the compulsory requisitioning of grain. This was a retreat in face of massive petty bourgeois pressure. War Communism ended and a New Economic Policy was launched.*

Lenin understood the real significance of the Krondstadt events. He told the Tenth Party Congress that his 'report tied in everything – from beginning to end – with the lessons of Krondstadt'.[32] Although he insisted that the White émigrés had played an important role, he realized that the rising was not a mere repetition of the White movements of the civil war. He saw it as a sign of the gulf separating the mass of the peasantry from the Bolshevik government, and affecting the workers as well.

The crisis was rooted in two contradictory factors: the weakness of the industrial proletariat and the need to maintain

---

* See further Chapter 23.

some agreement with the petty bourgeois peasantry. Lenin told the Tenth Congress of the two conditions necessary for the victory of socialism in backward Russia:

> here industrial workers are in a minority, and the petty farmers are the vast majority. In such a country, the socialist revolution can triumph only on two conditions. First, if it is given timely support by a socialist revolution in one or several advanced countries . . . The second condition is agreement between the proletariat, which is exercising its dictatorship, that is, holds state power, and the majority of the peasant population.[33]

By 1921 neither of these conditions had been fulfilled. 'What is needed now is an economic breathing space,' Lenin said.[34]

> Basically the situation is this: we must satisfy the middle peasantry economically and go over to free exchange; otherwise it will be impossible – economically impossible – in view of the delay in the world revolution, to preserve the rule of the proletariat in Russia.[35]

Three years earlier, in March 1918, Lenin had made a similar retreat on the international front, when he signed the treaty of Brest–Litovsk in order to obtain a 'breathing space'. Now, on 15 March, the Tenth Congress of the Party adopted what one delegate, Riazanov, called a 'Peasant Brest'.[36]

Tightening Discipline: Banning all Factions

The general crisis severely affected the party's internal regime. In the face of its general isolation, and forced to retreat to carry out a peasant Brest, this regime was very close to collapse. Leading a retreating army, Lenin argued, demands the greatest discipline, the greatest stringency. And so, for the first time in the history of Bolshevism, factions were banned within the party.

During the trade union debate before the Tenth Congress, in an article entitled 'The Party Crisis', Lenin wrote (on 19 January 1921), not mincing his words: 'We must have the courage to face the bitter truth. The party is sick. The party is down with fever.'[37] In a speech at a meeting of Moscow party activists on 24 February 1921 he said: 'We have to rally and realize that one more step in the discussion and we are no longer a party.'[38]

In his opening speech to the congress, Lenin declared: 'there should not be the slightest trace of factionalism – whatever its manifestations in the past. That we must not have on any account.'[39]

> this is no time to argue about theoretical deviations when [there is a] . . . tremendous preponderance of peasants in the country, when their dissatisfaction with the proletarian dictatorship is mounting, when the crisis in peasant farming is coming to a head, and when the demobilization of the peasant army is setting loose hundreds and thousands of broken men who have nothing to do, whose only accustomed occupation is war and who breed banditry . , . The atmosphere of the controversy is becoming extremely dangerous and constitutes a direct threat to the dictatorship of the proletariat.[40]

Above all Lenin feared a split in the party, which, he told the Tenth Congress, was very close. 'Have we had at previous congresses, even amidst the sharpest disagreements, situations which, in one aspect, verged on a split? No, we have not. Do we have such a situation now? Yes, we do.'[41] He then moved a resolution 'On Party Unity' that banned all factions.

> The congress . . . hereby declares dissolved and orders the immediate dissolution of all groups without exception formed on the basis of one platform or another (such as the Workers' Opposition group, the Democratic Centralism group, etc.). Non-observance of this decision of the congress shall entail unconditional and instant expulsion from the party.

To this was added a secret article giving the Central Committee unlimited disciplinary discretion: 'the congress authorizes the Central Committee, in cases of breach of discipline or of a revival or toleration of factionalism, to apply all party penalties, including expulsion.' Members of the Central Committee could be expelled from the party by a two-thirds vote at a combined meeting of the Central Committee and the Party Control Commission.[42]

A year later, at the Eleventh Party Congress, in March 1922, the last which Lenin attended, he explained again why extreme measures of party discipline were necessary, and why the banning of factions was unavoidable:

> During a victorious advance, even if discipline is relaxed, everybody presses forward on his own accord. During a retreat, however, discipline must be more conscious and is a hundred times more necessary, because, when the entire army is in retreat, it does not know or see where it should halt. It sees only retreat; under such circumstances a few panic-stricken voices are, at times, enough to cause a stampede. The danger here is enormous. When a real army is in retreat, machine-guns are kept ready, and when an orderly retreat degenerates into a disorderly one, the command to fire is given, and quite rightly too.
>
> If, during an incredibly difficult retreat, when everything depends on preserving proper order, anyone spreads panic – even from the best of motives – the slightest breach of discipline must be punished severely, sternly, ruthlessly.[43]

The banning of factional activity was not regarded as an absolute measure. When Riazanov proposed an amendment to rule out elections to the Central Committee on the basis of separate groups, each standing on its separate platform, Lenin objected.

> We cannot deprive the party and the members of the Central Committee of the right to appeal to the party in the event of disagreement on fundamental issues . . . Supposing we are faced with a question like, say, the conclusion of the Brest peace? Can you guarantee that no such question will arise? No, you cannot. In the circumstances, the elections may have to be based on platforms.[44]

That the banning of factions did not mean the banning of all inner-party opposition was clear not only from this exchange between Lenin and Riazanov, but also from the fact that the resolution 'On Party Unity' itself invited dissidents to state their views in the Bolshevik press as well as in special discussion sheets.

Lenin also went out of his way to emphasize that there was substance in the Workers' Opposition's criticisms of the situation in the party and state. He referred to 'the services of the Workers'

Opposition'. In the resolution on party unity he included the following:

> the congress at the same time declares that every practical proposal concerning questions to which the so-called Workers' Opposition group, for example, has devoted special attention, such as purging the party of non-proletarian and unreliable elements, combating bureaucratic practices, developing democracy and workers' initiative, etc., must be examined with the greatest care and tested in practice.[45]

Even in the darkest days of the civil war factions had not been banned in the Bolshevik Party. The Mensheviks and Socialist Revolutionaries were harrassed, now outlawed, now allowed to come out into the open. Such policy changes were dictated by the circumstances of the war, and by the vacillations of these parties. Now not only were these parties outlawed, but so also were factions inside the ruling Bolshevik Party. There was a feeling among the Bolsheviks that there was no alternative. Perhaps the attitude of the party was best summed up in Radek's words to the Congress:

> In voting for this resolution, I feel that it can well be turned against us, and nevertheless I support it . . . Let the Central Committee in a moment of danger take the severest of measures against the best party comrades, if it finds this necessary. Let the Central Committee even be mistaken! That is less dangerous than the wavering which is now observable.[46]

23
The New Economic Policy

The transition from War Communism to the New Economic Policy (NEP) was rapid. In the summer of 1920, when Lenin read a remark by Varga inspired by the experience of the Hungarian revolution, that 'requisitions do not lead to the goal since they bring in their train a decrease of production', he put two question marks beside it.[1] A few months later, beside a statement in Bukharin's *The Economics of the Transition Period* that coercion of the peasantry was not to be regarded as 'pure constraint', since it 'lies on the path of general economic development', he wrote 'very good'.[2]

As late as December 1920 Lenin still supported compulsory requisitioning. As he said to the Eighth Congress of the Soviets on 22 December 1920: 'In a country of small peasants, our chief and basic task is to be able to resort to state compulsion in order to raise the level of peasant farming.'[3]*

On 8 February 1921, however, in a Politbureau discussion on the agrarian question, Lenin wrote the draft of a thesis which stated:

1. Satisfy the wish of the non-party peasants for the substitution of a tax in kind for the surplus appropriation system (the confiscation of surplus grain stocks).
2. Reduce the size of this tax as compared with last year's appropriation rate.

---

* It is interesting that Trotsky had by February 1920 reached the conclusion that food requisitions led to a cul-de-sac. After his economic inspection trip to the Urals, he wrote to the Central Committee:
'The present policy of the requisition of food products is lowering agricultural production, bringing about the atomization of the industrial proletariat and threatens to disorganize completely the economic life of the country.'
As a fundamental practical measure, Trotsky proposed: 'To replace the requisitioning of the surpluses by a levy proportionate to the quantity of production (a sort of progressive income tax) and set up in such a manner that it is nevertheless more profitable to increase the acreage sown or to cultivate it better.'[4]
The Central Committee, however, refused to move towards a more liberal agricultural policy. Giving way to the opposition of Lenin and the other leaders of the party, Trotsky turned towards a stricter execution of the War Communism policy, in the form of an extreme militarization of labour. Though he was right in February, Trotsky did not persevere in the way Lenin did when he was in a minority.

3. Approve the principle of making the tax commensurate with the farmer's effort, reducing the rate for those making greater effort.

4. Give the farmer more leeway in using his after-tax surpluses in local trade, provided his tax is promptly paid up in full.[5]

On 11 February a Siberian peasant named Chernov was permitted to express the viewpoint in *Pravda* that it would be to the benefit of the state to institute a food tax, leaving the peasant free to dispose of his surplus. Two Moscow communists, Sorokin and Rogov, contributed an article to *Pravda* on 17 February, repeating Chernov's suggestion, and declaring that efforts to force the peasants to cultivate fields would not yield results. On 24 February a detailed draft worked out by the Politbureau on the lines of Lenin's thesis was submitted to the Central Committee. On 28 February, in a plenary session of the Moscow Soviet, Lenin said he saw the point of a delegate's argument to the effect that the peasants needed to know what they had to deliver to the state, i.e. that the seizure of 'surpluses' should be replaced by a tax in kind: 'we are inclined to take this idea into account and we shall place this question before the party congress due to be held in a week's time, sort it out and take a decision satisfactory to the non-party peasant and to the mass of the people'.[6]

The change in economic policy was very sudden indeed. When the question was raised by Lenin at the Tenth Congress, it had not been discussed before in the party. Even at the congress Lenin did not bring the question up until the very end of the session and it was hardly debated. The discussion of this weighty issue occupied some 20 of the 330 pages of the report of the congress. After Lenin's and Tsiurupa's official proposals only 4 ten-minute speeches followed and the new policy was adopted almost unanimously (only 30 voted against). The reason was quite obvious. The regime was very close to complete collapse, and the need for immediate rescue measures was clear to everybody. As Lenin put it in his summing-up speech:

> The Central Committee's decision to substitute a tax for the surplus-grain appropriation system was adopted with such obvious unanimity – and what is most important, we saw at

once, even before the congress opened, that various comrades in the localities had arrived at the same conclusions independently of this decision, on the basis of their own practical experience – that it is essentially impossible to doubt that as a measure it is proper and necessary.[7]

It became clear to Lenin that the Bolsheviks had to retreat in the face of the peasants' pressure. One note he wrote at the time reads: '1794 versus 1921'.[8] In 1794 in France the beneficiaries of the revolution, especially the more prosperous peasants, pressed for relaxation of Jacobin control and demanded freedom of trade. This demand swept away Robespierre, and the whole revolution moved to the right after Thermidor (the month of Robespierre's downfall). Lenin's note shows that he intended to carry out an economic retreat so as to avoid a head-on clash with the forces equivalent to those which broke Robespierre. He still saw this as a purely temporary retreat, a manœuvre by a workers' state encircled by capitalism and banking firmly on revolutionary developments in Europe.

'Learn to Trade'

With NEP Lenin applied his customary 'stick-bending'. The need now was to replace sweeping revolutionary changes with meticulous reforms, and day-to-day execution of decisions.

In moving from War Communism to NEP one of the main dangers was that the party and its members would not adapt themselves to the new needs. Enthusiasm, which had been a source of strength during the civil war, was far from enough to solve the new economic problems. In a number of speeches following the launching of NEP Lenin repeatedly returned to the theme: Communists must learn to trade.

In a speech to the Ninth Congress of Soviets on 23 December 1921 he spoke of 'a French proverb which says that people's faults are usually connected with their merits'. 'A man's faults are, as it were, a continuation of his merits,' and he went on to say:

> But if the merits persist longer than they are needed . . . they become faults . . . Our great merit was that in the political and military fields we took a step of historic importance, that

has gone down in world history as a change of epochs . . . this is the undoubted, unalterable, inalienable merit, which no efforts or onslaughts of our enemies can take away from us, but which if it persists where it is no longer needed becomes a most dangerous fault.
A burst of enthusiasm on the part of the workers and peasants . . . was sufficient to solve political and military problems.
Now enthusiasm will not do. What is needed is 'forbearance, bitter experiences, long effort, punctuality and perseverance'.[9]

Communists must learn to trade.
The proletarian state must become a cautious, assiduous and shrewd 'businessman', a punctilious *wholesale merchant* – otherwise it will never succeed in putting this small-peasant country economically on its feet.[10]

The whole point is that the responsible communists, even the best of them, who are unquestionably honest and loyal, who in the old days suffered penal servitude and did not fear death, do not know how to trade, because they are not businessmen, they have not learnt to trade.[11]

The communists, the heroes of the underground and the civil war, must now learn to trade.

Communism and trade?! It sounds strange. The two seem to be unconnected, incongruous, poles apart. But if we study it from the point of view of *economics*, we shall find that the one is no more remote from the other than communism is from small-peasant, patriarchal farming.[12]

State Capitalism, Yet Again

While not hiding the fact that NEP was a retreat forced on the Bolsheviks by the petty bourgeois peasantry, Lenin also argued that it was a resumption of the policy he had developed in the spring of 1918, which had been interrupted by the outbreak of the civil war. He quoted what he wrote in April 1918:

It is not enough to be a revolutionary and an adherent of socialism or a communist in general. You must be able at each particular moment to find the particular link in the chain which you must grasp with all your might in order to hold the whole chain and to prepare firmly for the transition to the next link; the order of the links, their form, the manner in which they are linked together, their difference from each other in the historical chain of events are not as simple and not as senseless as those in an ordinary chain made by a smith.

He now went on to say:

> At the present time, in the sphere of activity with which we are dealing, this link is the revival of home *trade* under proper state regulation (direction). Trade is the 'link' in the historical chain of events, in the transitional forms of our socialist construction in 1921-22, which we, the proletarian government, we, the ruling Communist Party, '*must grasp with all our might*'. If we 'grasp' this link firmly enough *now* we shall certainly control the *whole* chain in the very near future. If we do not, we shall not control the whole chain, we shall not create the foundation for socialist social and economic relations.[13]

This policy of spring 1918 was summed up by the term 'state capitalism' (see Vol.3, Chapter 6). State capitalism under the dictatorship of the proletariat would be the bridge between the petty-bourgeois individualist peasantry and socialism. Lenin re-iterated and redeveloped the line of action he suggested in 1918:

> Over the next few years we must learn to think of the intermediary links that can facilitate the transition from patriarchalism and small production to socialism. 'We' continue saying now and again that 'capitalism is a bane and socialism is a boon'. But such an argument is wrong, because it fails to take into account the aggregate of the existing economic forms and singles out only two of them.
> Capitalism is a bane compared with socialism. Capitalism is a boon compared with medievalism, small production, and the evils of bureaucracy which spring from the dispersal of the small producers. Inasmuch as we are as yet unable to pass directly from small production to socialism, some capitalism is inevitable as the elemental product of small production and exchange; so that we must utilize capitalism (particularly by directing it into the channels of state capitalism) as the intermediary link between small production and socialism, as a means, a path, and a method of increasing the productive forces.[14]

Not Hiding the Dangers

To argue that NEP was a necessary bridge between 'medievalism, small production' on the one hand, and socialism on the other, did not mean glossing over the dangers involved in the new policy. Lenin was not one to avoid confronting danger boldly and openly, soberly weighing up the forces in the proletarian camp and in the enemy camp. In his report to the Tenth Congress, he made it clear that NEP would strengthen capitalism in the countryside: 'the switch from the appropriation of surpluses to the tax will mean more kulaks [rich peasants] under the new system. They will appear where they could not appear before'.[15] In his summing up of the debate on his report, he said: 'Speakers here have asked, and I have received written questions to the same effect: "How will you retain the workers' state, if capitalism develops in the rural areas?" This peril . . . is an extremely serious one.'[16]

In a speech delivered at the All-Russia Congress of Transport Workers a fortnight after the Tenth Congress, Lenin said:

> We know from our own experience – and revolutions all over the world confirm it if we take the modern epoch of, say, a hundred-and-fifty years – that the result has always been the same everywhere . . . Once the small proprietors become owners of the means of production and land, exchange between them necessarily gives rise to capital, and simultaneously to the antagonisms between capital and labour. The struggle between capital and the proletariat is inevitable; this must be accepted by anyone who refuses to fool himself.[17]

As a matter of fact in the months and years following the inauguration of NEP, an accelerated process of class differentiation took place in the countryside. Rich peasants became richer. A section of the middle peasants, those who possessed sufficient animals and implements, benefited greatly from the new policy. At the same time the weak or impoverished part of the peasantry, most of whom had no horses, found themselves in a difficult position. They had to hire horses, obtain loans of seed, and so on, and thus became economically dependent on the well-to-do. More and more often they lost their hold on their strips of land and became agricultural labourers.

The peasants went beyond the limits Lenin tried to fix for them. When NEP was launched originally, it was intended that trade would be confined to local markets, and to exchange in kind between agriculture and industry. But those constraints were not observed. A general free trade developed. Lenin admitted defeat on this point when he said on 29 October 1921 :

> We intended to stimulate 'commodity exchange'. What was implied by that term? . . . It implied a more or less socialist exchange throughout the country of the products of industry for the products of agriculture, and by means of that commodity exchange the restoration of large-scale industry as the sole basis of socialist organization. But what happened? . . . this system of commodity exchange has broken down; it has broken down in the sense that it has assumed the form of buying and selling . . . Nothing came of commodity exchange; the private market proved too strong for us; and instead of the exchange of commodities we got ordinary buying and selling, trade.[18]

Linked to the rich peasant, the *kulak*, were the NEPmen, the prosperous traders. In 1922, 78 per cent of all retail trade was in the hands of these private traders. The NEPmen also became agents of nationalized factories and state institutions. They found their way into the co-operatives. Some of the co-operatives became mere façades for private trading concerns.

> Even the consumers' co-operatives in 1922-3 purchased nearly one-third of the supplies for their urban shops through private traders. It has been estimated that about nine-tenths of all retail trading outlets (including kiosks and stalls as well as shops) about this time were private and that three-quarters of the retail turnover was in private hands.[19]

At the Thirteenth Party Conference in January 1924, Preobrazhensky estimated that between a third and a half of the net profits of trade and industry in the previous year had gone into the hands of NEPmen or capitalists. In his view, the question of whether the NEPmen would strengthen their influence with the peasants and form an economic alliance to stem the drift to socialism, or whether the workers' state would be strong enough to break such an alliance and convert the private trader into a dependent agent of State industry, was a pressing one.[20]

For Lenin, NEP did not mean only co-operation between the state sector of the economy and the private sector, but above all *competition and struggle between them*. Co-operation and struggle were dialectically united: the state should restrict the private sector while protecting and expanding the state sector. In the mixed economy, the private sector should be subordinated to the state sector, and not the other way round. The planned, state sector under NEP should seek to expand and achieve greater control over its rival, the commodity-producing private sector, while the latter would naturally resist the incursion and strive for more or less normal 'free' market production. Lenin saw in NEP 'a desperate life and death struggle between capitalism and communism'.

The Proletariat in Retreat ...

That NEP meant a compromise with the peasantry was obvious from the outset. But it was not so clear what it would mean to the proletariat – in terms of its economic, social and political power. In fact the effect was far-reaching. The concessions to the peasantry were made at the cost of the proletariat.

The introduction of *khozraschet* (the principle of 'cost accountancy' or 'economic accountancy'), which Lenin described as a 'transition to commercial principles' was an inescapable element of NEP. One immediate result was that industrial managements started sacking workers.

> The process of dismissing superfluous staffs proceeded at a cumulative rate. The number of railway workers was reduced from 1,240,000 in the summer of 1921 to 720,000 in the summer of 1922; the number of workers and employees per 1,000 spindles in a leading textile factory was reduced from 30 in 1920-21 to 14 a year later.[21]

The number of unemployed workers rose very steeply:

January 1922	175,000
January 1923	625,000
January 1924	1,240,000[22]

These figures might not seem very serious; after all, unemployment in Britain was of about the same magnitude at the time, and Britain was a much smaller country. However, this would be a misleading impression. The vast majority of the population of Russia were peasants. As a percentage of labour employed, 1,240,000 was a very high figure indeed: there were only 8½ million 'workers and employees' in 1924, less than the 1913 total.

If the scourge of unemployment was not enough, another whip lashed the industrial workers – the 'red managers'. Their power was massively increased by NEP. They came increasingly from traditional managerial sections and were increasingly integrated into the party hierarchy.

> Statistics collected from the major trusts and syndicates in the latter part of 1923 showed that, whereas in 1922 65 per cent of the managing personnel were officially classified as 'workers' and 35 per cent as 'non-workers' (only one in seven of these being party members), a year later these proportions had been almost exactly reversed, only 36 per cent being 'workers' and 64 per cent 'non-workers', of whom nearly one-half were now party members. Two significant processes were thus at work: the management of industry was passing back into the hands of former bourgeois managers and specialists, and a higher proportion of these were acquiring the dignity and security of party membership.[23]

The managers acted in a more and more high-handed fashion towards the workers. In August 1922 the trade union paper *Trud* launched a strong attack on the new 'united front' of managers, which it accused of aiming at 'a diminution in the role of the unions', especially in the engagement and dismissal of workers, and of wanting ' "free trade" in matters of hiring and firing'. The article ended with a rhetorical question: 'Have our managers so far entered into the role of the 'masters' that they prefer unorganized workers to organized and disciplined members of trade unions?'

A few days later another article diagnosed a reversion among the new managers to the traditional attitudes of employers towards their workers: 'our managers, even the best of them, have been wonderfully quick in adopting the manners and tastes of our former capitalists'. *Trud* even published a cartoon depicting a Red industrialist, with a cigar in his mouth and all the attributes commonly ascribed by Soviet art to the capitalist, sitting in a cart drawn by a worker and complaining that 'labour legislation' stood in the way of a revival of industry.[24]

What about the workers wages? The real earnings of workers in 1922-23 were still only half those of 1913. The average wage of workers in constant rubles was as follows:

	Monthly (rubles)	Hourly (kopecks)
1913	30·49	14·2
1920-21	10·15	5·4
1921-22	12·15	7·3
1922-23	15·88	8·9[25]

The red managers went on the offensive in 1923 to cut workers' wages. A leading article in *Trud* on 11 March 1923, under the title 'Wages are, However, Falling', diagnosed a general decline since December, referred to 'the campaign of the industrialist for a gradual reduction in wages', and complained of the passivity of 'some' trade unions. In a resolution of 14 April 1923, on the eve of the Twelfth Party Congress, the central council of trade unions admitted that wages were 'falling in real terms' and called for action to arrest the decline.[26]

One ploy which management resorted to was postponing the payment of wages so as benefit from the depreciation of the ruble. As early as the winter of 1921-22 complaints had been heard of wage payments falling into arrears, especially in regions remote from the centre. With a currency frequently depreciating by as much as 30 per cent in a month, the loss to the worker was severe. For the last three months of 1922 the workers in the Don were reported to have lost 34, 23 and 32 per cent respecively of their real wages through currency depreciation. In January 1923 the trade union newspaper alleged that 'cases of failure to pay in full for two or three months are more and more becoming daily occurrence'.[27]

NEP seems to have opened the door to many abuses; nepotism flourished, and an applicant had to know the foreman or manager to get a job at all.[28] Tomsky, the leader of the trade unions, lamented: 'Haven't we got unfair dismissals, cringing, servility, respect for rank in our state apparatus?'[29]

E.H.Carr sums up the situation :

While the standard of living of the industrial worker in 1923 was higher than in the harsh years of War Communism, there had been no time since the revolution when discrimination was so overtly practised against him, or when he had so many legitimate causes of bitterness against a regime which claimed to govern in his name.[30]

The Role of Trade Unions Under NEP

At the beginning of January 1922 Lenin wrote a 'Draft Thesis on the Role and Functions of the Trade Unions under the New Economic Policy' for the Central Committee. This resolution emphasized the role of the trade unions as defence organizations of workers against management:

one of the main tasks that will henceforth confront the trade unions is to protect in every way the class interests of the proletariat in its struggle against capital. This task should be openly put in the forefront, and the machinery of the trade unions must be recognized, modified or supplemented accordingly: strike funds, and so on should be formed, or rather, built up.

The new role of the unions is especially necessary because industry under NEP is bound to be ruled by the capitalist principle of *khozraschet*.

The conversion of state enterprises to what is called the profit basis is inevitably and inseparably connected with the New Economic Policy; in the near future this is bound to become the predominant, if not the sole, form of state enterprise . . . This circumstance, in view of the urgent need to increase the productivity of labour and make every state enterprise pay its way and show a profit, and in view of the inevitable rise of narrow departmental interests and excessive departmental zeal, is bound to create a certain conflict of interests between the masses of workers and the directors and managers of the state enterprises, of the government departments in charge of them. Therefore, it is undoubtedly the duty of the trade unions, in regard to the state enterprises as well, to protect the class interests of the proletariat and the working masses against their employers . . . As long as classes exist, the class struggle is inevitable.

It follows from this that at the present moment we can under no circumstances abandon the idea of the strike struggle, we cannot, as a matter of principle, conceive the possibility of a law that makes compulsory state mediation take the place of strikes.[31]

Following those arguments, at the Fifth Trade Union Congress (1922) Schmidt, the Commissar for Labour, declared that with NEP 'the trade unions had to transfer the centre of gravity of their activity to the work of defending the interests of their members'.[32]

In fact under NEP the trade unions developed very differently from the way Lenin visualized. They lost much of their importance as a result of NEP. Under War Communism they were indispensable not only in themselves, but also as collaborators in the state management of industry. They were integrated into the Commissariat of Labour and into VSNKh. Now, under NEP, the unions were deprived of the right to intervene in management's administration of industry.

The Eleventh Congress of the Party, in March 1922, made clear the implications of NEP for the trade unions – they were to have no role in industrial management.

> Individual management instead of management by committee was now to be firmly established. 'The main . . . task of the proletariat after it has conquered power . . . is to increase the volume of output and to raise . . . the productive forces of society . . . [This] demands that the managements of the factories should concentrate full power in their hands . . . Any direct interference of the trade unions with the management of enterprises must in such circumstances be regarded as absolutely harmful and inadmissible.'

Even in privately owned industry the unions were to have no power to intervene in management: 'the trade unions should not assume directly any functions of control over production in private businesses and in businesses leased to private hands'.[33]

National minimum wages were no longer to be fixed by the All-Russian Central Council of Trade Unions, but by the Commissariat of Labour. At the end of 1922 the Commissariat was given the right to arbitrate in disputes. Margaret Dewar, a historian of labour relations in Soviet Russia, summed up the situation thus:

> The workers and their unions had, in fact, lost all the control over industry which they had exercised during the civil war, and which – so they were promised – would gradually be extended until they became the administrators of industry. They were, in fact, reduced to the role of the executors of production plans decided upon by the government and the private agencies without their participation; they were threatened by unemployment, and in their struggle for higher wages and better working conditions they were handicapped by political loyalties and by the law.[34]

(In addition the administration of social insurance against sickness and unemployment was transferred from the trade unions to the Commissariat of Labour.)

How did the trade unions react to workers' demands? 'Demands for higher pay were frequently opposed by the union leaders, especially in state financed industries with very low wages, such as coal, iron and steel.'[35]

A resolution on wages of the Fifth Congress of Trade Unions in September 1922 declared 'against the illusion that it is possible in the very near future to raise wage rates to the level of the pre-war minimum standard'. On 25 February 1923 *Trud* called a halt to any wage increases.

> The present economic situation makes objectively impossible a general rise in wages in industry . . . the attention of the unions in the immediate future should be concentrated on maintaining the present level of wages and not permitting a reduction of real wages in future agreements.[36]

One result of workers' frustration was a decline in trade union membership. Over 50 per cent of the workers left their unions between July 1921 and August 1922.[37] Another consequence was the outbreak of numerous unofficial strikes in July-September 1923. The seriousness of the situation can be seen from a speech by Stalin on 2 December 1923, when he said: 'what has caused the question of internal party policy to become so acute precisely in the present period, in the autumn of this year? How is this to be explained?' One explanation he gave was 'the wave of discontent and strikes over wages that swept through certain districts of the republic in August of this year. The fact of the matter is that this strike wave exposed the defects in our organizations; it revealed the isolation of our organizations – both party and trade-union – from the events taking place in the factories'.[38]

Any threat by workers to strike in order to draw attention to grievances was treated as a breach of trade union discipline and punished by exclusion of those responsible from the union, which meant automatic dismissal from the factory and inability to obtain another job. In practice, therefore, the trade union representatives and factory committees tended to find themselves co-operating with the managers and the police to maintain discipline among the workers, to prevent strikes and to suppress disturbances. When stoppages occurred, the secret police at once intervened, at the request of the management and with the tacit or explicit assent of the unions, to arrest 'ringleaders' and 'instigators'. Protests and demonstrations by the workers were ruthlessly met with force. In the first half of 1923, when strikes were freely reported, *Trud* frequently recorded the exclusion of strikers from the unions as a penalty.[39]

The union leaders, who were completely subordinated to the party-state leadership, did not defend workers, but increasingly collaborated with management in disciplining them.

'At the end of 1923 the Russian proletariat, dispersed and neglected, subjected to a long process of quantitative and qualitative deterioration, seemed to have touched the nadir of its prestige and influence.'[40]

Abuse of Privileges

As we saw in Vol.3 Chapter 13, the privileged and the corrupt had had to conceal their affluence during the War Communism. Under the prevailing standards of public morality any opulence was unseemly, stolen fruit that could be enjoyed only surreptitiously.

With NEP the situation changed radically. Inequality became widespread. Wealth and luxury became legitimate. There was no longer any need to conceal opulence. *Parvenus* with little

culture and fat wallets showed no restraint at all. In the atmosphere of feverish speculation, when it was not clear how
long they would be free to make money, the NEPmen and kulaks
were guided by one slogan: 'Seize the time'. They hurried to
make money and to squander it. Wealth and luxury osten-
tatiously paraded everywhere.

Soviet novels of the time frequently dealt with the disillusionment of revolutionaries with NEP, while privileges
proliferated. In *The Thief* by Leonid Leonov, the central figure
Mitka Vekshin, an engineer and party member who was active
in the October revolution and then played a heroic role in the
long and bitter civil war as a communist in the Red Cavalry. 'He
led his regiment as though he had a dozen lives, and indeed
fought like a dozen Vekshins.' But now, with NEP, Vekshin
suffered terrible disappointment.

> The shops were being rapidly repaired in the squares, the lights
> of the pleasure resorts flared up, and laughter was oftener
> heard. The demobilized soldiers of the revolution watched with
> sullen contempt shop windows which only yesterday had been
> riddled with bullets, rising up more glittering and luxurious
> than ever. But today these shop windows only aroused feelings
> of hunger, or terror, or amazement.

One incident completed Vekshin's bitterness. He was standing before a grocery store.

> It was hot, and in the shop window the fat was dripping from
> a headless sturgeon: Vekshin was hungry. An elegantly dressed
> woman wanted to go into the shop, and he politely reached
> out his hand to open the door for her, but she misunderstood
> him. She struck him with her glove on the hand grasping the
> latch, and would have struck again if he had not awkwardly
> withdrawn.
> Snaka Babkin [Vekshin's mate] who had witnessed his former
> glory and now was to see his humiliation, was overwhelmed
> by the look of horror on Mitka's face. The woman, an official's
> wife, had in the meantime passed into the shop.
> That evening Mitka got drunk. In one of the remoter quarters
> of the city, in a thieves' den, he drank in gulps a bitter,
> poisonously intoxicating drink from which there streamed a
> stench of corruption.

And so Mitka Vekshin became a thief and leader of a gang of criminals.

In contrast to Vekshin was his next-door neighbour, the petty bureaucrat debt collector Pyotr Gorbidonich Chikelyov.

> In his official work it was only through heavy, laborious toil that he ever won the approval of his superiors, although they valued highly his talent for collecting debts. 'I can squeeze money from a stone,' he often used to say facetiously. On the dull green breast of his coat there always hung an array of tin medals as a sign of respectability. Every evening he read a few lines in some political manual and learnt them by heart, hoping by means of them to reach a higher position. He was crafty and painstaking, and he managed to burrow a modest place for himself in the new society, just as he had done once in the old one. (He had been proposed for the Order of Anna, but in consequence of the revolution never received it.) Now he was chairman of the House Committee, quite a distinguished post for a small man and his official career still held further hopes.[41]

More evidence of the social corruption of the time can be found in the reminiscences of an American journalist, whose grasp of politics was poor, but whose reportage of life in Russia in the early 1920s was unsurpassed. He described the life of the privileged in Moscow during the NEP as *La dolce vita*. Champagne and vintage wines from France and Germany, 50-year-old cognac, fragrant coffee, meat and chicken – everything from fresh caviar to sugar and peaches was available. People gorged themselves with the sweets of pleasure, trying to 'tear from life the joys they had been denied so long'.

> It was a strange sight, this *Praga*, in the centre of the world's first Proletarian Republic. Most of the men looked like . . . the low-class jackals and hangers-on of any boom . . . but there were [also] former nobles in faded broadcloth and Red Army soldiers in uniform . . . eager for Moscow's fleshpots and a flutter at the tables. A smattering, too, of foreigners, fixers, agents and the commercial vanguard of a dozen big firms attracted by Lenin's new policy of concessions, hurrying to see if [it] was true that Russia might again become a honey-pot for alien wasps. And women of all sorts . . . mostly daughters of joy whom NEP had hatched in flocks, noisy . . . as sparrows.

Later in increasing numbers the wives and families of NEPmen, the new profiteers, with jewels on their stumpy fingers.[42]

He described another place, 'a restaurant called "Bar" not far from the Savoy Hotel'.

> By the fall of 1922, 'Bar' was doing a roaring trade as a snappy restaurant, night club and brothel all in one. The sale of wine and beer became legal that year, but at 'Bar' there were vodka and liquers as well. In the winter of 1922-23 they went further and cocaine and heroin were to be had, for a price, by clients in the know. A merry little hell it was in the spring of 1923 . . . No better than 'Bar', if less flagrant and luxurious, less 'protected' and profitable, was the red light district . . . near the Trubny Square . . . In the . . . big tenement houses . . . were corridors . . . where . . . beside the name and number of the small . . . rooms was tacked a photograph of its fair occupant in the scantiest of costume.[43]

With open cynicism Ilya Ehrenburg wrote in 1921: 'The French have written Liberty – Equality – Fraternity on the walls of their prisons; here, on the ten-thousand-ruble bonds with which the speculators and contractors are stuffing their pockets, the revolutionary slogan is "workers of the world, unite".'[44]

Prostitution, the complete degradation of women in the interests of men with money, not only appeared in brothels and bars, but was admitted as a commonplace in contemporary Soviet literature. For instance, Isaac Babel wrote a number of stories dealing with prostitutes, such as 'My First Fee' (1922), 'The Chinaman' (1923), and 'Through the Fanlight' (1923).

Society was sinking into a cesspool.

How Long the Retreat? How Long the NEP?

In the period following War Communism there were signs that Lenin lacked clarity and decisiveness in answering these questions. He gave a number of different and contradictory answers. He was still testing the ground, searching for experience which would tell him when the retreat could be halted.

At the Tenth Party Conference of May 1921, summoned to explain the new course to party activists, Lenin insisted that the NEP had been established 'seriously and for a long time'.

The policy is a long-term one and is being adopted in earnest. We must get this well into our heads and remember it, because, owing to the gossip habit, rumours are being spread that we are indulging in a policy of expedients, that is to say, political trickery, and that what is being done is only for the present day. That is not true.[45]

The conference resolution described it as 'established for a long period to be measured in terms of years'.[46]

In a speech delivered to the Third All-Russian Food Conference on 16 June 1921, Lenin said that the New Economic Policy would continue 'until we fully restore large-scale industry'.[47]

However, in a speech on 11 July 1921 Lenin said that NEP was not intended to last long: 'I am sure that if we act more cautiously, if we make concessions in time, we shall win this war too, even if it lasts over three years.'[48]

Again, in an article entitled 'The Importance of Gold' written on 5 November 1921, he stated: 'There are visible signs that the retreat is coming to an end; there are signs that we shall be able to stop this retreat in the not too distant future.'[49] However, on 23 December, Lenin talked about NEP continuing for quite a long time: 'we shall carry out this policy in earnest and for a long time, but, of course . . . not for ever'.[50]

The territory was unknown, experience was meagre. Hence formulations were contradictory. But with all this lack of clarity, a few points are indisputable. From the fact that Lenin called NEP a 'retreat' and a 'defeat', it is clear that he (a) tried to minimize the extent of the retreat in the framework of NEP, and (b) was looking for a way to end NEP as soon as possible.

On 27 March 1922 he gave the last speech of his life to the Eleventh Party Congress. It was a rambling one, for which he apologized, and 'for a variety of reasons, in large part through illness', he could not elaborate his report. He said:

The Central Committee approved my plan, which was, that in the report of the Central Committee to the present congress strong emphasis should be laid on calling a halt to this retreat and that the congress should give binding instructions on behalf of the whole party accordingly. For a year we have been retreating. On behalf of the party we must now call a halt.[51]

In notes for his speech at the congress, Lenin summed up his position thus: 'Halting the retreat . . . Preparation for the offensive *against private capital* – the watchword.'[52]

From Retreat . . . To Rout?

Lenin became increasingly worried in case the retreat started by NEP turned into a general rout of communism. In his speech to the Eleventh Party Congress he pointed to the failure of the state and party in the year since NEP had been introduced.

> During the past year we showed quite clearly that we cannot run the economy. That is the fundamental lesson. Either we prove the opposite in the coming year, or Soviet power will not be able to exist.[53]

> We have some successes, even if only very tiny ones, to record for the past year, but they are insignificant.[54]

A former Cadet minister in the Kolchak government, Ustrialov, asked in the journal *Smena Vekh* (A Changing of Landmarks) published in Prague: What is the Bolsheviks' New Economic Policy – evolution or tactics? Lenin, at the congress, paraphrased his question thus:

> 'What sort of state is the Soviet government building? The communists say they are building a communist state and assure us that the new policy is a matter of tactics: the Bolsheviks are making use of the private capitalists in a difficult situation, but later they will get the upper hand. The Bolsheviks can say what they like; as a matter of fact it is not tactics but evolution, internal regeneration; they will arrive at the ordinary bourgeois state, and we must support them. History proceeds in devious ways.'

Lenin was far from being glibly optimistic. History might prove Ustrialov right.

> We must say frankly that the things Ustrialov speaks about are possible. History knows all sorts of metamorphoses. Relying on firmness of convictions, loyalty, and other splendid moral qualities is anything but a serious attitude in politics . . .

The enemy is speaking the class truth and is pointing to the danger that confronts us, and which the enemy is striving to make inevitable. *Smena Vekh* adherents express the sentiments of thousands and tens of thousands of bourgeois, or of Soviet employees whose function it is to operate our New Economic Policy. This is the real and main danger. And that is why attention must be concentrated mainly on the question: 'Who will win?' . . . No direct onslaught is being made on us now; . . . today we are not being subjected to armed attack. Nevertheless, the fight against capitalist society has become a hundred times more fierce and perilous, because we are not always able to tell enemies from friends.[55]

For Lenin, whose Marxism was never mechanical or fatalistic, the definition of the dictatorship of the proletariat as a *transition period* meant that there could be *two* outcomes of this phase: going forward to socialism, or backsliding to capitalism. The policy of the party would tip the balance.

Bureaucratization Advances Further Under NEP

At the Eleventh Party Congress Riazanov said:

Our Central Committee is altogether a special institution. It is said that the English parliament is omnipotent; it is only unable to change a man into a woman. Our Central Committee is more powerful: it has already changed more than one very revolutionary man into an old lady and the number of these old ladies has increased incredibly.[56]

He also accused it of intervening in all aspects of party life. V.Kosior gave many examples of local leaders both of the party and of the trade unions being removed by decisions of the Political Bureau or the Orgbureau:

During this year not only was there no more linking and welding inside the party organizations, or more links with the working masses, but, on the contrary, the working masses are leaving the party. Many workers are leaving the party. How to explain this? This, dear comrades, is to be explained by the 'strong arm' regime, which has nothing in common with real party discipline and which is cultivated among us. Our party carries wood, sweeps the streets and even votes, but decides no questions . . . the not very healthy proletariat finds itself in these surroundings, and cannot stand it.[57]

At the Twelfth Congress (April 1923) Preobrazhensky complained that 30 per cent of the secretaries of the *guberniia* party committees were 'recommended' for their positions by the Central Committee of the party,[58] thus violating the principle of election of all party officials. In a speech to Moscow party members in 1923, Bukharin described the appointment methods to local party bodies thus:

As a rule the voting takes place according to a definite pattern. They come into the meeting and ask: 'Is anyone opposed?' And since everyone is more or less afraid to voice dissent, the individual who was appointed becomes secretary of the cell bureau . . . in the majority of cases the elections in our party organizations have in fact been transformed into mockery of elections, because the voting takes place not only without preliminary discussion, but, again, according to the formula, 'Is anyone opposed?' And since it is considered bad form for anyone to speak against the 'leadership', the matter is automatically settled. This is what elections are like in the local cells.

Let us now speak of our party meetings. How are they conducted? I myself have taken the floor at numerous meetings in Moscow and I know how the so-called discussion takes place in our party organizations. Take for example the election of the meeting's presiding committee. One of the members of the district committee presents a slate and asks: 'Is anyone opposed?' Nobody is opposed, and the matter is considered settled. The presiding committee is elected and the same comrade then announces that the presiding committee was elected unanimously.[59]

Lenin returned repeatedly to a problem with which, as we have seen, he had been grappling since the revolution: that of the growing and corrupt bureaucracy.* Under the conditions of NEP an alliance of state and party bureaucrats with NEPmen and kulaks could deprive the proletariat of all power. In his speech to the Eleventh Party Congress, already quoted, Lenin said:

---

* See pp. 158-61.

we have lived through a year, the state is in our hands; but has it operated the New Economic Policy in the way we wanted in this past year? No . . . How did it operate? The machine refused to obey the hand that guided it. It was like a car that was going not in the direction the driver desired, but in the direction someone else desired; as if it were being driven by some mysterious, lawless hand, God knows whose, perhaps of a profiteer, or of a private capitalist, or of both. Be that as it may, the car is not going quite in the direction the man at the wheel imagines, and often it goes in an altogether different direction.[60]

What then is lacking? Obviously, what is lacking is culture among the stratum of the communists who perform administrative functions. If we take Moscow with its 4,700 communists in responsible positions, and if we take that huge bureaucratic machine, that gigantic heap, we must ask: who is directing whom? I doubt very much whether it can truthfully be said that the communists are directing that heap. To tell the truth, they are not directing, they are being directed. Something analogous has happened here to what we were told in our history lessons when we were children: sometimes one nation conquers another . . . If the conquering nation is more cultured than the nation conquered, the former imposes its culture upon the latter; but if the opposite is the case, the vanquished nation imposes its culture upon the conqueror. Has not something like this happened in the capital of the RSFSR? Have the 4,700 communists . . . come under the influence of an alien culture? . . . Their culture is miserable, insignificant, but it is still at a higher level than ours. Miserable and low as it is, it is higher than that of our responsible communist administrators.[61]

It seemed that Ustrialov might prove to be right.

24

The Defeat of the German Revolution

The Revolutionary Situation

While in Russia under NEP the proletariat was on the retreat, a new hope of revolution arose in Germany. A victory for the German working class would have ended the isolation of the Russian proletariat and radically changed the whole international situation.

In 1923 fierce class struggle broke out in Germany, as a result of a serious crisis. The immediate cause was the occupation of the Ruhr by France on 11 January 1923 in retaliation for Germany falling behind with its reparations payments. Two days later the German government, led by the conservative Cuno, issued an appeal to the population of the Ruhr for 'passive resistance' and non-co-operation with the occupying authorities. The immediate result was an increase in German resistance, ranging from strikes to acts of sabotage. A crucial by-product of the French occupation and German resistance was an acceleration of the rate of inflation of the mark to astronomic proportions. The changes in its exchange rate with the dollar tell the story:

January	1923	17,920	July	1923	349,000
February	1923	20,000	August	1923	4,600,000
May	1923	48,000	September	1923	98,860,000
June	1923	110,000	October	1923	25,260,208,000
			November	1923	4,200,000,000,000[1]

The result was the absolute pauperization of the whole of the working population; ruin for the petty bourgeoisie; the rapid enrichment of the owners of capital; massive speculation and corruption; the closing of all social safety valves. Never had a highly industrial society been in such deep economic, social and political turmoil.

The traditional reformist working-class organizations were impotent in this situation. One writer, Evelyn Anderson, stated:

> In those days . . . the influence of the Social Democrats and the trade unions was waning. Although membership of the unions was larger than ever before, the inflation had robbed them of all funds with which to support their members, to finance strikes or even to pay their officials. Moreover, normal Trade Union activity had become quite impossible in a situation in which nominal wages and salaries had lost all meaning.[2]

Pierre Broué, in his monumental history of the German revolution, *Révolution en Allemagne (1917-1923)*, wrote:

> The traditional trade union practice of Social Democracy was empty of all meaning, trade unionism was impotent, collective agreements derided. The workers left the trade unions and often directed their anger against them, blaming them for their passivity, sometimes for their complicity. The collapse of the trade union apparatus and Social Democracy was paralleled by that of the state. What became of notions of property, order and legality? How in such an abyss, can one justify an attachment to parliamentary institutions, to the right to vote, to universal suffrage? Neither the police nor the army were free of sickness. A world was dying.[3]

From May onwards massive spontaneous strikes took place throughout the country. They were denounced by trade union leaders and opposed by the Social Democrats. The authority of the factory committees leading the struggle increased dramatically. Their national action committee began to represent an alternative workers' leadership, a serious counterbalance to the trade union leaders.

On 16 June, in the name of the factory councils, its president Grothe addressed a solemn appeal to the workers, employees and intellectuals. Describing the catastrophe that was threatening German society, he reaffirmed that the working class could prevent it by getting rid of the capitalist system:

> Only the struggle of all, only the class struggle can bring you what you need simply in order to assure your survival. The whole working people is in motion. In this flood that the trade unions today try to dam and sabotage, important tasks and initiatives fall to the factory councils.

He invited the factory councils to form local and regional organizations to give the working masses 'objectives and leadership' in the coming struggles. Committees for the control of prices and proletarian defence organizations – Proletarian Hundreds – were needed: with factory councils, they would form the base for a workers' government, which alone could produce a positive outcome to the crisis.

Strikes and demonstrations followed. Workers demonstrated at Bautzen on 2 June, at Dresden and at Leipzig on 7 June. On this date more than 100,000 miners and engineers were on strike in upper Silesia, under the leadership of an elected strike committee which included six communists out of a total of 26 members. On 11 June there broke out a historically unique strike of 100,000 agricultural workers in Silesia, soon followed by 10,000 Brandenburg day workers. On 11 June a merchant marine strike also began at Emden, Bremen, Hamburg and Lübeck, on the initiative of the Federation of Seamen, which belonged to the communist-led Profintern, the red international of trade unions.

In Berlin it was the engineering workers who took action. 153,000 of the total of 250,000 engineers were organized in trade unions. First workers' pressure achieved a referendum in the union on the strike. The result was massively in favour. The union then organized a second referendum open to non-trades-unionists. The majority in favour was even greater. Finally 60 enterprises called for the strike. Immediately the employers began to negotiate. On 10 July 150,000 engineers struck and the trade union leadership was overthrown in many factories. On the same day the management agreed to a rise in wages, from 9,800 marks for the second week of June to 12,000 for the first week of July. One clause of the agreement proposed to set up a parity commission to establish a price index that would serve as the basis for indemnity against inflation. At the demand of the employers, to prevent the idea from spreading, this remained secret. The results, however, were visible: the wages of the engineers after 10 June were 38 per cent higher than the figure demanded by the unions and rejected on 3 June. It was soon the turn of the building workers, and then the woodworkers in the capital. Everywhere the communists were in the forefront in launching the strikes and also in the return to work, not only in trade union meetings where they were often in the majority, but in the 'workers' assemblies' which they had forced the trade union leaders to call, which were open to all.[4]

For the first time (and, as history was to show, the last) the Communist Party of Germany had the majority of the proletariat under its influence. According to one historian: 'In the summer of 1923 the KPD undoubtedly had the majority of the German proletariat behind it.'[5]

Thus, over a period of about five years – from December 1918 to the summer of 1923 – the KPD changed from a party representing a tiny minority of the working class into a mass party with influence over the bulk of the class.

Commotion in the Streets

'Bread riots became commonplace: in Berlin, Dresden, Frankfurt am Main, Mannheim, Cologne.'[6] The bourgeois state machine was under tremendous strain:

> This disruption of economic life endangered the legal structure of the Weimar Republic. Civil servants lost their ties to the state; their small salaries had no relation to their daily needs; they felt themselves in a boat without a rudder. Police troops, in sympathy with the rioting populace, lost their combative spirit against the hunger demonstrations and closed their eyes to the sabotage groups and clandestine military formations mushrooming throughout the Reich. Hamburg was so tense that the police did not dare interfere with looting of foodstuffs by the hungry masses. In August, large demonstrations of dock workers in the Hamburg harbour led to rioting. 'Parts of the police,' [a leading Hamburg communist] wrote, 'are regarded as unreliable; they sympathize with the working class.'[7]

On 8 August things came to a head. Chancellor Cuno justified his policies to the Reichstag in a lengthy speech. The debate went on until the next day. The Reichstag was then besieged by workers' delegations, which it refused to receive. The debate ended on 10 August with a vote of confidence for the government, the Social Democrats abstaining and the Communists voting against. The Communist Wilhelm Könen addressed the German workers from parliament, calling for 'the mass movement of the workers to go over the head of parliament, and form a workers' revolutionary government'. The strike movement gained momentum. The tram workers in Berlin went on strike. A few minutes later it was the turn of the printers, who followed the call of the communist cell, and whose strike included the 8,000 workers at the national mint. The production of notes stopped : in a few hours, the government would not even have money at its disposal. The workers in big enterprises followed the movement, led by those of Siemens and Borsig. The workers of eleven striking Berlin enterprises took up communist demands for the resignation of Cuno and for the formation of a workers' government. Urban transport was completely at a standstill, gas and electricity cut off. In Hamburg all building work ground to a halt, and there were workers' demonstrations at Krefeld and Aachen: the police intervened and there were some deaths. The midday editions of the newspapers announced that the Reichsbank was going to close due to lack of notes.[8]

On 11 August a hastily summoned conference of the Berlin factory councils proclaimed a general strike in the city and urged the working class throughout the country to join the strike. The proclamation was carried by a special edition of *Die Rote Fahne*, but the entire issue was promptly confiscated by the authorities, who invoked a one-day-old government decree 'for the protection of public order'. Despite this, the communists succeeding in eliciting a strong response from several groups of workers in the city. Moreover, sporadic wildcat strikes erupted on this and subsequent days in various parts of the country. There was a distinct possibility that these intermittent strikes would turn into a general one, as had happened in March 1920 during the Kapp putsch.[9]

There was a radical difference, however, between the Cuno strike and the Kapp strike. As Evelyn Anderson, put it in her book *Hammer or Anvil*:

> In March 1920 German workers had responded to the joint appeal of their unions and parties. In August 1923 no such appeal had been issued, either by the unions or by any of the

working-class parties. The Cuno strike was entirely spontaneous, and as such it was a unique action in the history of the German labour movement. Shop stewards and local workers' representatives took the initiative and led the movement. The parties began to realize what was happening only after this movement of the masses had created an accomplished fact. All this had important consequences. The movement exhausted and spent itself once it had achieved the maximum that spontaneous and unguided action of this kind could possibly achieve, i.e. the resignation of the government. To exploit this success for more positive and constructive ends would have been the task of the political working-class parties.

Regrettably, however, 'None of the existing parties was up to this task.'[10]

The Policy of the KPD

During the first seven months of 1923 – between the start of the occupation of the Ruhr by French troops and the collapse of the Cuno government on 11 August – the policy of the KPD lacked cohesion and clear direction. Throughout these months the Communist leaders were deeply pessimistic. Thus on 17 March, at an international conference in Frankfurt, Brandler, Chairman of the KPD, said:

> While we experienced then [in 1918] a rising revolutionary tide on account of the Russian revolution, we face today a receding tide because of the seizure of power by the bourgeoisie, and now our primary task is to rally the proletariat.[11]

Throughout 1923 the KPD leadership lacked independence and was totally subservient to the orders of the Comintern in Moscow. This was the catastrophic result of the *Märzaktion* in 1921, since when Brandler, Thalheimer, Walcher, Ernest Meyer, had become, in Broué's description,

> 'rightists', systematically, obstinately prudent, armed with precautions against any tendency towards putschism and even the simple leftist reflex. Convinced by the leaders of the International of the grave fault they had committed, the lost confidence in their capacity to think and often surrendered their own point of view entirely in order to agree with the Bolsheviks who, at least, had known how to win.[12]

In contrast with Brandler's pessimism regarding the immediate prospect of revolution, the bourgeois press was convinced that the revolution was imminent! On 26 July *Kreuz-Zeitung* wrote: 'We are now without doubt – who can fail to see this after what we have seen before our very eyes – on the eve of a new revolution.' *Germania* the next day reported: 'Trust in the Reich government is seriously shaken . . . Discontent has reached a dangerous degree. The fury is general. The air is charged with electricity. Any spark and it would explode . . . We have the state of mind of 9 November,'[13] i.e. the day the Kaiser was deposed.

Every paper in Germany was using the expression '*Novemberstimmung*' (the mood of November), with the exception of the communist press.

In late April or early May representatives of the various factions in the KPD leadership arrived in Moscow to ask the Bolshevik leaders to arbitrate between them once again. The ECCI was represented by Trotsky, Radek, Bukharin and Zinoviev. The question of the united front policy was discussed at the conference, but a communist seizure of power was not even mentioned.[14] In June an enlarged executive meeting of the Comintern took place. It did not discuss the situation in Germany except in very general terms. After the meeting was over, most of the senior members of the Politbureau of the Russian party and of the ECCI went on holiday.

Even after the massive strikes that overthrew the Cuno government, and after a new government under Stresemann – a coalition with a number of Social Democrats in key positions (Hilferding being the Finance Minister) – had been established, which had taken decisive measures against the inflation and was considering reaching agreement with France by stopping passive resistance, Radek still argued for a policy of waiting. He wrote in *Die Rote Fahne*:

> A relative truce is now maintained: it must give the broad coalition the time to discredit itself more completely in the eyes of the petty bourgeoisie and the backward workers to whom the name of a Hilferding still inspires some sort of vague hope.[15]

Finally, on 15 August Zinoviev, President of the Comintern, communicated with Moscow from the Caucasus to the effect that the KPD should take stock of the approaching revolutionary crisis, as 'a new and decisive chapter is beginning in the activity of the German Communist Party and, with it, the Comintern'.[16]

Trotsky was by far the most enthusiastic about the news from Germany. When he learned of the Cuno strike and the new Stresemann government, he concluded that developments in Germany were, indeed, pointing toward a domestic crisis which the KPD ought to exploit. Eager to receive additional information, he invited two members of the German party, August Enderle and Jakob Walcher, to visit him at once in in southern Russia. They were currently in Moscow as KPD delegates to the Executive Committee of the Profintern. At the end of the conversation Trotsky sent one of them back to Berlin, presumably to act as his contact man and on-the-spot observer.

During the following week the Russian leaders broke off their vacations and returned to Moscow. On 23 August the Politbureau met for a secret session which was also attended by Radek, Piatakov – then deputy chairman of VSNKh – and possibly Tsiurupa, later president of Gosplan.[17]

We shall go on to describe the discussions in Moscow and the policies emanating from them. But first we need to deal with an issue that had a seriously detrimental effect on the policy of the KPD: 'the Schlageter affair'.

The Schlageter Diversion

Clear proof of the extent to which the Comintern leaders failed to understand the revolutionary crisis in Germany was contained in a speech made by Radek at the June session of the enlarged ECCI, which set the KPD off on an irrelevant and reactionary course. Radek hailed one Schlageter as an ally, although he was 'the brave soldier of the counter-revolution'.

A.L.Schlageter was an extreme right-wing officer who fought the Bolsheviks in the Baltic and the workers in the Ruhr. He attempted to blow up a railway line in the Ruhr which was under French control. He was immediately caught, court martialled and on 26 May 1923 shot. General Ludendorff spoke at his funeral in Munich. Schlageter was a hero of the Nazi movement.

Now Radek tried to use him as a symbol for an alliance between communists and nationalists. 'Where will the path of these young people lead?' he asked his Moscow listeners. There were only two ways forward for Germany – with Russia against France, or with France against Russia. If Germany chose the second alternative the national ideals of the activists of the right would be vacuous; only if Germany joined hands with Russia would German nationalism have a chance. Schlageter's friends must answer the vital question:

> Against whom do the German nationalists want to fight: against Entente capital or the Russian people? With whom do they want to ally themselves? With the Russian workers and peasants to shake off together the yoke of Entente capital or with Entente capital to enslave the German and Russian people?

Radek invoked the historic example of Scharnhorst and Gneisenau who, after the humiliation of Jena by Napoleon, had seen that the emancipation of the peasants was a condition of the liberation and restoration of Prussia. The liberation of Germany from the yoke of Versailles could be achieved only through the emancipation of the workers. The KPD 'is not the party merely of the struggle for the industrial workers' loaf of bread, but the party of struggling proletarians who fight for their freedom, for *a freedom which is identical with the freedom of their whole people, with the freedom of all who work and suffer in Germany*'.

Radek could not possibly have spoken on his own initiative on such a question. He stated afterwards that he had obtained 'not only the tacit, but the written assent' of Zinoviev to his speech, and that Zinoviev afterwards described his Schlageter articles as 'correct and good'.[18]

After this speech the KPD embarked on a number of weeks of public debates with nationalists, including the Nazis. In Berlin a debate was organized before a student audience between communists and Nazis on the subject: 'For What Did Schlageter Die?'

According to the report in *Die Rote Fahne*, this discussion lasted several hours without leading to any incidents. The communist leader Ruth Fischer stated that 'the giant, who is going to liberate Germany, is here . . . The giant is the German proletariat, to which you belong and with which you should align yourselves'. This was greeted, so the paper says, with 'loud applause'. Then the meeting broke up, and the opposing groups separated 'not exactly conciliated, but with a feeling of mutual respect'. The Social Democratic paper, *Vorwärts*, threw an interesting sidelight on this particular performance of Ruth Fischer. Quoting an eye-witness account, the paper claimed that the communist speaker appealed openly to the anti-Semitic sentiments of her audience.

> Whoever cries out against Jewish capital . . . is already a fighter for his class, even though he may not know it. You are against the stock market jobbers. Fine. Trample the Jewish capitalists down, hang them from the lampposts . . . But . . . how do you feel about the big capitalists, the Stinnes, Klöckner? . . . Only in alliance with Russia . . . can the German people expel French capitalism from the Ruhr region.

Anti-Semitic remarks, innuendos rather than open expressions, appeared occasionally in the communist press during this period. *Die Rote Fahne* printed a small item on 7 August on 'Stresemann's Jewish *Kommerzienräte*' (Councillors of Commerce, a title conferred on distinguished financiers), in which it drew attention to the fact that such prominent Social Democrats as Friedrich Stamfer, the editor of *Vorwärts*, Carl Severing and Hermann Müller were closely connected with these Jewish capitalists.

Although the communists tried on the whole to keep clear of the anti-Semitic issue, they could not always avoid it, especially when it was raised by nationalist hecklers during joint discussion meetings. This was clearly demonstrated in the case of Hermann Remmele, a member of the Central Committee of the KPD, who on 2 August addressed a mixed audience of communists and Nazis in Stuttgart. When he told his listeners that anti-Semitism was an age-old device which those in power employed to distract the attention of the blind and ignorant masses from the real causes of their misery, he was interrupted by shouts from the floor.

Remmele continued: 'How such anti-Semitism arises I can easily understand. One merely needs to go down to the Stuttgart cattle market in order to see how the cattle dealers, most of whom are Jewish, buy up cattle at any price, while the Stuttgart butchers have to go home again, empty-handed, because they just don't have enough money to buy cattle.' ('Quite right' from the Fascists.)

A little later in his speech, Remmele again touched on this subject, and again with the apparent purpose of appeasing the audience in order to put his own point across: 'You, the Fascists, now say [that you want] to fight Jewish finance capital. All right. Go ahead! Agreed! (Stormy applause from the Fascists.) But you must not forget one thing, industrial capital! (Interjections from the Fascists: 'We fight that too!') For finance capital is really nothing else but industrial capital.'

How eager the KPD was to use any expedient to reach common ground with the nationalists was evident from another public debate in which Remmele participated on 10 August. Besides Remmele, a speaker each from the Nazis and the Social Democrats had been invited by the communists to participate in the discussion. The SPD, however, turned down the invitation. In his eagerness to win the sympathies of the Nazis, Remmele made a number of statements which were in flagrant violation of the party's official united front policy. Thus he told his 8,000 listeners that he considered an alliance with the Nazis less objectionable than one with the Social Democrats, and then added that the communists would even be willing to co-operate with the murders of Liebknecht and Luxemburg.[19]

The Schlageter line was a complete failure: no Nazi supporters could be attracted to communism by intellectual debate on the question of who was the better defender of the national interests of Germany. And this line was put forward at a moment of deep revolutionary crisis!

The Schlageter episode seems like a macabre anecdote, but

it cannot be erased from history; an obscenity that throws light on the degeneration of the Comintern leadership while Lenin was still alive.

The ECCI Wakes Up

The leaders of the Comintern were taken unawares by the strike against Cuno, which found them in the middle of their holidays. None of them expected a movement of such magnitude which so clearly condemned the temporising of the June session of the ECCI. The Moscow leadership now awoke with a start. Broué writes:

> It was clear that around 10 August the masses were ready for a battle that the leaders thought was a long way off. But the tension could not be prolonged indefinitely and the balance between the classes marked by the formation of a broad coalition government could not last. Thus, from the middle of August, the leaders of the International worked for the preparation of the German insurrection, a race against time aimed at catching up on time lost since May.[20]

Brandler had been in Moscow since the end of August, waiting for the Bolshevik leaders to make up their minds about policies for Germany. The leaders of the Left in the KPD, Arkadi Maslow, Ruth Fischer and Ernest Thälmann, were summoned to Moscow. Edwin Hoernle and Clara Zetkin, two members of the Zentrale, were also stationed in Moscow at the time, as delegates of the KPD to the ECCI. In a meeting between these German leaders and the Politbureau of the Russian party, Trotsky argued that the situation was so ripe for revolution that a date had to be fixed for the insurrection – as had been done in Russian on the eve of the October revolution. Elaborating on his views in an article published in Pravda on 23 September (and reprinted as a special issue of the central journal of the Comintern International Presse-Korrespondenz), entitled 'Is it Possible to Fix a Definite Schedule for a Counter-revolution or a Revolution?' Trotsky wrote:

> Obviously, it is not possible to create artificially a political situation favourable for a . . . coup, much less to bring it off at a fixed date. But when the basic elements of such a situation

are at hand, then the leading party does . . . choose beforehand a favourable moment, and synchronizes accordingly its political, organizational, and technical forces, and – if it has not miscalculated – deals the victorious blow.

. . . let us take our own October revolution as an example . . . From the moment when the Bolsheviks were in the majority of the Petrograd, and afterward in the Moscow Soviet, our party was faced with the question – not of the struggle for power in general but of preparing for the seizure of power according to a definite plan, and at a fixed date. The chosen day, as is well known, was the day upon which the All-Russian Congress of the Soviets was to convene.[21]

Using this argument, Trotsky insisted on fixing a date for the German insurrection. Against the protest of Brandler, whose misgivings were shared by Radek, 9 November was chosen. It was a historic date: the Russian revolution of 1917 took place on 7 November, and the German revolution of 1918 on 9 November.

When Brandler refused to budge, Zinoviev suggested a compromise: the date to serve merely 'for orientation', and the insurrection was to take place some time during the next four to six weeks. While the debates were taking place at the end of September, early November remained the target date.

With Brandler and Radek irresolute and sceptical and Zinoviev, as was his habit, prevaricating, Stalin, in one of his few incursions into Comintern affairs at the time, came out in support of a policy of restraint for the KPD. In a letter to Zinoviev and Bukharin in August on the situation in Germany, he said:

Should the Communists strive [at the given stage] to seize power without the Social Democrats? Have they sufficiently matured for that – that's the question as I see it. Upon our taking power, we had in Russia such reserves as (a) peace; (b) land to the peasants; (c) the support of the vast majority of the working class; (d) the sympathy of the peasants. The German communists have at present nothing of the sort. They have, of course, contiguous to them the land of the Soviets, which we did not have, but what can we give them at the present moment? Should the power in Germany, so to speak, drop now, and should the communists catch it up, they'll fall through with a crash. That's 'at best'. But if it comes to the worst – they will be smashed to pieces and beaten back. The gist of the matter does not lie in Brandler's desire to 'teach the masses'; the gist of the matter is that the bourgeoisie plus the Right Social Democrats would surely convert the practice-demonstation into a general battle (they still have all the odds on their side for that) and would crush them. The Fascists, of course, are not napping, but it is to our advantage to let the Fascists attack first: this will fuse the entire working class around the communists . . . Moreover, the Fascists, according to all reports, are weak in Germany. In my opinion the Germans should be restrained and not encouraged.'[22]

Thus in August 1923, when the German revolution was knocking hard at all the doors, Stalin believed that the KPD should be restrained rather than encouraged. His passive fatalism was camouflaged by the consoling prognosis that time was on the side of the revolution, and that the strength of the revolutionary forces was bound to go on growing, ignoring the possibility that the hopes of the masses could change into disillusionment if the revolutionary party was not decisive in seizing power. Lenin was absolutely right when he argued in September and October 1917 that a delay of a few weeks might ruin the revolution, that it was *now or never*! 'The success of both the Russian and the world revolution depends on two or three days' fighting,' as he wrote on 8 (21) October 1917.[23]

Another question had to be settled before the deliberations of the German and Russian leaders could end. It was raised by Brandler and concerned the supreme command of the proposed revolution. Brandler, as he himself put it, was not 'a German Lenin', and he asked both Trotsky and Zinoviev whether Trotsky could not take charge of the German operation – come incognito and establish himself in Germany. Trotsky was eager for this assignment. But the anti-Trotsky 'troika' in the Russian Politbureau, Zinoviev, Kamenev and Stalin, would not let him go. Had he done so and succeeded, he would have dwarfed them as the acknowledged leader of both the Russian and the German revolutions.

They evaded this difficulty by turning the delicate scene into a farce. Zinoviev replied that he himself, the President of the Communist International, would go to Germany 'as a soldier of the revolution' instead of Trotsky. Then Stalin intervened, and with an air of bonhomie and common sense said that the Politbureau could not possibly dispense with the services of either of its two most eminent and well-loved members.[24]

The strategic plan for the revolution was now drawn up by the Russian and German leaders. The launching-pad was to be Saxony. Here a government headed by the left-wing Social Democrat Zeigner had been collaborating for months with the communists. The Russians, and notably Zinoviev, believed that the communists should enter this government, and from this strategic position lay the groundwork for an armed uprising. The problem was later put succinctly by Radek:

> The proletariat concentrates its strength in Saxony, taking its start from the defence of the workers' government, into which we enter; and it will attempt in Saxony to use the state power in order to arm itself and to form, in this restricted proletarian province of central Germany, a wall between the southern counter-revolution in Bavaria and the Fascism of the north. At the same time the party throughout the Reich will step in and mobilize the masses.

The key words emphasized by Radek were '[the proletariat] will attempt in Saxony to use the state power in order to arm itself'.[25]

On 1 October a telegram signed by Zinoviev on behalf of the ECCI was despatched to the Zentrale of the KPD:

> Since we estimate the situation to be such that the decisive moment will arrive not later than in four-five-six weeks, we think it necessary to occupy at once every position which can be of immediate use [for our purposes]. On the basis of the [present] situation we must approach the question of our entry into the Saxon government in practical terms. We must enter [the Saxon government] on the condition that the Zeigner people are actually willing to defend Saxony against Bavaria and the Fascists. 50,000 to 60,000 workers have to be immediately armed; ignore General Müller.* The same in Thuringia.

---

* General Müller was the newly appointed commander of the Reichswehr for Saxony.

According to Brandler, he opposed, to no avail, the sending of Communists into the governments of Saxony and Thuringia:

> I strongly objected to the attempt to hasten the revolutionary crisis by including communists in the Saxon and Thuringian governments – allegedly in order to procure weapons. I knew, and I said so in Moscow, that the police in Saxony and Thuringia did not have any stores of weapons. Even single sub-machine guns had to be ordered from the *Reichswehr's* arsenal near Berlin. The workers had already seized the local arsenals twice, once during the Kapp putsch, and again in part in 1921. I declared further that the entry of the communists into the government would not breathe new life into the mass actions, but rather weaken them; for now the masses would expect the government to do what they could only do for themselves.
> In answer to that Zinoviev thundered, banged his fist on the table and so on.

Outvoted, Brandler declared that he would submit to the decisions of the Comintern. This is how he explains his motives:

> I told myself that these people had made three revolutions. To me their decisions seemed nonsensical. However, not I but they were considered seasoned revolutionaries who had achieved victory. They had made three revolutions and I was just about to try to make one. Well, I had to follow their instructions. During my return journey from Moscow to Berlin I bought a newspaper at the railway station in Warsaw. From this newspaper I learned that I had become a Minister in the Saxon government. What a situation! Things were being done behind my back and I knew nothing. All this was meant to put me before a *fait accompli*.[26]

Early in October all the KPD leaders in Moscow except Maslow went back to Germany to execute the agreed plan. A Comintern delegation was also appointed to go to Germany to direct the proceedings: Radek in charge of party matters; Piatakov to supervise military affairs generally in conjunction with Generals Skobolevsky and Guralsky, who were already on the spot; and Schmidt to establish contacts with the trade unions.

On 12 October three communist leaders joined the Saxon

government. The communists wanted one of these to head the Ministry of the Interior, which controlled the police. This Zeigner would not grant and the communists had to be satisfied to have one of their number – it happened to be Brandler – appointed *Ministerialdirektor* (Assistant Secretary) in charge of the state chancellery, an appointment which allowed them at least an indirect influence over the police. It was also agreed that the communist Paul Böttcher, should become Minister of Finance, and the communist Fritz Heckert Minister of the Economy.[27]

The national government was not slow to attack the new government in Saxony. On 13 October an ultimatum was sent demanding that the 'Proletarian Hundreds' be dissolved. The Saxon government defied the order. The communists were elated by the fact that they had come to terms with the Thuringian government on the same day. Here too a coalition of left-wing socialists and communists was set up with two communists joining the government – as Ministers of Education and Economy. Berlin reacted by informing the Zeigner government that from 16 October the Saxon police were to be placed under the immediate authority of the Reichswehr (national army). With the police removed from his control Zeigner was powerless, and Brandler became a *Ministerialdirektor* in charge of meaningless police files.[28] On 20 October the Reichswehr marched into Saxony.

On 21 October a conference of factory committees was convened in Chemnitz. Brandler delivered a speech ending with a call for a general strike. But one of the Social Democratic ministers in the coalition government threatened to withdraw from the conference if the proposal was passed, and the conference degenerated into a fiasco. The demand for a general strike was politely buried by a resolution to set up a commission to examine the proposals. Brandler drew the logical conclusion. He called off the proposed insurrection. (Radek and the other Comintern agents, who were not present in Chemnitz, concurred with this decision.)

In retrospect Ruth Fischer wrote, quite justifiably, about the refusal of the Chemnitz conference to call a general strike in Saxony:

The doubts of the Social Democrats at Chemnitz . . . were completely justified; it was a stupid plan to load the weight of a collision with the Reichswehr entirely on the shoulders of the Saxon workers. Successful action was possible only if led by the key centres of proletarian strength – by Hamburg, Berlin, the Ruhr . . . In every one of these regions the Communist Party was stronger than in Saxony, and its choice of this state was interpreted by the Social Democratic delegates as an attempt to spare the communist cadres.[29]

The whole idea of a coalition government in Saxony was absurd. The notion of communists joining a coalition government with Social Democrats, accepting responsibility for a government they did not control, and at the same time preparing for an insurrection, was now exposed in all its contradictions.

The leaders of the Comintern and the KPD overlooked the fact that a policy of a united front involves not only advantages but also, if wrongly applied, dangers. It can easily give rise to understandings between leaders behind the backs of the masses, to passive adaptation to reformist elements, to opportunist vacillation.

A tragic, grotesque finale to the failure of the German October was provided by the communist uprising in Hamburg. Couriers, who had been waiting in Chemnitz to carry to expectant communists throughout Germany the order to act, were despatched to countermand the preparations. By a tragic blunder which has never been satisfactorily explained, two members of the party Central Committee, Thälmann and Remmele, left Chemnitz before the conference ended, under the impression that its success was assured, and, arriving in Hamburg on the evening of 22 October, gave the word for the rising to begin. Early next morning, while the Reichswehr was advancing unopposed on Dresden, the capital of Saxony, to depose the coalition government, a few hundred Hamburg communists attacked and occupied several police stations, seizing their stocks of arms and remaining in control of part of the city for forty-eight hours; they fought with desperation against the police and the troops who quickly arrived to crush their insurrection.[30]

Thus the German revolution ended, as a tragic fiasco.

The Fourth Comintern Congress Sows the Seed

There was a great deal of confusion at Comintern head-quarters when they talked about a 'workers' government' as something distinguishable from the dictatorship of the proletariat. In instructing the KPD leaders to join coalition governments with Social Democrats in Saxony and Thuringia, Zinoviev invoked the resolution of the Fourth Congress of the Comintern about workers' governments. This is why no-one in the leadership of the Comintern, including the Russian party, opposed the creation of coalition governments in Germany in 1923.

It should be noted in passing that neither Lenin nor Trotsky participated in the Fourth Congress debate on the important subject of workers' government. Lenin was very ill indeed, and the only contribution he made to the congress was one speech on the fifth anniversary of the October revolution, a speech that was very disjointed and rambling. (He was so ill that Radek had to come to his assistance in delivering the speech – not that Lenin's German, the official language of the congress, was in any way faulty.) Trotsky did make a number of important contributions to the congress, but he did not participate in the debate on workers' government.

The main speakers on the subject were Zinoviev and Radek. Both argued strongly that the battle for a joint Socialist-Communist government was the logical outcome of agitation for a workers' united front. They implied that such a government would almost automatically lead to a deeper level of struggle and from there to the dictatorship of the proletariat. Thus Radek stated :

> When the Labour government comes into existence, it will merely be a stepping stone to the dictatorship of the proletariat, for the bourgeoisie will not tolerate a Labour government even though founded on democratic principles. The Social Democratic worker will find himself compelled to become a communist, in order to defend his rule.[31]

This was mechanistic nonsense : as if capitalism could not survive reformist governments without bourgeois participation !

It is true the Congress resolution was much more guarded

than Radek's speech. But it was still very ambiguous and left room for opportunist conclusions to be drawn.

Apparently the leadership of the Comintern at the Fourth Congress overlooked the intransigent opposition of Lenin and the Bolsheviks to the provisional government of Kerensky, which had not wavered even when the government's existence was threatened by General Kornilov. Even in such circumstances, Lenin argued, the Bolsheviks should not take any responsibility for the government's behaviour, and should on no account bury their differences with the Mensheviks and SRs. In a letter to the Central Committee of the Bolsheviks of 30 August (12 September) 1917, he stated:

> Even now we must not support Kerensky's government. This is unprincipled. We may be asked: aren't we going to fight against Kornilov? Of course we must! But this is not the same thing; there is a dividing line here . . .
> We shall fight, we are fighting against Kornilov, *just as* Kerensky's *troops do*, but we do not support Kerensky. *On the contrary*, we expose his weakness. There is the difference. It is rather a subtle difference, but it is highly essential and must not be forgotten.[32]

Lenin always held that practical, temporary agreements with reformists were sometimes necessary. But in such agreements no trust should be placed in the reformists, no blurring of the differences between communists and reformists should be allowed, and the rule should be followed: march separately, strike together. Lenin always insisted that one must keep a wary eye on the temporary ally as well as on the foe. A policy of united front with reformists can be limited to partial tasks only, in particular to defensive struggles. It is out of the question to accomplish the socialist revolution through a united front with Social Democrats. Between the bourgeois order and the dictatorship of the proletariat there cannot be any intermediary revolutionary regime.

The idea of a coalition government between communists and Social Democrats, as accepted by the Fourth Congress of the Comintern in November 1922 and realized a year later in Germany, completely contradicted Lenin's mistrust of Social Democracy and his intransigent opposition to it.

The Defeat of the German Revolution
and the Consolidation of Bureaucracy in Russia

The excitement of the German revolution gripped people throughout Russia. Ruth Fischer describes Moscow in September 1923: It was

> plastered with slogans welcoming the German revolution. Banners and streamers were posted in the centre of the city with such slogans as 'Russian Youth, Learn German – the German October Is Approaching.' Pictures of Clara Zetkin, Rosa Luxemburg and Karl Liebknecht were to be seen in every shop window. In all factories, meetings were called to discuss 'How Can We Help the German Revolution?'[33]

Such discussions were not mere formalities. The Russian workers were expected by the government to make genuine sacrifices for the German revolution. According to the records of the ECCI, 'the Russian working classes agreed to suspend the increase of their wages and to submit to reductions if it were necessary in the interest of the German revolution'. The workers were told that a defeat for the German proletariat would constitute a defeat of the Russian workers as well. Women were asked at public meetings to donate their wedding rings and other valuables for the German cause. The Trade Commissariat distributed circulars which stated that 'the advance of the German revolution confronted the Trade Commissariat with new problems; the present routine of trading must be replaced by the establishment of two German reserves: gold and corn, for the benefit of the victorious German proletariat;' and the agencies of this Commissariat in the individual Soviet republics were ordered to send a total of 60 million pud of grain towards Russia's western frontiers. The Russian Communist Party, by order of the Politbureau, drew up lists of members who spoke German in order to create a commuunist-trained reserve corps which could, at the appropriate moment, be transferred to Germany, where it would assist the revolution. Special attention was paid to the mobilization of Russia's Communist youth organizations, whose members were told that they might have to risk their lives on behalf of the German proletariat and the cause of revolution. In October revolutionary slogans became current: 'Workers' Germany and our Workers' and Peasants' Union are the bulwark of peace and labour'; 'German Steam Hammer and Soviet Bread will Conquer the World'. Soviet newspapers wrote that, if the German workers were successful, the new German government would join with Soviet Russia and thereby 'unite in Europe the tremendous power of 200 million people, against which no war in Europe will be possible . . . because no one would be able to face such a force'.[34]

The Great Whitewash

These hopes aroused among the Russian workers turned to ashes.

How did the Moscow leadership react to the turn of events in Germany? Trotsky had not doubt that the German proletariat had suffered an extremely severe defeat. He held that a revolutionary situation had existed in Germany from May, or at any rate from July to November. In January 1924 he wrote:

> It is now incontestable that the period running from May (beginning of the resistance in the Ruhr) or July (collapse of this resistance) to November, when General Seeckt took over power, was a clearly marked phase of crisis without precedent in the life of Germany.

However, the communist leadership had let the opportunity slip:

> If the Communist Party had changed abruptly the pace of its work and had profited by the five or six months that history accorded it for a direct political, organizational, technical preparation for the seizure of power, the outcome of events could have been quite different from the one we witnessed in November . . . The proletariat should have seen a revolutionary party at work marching directly to the conquest of power.
>
> But the German party continued, at bottom, its propaganda policy of yesterday even if on a larger scale.[35]

In a later and famous essay of September 1924, *Lessons of October*, Trotsky declared: 'we witnessed in Germany a classic demonstration of how it is possible to miss a perfectly exceptional revolutionary situation of world-historic importance'.[36]

Unlike Trotsky, Zinoviev and his friends in the Comintern leadership tried to belittle the importance of the setback and at the same time to find scapegoats in the persons of Brandler and Radek. In contrast with Lenin, who insisted that revolutionary leaders should tell the truth to the workers, so that even if a sharp turn was necessary it should be done in such a way as to leave a clear, forceful imprint in the workers' consciousness, Zinoviev did everything to obscure the meaning of the defeat in Germany and its tremendous international implications.

Between 12 October and 1 November 1923 he wrote ten articles in *Pravda* under the title 'Problems of the German Revolution'. They were controlled in tone and content and portended no change of attitude. The first optimistically hailed the impending German revolution:

> Only a short space of time, and it will become clear to everyone that the autumn months of 1923 were a turning-point not only in the history of Germany, but through it also for the whole of mankind. With trembling hand the German proletariat turns the most important page in the history of the world struggle of the working class. The hour strikes. A new chapter in the history of the world proletarian revolution has begun.

The fifth article argued that, in spite of difficulties, 'the German proletariat will maintain itself in power' – an allusion to Lenin's famous pamphlet of September 1917, *Will the Bolsheviks Retain State Power?* The sixth discussed 'the Achilles heel of the German revolution', the danger of foreign intervention. The seventh, written on 22 October (the day after the collapse of the Chemnitz conference), asserted that 'there is not the slightest doubt that the German Communist Party has by and large applied the tactics of the united front with great success', and that 'the objections of the "Left" communists . . . miss the mark'.

On 26 October *Pravda* published an article by Zinoviev, which stated:

> From the very outset, the proletarian revolution in Germany will be of even greater international significance than the Russian revolution was. Germany is more of an industrial

country than Russia. Germany lies at the very centre of Europe . . . Germany possesses a powerful proletariat which, when it stretches its limbs, will thereby destroy the equilibrium in any bourgeois country that decides to strike a blow against German revolution.

On 31 October Zinoviev stated that the German revolution was still on the upswing: 'One must be blind not to see that in Germany the fate of Europe will very shortly be determined.'

Not till the tenth and last article, published on 1 November, with the sub-title *No Illusions*, was any reference made to the disasters in Saxony and Hamburg. The diagnosis was that 'the SPD opened the way for the Fascists to a "peaceful" conquest of power'; the coalition government in Saxony had 'not been able to carry out' the tasks assigned to it because of the obstruction of the Social Democrats. No censure of the KPD leadership was suggested, either in the articles or in the preface, written on 2 November, for a German translation to be published in Germany as a pamphlet.

A few weeks later Zinoviev found it necessary to distance himself from the KPD leadership. He wrote a letter to the Central Committee of the KPD on behalf of the ECCI accusing them 'of having failed to use the situation in Saxony as the starting-point for armed action', and having 'converted participation in the Saxon government into a banal parliamentary combination with the social democrats'.[37] He conveniently overlooked the fact that Brandler and the majority of the Zentrale were very reluctant to join the Saxon government and did so only under pressure from the ECCI.

Zinoviev continued to underemphasize the defeat in Germany. On 25 January 1924, at the Thirteenth Conference of the CPSU, he declared: 'The Executive Committee of the Communist International must say to you that should similar events repeat themselves, we would do the very same thing in the very same situation.'

On 2 February 1924, at a conference of the International Red Aid, he declared that the situation in the whole of Europe was such that 'we must not expect there a period now, no matter how brief, of even an external pacification, any lull whatever . . .

Europe is entering into the phase of decisive events . . . Germany is apparently marching towards a sharpened civil war'.

Early in February 1924, the Presidium of the ECCI stated in its resolution on the lessons of the German events: 'The Communist Party of Germany must not remove from the agenda the question of the uprising and the seizure of power. *On the contrary* [!] this question must stand before us in all its concreteness and urgency.'[38] On 26 March the ECCI wrote to the KPD:

> The proletarian revolution in Germany is inevitable. The mistakes in estimating the tempo of events committed in October 1923 created many difficulties for the party. They are nevertheless merely an episode. The basic estimate remains unchanged. The revolution is approaching . . . [The party] must now put before the German working class, more sharply than ever before, the most important of all tasks – the preparation for the direct struggle for power, for the proletarian dictatorship.[39]

Zinoviev concealed the serious mistakes committed by the leadership. As frequently happens in history, tailism was turned into its opposite, adventurism. And following the defeat in Germany, Zinoviev encouraged an extreme ultra-left turn in the KPD. This prepared the ground for the defeat of the German proletariat by the Nazis a few years later. To quote from a statement of the ECCI on 19 January 1924 regarding the events in Germany:

> The leading strata of German Social Democracy are at the present moment nothing but a fraction of German Fascism wearing a socialist mask . . . It is not just now that these leaders of German Social Democracy have gone over to the side of capital. At bottom they have always been on the side of the class enemies of the proletariat, but it is only now that this has been revealed to the masses in a glaring light, by the completion of the transition from capitalist democracy to capitalist dictatorship. This circumstance induces us to modify the united front tactics in Germany. There can be no dealings with the mercenaries of the White dictatorship. This must be clearly grasped by all German communists and solemnly and loudly announced to the entire German proletariat.
> Even more dangerous than the right-wing SPD leaders are the

left . . . The slogan of the united front tactic in Germany is now: Unity from below![40]

The term 'united front from below' meant simply that communists must denounce the socialist leaders and ask the supporters of the socialist parties to join their own ranks.

To protect himself from criticism for the German debacle, Zinoviev also resorted to a very distasteful innovation – sacrificing the KPD leadership as scapegoats. Brandler's removal from the chair of the KPD saved Zinoviev's skin.

Trotsky, who criticized Brandler's conduct consistently, nevertheless objected in principle to Moscow instituting a guillotine for foreign communist leaders. He said some time after the events:

> In this case, as in others, I fought against the inadmissible system which only seeks to maintain the infallibility of the central leadership by periodic removals of national leaderships, subjecting the latter to savage persecutions and even expulsions from the party.[41]

Foreign parties, Trotsky argued, must be allowed to learn from their own experience and mistakes, to manage their own affairs, and elect their own leaders. Brandler's removal established a very bad precedent.

Lenin did not play any part in the formation of policy for the German Communist Party in 1923, because he was seriously ill. After 10 March he was near death, after a stroke that paralyzed half of his body and deprived him of speech. Lenin's political activity was over, although he lingered on for another nine months – until 21 January 1924.

The reader may well ask: if Lenin played no role at all in the German events of 1923, why should this chapter on the German revolution be included in Lenin's political biography? The answer is that there is no alternative. The catastrophe in Germany in 1923 was the most important item on the balance sheet of Lenin's Comintern. An account of the tragic event is a vital part in our account of Lenin's work as leader of the Communist International.

The German debacle of 1923 also throws light on a very

serious weakness besetting Lenin's Comintern. Lenin had based the Comintern on two assumptions: first, that the world working class is one and indivisible; and second that the law of uneven development applies to it, and that its advanced sections should lead and support the more backward ones. For a time the role of the vanguard in the Communist International would be played by the Russian party.

However, in such a world army impact and influence cannot flow in only one direction: not only must the vanguard party influence the more immature, inexperienced parties, but the latter must also affect the former. Russian Bolshevism profoundly influenced the communist parties of western and central Europe, and vice versa. The interaction between communist parties of different countries affected the internal struggles in each party, because of the unevenness within each.

The whole history of Bolshevism was one of debates and inner party struggles. The Bolshevik Party had not only its Lenin and Sverdlov, but also its ultra-lefts, Bogdanov and Lunacharsky (1907-10); its 'Conciliators', Rykov and Dubrovinsky (1911-12); and its extreme right, in the persons of Zinoviev and Kamenev (at the time of the Russian revolution).

The interaction between the Russian party and the communist parties of central and western Europe meant that while the immature leaders of the latter parties provided grist for Zinoviev's mill, the President of the International was also able to discourage the advance training of independent, self-reliant leaders throughout the International. A process of natural selection of the unfittest was encouraged by Zinoviev. It is true that Paul Levi was not a Lenin, but neither was he a Zinoviev or a Bela Kun. Zinoviev preferred lieutenants who would be over-awed by the mantle of October that he wore. The clearest result of the Zinoviev leadership was the 1923 catastrophe in Germany.

25

Lenin Fights for his Life-Work

Lenin Falls Ill

The history of Bolshevism and the biography of Lenin were always intertwined. Now, during the NEP period, when the division between the dream and reality was at its widest and deepest, the tragedy of individual impotence, in the face of massive social forces, was accompanied by a sickness, not only of the proletariat and the party, but of the man himself.

The years of the revolution and civil war had taken their toll of Lenin's health. But his indomitable will power was unshaken and his determination to work unabated. He continued to work hard, and engaged in a wide variety of activities. On 1 September 1920 he modestly begged the Rumiantsev Library to lend him two Greek dictionaries: Greek–German, Greek–French, Greek–Russian or Greek–English; a history of Greek philosophy; and the best philosophical dictionaries, whether German, French, Russian or English. This was in the midst of the most terrible suffering and heroic struggles in Russia. (Lenin knew that reference books could not be taken out of the library. But he asked if he could have some of these volumes 'for an evening, for the night, when the library is closed. I will return them by morning'.)[1]

He was tense and worked through most nights, so it was not surprising that his health deteriorated. On 28 December he wrote: 'today I feel quite ill from insomnia'.[2] In 1921 his health continued to deteriorate. On 9 August he wrote to Gorky: 'I am so tired that I am unable to do a thing.'[3]

He first fell seriously ill on 6 December 1921, when he was suffering from chronic insomnia. He took sick leave and moved to Gorki, a suburb of Moscow. After a couple of weeks he returned to work, but on 1 January 1922 he took another six weeks' leave. Back at his desk for another few weeks, he again had to take a vacation from 6 March until 25 March. On 23

April he was operated on to remove one of the two bullets fired at him in April 1918 by the Socialist Revolutionary Dora Kaplan. On 25 May he suffered a stroke that led to partial paralysis and the loss of his ability to speak. 'You understand,' Lenin later remarked to Trotsky, 'I could not even speak or write, and I had to learn everything all over again.'[4] His robust constitution saved him, but he did not return to work until 2 October, and never fully regained his health. On 20 November he delivered his last public speech (at a session of the Moscow Soviet). On 7 November he left for Gorki. On 13 December he suffered two dangerous strokes. On the night of 22-23 he was again half paralyzed, and was confined to his bed in a small room of his Kremlin apartment.

Throughout this period, Lenin's industry was astonishing. As late as 10 February 1923, after a number of strokes, when his secretary, Fotieva, described his condition in her diary: 'Looks tired, speaks with great difficulty, losing the thread of his thoughts and confusing words. Compress on his head',[5] he asked for a whole list of books.*

On 6 March 1923 Lenin's health worsened markedly. On 10 March a further stroke paralyzed half his body and completely deprived him of speech. His political activity was ended. On 15 May he was moved from his apartment in the Kremlin to

---

* V.S.Rozhitsin, *Modern Science and Marxism*, Kharkov, 1922; S.Y.Semkovsky, *Marxism as a Teaching Subject. Report at the All-Ukraine Pedagogical Conference* (July 1922), Kharkov, 1922; M.Alsky, *Our Finances During the Civil War and NEP*, Moscow, 1923; S.N.Faulkner, *Turning-Point in the Crisis of World Industry*, Moscow, 1922; G.Tsiperovich, *By Ourselves! (Results of 5 years of Economic Development)*, Petrograd, 1922; L.Axelrod (Orthodox), *Against Idealism: A Criticism of Certain Idealistic Trends in Philosophical Thought: Collection of Articles*, Moscow–Petrograd, 1922; Arthur Drews, *Die Christumsmythe*, Moscow, 1923; P.G.Kurlov, *The End of Russian Tsarism: Reminiscences of an ex-Commander of the Gendarmerie*, Moscow–Petrograd, 1920; S.I.Kanatchikov, *Topics of the Day (Pages of Proletarian Ideology)*, Petrograd, 1923; I.A.Modzalevsky, *Proletarian Mythmaking (On Ideological Deviations in Modern Proletarian Poetry?)*, Semipalatinsk, 1922.[6]

Gorki. Two months later, suddenly, as if by a miracle, his health started to improve again. He began to take walks and practise writing with his left hand. Before long he was able to read books. It was usually Krupskaya who read the newspaper to him. Apparently, however, he did not recover his speech. On 21 January 1924 his health suddenly deteriorated and he died.

In the last few months of his active political life Lenin faced the greatest challenge of all – the defence of his whole life's work, from reaction growing within the Soviet regime, which he had founded. The articles he dictated in those days are among the best he ever wrote, and are both sharp and clear. While the flow of writing was very small, the quality was as high as ever.

Tragically, the owl of wisdom was heard only after the sun had set; only after the time for action had passed, in the twilight of his life, did Lenin grasp the real depth of social reaction in Russia. As ever, he was clear, seeing to the root of things.

Repulsing Encroaching Capitalism

We have seen (in Chapter 8) that Lenin defined NEP as a retreat imposed on the Soviet regime by the forces of capitalism, a 'peasant Brest' which would inevitably intensify the struggle between the kulaks and NEPmen on the one hand, and the proletariat and the state on the other. We have seen that the peasants went far beyond the limits which he tried to set when he launched NEP.

At the same time the workers were forced into a substantial retreat. Mass unemployment overtook them. Red managers, integrated into the party hierarchy, attacked their standards, imposing strict labour discipline, and subjecting them to unfair dismissals.

The trade unions did not play the role which Lenin had hoped they would. They lost much of their power and standing when they were denied any influence over the fixing of wages in industry, not to mention participation in management. Instead of defending the workers against the employers – whether private or state – the unions took a growing part in imposing discipline on the workers, and collaborated with management against them.

Privileges were more and more openly flaunted in a situation of general poverty. NEPmen displayed wads of banknotes, frequented brothels and gambling houses, and their wives showed off their jewellery. Members of the Workers' Opposition said that NEP stood for the New Exploitation of the Proletariat, a quip which became a popular slogan.

Again and again in 1921 and 1922 Lenin posed the questions: How long the retreat? How long NEP? He emphasized increasingly the need to check the retreat. He wrestled with the fear that perhaps the White Guard ex-Minister Professor Ustrialov would prove right and the NEP would turn from a tactic into an *evolution*. Lenin was well aware of the dialectical principle which occupies a central place in Marxism: that quantitative changes, whether in nature or society, at certain points turn into qualitative changes. He was afraid that this might happen to the regime under NEP.

He saw the bureaucratization of state and party increasing under NEP, and the state slipping out of revolutionary hands: 'the machine refuses to obey the hand that guided it', and is 'driven by some mysterious, lawless hand, God knows whose, perhaps of a profiteer, or of a private captitalist, or of both'. He was anxious in case the proletariat lost its hold on the state machine.

Defending the Monopoly of Foreign Trade

The question of how far the Soviet state would retreat under pressure from capitalism was posed concretely by the issue of the state monopoly of foreign trade.

This monopoly was established on 22 April 1918. During the civil war the question of its abolition never arose (not that there was any foreign trade to speak of). However, towards the end of 1921 Miliutin, the Soviet delegate to the Baltic Economic Conference held in Riga, promised that this monopoly would be abolished. A number of other Bolshevik leaders supported Miliutin in this. Sokolnikov, Bukharin and Piatakov opposed the retention of the monopoly of foreign trade; Zinoviev, Kamenev and Stalin wanted it relaxed. On 3 March 1922 Lenin wrote to Kamenev:

The foreigners are already buying up our officials with bribes, and 'carting out what there is left of Russia'. They may well succeed.

[We must] publish right away . . . a firm, cold, fierce statement that we do not intend to retreat in the economy any further, and that those who attempt to cheat us (or circumvent the monopoly, etc,) will face terrorism.'

On 15 May 1922, Lenin wrote a draft decision for the Politbureau on the subject, stating, 'The CC reaffirms the monopoly of foreign trade'.[8] He also wrote in a letter to Stalin that 'a formal ban should be put on all talk and negotiations and commissions etc. concerning the relaxation of the foreign trade monopoly'. Stalin wrote on Lenin's letter: 'I have no objections to a "formal ban" on measures to *mitigate* the foreign trade monopoly at the *present* stage. All the same, I think that *mitigation* is becoming indispensable.'[9]

The discussion continued. On 22 May Lenin's theses were adopted by the Politbureau. But later, during his absence after the stroke that paralyzed him on 25 May, the opponents of the monopoly won the day. On 6 October a plenum of the Central Committtte ratified Sokolnikov's proposal that the monopoly should be considerably relaxed. Lenin reacted sharply, and on 16 October the Central Committee agreed to put the question on the agenda again at the next plenum on 25 December. On 11 October Lenin asked Trotsky to confer with him on this problem in particular. Two days earlier he had sent an urgent letter to all Politbureau members demanding the reversal of the decision. Once again Stalin appended a note to Lenin's letter: 'Comrade Lenin's letter has not made me change my mind as to the correctness of the decision of the plenum of the Central Committee of the 6 October concerning foreign trade.'[10] The lion was mortally wounded, and the jackal raised his head. On 12 December Lenin suggested to Trotsky that they should join forces in defence of the foreign trade monopoly. 'Comrade Trotsky: I am sending you Krestinsky's letter. Write me as soon as possible whether you agree: at the plenum, I am going to fight for the monopoly. What about you? Yours, Lenin.'[11]

Three days later, in a letter to Stalin Lenin wrote: 'I have

. . . come to an agreement with Trotsky on the defence of my views on the monopoly of foreign trade.' He added: 'any further vacillation over this extremely important question is absolutely impermissible and will wreck all our work'.[12]

How central Lenin felt the question of the monopoly of foreign trade to be to the question of the limits of the retreat under NEP is clear from his criticism of a letter from Bukharin suggesting a relaxation of the monopoly.

> In practice, Bukharin is acting as an advocate of the profiteer, of the petty bourgeois and of the upper stratum of the peasantry in opposition to the industrial proletariat, which will be totally unable to build up its own industry and make Russia an industrial country unless it has the protection, not of tariffs, but of the monopoly of foreign trade. In view of the conditions at present prevailing in Russia, any other form of protection would be absolutely fictitious; it would be merely paper protection, from which the proletariat would derive no benefit whatever. Hence, from the viewpoint of the proletariat and of its industry, the present fight rages around fundamental principles.[13]

The Lenin–Trotsky partnership on the question of the monopoly led the Central Committee to reverse its decision of 6 October. On 21 December, therefore, Lenin could write to Trotsky: 'It looks as though it has been possible to take the position without a single shot, by a simple manœuvre. I suggest that we should not stop and should continue the offensive.'[14]

Lenin frequently emphasized that NEP was a concession to the petty capitalist peasantry. Such concessions would lead to catastrophe without certain safeguards. There must be no freedom of foreign trade. Such freedom would deprive the state of any means of controlling either prices or the peasantry.

The Need for Planning

It was clear to Lenin that the weakness of the proletariat was due to the weakness of industry. The balance of power between the proletariat and the peasantry, and the strength of the NEPmen, depended above all on the relative strength of industry and agriculture.

At the Fourth Congress of the Comintern, in the penultimate speech of his life, on 13 November 1922, Lenin argued that 'all commanding heights' of the economy were in the hands of the state. But how 'commanding' was industry? While agricultural output in 1922 was at three-quarters of its pre-war level, industry had achieved only a little more than a quarter of pre-war production: small industry – rural and artisan – was at 54 per cent of its pre-war level, while large-scale industry was at only 20 per cent. The 1922 output of the metallurgical industry, the largest of Russia's pre-war industries, and the basis of all large-scale industry, was only 7 per cent of its 1912 level.[15]

Lenin therefore sounded a note of alarm in his speech to the Fourth Congress of the Comintern in November 1922:

> The salvation of Russia lies not only in a good harvest on the peasant farms – that is not enough; and not only in the good condition of light industry, which provides the peasantry with consumer goods – this, too, is not enough; we also need *heavy* industry. And to put it in a good condition will require several years of work.
>
> Heavy industry needs state subsidies. If we are not able to provide them, we shall be doomed as a civilized state, let alone as a socialist state.[16]

Towards the end of his last published article, Lenin wrote of the need 'to change from the peasant, *muzhik* horse of poverty, from the horse of an economy designed for a ruined peasant country, to the horse which the proletariat is seeking and must seek – the horse of large-scale machine industry, of electrification, of the Volkhov power station, etc.' He called this 'the general plan of our work, of our policy, of our tactics, of our strategy'.[17] Building heavy industry was directly related to economic planning.

Even in the midst of civil war, Lenin wrote about the need for economic planning. For instance, the new party programme adopted by the Eighth Congress, in March 1919, demanded 'the maximum union of the whole economic activities of the country in accordance with one general state plan'. But this was only a verbal affirmation, without immediate practical consequences: under the prevailing conditions every economic activity was subordinated to the immediate needs of the front, and therefore could not but be dictated by expediency.

In February 1920, in a speech to YTsIK, Lenin argued that electrification should be planned and should form the base for a general planned development of the economy. At the end of the session VTsIK resolved that the time had now come to 'take steps towards a more regularly planned economic construction, towards the scientific working out and consistent execution of a state plan for the whole national economy'. Taking into account the 'primary significance' of electrification for industry, agriculture and transport, it instructed VSNKh to prepare a project for the building of a 'network of electric power stations' and to set up a commission for the electrification of Russia (Goelro).[18]

At the Eighth Congress of Soviets, in December 1920, Lenin declared: 'Communism is soviet power plus the electrification of the whole country', and added that the electrification plan 'is the second programme of our party'.[19]

From the beginning of NEP it was Trotsky who increasingly insisted that what was needed was not only planned electrification, but a *general* economic plan. He demanded the strengthening of the power of Gosplan, the State Planning Commission. Lenin was less than enthusiastic about the idea. He was worried that the plan would remain on paper, that it would be make-believe encouraged by 'communist conceit'. He wrote to G.M.Krzhizhanovsky on 19 February 1921: 'We are beggars. Hungry, ruined beggars. A complete, integrated, real plan for us at present – "a bureaucratic Utopia".'[20] So he did not support Trotsky's stand, either before his first stroke in May 1922 or after he returned to work in the autumn.

On 23 August 1922 Trotsky reproached Lenin with the fact that because of the lack of economic planning the government was not tackling urgent economic matters with the necessary urgency:

The most vital and urgent administrative–organizational economic measures are adopted by us with, what I estimate to be on an average, a delay of a year and a half to two years . . . With the change-over to the new economic policy State funds are a vital lever in the economic plan. Their allocation is predetermined by the economic plan. Outside of fixing the volume of monetary issues and allocating financial resources between departments there is not and cannot be any economic plan at the moment. Yet, as far as I can judge, Gosplan has no concern with these fundamental questions . . . How can one require efficiency and proper accountability from individual departments and organs if they do not have the slightest certainty as to what to-morrow will look like? How can one ensure even minimum stability of operation without at the least some rough and approximate, albeit short-term, plan? How can one institute even a rough, short-term plan without a planning organ, one which does not have its head in the academic clouds but is directly engaged on controlling, knitting together, regulating and directing our industry?[21]

He stressed the need for planning as a means for rapid industrialization, creating a firm base for the dictatorship of the proletariat.

Finally Trotsky, and the clouds gathering in the NEP sky, persuaded Lenin to change his mind. On 27 December he dictated from his sickbed a memorandum to the Politbureau, in which he declared himself converted to Trotsky's view on this point. He wrote:

Granting Legislative Functions to the State Planning Commission. This idea was suggested by Comrade Trotsky, it seems, quite a long time ago. I was against it at the time, because I thought that there would then be a fundamental lack of co-ordination in the system of our legislative institutions. But after closer consideration of the matter I find that in substance there is a sound idea in it, namely: the State Planning Commission stands somewhat apart from our legislative institutions, although, as a body of experienced people, experts, representatives of science and technology, it is actually in a better position to form a correct judgment of affairs . . . I think that we must now take a step towards extending the competence of the State Planning Commission.[22]

A few weeks earlier, on 25 November, Lenin had proposed to the Political Bureau that Trotsky's thesis on NEP for the Fourth Congress of the International should be published as a pamphlet and widely distributed.[23] This argued that planning of the economy should be undertaken on the foundations of NEP:

The workers' state [Trotsky wrote], while shifting its economy to the foundations of the market, does not, however, renounce the beginning of planned economy, not even for the period immediately ahead . . . The state is centring its attention more and more on heavy industry and transport, as the foundations of economic life, and adjusts its policy with regard to finances, revenues, concessions and taxes to a great degree to the requirements of heavy industry and transport. Under the conditions of the present period the state economic plan does not set itself the Utopian task of substituting omniscient prescience for the elemental interplay of supply and demand. On the contrary, taking its starting point from the market, as the basic form of distribution of goods and of regulation of production, our present economic plan aims at securing the greatest possible preponderance of state enterprises in the market by means of combining all the factors of credit, tax, industry and trade; and this plan aims at introducing in the reciprocal relations between the state enterprises the maximum of foresight and uniformity so that by basing itself on the market, the state may aid in eliminating the market as quickly as possible, above all in the sphere of the reciprocal relations between the state-owned enterprises themselves.[24]

Insofar as NEP was a struggle between capitalist and socialist tendencies in the economy, its outcome was still in the balance: the decisive factor was the development of the international revolution. The press frequently referred to the state sector as an island of socialism in a sea of peasant capitalism – an image reflecting the fear that the continuation of NEP might bring about a total submersion of this island. As a transition stage, including both struggle and collaboration between capitalist and socialist elements, NEP could lead either to socialism or capitalism. Ustrialov could still prove right. Tactics could turn into evolution, a retreat into a rout. Lenin continued to ask the question: *Kto kogo?* – Who will win?

Great Russian Chauvinism Breaks Out

Suddenly, to the many elements of economic and social reaction under NEP, a new menace was added – Great Russian Chauvinism – and this in the leadership of the party. It was a shattering experience for Lenin. He always felt deeply sympathetic towards the oppressed nationalities. He detested chauvinism, and especially abhorred the Great Russian variety.

For a number of years there had been covert symptoms of Great Russian chauvinism in state and party. With the increasing centralization of administration, and the appointment of more and more state and party officials by Moscow, the workers of other nationalities were bound to appear as second-class. Thus administrative convenience played into the hands of Moscow centralism and Great Russian chauvinism. NEP, which gave economic and social power back to the Russian merchants and officials who had been identified with national oppression under the Tsarist regime strengthened the development of Great Russian chauvinism.

Lenin was alarmed. As early as the Ninth Party Congress in March 1920 he stated: 'Scratch some communists, and you will find Great Russian chauvinists.'[25] At the tenth Party Congress in March 1921, Sakharov, one of the delegates from Turkestan, analysed the composition of the local party and demanded a more active struggle both against Great Russian chauvinism and against Moslem nationalism.[26] The Tenth Congress was the first to recognize Great Russian chauvinism in the communist apparatus by including in its resolutions a strongly worded condemnation of it.[27]

On 2 November 1920 Trotsky, in a message to Lenin and the Politbureau, bluntly stated that the Soviet administration in the Ukraine had from the outset been based on people sent from Moscow and not on local elections.

> The Soviet regime in the Ukraine has maintained itself in being up to now (but feebly at that) largely by virtue of the authority of Moscow, the Great-Russian communists and the Russian Red Army . . . Economically the Ukraine still is the embodiment of anarchy sheltering under the bureaucratic centralism of Moscow.[28]

He demanded a radical break with this method of government.

At the Eleventh Party Congress (March-April 1922), the veteran Ukrainian Bolshevik N.Skrypnik argued that the Communist Party apparatus was infiltrated with adherents of *Smena Vekh* ready to violate the party's solemn pledge to defend

Ukrainian independence. 'The one and indivisible Russia is not our slogan,' he exclaimed – at which point a voice from the audience shouted back ominously: 'The one and indivisible Communist Party!'[29]

The fact that the party membership was overwhelmingly Russian facilitated Great Russian chauvinism. (In 1922 72 per cent of all members were Great Russians.) The right of nations to self-determination was inevitably threatened in a situation where there was only *one* party – particularly as it was highly centralized and dominated by officials from the dominant nation. Since the Central Committee in Moscow – or increasingly the Secretariat – imposed its will on the Central Committees of the national republics, little in real terms remained of national independence.

In August 1922 two associated topics brought the question of Great Russian chauvinism to a head in the Moscow party leadership. One was the establishment of the USSR, the other the national question in Georgia.

On 10 August 1922 the Politbureau directed the Orgburo to set up a commission to investigate relations between the RSFSR and the Soviet Republics of Ukraine, Belorussia, Georgia, Armenia, and Azerbaidzhan. Stalin drafted the Commission's resolution 'On the Relations between the RSFSR and the Independent Republics'.

He treated the government of RSFSR as the *de facto* government of all the six republics, without even formally recognizing the legal fiction of independence. The government organs of the RSFSR, VTsIK, Sovnarkom and STO (Council of Labour and Defence) were to take over the functions of the leading bodies of the six republics. Key commissariats (foreign affairs and foreign trade, military affairs, transport and communications) were to be taken over by the Russian government, while others (finance, labour and national economy) had to operate under the control of the corresponding agencies of RSFSR, and only an insignificant few were to be entrusted entirely to the autonomous republics. Nearly all the national commissariats were to become mere extensions of the Moscow administration.

Point 6 of the resolution proposed that the documents should be kept secret until after the various VTsIKs agreed; there was to be no consultation of congresses of soviets, let alone of the masses of workers and peasants.[30]

On 15 September 1922 the Central Committee of the Georgian Communist Party rejected this resolution. The secretariat, i.e. Stalin, then acted improperly, by sending the Commission's resolution to all members and candidate members of the party Central Committee without the question having been considered by the Politbureau. To add insult to injury on 28 August, even before his plans had been discussed by the Politbureau of the Central Committee, Stalin appears to have sent a telegram to Mdivani, a leader of the Georgian opposition to Stalin, informing him that the decisions of the highest governing bodies of RSFSR (VTsIK, Sovnarkom and STO) were henceforth binding on all the republics.[31]

When Lenin received the Commission resolution he was furious. It violated any concept of national equality, and openly formalized the hegemony of the RSFSR over the other republics. On 26 September he wrote to Kamenev: 'we consider ourselves, the Ukrainian SSR and others, equal, and enter with them, on an equal basis, into a new union, a new federation, the Union of the Soviet Republics of Europe and Asia'. He demanded the creation of an All-Union Central Executive Committee, Sovnarkom and STO, to supersede those of the RSFSR.[32]

Stalin was truculent and opposed the sick old man. He and Kamenev, probably at a meeting of the Politbureau, exchanged two brief notes on the subject of Lenin's memorandum. Kamenev's note reads: 'Ilyich is going to war to defend independence.' Stalin replied: 'In my opinion we have to be firm against Lenin.'[33]

On 27 September Stalin replied to Lenin. Among other hurtful remarks he accused Lenin of 'national liberalism'.[34] This annoyed Lenin very much.

On 6 October Lenin wrote a memorandum to the Politbureau 'On Combating Dominant National Chauvinism':

I declare war to the death on dominant nation chauvinism . . .
It must be *absolutely* insisted that the Union Central Executive

Committee should be *presided over* in turn by a
Russian,
Ukrainian,
Georgian, etc.
Absolutely![35]

Recognizing that he would be in a minority on the Central
Committee, Stalin accepted Lenin's amendment to the Commission's resolution. But, this was only a Pyrrhic victory for
Lenin, as the issue of Georgia, around which the national question
next arose, showed.

Stalin and Ordzhonikidze, political and military leaders of
the Caucasian front during the civil war, wanted to combine
the republics of Georgia, Azerbaidzhan and Armenia into a
Caucasian Federation, violating the autonomy of the national
republics. The local Georgian leaders, headed by Budu Mdivani,
one of the earliest Bolsheviks in the Caucasus, and Filipp
Ieseevich Makharadze, a member of the Central Committee of
the Russian Communist Party and a Marxist since 1891, opposed
the suggested Federation. The conflict turned into a political
and personal clash between two groups of Georgians: on the
one hand Ordzhonikidze and his mentor Stalin, on the other the
Georgian Communist Party Central Committee.

On 22 October the Central Committee of the Georgian
Communist Party resorted to the unprecedented step of tendering
its resignation to the Cenral Committee of the Russian party.
The resignation was accepted and Ordzhonikidze appointed a
new Central Committee, made up of incompetent but docile
young men who accepted the Federation without protest. The
secretariat in Moscow eagerly accepted the resignation of the
old Georgian Central Committee and the new appointment.

But the members of the old Central Committee did not give
up the struggle. A small but significant incident took place that
opened Lenin's eyes to the real meaning of the conflict around
the Georgian question. In the course of the continual debates
and confrontations, Ordzhonikidze, losing his temper, went so far
as to use physical violence against another party member, a
supporter of Mdivani. It happened at a private session held at
Ordzhonikidze's house, while Rykov, Lenin's deputy and a mem-

ber of the Politbureau, was present. When a new request to reopen the inquiry, signed by Makharadze and others, reached Moscow, it could not be ignored. At this point Lenin was beginning to be anxious about the situation. He was suddenly alarmed by a letter from Okudzhava, a prominent member of the old Georgian Central Committee, accusing Ordzhonikidze of personally insulting and threatening the Georgian comrades.

Lenin's incapacity gave Ordzhonikidze and Stalin the opportunity to take the offensive against their Georgian opponents. On 21 December the Central Committee of the Russian Communist Party ordered the opposition leaders, Mdivani, Makharadze, Tsintsadze and Kavtaradze, to leave Georgia.[36]

Lenin, when he recovered from his stroke towards the end of December, decided to return to the Georgian question. But his decision to resume work met with obstacles, firstly, from his doctors. Visitors were forbidden. Lenin was allowed to see only his wife, Krupskaya, his sister Maria and three or four secretaries, apart, of course, from the medical staff. His entourage was forbidden to talk to him about current state business. On 24 December the Politbureau issued the following instruction:

> 1. Vladimir Ilyich is granted permission to dictate for five to ten minutes a day, but it ought not to have the character of a correspondence and Ilyich must not expect replies to these notes. Visits are forbidden.
> 2. Friends and servants are forbidden to communicate anything to Lenin concerning political life, in order not to give him cause for reflection and anxiety.[37]

How far this was an effort to protect Lenin, and how far an attempt to protect the Secretariat from Lenin, is not clear. That Lenin felt himself besieged is clear from the following entry by L.A.Fotieva in the *Journal* of 1 February 1923:

> Today Vladimir Ilyich sent for me . . . Vladimir Ilyich said: 'If I were at large (at first he made a slip, then repeated, laughing: If I were at large)'.[38]

The secretariat put great pressure on Lenin's private secretaries. Thus an entry by Fotieva on 3 February had this to say:

Asked whether this question [of Georgia] had been up before the Politbureau, I answered that I had no right to talk about it. Asked: 'Have you been forbidden to speak precisely and particularly about this?' 'No, I have no right generally to talk about current business.' 'So this is current business?' I realised that I had made a slip. I repeated that I had no right to talk.[39]

However ill he was, Lenin was not a man to be fobbed off. He persevered in his search for information on the Georgian affair. He could rely only on a few dedicated women in his private secretariat. He may have lost a great deal of his ability to work, but not his willpower. He knew that his time was nearly up, and he had a duty to fulfil: to tell the truth to the party and the country. He took advantage of the permission to dictate to put out several important memoranda, including one on the nationalities question which deserves to be quoted at length. On 30 December 1922 he dictated the following:

> I suppose I have been very remiss with respect to the workers of Russia for not having intervened energetically and decisively enough in the notorious question of autonomization, which, it appears, is officially called the question of the union of Soviet Socialist Republics . . .
> It is said that a united apparatus was needed. Where did that assurance come from? Did it not come from that same Russian apparatus which . . . we took over from Tsarism and slightly anointed with Soviet oil? . . .
> It is quite natural that in such circumstances the 'freedom to secede from the union' by which we justify ourselves will be a mere scrap of paper, unable to defend the non-Russians from the onslaught of that really Russian man, the Great Russian chauvinist, in substance a rascal and a tyrant, such as the typical Russian bureaucrat is. There is no doubt that the infinitesimal percentage of soviet and sovietized will drown in that tide of chauvinistic Great Russian riffraff like a fly in milk. . . . were we careful enough to take measures to provide the non-Russians with a real safeguard against the truly Russian bully? I do not think we took such measures although we could and should have done so.

Lenin went on to refer to Stalin:

> I think that Stalin's haste and his infatuation with pure administration, together with his spite against the notorious

'nationalist socialism', played a fatal role here. In politics spite generally plays the basest of roles.[40]

Next day, on 31 December, Lenin went on to dictate a bitter attack on Great Russian chauvinism.

we, nationals of a big nation, have nearly always been guilty, in historic practice, of an infinite number of cases of violence; furthermore, we commit violence and insult an infinite number of times without noticing it . . . internationalism on the part of oppressors or 'great' nations, as they are called (though they are great only in their violence, only great as bullies), must consist not only in the observance of the formal equality of nations but even in an inequality of the oppressor nation, the great nation, that must make up for the inequality which obtains in actual practice . . . What is needed . . .? Not merely formal equality . . . it is necessary to compensate non-Russians for the lack of trust, for the suspicion, and the insults to which the government of the 'dominant' nation subjected them in the past.[41]

In another note dictated on the same day, he went on to deal with the misdeeds of Ordzhonikidze: 'exemplary punishment must be inflicted on Comrade Ordzhonikidze.' He continued,

The political responsibility for all this truly Great Russian nationalist campaign must, of course, be laid on Stalin and Dzerzhinsky [the head of the Cheka].

Unless Great Russian chauvinism was fought to the death, the party's support of anti-imperialist nationalist liberation movements would be completely hypocritical.

we ourselves lapse . . . into imperialist attitudes towards oppressed nationalities, thus undermining all our principled sincerity, all our principled defence of the struggle against imperialism![42]

The Georgian question was uppermost in Lenin's mind throughout his last few weeks of political activity. His secretary, Fotieva, in the *Journal* entry of 14 February 1923, wrote: 'Called me in again. Impediment in speech, obviously tired. Spoke again on the three points of his instructions. In special detail on the subject that agitated him most of all, namely the Georgian question. Asked to hurry things up.'[43]

On 5 March he dictated the following letter to be telephoned to Trotsky:

> Top secret
> Personal
>
> Dear Comrade Trotsky: It is my earnest request that you should undertake the defence of the Georgian case in the party CC. This case is now under 'persecution' by Stalin and Dzerzhinsky, and I cannot rely on their impartiality. Quite to the contrary. I would feel at ease if you agreed to undertake its defence. If you should refuse to do so for any reason, return the whole case to me. I shall consider it a sign that you do not accept.
>
> With best comradely greetings,
> Lenin.[44]*

With this letter Lenin forwarded to Trotsky his memorandum on the national question. The following day Lenin sent a brief but very significant message to the leaders of the Georgian opposition.

> To P.G.Mdivani, F.Y.Makharadze and others
>
> Top secret
>
> Copy to Comrades *Trotsky and Kamenev*
> Dear Comrades:
> I am following your case with all my heart. I am indignant over Ordhonikidze's rudeness and the connivance of Stalin and Dzerzhinsky. I am preparing for you notes and a speech.
>
> Respectfully yours,
> Lenin
>
> 6 March 1923.[45]

This was the last document Lenin dictated.

On 7 March he suffered his third serious stroke. By 10 March half his body was paralyzed. He never recovered the power of speech. His political life was over. Stalin and Ordzhonikidze were saved by this stroke.

---

* The closing words of the letter were so warm that Stalin, when forced to read it out before the Central Committee in July 1926 – by which time his position was unassailable – changed them to 'With communist greetings'.

26

Fighting to the Last Breath . . .

Rabkrin

While he was dealing with the Georgian question, Lenin became increasingly aware that it was only a symptom of a much deeper and more general sickness – the rule of the bureaucracy.

If this sorry affair brought him into conflict with Stalin, his examination of the Workers' and Peasants' Inspectorate (Rabkrin) brought the two men into further conflict. This institution was designed to fight bureaucracy. In the words of the resolution of the Ninth Party Conference, (September 1920), its task was to

> fight encroaching bureaucratism, careerism, the abuse of their party and soviet positions by party members, the violation of comradely relations within the party, the spread of unfounded and unverified rumours and insinuations, which discredit the party or its individual members, and other such reports that damage the party's unity and authority.'[1]

Stalin headed Rabkrin from 1919 until the spring of 1922, when he was appointed General-Secretary. But he continued to exercise a strong influence on it for some time. The Inspectorate's functions were very wide: it was entitled to inspect the work of the commissariats and the civil servants, to oversee the efficiency and morale of the whole administration. Lenin intended Rabkrin as a super-commissariat fighting bureaucracy and imposing democratic control. It acted through teams of workers and peasants who were free at any time to enter any government office. Unfortunately working in offices turned the workers themselves into bureaucrats. As Deutscher put it, Stalin transformed Rabkrin 'into his private police within the government'.[2] As its Chief, he came to control the whole state machinery, its working and personnel, far more closely than any other commissar.

Trotsky attacked Rabkrin as inefficient as early as 1920. He was not supported by Lenin, who continued to defend Rabkrin as late as 5 May 1922.[3] However, his conflict with Stalin on the Georgian issue opened his eyes. In his last article, 'Better Fewer but Better', he declared war on Rabkrin.

> Let us say frankly that the People's Commissariat of the Workers' and Peasants' Inspection does not at present enjoy the slightest authority. Everybody knows that no other institutions are worse organized than those of our Workers' and Peasants' Inspection, and that under present conditions nothing can be expected from this People's Commissariat.[4]

He continued:

> Indeed, what is the use of establishing a People's Commissariat which carried on anyhow, which does not enjoy the slightest confidence, and whose word carried scarcely any weight. Our main object . . . is to avoid all this . . . we must really set to work . . . to create something really exemplary, something that will win the respect of all and sundry for its merits, and not only because of its rank and title.[5]

Lenin's final remarks on the qualities desirable in a reformed Rabkrin reflected its defects under Stalin's leadership. 'Let us hope that our new Workers' and Peasants' Inspection will abandon what the French called *pruderie*, which we may call ridiculous primness, or ridiculous swank, and which plays entirely into the hands of our soviet and party bureaucracy.'[6]

Lenin's criticism of Rabkrin did not meet with unanimous support among the party leadership. Trotsky recalled:

> how did the Political Bureau react to Lenin's project for the reorganization of Rabkrin? Comrade Bukharin hesitated to print Lenin's article, while Lenin, on his side, insisted upon its immediate appearance. N.K.Krupskaya told me by telephone about this article and asked me to take steps to get it printed as soon as possible. At the meeting of the Political Bureau, called immediately upon my demand, all those present – comrades Stalin, Molotov, Kuibyshev, Rykov, Kalinin, Bukharin – were not only against comrade Lenin's plan but against the very printing of the article. The members of the secretariat were particularly harsh and categorical in their opposition. In view of the insistent demand of comrade Lenin that the article should be

shown to him in print, comrade Kuibyshev, afterwards the head of Rabkrin, proposed at the above-mentioned session of the Political Bureau that one special number of *Pravda* should be printed with Lenin's article and shown to him in order to placate him, while the article itself should be concealed from the party . . . I was supported only by comrade Kamenev who appeared at the meeting of the Political Bureau almost an hour late.

The chief argument which induced them to print the article was that an article by Lenin could not be concealed from the party in any case.[7]

On 4 March 1923 *Pravda* published Lenin's article.

The Prescription

In the autumn of 1922 Lenin returned as if from the grave. He could see with crystal clarity what was happening around him, and the disastrous growth of bureaucracy, one of the main problems being that 'we have bureaucrats in our party offices as well as in soviet offices'. He also perceived that by far the greatest source of malignancy was in the supreme body – the Central Committee of the party. Conscious that his life was running out, he was spurred on to draw up a number of practical proposals to fight the bureaucratic cancer at the centre.

One important recommendation which Lenin made on 23 December 1922 was that the Central Committee should be increased in size – to 100. This 'must be done in order to raise the prestige of the Central Committee, to do a thorough job of improving our administrative machinery and to prevent conflicts between small sections of the CC from acquiring excessive importance for the future of the party'.[8]

In a further note, written on 26 December, he explained that one of the main advantages of enlarging the Central Committee would be to improve its social composition.

> The enlistment of many workers to the CC will help the workers to improve our administrative machinery, which is pretty bad . . . I think that a few dozen workers, being members of the CC, can deal better than anybody else with checking, improving and remodelling our state apparatus . . .
> The working-class members of the CC must be mainly workers

of a lower stratum than those promoted in the last five years to work in soviet bodies; they must be people closer to being rank-and-file workers and peasants . . . I think that by attending all sittings of the CC and all sittings of the Political Bureau, and by reading all the documents of the CC, such workers can form a staff of devoted supporters of the soviet system, able, first, to give stability to the CC itself, and second, to work effectively on the renewal and improvement of the state apparatus.[9]

Another reform was Lenin suggested was that Rabkrin, i.e. a state institution, should be combined with the party's Central Control Commission.

I propose that the Congress should elect 75 to 100 new members to the Central Control Commission. They should be workers and peasants, and should go through the same party screening as ordinary members of the Central Committee, because they are to enjoy the same rights as the members of the Central Committee.[10]

This new Central Control Commission, together with the Central Committee, would assemble as a 'supreme party conference' once every two months.

The presidium of the Central Control Commission would take part in the work of the Politbureau, so as to check all its working scrupulously:

the members of the Central Control Commission, whose duty it will be to attend all meetings of the Political Bureau in a definite number, will have to form a compact group which should not allow anybody's authority, without exception, neither that of the General Secretary nor of any other member of the Central Committee, to prevent them from putting questions, verifying documents, and, in general, from keeping themselves fully informed of all things and from exercising the strictest control over the proper conduct of affairs.

A larger Central Committee, closely related to the re-structured Central Control Commission, would be more in touch with the masses.[11]

How were these reforms to be effected? As his health did not permit Lenin to carry out the struggle for reform himself, he turned to Trotsky for help. Trotsky remembers his last conversation with Lenin. Not long before his third stroke:

> Lenin summoned me to his room in the Kremlin, spoke of the terrible growth of bureaucratism in our Soviet apparatus and of the necessity of finding a lever with which to get at that problem. He proposed to create a special commission of the Central Committee and asked me to take an active part in the work. I answered him: 'Vladimir Ilyich, it is my conviction that in the present struggle with bureaucratism in the soviet apparatus, we must not forget that there is taking place, both in the provinces and in the centre, a special selection of functionaries and specialists, party and non-party, around certain ruling party personalities and groups – in the provinces, in the districts, in the party locals and in the centre – that is, the Central Committee. Attacking a functionary you run into the party leader. The specialist is a member of his retinue. Under present circumstances, I could not undertake this work.
> Vladimir Ilyich reflected a moment and – here I quote him verbatim – said 'That is, I propose a struggle with soviet bureaucratism and you are proposing to include the bureaucratism of the Organization Bureau of the party?'
> I laughed at the unexpectedness of this, because no such finished formulation of the idea was in my mind.
> I answered: 'I suppose that's it.'
> Then Vladimir Ilyich said: 'Very well, then, I propose a bloc.'
> I said: 'It is a pleasure to form a bloc with a good man.'
> At the end of our conversation, Vladimir Ilyich said that he would propose the creation by the Central Committee of a commission to fight bureaucratism 'in general', and through that we would be able to reach the Organization Bureau of the Central Committee. The organizational side he promised to think over 'further'! At that we parted. I then waited two weeks for the bell to summon me but Ilyich's health became continually worse and he was soon confined to bed. After that Vladimir Ilyich sent me his letters on the national question through his secretaries. And so that work was never carried through.[12]

A dying man, making desperate efforts to save the revolution, Lenin turned to Trotsky as an ally. Again, as in 1917 and during the civil war, an intimate Lenin–Trotsky alliance was being forged.

But the reforms which Lenin suggested to fight the bureaucracy were bound to be extremely ineffective. They existed in a vacuum. Not that they could be faulted in themselves as *technical* measures. They were, however, not connected with any mobilization of *workers* into action, and as we have seen throughout his political activity, it was in his capacity to mobilize workers that Lenin's strength lay.

The Central Control Commission (Rabkrin) which Lenin proposed was to be independent of the state structure, but dependent on the party congress. But the congress became more and more dependent on the Secretary-General, who had the power to appoint almost all holders of office in the Party.

The Central Committee was to be filled with rank-and-file workers, but once they achieved this lofty position, there was no way to prevent them from turning into bureaucrats themselves. Would not an enlarged Central Committee, made up mainly of obscure new members, only make it easier for the Secretary-General to overpower the Politbureau, which was composed of old Bolsheviks who had too much prestige for him to crush them directly and immediately? With no factions allowed in the party, and the Secretary-General claiming that any disagreement constituted a faction, the power of democratic control over the bureaucracy was even more empty.

Lenin's suggested anti-bureaucratic measures thus lacked muscle to back them. In the event, the power of the secretariat did not decrease in the enlarged Central Committee which the Twelfth Congress (April 1923) created; quite the contrary. In fact, *all* Lenin's suggestions as regards Rabkrin were carried out by Stalin at the Twelfth Party Congress. At the same time he strengthened his hold over the machine, and consolidated the power of the bureaucracy generally. To add insult to injury, who should be appointed as Chairman of the Central Control Commission but Ordzhonikidze?

Lenin's Testament

In the last few days of his political life Lenin was haunted by the question of his successor. Who would take his place at the head of the party and the state? He wrote about the subject. He undertook an analysis of the personnel of the top leadership of the party, which seemed to him to be of serious importance because of the perilous situation of the soviet regime. The question constitutes a crucial element of Lenin's 'Testament'.

This 'Testament' consists of notes dictated between 23 and 31 December 1922, with a supplement dictated on 4 January. In Lenin's *Works*, published after Khrushchev's revelations, they are called 'Letter to the Congress'.

The notes propose changes in the Central Committee, the Central Control Commission and Rabkrin, and then present an analysis of the top leadership of the party. Lenin argues that a threat to the stability of the soviet regime can exist first of all at its base – in the danger of a split between the proletariat and the peasantry.

> Our party relies on two classes and therefore its instability would be possible and its downfall inevitable if there were no agreement between these two classes . . . No measures of any kind could prevent a split in such a case.

This is a threat in the long run. In the short run Lenin foresees the greater danger of a split resulting from *personal* relationships within the party leadership.

> I think that from this standpoint the prime factors in the question of stability are such members of the CC as Stalin and Trotsky. I think relations between them make up the greater part of the danger of a split.

After this prophetic judgment Lenin proceeds to sketch portraits of six of the leaders: Stalin and Trotsky, Zinoviev and Kamenev, Bukharin and Piatakov.

> Comrade Stalin, having become Secretary-General, has unlimited authority concentrated in his hands, and I am not sure whether he will always be capable of using that authority with sufficient caution. Comrade Trotsky, on the other hand, as his struggle against the CC on the question of the People's Commissariat for Communications has already proved, is distinguished not only by outstanding ability. He is personally perhaps the most capable man in the present CC, but he has displayed excessive self-assurance and shown excessive pre-occupation with the purely administrative side of the work.
> These two qualities of the two outstanding leaders of the

present CC can inadvertently lead to a split, and if our party does not take steps to avert this, the split may come unexpectedly.

Only a single remark is made about Zinoviev and Kamenev. 'I shall just recall that the October episode with Zinoviev and Kamenev was, of course, no accident.'

Of the two youngest men, Bukharin and Piatakov, Lenin writes:

> They are, in my opinion, the most outstanding figures (among the youngest ones), and the following must be borne in mind about them: Bukharin is not only a most valuable and major theorist of the party; he is also rightly considered the favourite of the whole party, but his theoretical views can be classified as fully Marxist only with great reserve, for there is something scholastic about him (he has never made a study of dialectics, and I think, never fully understood it).
>
> As for Piatakov, he is unquestionably a man of outstanding will and outstanding ability, but shows too much zeal for administrating and the administrative side of the work to be relied upon in a serious political matter.[13]

At this stage – on 23 and 25 December – Lenin suggested that a collective leadership should be preserved, based largely on the pre-eminence of Trotsky and Stalin, and with the safeguards of a larger Central Committee, etc.

However, ten days later, after dictating the above, Lenin wrote an addendum that completely shifted the balance: a sharp, bitter attack on Stalin. This change of mind can be seen as a result of the Georgian affair, for Lenin now accused Ordzhonikidze and Stalin of acting like Great Russian bullies; and also as a result of an incident involving Stalin and Krupskaya.

On 22 December Stalin used offensive language against Krupskaya, and threatened to take her to the Control Commission for having taken down a letter Lenin dictated to Trotsky on the question of the monopoly of foreign trade, thus breaking the medical regimen ordered for Lenin. On 23 December Krupskaya wrote to Kamenev:

> Lev Borisovich! Stalin subjected me to a storm of the coarsest abuse yesterday about a brief note that Lenin dictated to me,

with the permission of the doctors. I didn't join the party yesterday. In the whole of these last thirty years I have never heard a single coarse word from a comrade. The interests of the party and of Ilyich are no less dear to me than to Stalin. At the moment I need all the self-control I can muster. I know better than all the doctors what can and what cannot be said to Ilyich, for I know what disturbs him and what doesn't, and in any case I know this better than Stalin.

Krupskaya asked to be protected 'from gross interference in her private life, unworthy abuse and threats'. She continued:

I have no doubt as to the unanimous decision of the Control Commission with which Stalin takes it upon himself to threaten me, but I have neither the time nor the energy to lose in such a stupid farce. I too am human and my nerves are at breaking-point. N.Krupskaya.[14]

It was a day later, on 4 January 1923, that the addendum about Stalin's rudeness was added by Lenin to his Testament.

Addition to the Letter of 24 December, 1922
Stalin is too rude and this defect, although quite tolerable in our midst and in dealings among us communists, becomes intolerable in a Secretary-General. That is why I suggest that the comrades think about a way of removing Stalin from that post and appointing another man in his stead who in all other respects differs from Comrade Stalin in having only one advantage, namely, that of being more tolerant, more loyal, more polite and more considerate to the comrades, less capricious, etc. This circumstance may appear to be a negligible detail. But I think that from the standpoint of safeguards against a split and from the standpoint of what I wrote above about the relationship between Stalin and Trotsky it is not a detail, or it is a detail which can assume decisive importance.[15]

The personal affront to Krupskaya would not in itself have caused Lenin to attack Stalin. Personal grudges were never an element in his political relations with friend or foe. We have seen elsewhere that his personal regard for Vera Zasulich (and Martov) did not prevent Lenin from taking the harshest measures against them. 'Lenin was far too honest intellectually, too devoted to the cause, to sacrifice the needs of the organization to his own sentiments.'[16] Now, at the end of his life, Lenin did not change his attitude.

Politics must outweigh all other considerations. But the personal rudeness of Stalin, added to the issues of Georgia, Rabkrin, etc., probably constituted a warning signal that Stalin might do great damage to the communist cause.

The incident with Krupskaya was bound to have a sequel. On 5 March 1923, two days before the stroke that finally removed Lenin from the political scene, he wrote the following letter to Stalin, with a copy to Kamenev and Zinoviev.

> Dear Comrade Stalin,
> You have been so rude as to summon my wife to the telephone and use bad language. Although she had told you that she was prepared to forget this, the fact nevertheless became known through her to Zinoviev and Kamenev. I have no intention of forgetting so easily what has been done against me, and it goes without saying that what has been done against my wife I consider having been done against me as well. I ask you, therefore, to consider whether you are prepared to withdraw what you have said and to make your apologies, or whether you prefer that relations between us should be broken off.
> Respectfully yours,
> Lenin[17]

Lenin did not shirk his own responsibility for Stalin's appointment to high office. He must have remembered what he himself had said on 30 December 1920:

> A political leader is responsible not only for the quality of his leadership but also for the acts of those he leads. He may now and again be unaware of what they are about, he may often wish that they had not done something, but the responsibility still falls on him.[18]

Lenin's Testament looks, on the face of it, like a non-Marxist document – a personal fight against Stalin instead of a general political-social statement. However, Lenin well knew that politics develops by and through people. Personal traits in the party and state leadership may well become the expression of alien social forces.

The tragedy of Lenin's position pervades the whole of his

'Testament' – that he had to rely on personal changes as the *main weapon of politics*, when throughout his revolutionary activity he had relied on the rank and file to put the necessary pressure on the conservative party machine.

Lenin could not turn to the proletarian element in the party, because it was a small minority. He could not rely on inner-party democracy – even if by a miracle it had been restored – because the party was made up largely of factory managers, government officials, army officers, party officials, etc.; such a democracy would have reflected the aspirations of the bureaucracy. Lenin could not call on the 'Old Guard', first because they were a tiny minority in the party – a mere 2 per cent – and secondly because many of them made up an important part of the bureaucratic caste.

The measures with which Lenin proposed to fight bureaucracy were all substitutes for the non-existent active proletariat: one is 'incapable of making correct calculations . . . when one is heading for destruction', Lenin wrote in a different context. Unfortunately, this remark now applied to him.

This objective situation explains the indecisiveness plaguing Lenin in the last few days and weeks of his active political life. He was groping for a direction. After every spell of illness, when he returned, from his sickbed to watch over the movements of the state and party machines, his alarm grew, and with pathetic determination he struggled to grasp the helm in his faltering hands.

Above all Lenin knew that the bureaucracy had arisen in the soviet state to fill a political and administrative vacuum, created by the exhaustion and dispersal of the revolutionary proletariat which had resulted from the cumulative suffering of the first world war, the revolution, the civil war and the accompanying devastation, famine, epidemics and physical annihilation.*

---

*The rise of the bureaucracy in party and the state, as the present volume shows, was a very long process starting during the period of civil war, accelerated during the NEP, and

27
The Final Defeat

Trotsky Procrastinates

We have seen that Lenin and Trotsky agreed to unite against Stalin and against the bureaucracy, concentrating their attack on two main issues: Georgia and Rabkrin. Trotsky reported a remark of Fotieva: 'Vladimir Ilyich is preparing a bomb for Stalin at the congress.' The word 'bomb' was Lenin's, not hers. 'Vladimir Ilyich asks you to take the Georgian case in your hands; he will then feel confident.'[1]

What would Trotsky do? On 6 March 1923 Kamenev came to see him. He was crestfallen and anxious to mollify him. Trotsky showed magnanimity and forgiveness. Forgetting Lenin's words, he jumped at a 'rotten compromise'. He told Kamenev that he had decided not to take any action against Stalin, despite Lenin's clear stand. In his autobiography he described his attitude to Kamenev:

'I am against removing Stalin, and expelling Ordzhonikidze . . . But I do agree with Lenin in substance. I want a radical change in the policy on the national question, a discontinuance of persecutions of the Georgian opponents of Stalin, a discontinuance of the administrative oppression of the party, a firmer policy in matters of industrialization, and an honest co-operation in the higher centres . . . it is necessary that Stalin should

---

culminating at the time of Lenin's departure from the political arena. There was nevertheless a gap between the victory of the bureaucracy and the establishment of a bureaucratic state capitalist regime in Russia. The latter took place when the bureaucracy adopted a policy of massive industrialization and forced collectivization of agriculture; only then did the bureaucracy usurp the historical function of capitalism – capital accumulation. On this question see further T. Cliff, *State Capitalism in Russia*, London, 1974.

write to Krupskaya at once to apologize for his rudeness, and that he revise his behaviour. Let him not overreach himself. There should be no more intrigues, but honest co-operation . . .' Kamenev gave a sigh of relief. He accepted all my proposals. His only fear was that Stalin would be obstinate: 'He's rude and capricious.'

'I don't think,' I answered, 'that Stalin has any alternative now.' Late that night Kamenev informed me that he had been to see Stalin in the country, and that Stalin had accepted all the terms.[2]

While Kamenev was acting as go-between, Lenin succumbed to another stroke. He was to survive it by ten months, but paralysed, speechless most of the time, and suffering from spells of unconsciousness. When it became clear that Lenin had finally left the political scene, Stalin took his own path with a vengeance.

The first and by far the most important opportunity for Trotsky to make use of the 'bomb' against Stalin was the Twelfth Party Congress (17-25 April 1923). But no attempt was made to do so.

Stalin himself presented the report on the national question to the Twelfth Congress. Lenin's attacks on Stalin and Ordzhonikidze over the national question were kept from the delegates. Stalin viciously attacked the Georgian communists, accusing them of 'Georgian chauvinism'.

> It is on to this dangerous path that our comrades, the Georgian deviators, are pushing us by opposing federation in violation of all the laws of the party, by wanting to withdraw from the federation in order to retain an advantageous position. They are pushing us on to the path of granting them certain privileges at the expense of the Armenian and Azerbaijanian republics. But this is a path we cannot take, for it means certain death to our entire policy and to soviet power in the Caucasus.
>
> . . . under present conditions it is impossible to maintain peace in the Caucasus, impossible to establish equality, without the Transcaucasian Federation. One nation must not be allowed more privileges than another. This our comrades have sensed. That is why, after two years of contention, the Mdivani group is a small handful, repeatedly ejected by the party in Georgia itself.

To add insult to injury Stalin cited Lenin in support of his policy.

> It was also no accident that Comrade Lenin was in such a hurry and was so insistent that the federation should be established immediately. Nor was it an accident that Our Central Committee on three occasions affirmed the need for a federation in Transcaucasia.[3]

In vain did the Georgian delegates demand that Lenin's notes on the subject should be read out. The only member of the Polit-bureau to take up their case was Bukharin. Criticizing Stalin and Zinoviev by name, and alluding to Lenin's supposed notes, he exposed Stalin's campaign against 'local deviations' as a fraud. Why, he asked, did Lenin 'sound the alarm' only against Great Russian chauvinism?

> Why did Comrade Lenin begin to sound the alarm with such furious energy on the Georgian question? And why did Comrade Lenin say not a word in his letter about the mistakes of the deviators, but on the contrary direct all his strong words against the policy which was being carried out against the deviators?[4]

Bukharin was supported in his attack on Great Russian chauvinism by Rakovsky, quoting the conduct of a high Ukranian official who, as he was leaving a congress at which he had voted for a resolution asserting the equal rights of the Ukrainian language, replied curtly to a question addressed to him in Ukrainian: 'Speak to me in an intelligible language.'[5]

But the impact of Bukharin's and Rakovsky's speeches was minimal. Stalin in reply dared to say:

> Many speakers referred to notes and articles by Vladimir Ilyich. I do not want to quote my teacher, Comrade Lenin, since he is not here, and I am afraid that I might, perhaps, quote him wrongly and inappropriately.[6]

And what was Trotsky doing? He absented himself completely from the debate on the national question, explaining that he had been occupied with amendments to his resolution on industry![7] Stalin's resolution on the nationalities question was adopted unanimously.

Again, who presented the organization report of the Central Committee, including the report on Rabkrin? Stalin!

Lenin's denunciation of Rabkrin, although known to delegates, as it had been published in *Pravda*, and referred to by one delegate as 'something like a bombshell',[8] was easily defused by Stalin. In his report on party organization he repeated and endorsed Lenin's condemnation of bureaucracy:

> [Lenin] said that our policy was correct, but the apparatus was not working properly and, therefore, the car was not running in the right direction, it swerved. I remember that Shliapnikov, commenting on this, said that the drivers were no good. That is wrong, of course, absolutely wrong. The policy is correct, the driver is excellent, and the type of car is good, it is a soviet car, but some of the parts of the state car, i.e. some of the officials in the state apparatus, are bad, they are not our men. That is why the car does not run properly and, on the whole, we get a distortion of the correct political line . . . That is why the apparatus as a whole is not working properly. If we fail to repair it, the correct political line by itself will not carry us very far . . . These are the ideas Comrade Lenin elaborated as far back as a year ago, and which only this year he formulated in a harmonious system in the proposal to reorganize the Central Control Commission and the Workers' and Peasants' inspection.[9]

The time had come, according to Stalin, to train up a generation of 'young leaders to take the place of the old . . . to draw new, fresh forces into the work of the Central Committee . . . to promote the most capable and independent of them?[10] He submitted to the congress a resolution along the lines of Lenin's proposal for the fusion of Rabkrin and a much enlarged Central Control Commission of the party.[11] It was unanimously adopted.

While carrying out Lenin's wish to enlarge and combine the Central Control Commission and Workers' and Peasants' Inspection, Stalin made this body, apart from the secretariat itself, the most solidly reliable instrument at his command.

In his reply to the discussion of the Central Committee Organizational Report, after another vicious attack on the Georgian communists, Stalin ended with the following words:

In conclusion, a few words about the present congress. Comrades, I must say that I have not for a long time seen a congress so united and inspired by a single idea as this one is. I regret that Comrade Lenin is not here. If he were here he would be able to say: 'I tended the party for twenty-five years and made it great and strong.' *(Prolonged applause.)*[12]

Trotsky again did not intervene in the discussion of this item. He spoke at the congress only on his industrial report. He did not give even a hint of any disagreement with Stalin.

What about the publication of Lenin's 'Testament'? Members of the Politbureau and the Presidium of the Central Control Commission were asked for their views at the beginning of June 1923.

Zinoviev was against publication. Stalin said: 'I submit that there is no necessity to publish, the more so since there is no sanction for its publication from Ilyich'. Kamenev's comment was: 'It must not be printed. It is an undelivered speech meant for the Politburo. No more. Personal description is the basis and content of the article.' Tomsky affirmed: 'I am for Comrade Zinoviev's proposal – that only the members of the CC be informed. It should not be published for no one among the public at large will understand anything of this.' A.Solts, of the Presidium of the Central Control Commission, said: 'This note by V.I. had in view not the public at large by the CC and that is why so much space is allotted to the description of persons . . . It should not be printed.' The same position was taken by Bukharin, Rudzutak, Molotov and Kuibyshev. The only person in favour of publication was Trotsky.[13]

But Trotsky was too late. Having remained silent at the Twelfth Congress, he was in no position to insist on publishing Lenin's 'Testament' two months later.*

---

* That Trotsky was later very embarrassed by his behaviour at the Twelfth Congress is clear from the fact that no reference at all to the congress can be found in his autobiography (while four pages are devoted to describing duck-hunting in precisely the place where a description of the congress would be expected). Some time after the congress he even went as far

(continued overleaf)

Why Did Trotsky Keep Quiet?

In later days Trotsky was convinced that if he had spoken up at the Twelfth Congress, relying on the documents Lenin supplied him with, he could probably have defeated Stalin quickly, even if in the long run this would not have prevented the victory of the bureaucracy.

> Our [Lenin's and Trotsky's] joint action against the Central Committee at the beginning of 1923 would without a shadow of a doubt have brought us victory. And what is more, I have no doubt that if I had come forward on the eve of the Twelfth Congress in the spirit of a 'bloc of Lenin and Trotsky' against the Stalin bureaucracy, I should have been victorious even if Lenin had taken no direct part in the struggle. How solid the victory would have been is, of course, another question. To decide that, one must take into account a number of objective processes in the country, in the working class, and in the party itself. That is a separate and large theme . . . In 1922-2 . . . it was still possible to capture the commanding position by an open attack on the faction then rapidly being formed of national socialist officials, or usurpers of the apparatus, of the unlawful heirs of October, of the epigones of Bolshevism.[15]

---

as to deny the existence of Lenin's 'Testament'. In May 1925 Max Eastman published a book, *Since Lenin Died*, containing the first published report of the 'Testament'. Two months later the book reached Moscow and created something of a scandal. Under pressure from his colleagues in the Politbureau. Trotsky dissociated himself from Max Eastman.

Eastman asserts in several places that the Central Committee has 'concealed' from the party a large number of documents of extraordinary importance, written by Lenin during the last period of his life. (The documents in question are letters on the national question, the famous 'Testament', etc.). This is pure slander against the Central Committee of our party. Eastman's words convey the impression that Lenin wrote these letters, which are of an advisory character and deal with the inner-party organization, with the intention of having them published. This is not at all in accordance with the facts . . . If all these letters have not been published, it is because their author did not intend them to be published. Comrade Lenin has not left any 'Testament'; the character of his relations to the party, and the character of the party itself, preclude the possibility of such a 'Testament'.[14]

'If . . . if . . .' It is very difficult to speculate what would have happened if a certain action had been taken, how a change of one link in the historical chain of events would have shaped the rest of the chain. With this reservation in mind one might say : accepting Trotsky's estimate that his intervention against Stalin in the spirit of a bloc with Lenin would have succeeded – even temporarily – this would have affected the policies carried out by the Comintern in Germany in the autumn of 1923 when the CP was on the verge of taking power, but was hindered by poor leadership, not least in Moscow. As Trotsky argued in his *Lessons of October*, this of course would have radically changed the situation of the proletarian revolution in Russia, with enormous consequences.

What was the reason for Trotsky's silence at the Twelfth Congress ? There are a number of explanations, one of them given by Trotsky : he avoided coming out against Stalin as this could have been interpreted as fighting for personal power while Lenin was still alive. This is what Trotsky wrote in his autobiography :

> The chief obstacle was Lenin's condition. He was expected to rise again as he had after his first stroke and to take part in the Twelfth Congress as he had in the Eleventh. He himself hoped for this. The doctors spoke encouragingly, though with dwindling assurance . . . Independent action on my part would have been interpreted, or, to be more exact, represented as my personal fight for Lenin's place in the party and the state. The very thought of this made me shudder. I considered that it would have brought such a demoralization in our ranks that we would have had to pay to painful a price for it even in case of victory. In all plans and calculations, there remained the positive element of uncertainty – Lenin and his physical condition. Would he be able to state his own views? Would he still have time? Would the party understand that it was a case of a fight by Lenin and Trotsky for the future of the revolution, and not a fight by Trotsky for the place held by Lenin, who was ill?[16]

Another much less flattering explanation of Trotsky's astonishing behaviour was given by his close friend and admirer, Adolf Ioffe. In a letter written to Trotsky written an hour before he committed suicide in 1927, Ioffe wrote :

I have never doubted the rightness of the road you pointed out, and as you know I have gone with you for more than twenty years, since the days of 'permanent revolution'. But I have always believed that you lacked Lenin's *unbending will*, his *unwillingness to yield*, his readiness even to remain alone on the path that he thought right in the anticipation of a future majority, of a future recognition by every one of the rightness of his path . . . you have often *abandoned your rightness* for the sake of an overvalued agreement, or compromise. This is a mistake . . . the guarantee of the victory of your rightness lies in nothing but the extreme unwillingness to yield, the strictest straightforwardness, the absolute rejection of all compromise; in this very thing lay the secret of Lenin's victories.[17]

There is no doubt that Lenin, with his sense of urgency, of the need to concentrate on the decisive link in the chain of events at the time, even at the cost of secondary elements, would not have been influenced by such secondary considerations as how his fight against Stalin would look to bystanders.

Yet another reason for Trotsky's behaviour was his belief that *no faction fight inside the party was justified*. On 22 December 1923, in an article entitled 'Groups and Factional Formations', he wrote:

We are the only party in the country and, in the period of the dictatorship, it could not be otherwise . . . The party does not want factions and will not tolerate them. It is monstrous to believe that it will shatter or permit anyone to shatter its apparatus.[18]

Again, in his speech to the Thirteenth Party Congress on 26 May 1924, he said:

I have never recognized freedom for groupings inside the party, nor do I now recognize it, because under the present historical conditions groupings are merely another name for factions.

One might disagree with the party leadership, but there was no salvation outside the party:

Comrades, none of us wants to be or can be right against the party. In the last analysis, the party is always right, because the party is the sole historical instrument that the working class possesses for the solution of its fundamental tasks . . .
The English have a proverb: My country right or wrong. We

can say with much greater historical justification: Whether it is right or wrong in any particular, specific question at any particular moment, this is my party.[19]

(Stalin dismissed Trotsky's statement sarcastically, saying that the party made no claim to infallibility.)

Trotsky's fetishization of the party was probably partly due to the fact that he had joined it late in the day.

There may yet be another explanation for his behaviour. As Deutscher writes:

> The truth is that Trotsky refrained from attacking Stalin because he felt secure. No contemporary, and he least of all, saw in the Stalin of 1923 the menacing and towering figure he was to become. It seemed to Trotsky almost a bad joke that Stalin, the wilful and sly but shabby and inarticulate man in the background, should be his rival. He was not going to be bothered about him, he was not going to stoop to him or even to Zinoviev; and, above all, he was not going to give the party the impression that he, too, participated in the undignified game played by Lenin's disciples over Lenin's still empty coffin.[20]

Trotsky's disdainful attitude towards Stalin was of long standing. He wrote later that he was hardly aware of Stalin's existence until after the October revolution.[21] Yet Stalin had been the editor of the party's paper, and one of the most important members of the Central Committee. Trotsky's attitude reveals how far he was from Lenin in grasping the personal-administrative elements in the Bolshevik Party that he belatedly joined.

Above all, Trotsky's hesitation in carrying Lenin's struggle against Stalin into the open was due to his fear of splitting the party and encouraging the counter-revolution. His vast knowledge of the French revolution must have made him aware of this danger. He must have recalled how the extreme left, in the days following 9 Thermidor and the fall of Robespierre, motivated by sheer hatred of Robespierre, supported the right. Gracchus Babeuf, the first modern communist, went as far as to declare on 5 September 1794: '10 Thermidor was the end of our confinement; since then we have been in labour to be reborn into liberty'.[22] After a time Babeuf regretted having been one of the first to inveigh against the 'Robespierre system'.[23] But it was too late. Although there was no collusion between Babeuf and the neo-Hebertists on the one hand, and the Monarchist reactionaries and the Thermidorians on the other, the campaign of the former did help towards the success of the latter.

Yet another factor intervened to influence Trotsky, and to tip the scales against his coming out into the open with a denunciation of the bureaucracy. In the summer of 1923

> 'wild' strikes broke out in many factories, spread, and were accompanied by violent explosions of discontent. The trade unions were caught by surprise; and so were the party leaders. The threat of a general strike was in the air; and the movement seemed on the point of turning into a political revolt. Not since the Kronstadt rising had there been so much tension in the working class and so much alarm in ruling circles.[24]

Trotsky had to ask himself whether he could take responsibility for possibly sparking off a new Kronstadt rising. He clearly considered it the duty of revolutionaries, in the absence of any existing alternative, to remain loyal to the party of the revolution to the last possible moment. This was a weighty consideration, much easier to dismiss when the degeneration of the party had run its course than in the midst of the struggle.

The main influences on Trotsky's behaviour were the same circumstances that made Lenin's grasp so unsure, so vacillating – contradicting his whole character, his whole political past. Neither Lenin nor Trotsky could see a solution. There was a possibility of the seige of Russia eventually being lifted by the international revolution. But what to do in the meantime? The proletariat was weakened and atomized, and the party no longer enjoyed the working-class support it had commanded when it entered the civil war; a revolutionary party and government which had fought a cruel and devastating civil war could neither abdicate the day after its victory, nor submit to its defeated enemies and their revenge, even when it discovered that it could not rule according to its own principles.

Lenin and Trotsky knew very well that the workers were exhausted. Trotsky's own supporters, as he put it, were not spurred on by a hope of great and serious changes. On the other hand, the bureaucracy fought with extraordinary ferocity.[25] To fight with little hope is very difficult indeed. As Trotsky wrote many years later:

> The Left Opposition could not achieve power, and did not hope even to do so – certainly not its most thoughtful leaders. A struggle for power by the Left Opposition, by a revolutionary Marxist organization, was conceivable only under the conditions of a revolutionary upsurge. Under such conditions the strategy is based on aggression, on direct appeal to the masses, on frontal attack against the government. Quite a few members of the Left Opposition had played no minor part in such a struggle and had first-hand knowledge of how to wage it. But during the early twenties and later, there was no revolutionary upsurge in Russia, quite the contrary. Under such circumstances it was out of the question to launch a struggle for power.

Inability to foresee victory must engender paralysis of willpower. The 'danger was that, having become convinced of the impossibility of open association with the masses, even with their vanguard, the opposition would give up the struggle and lie low until better times'.[26]

Gramsci refers to 'the optimism of the will and the pessimism of the intellect'. The last few months of Lenin's active political life were such that neither he no Trotsky could point to any mass support to which to attach that *will*. The Russian proletariat was exhausted and isolated.

The Sequel in Parentheses

Towards the end of 1923 – seven months after Lenin left political life – Trotsky started organizing an opposition group. This story falls outside the scope of the present work. But it would be an injustice to Trotsky if we did not at least remark on the 17 years of hard struggle he led against the degeneration of the regime, and in defence of workers' interests. Thousands of revolutionary fighters followed him into Siberia and to prison, thousands died in labour camps, many were shot, many committed suicide (*all* Trotsky's four children – two boys and two girls – as well as his first wife, his two sons-in-law and one daughter-in-law, and all his grandchildren, with one exception, were murdered or driven to suicide).

Lenin's Death

On 19 January 1924 Lenin appeared extremely exhausted and showed signs that his sight was affected. On Monday 21 January, at six in the evening he had another severe stroke, and died fifty minutes later.

On 26 January the Congress of Soviets held a solemn session in honour of its dead leader. Stalin, who spoke fourth (after Kalinin, Krupskaya and Zinoviev)* gave a speech very much like a religious prayer: the announcement of each 'Commandment' by Lenin being followed by a uniform response of the worshippers:

> Comrades, we communists are people of a special mould. We are made of a special stuff. We are those who form the army of the great proletarian strategist, the army of Comrade Lenin. There is nothing higher than the honour of belonging to this army. There is nothing higher than the title of member of the party whose founder and leader was Comrade Lenin. It is not given to everyone to be a member of such a party. It is not given to everyone to withstand the stresses and storms that accompany membership in such a party. It is the sons of the working class, the sons of want and struggle, the sons of incredible privation and heroic effort who before all should be members of such a party. That is why the party of the Leninists, the party of the communists, is also called the party of the working class.
> DEPARTING FROM US, COMRADE LENIN ENJOINED US TO HOLD HIGH AND GUARD THE PURITY OF THE GREAT TITLE OF MEMBER OF THE PARTY. WE VOW TO YOU, COMRADE LENIN, THAT WE SHALL FULFIL YOUR BEHEST WITH HONOUR!
> DEPARTING FROM US, COMRADE LENIN ENJOINED US TO GUARD THE UNITY OF OUR PARTY AS THE APPLE OF OUR EYE. WE VOW TO YOU, COMRADE LENIN, THAT THIS BEHEST, TOO, WE SHALL FULFIL WITH HONOUR!
> DEPARTING FROM US, COMRADE LENIN ENJOINED US TO

---

*Trotsky missed Lenin's funeral as well as the meeting of the Congress of Soviets. Stalin misled Trotsky, who was far from Moscow, in Tiflis, about the date of Lenin's funeral, so as to make it impossible for him to attend it.[27]

His absence was interpreted by rumour and gossip in Moscow as intentional, which helped Stalin in his scheming against him.

STRENGTHEN WITH ALL OUR MIGHT THE ALLIANCE OF THE WORKERS AND PEASANTS. WE VOW TO YOU, COMRADE LENIN, THAT THIS BEHEST, TOO, WE SHALL FULFIL WITH HONOUR!

DEPARTING FROM US, COMRADE LENIN ENJOINED US TO STRENGTHEN AND EXTEND THE UNION OF REPUBLICS. WE VOW TO YOU, COMRADE LENIN, THAT THIS BEHEST, TOO, WE SHALL FULFIL WITH HONOUR!

DEPARTING FROM US, COMRADE LENIN ENJOINED US TO REMAIN FAITHFUL TO THE PRINCIPLES OF THE COMMUNIST INTERNATIONAL. WE VOW TO YOU, COMRADE LENIN, THAT WE SHALL NOT SPARE OUR LIVES TO STRENGTHEN AND EXTEND THE UNION OF THE WORKING PEOPLE OF THE WHOLE WORLD – THE COMMUNIST INTERNATIONAL![28]

The same session of the Congress of Soviets changed the name of Petrograd to Leningrad. It was decided to make 21 January, the anniversary of Lenin's death, a day of national mourning, to set up monuments to him in the principal cities of the USSR and to publish a collected edition of his works. The final decision was:

1. to preserve the body of Vladimir Ilyich Lenin in a mausoleum, making it accessible to visitors:
2. to construct the mausoleum under the Kremlin wall among the fraternal graves of the warriors of the October revolution.[29]

Krupskaya apparently learned by 29 January of the decision to keep him on display, or the probability of this decision, for the next day *Pravda* published an open letter from her which was an indirect protest.

'I have a great request to you,' she wrote, addressing herself to all the workers and peasants.

Do not permit your grief for Ilyich to take the form of external reverence for his person. Do not raise memorials to him, palaces named after him, splendorous festivals in commemoration of him, etc.: to all this he attached so little importance in his life, all this was so burdensome to him.[30]

But the workers and peasants remained silent, and continued to flock to the mausoleum.

Although she lost this battle, Krupskaya never publicly mentioned the mausoleum or its contents in her voluminous works, never visited it, nor stood on top of it during party festivals. Similarly, she persisted in referring to the city of Leningrad by its old nickname 'Piter' in her own correspondence.

While Lenin was politically active the word Leninism was never used. Lenin would certainly never have permitted its use. He always considered himself as a disciple and follower of Marx. Now a cult of Lenin was started, in which Lenin's writings were to be quoted against all dissent and criticism of the Secretary-General.

The fate of dead revolutionary leaders, as described in *State and Revolution*, now overtook Lenin:

> During the lifetime of great revolutionaries, the oppressing classes constantly hounded them, received their theories with the most savage malice, the most furious hatred and the most unscrupulous campaigns of lies and slander. After their death, attempts are made to convert them into harmless icons, to canonize them, so to say, and to hallow their *names* to a certain extent for the 'consolation' of the oppressed classes and with the object of duping the latter, while at the same time robbing the revolutionary theory of its *substance*, blunting its revolutionary edge and vulgarizing it.[81]

The Pharaohs of Egypt were mummified in order to keep the mass of the oppressed people in their place. Every Pharaoh mummified his father so as to preserve the foundation of his own rule. Lenin's mausoleum was built for Stalin to stand on during the trooping of the colour.

In Retrospect: The Moral Agony

In the last few weeks before he completely lost consciousness Lenin suffered not only from a terrible sense of isolation but from a moral agony almost unparalleled in the history of men and movements. Feelings of personal guilt pervaded all his utterances.

Was the Russian revolution a false spring? Did the Bolsheviks take power prematurely? Marx and Engels had repeatedly written about the tragic fate of revolutionaries who came to power before their time. Thus Engels wrote:

> The worst thing that can befall a leader of an extreme party, is to be compelled to take over a government in an epoch

when the movement is not yet ripe for the domination of the class which he represents and for the realization of the measures which that domination would imply . . . he necessarily finds himself in a dilemma. What he *can* do is in contrast to all his actions as hitherto practised, to all his principles and to the present interests of his party; what he *ought* to do cannot be achieved. In a word, he is compelled to represent not his party nor his class, but the class for whom conditions are ripe for domination. In the interests of the movement itself, he is compelled to defend the interests of an alien class, and to feed his own class with phrases and promises, with the assertion that the interests of that alien class are their own interests. Whoever puts himself in this awkward position is irrevocably lost.[32]

Lenin knew well that the question whether the Russian revolution was 'premature' could be answered only in the *international* arena. Was Russia the weakest link in the world capitalist chain, and would the snapping of this link lead to the possibility of other links following? Russia was a backward country, but was it not an element of the capitalist world system? Looking back over the first four years of the Comintern, the answer could only be that the October revolution *did* find a massive echo in revolutions and in revolutionary waves throughout Europe, and that the tiny communist sects of 1919 did grow into mass proletarian parties.

Were Lenin and Trotsky at fault in not giving enough of their time and energy to the training of inexperienced and immature leaders of the new communist parties, who were weighed down by reformist national traditions? Could they, in the midst of fighting a civil war in a ruined country, have devoted more time to the International? Had they any alternative, given the lack of leading personnel, but not to scrutinize too closely the credentials of those few who were willing to serve at the headquarters of the Comintern, like Zinoviev or Bela Kun? Of course, to such questions Lenin could not have given a single, cut-and-dried answer.

The replacement of the dictatorship of the proletariat by the dictatorship of the secretariat — was this a product of the nature of Bolshevism? To answer this question affirmatively is to give too much weight to Bolshevism and also to insult it: to claim for it a supra-historical prowess.

The Bolshevik party *did* succeed in leading a revolution and winning a civil war. Can the party, which is only one element in the historical process, be expected to be omnipotent, to be able to shape history even when the class of which it is a part is completely decimated and exhausted?

Was not one of the main sources of degeneration of the revolution the shameful role of the Old Bolsheviks, the committeemen, who, by and large, initially supported Stalin? Was not Lenin responsible for the role his own veteran cadres played in 1922-23?*

In April 1917 Lenin had to overcome the resistance of the 'Old Bolsheviks', as he himself called them, when he fought to persuade the party to aim for the socialist revolution; he did so again on the eve of the October revolution, when many of the same people baulked at insurrection. But in 1922-23, could rusty parts be used to explain why the machine was not working, when the rust was accompanied by an absence of power? Could even the most active committeemen sustain the revolution when the Russian proletariat was a spent force?**

In the Foreword to the second volume of *Lenin* I wrote: 'Lenin influenced the party, and the party influenced the class and vice versa. The proletariat created the party and the party shaped Lenin.'[34] Now, after the most exacting civil war, the sick

---

* The Old Bolsheviks, the majority of whom at first supported Stalin against Trotsky, later on regretted this. As we know, the whole generation of Old Bolsheviks was later exterminated by Stalin. This is proof, if any were needed, that Stalinism was not in any way a logical development of Leninism.

** Wary of the conservatism of the members of the old guard, Lenin knew that they would not accept Trotsky, who had been outside the party during the long years 1903-17. Hence in his 'Testament' he went out of his way to emphasize that Trotsky's non-Bolshevik past should not be held against him.[33] But it was just this that was used in the massive campaign against 'Trotskyism' which started towards the end of 1923 and continued for years thereafter. The *ésprit de corps* of the Old Bolsheviks became a very effective weapon in Stalin's hands.

proletariat, the sick party and the sick Lenin again interacted with each other. Who knows whether Lenin's physical illness – the excruciating, unrelieved insomnia and the strokes – was caused, or at least hastened, by his mental agony over the state of class and party? When he complained that the state was slipping from Bolshevik hands – 'the machine refuses to obey the hand that guided it' – was he not also hinting at his own personal incapacity to hold the steering wheel of party and state? Lenin never had illusions about being omnipotent. He was well aware that the quality of leadership crucially affected historical development. But it was only *one* factor, and in the last analysis it was not the decisive one.

Of course, the events and the situation which led to the complete victory of Stalin's bureaucracy appear in much bolder relief in retrospect than they did to their contemporaries. This lack of a clear vision probably largely accounts for Lenin's moral agony on his deathbed. But there was no fatalistic inevitability about the unfolding drama.

In 1921 the leading Bolshevik economist Evgenii Preobrazhensky wrote a semi-fictional book, *From NEP to Socialism: a Glance into the future of Russia and Europe.* He described how in 1970 in a hall of the Polytechnical Museum of Moscow, one of the main cities of the United Socialist States of Europe, a lecture took place on the history of the Russian revolution which opened the door to the victory of socialism in Europe. The lecturer recalled the difficult conditions of struggle during the first few years of the soviet state, the obstacles created by the rural character and backwardness of the country, and its isolation. He explained:

> If the revolution in the west had delayed too long, this situation could have led to an aggressive socialist war by Russia, supported by the European proletariat, against the capitalist west. This did not happen because the proletarian revolution was by this time already knocking at the door owing to its own inner development.[35]

After a long period of dual power, especially in Germany, the seizing of power by workers' councils in a number of industrial cities gave the signal for a civil war, from which the German workers emerged victorious. But this victory led to aggression by the capitalist governments of France and Poland. The Red Army of the Soviet Union repulsed the attack, while the imperialist regimes, undermined from within by revolutionary propaganda, collapsed under the onslaught of the German revolution. The European revolution triumphed, and the United Socialist States of Europe was established. The lecture ended with the following words:

> New, Soviet Europe opened a fresh page in economic development. The industrial technique of Germany was united with Russian agriculture, and on the territory of Europe there began rapidly to develop and become consolidated a new economic organism, revealing enormous possibilities and a mighty breakthrough to the expansion of the productive forces. And along with this, Soviet Russia, which previously had outstripped Europe politically, now modestly took its place as an economically backward country behind the advanced industrial countries of the proletarian dictatorship.[36]

Was this a realistic dream, or a Utopia? Was it possible for the German revolution of 1923 to be victorious? Possible, of course, does not mean inevitable. After all it is arguable that without Lenin – if he had not returned to Russia after the February revolution – the reorientation of the Bolshevik Party towards the socialist revolution and the victory of October would not have happened. The statement, 'No Lenin, no October', while contradicting the mechanistic, fatalistic school of 'Marxism' of Karl Kautsky, Otto Bauer and the like, does not contradict the real active concept of Marxism.[37] If Lenin had not been sick and out of action during the German revolution of 1923 . . . if Trotsky had had his way and been sent to Germany as the representative of the Comintern . . . if . . . if . . . The essence of the matter lies in that 'if'.

Was it too much to expect that the tragedy in which Lenin, the party and the proletariat were involved would remain an optimistic tragedy, and that all the sacrifices and sufferings would not be in vain?

Lenin never doubted that the October revolution was completely justified historically, that it was a magnificent achievement of the proletariat. Did the revolutionary proletariat of Russia have any choice but to do all it could to extract itself from the terrible world slaughter by putting an end to the imperialist war and to the social order that produced it? A revolutionary class and a revolutionary party which did not advance as far as possible in its attempt to shape society, up to and including state power, would have betrayed their mission. The world had become ripe – if not overripe – for socialism. Without a revolution humanity was threatened with decay and decomposition. The revolution broke out in Russia first because the world capitalist chain broke at its weakest link. Of course it would have been better if it had been victorious in a more advanced country than Russia, let us say the United States. However, proletarian revolutions are not made to order: they are the product of the irrationality of the capitalist system. If the 1917 revolution was 'premature', it was only because it was restricted to one country: the October revolution was not a mistake, but its failure to spread beyond the borders of Russia was; not just a mistake, but a crime for which the Social Democratic parties were primarily responsible.

The rich experience of the Bolshevik revolution, Lenin was confident, would be a legacy for generations to come. The Paris Commune demonstrated the heroism of the working class, its capacity to seize state power, and to try, however haltingly, to start to reshape society. The proletariat of Paris was tiny, mainly employed in small workshops, without a party to lead it, and without a clear theory to guide it. The memory of the Paris Commune is enshrined forever in the heart of the international working class. The Russian revolution, which brought to power a much more mature, better organized and conscious proletariat, was an even more inspiring example than the Paris Commune. The Russian proletariat displayed superhuman will and moral resources in the face of terrible suffering.

At the worst, Lenin and his friends would at least bequeath to their successors a set of ideas, a restatement of revolutionary policy, which would inspire generations of socialists as the Paris Commune had done. The memory of October and Bolshevism will pass from one generation to another. October showed the *potentialities* of the proletariat. Let us finally quote again the words of Rosa Luxemburg in summing up the historical essence of Bolshevism:

> Theirs is the immortal historical service of having marched at the head of the international proletariat with the conquest of political power and the practical placing of the problem of the realization of socialism, and of having advanced mightily the settlement of the score between capital and labour in the entire world. In Russia the problem could only be posed. It could not be solved in Russia. An in *this* sense, the future everywhere belongs to 'Bolshevism'.[38]

Notes

Chapter 1: The Bolshevik Government's First Steps

1. L.Trotsky, *My Life*, New York 1960, p.37
2. R.P.Browder and A.F.Kerensky, *The Russian Provisional Government 1917 – Documents*, Stanford 1961, Vol.3, p.1801
3. P.N.Miliukov, *Istoriia vtoroi russkoi revoliutsii*, Sofia 1923, Part 3, p.296
4. V.B.Stankevich, *Vospominaniia, 1914-1919 g.*, Berlin 1920, p.267
5. A.Kopp, *Town and Revolution*, London 1967, pp.1-2
6. I.V.Gessen, 'In Two Revolutions: Life Experience', *Arkhiv russkoi revoliutsii*, Vol.22, Berlin 1937, p.382
7. J.Bunyan and H.H.Fisher, *The Bolshevik Revolution, 1917-1918: Documents and Materials*, Stanford 1934, p.148
8. J.Reed, *Ten Days that Shook the World*, London 1961, p.97
9. N.N.Sukhanov, *The Russian Revolution 1917, A Personal Record*, London 1955, p.648
10. I.Getzler, *Martov*, Cambridge (Mass.) 1967, p.172
11. Reed, *op.cit.*, p. 28
12. Sukhanov, *op.cit*, p. 636
13. *ibid.* pp.639-40
14. V.I.Lenin, *Collected Works*, translated from the fourth Russian edition (henceforth referred to as *Works*), Vol.29, p.209
15. L.Trotsky, *On Lenin*, London 1971, p.122
16. Lenin, *Works*, Vol.44, p.206
17. Trotsky, *On Lenin*, *op.cit.* p.127
18. S.S.Pestovsky, 'On October Days in Peter', *Proletarskaia revoliutsiia*, No.10, 1922; Bunyan and Fisher, *op.cit.* pp.186-7
19. Reed, *op.cit.* p.102
20. *Vospominaniia o Vladimire Ilyiche Lenine*, Moscow 1963, Vol.3, pp.160-6
21. Bunyan and Fisher, *op.cit.* p.186
22. Lenin, *Works*, Vol.26, pp.249-50
23. *ibid.* pp.258-60
24. *ibid.* Vol.30, p.265
25. Y.Akhapkin, *First Decrees of Soviet Power*, London 1970, p.32
26. *ibid.* pp.36-8
27. *ibid.* pp.42-3
28. *ibid.* pp.63-5, 69-71
29. *ibid.* pp.88-9
30. W.H.Chamberlin, *The Russian Revolution*, New York 1965, Vol.1, p.355
31. Lenin, *Works*, Vol.44, pp.71-2
32. J.L.H.Keep, 'Lenin's Letters as an Historical Source', in B.W.Eissenstat (ed.), *Lenin and Leninism*, Lexington (Mass.) 1971, p.258
33. G.S.Ignatiev, *Oktiabr 1917 goda v Moskve*, Moscow 1964, p.4

34. J.Keep, 'October in the Provinces', in R.Pipes (ed.) *Revolutionary Russia*, Cambridge (Mass.) 1967, p.194

35. *ibid.* pp.195-6

36. *ibid.* p.197

37. R.W.Pethybridge, *The Spread of the Russian Revolution: Essays on 1917*, London 1971, p. 77

38. Reed, *op.cit.* pp.161-2

39. *ibid.* p.164

40. Pethybridge, *op.cit.* p. 17

41. *ibid.* p.22

42. *ibid.* p.23

43. Lenin, *Works*, Vol.26, p.294

44. V.Serge, *Year One of the Russian Revolution*, London 1972, p.79

45. Trotsky, *On Lenin, op.cit.* pp.151, 118

46. Lenin, *Works*, Vol.27, p.519

47. M.Latsis, *Chrezvychainaia komissiia po borbe s kontr-revoliutsiei*, Moscow 1920

48. Serge, *op.cit.* p.307

49. E.H.Carr, *The Bolshevik Revolution, 1917-1923*, Vol.1, London 1950, p.168

50. Serge, *op.cit.* p.189

51. Lenin, *Works*, Vol. 30, p. 223

52. *Vospominaniia o Vladimire Ilyiche Lenine, op.cit.* Vol.2, pp.435-8

53. Lenin, *Works*, Vol.26, pp.409, 415

54. *ibid.* p.261

55. *ibid.* p.288

56. *ibid.* p.365

57. *ibid.* p.459

58. *ibid.* p.404

59. Reed, *op.cit.* p.179

60. *ibid.* p.150

Chapter 2: The Consolidation of Power

1. *The Bolsheviks and the October Revolution: Minutes of the Central Committee of the Russian Social Democratic Labour Party (bolsheviks) August 1917-February 1918* (hereafter referred to as *CC Minutes*), London 1974, p.127

2. *ibid.* pp.129-34

3. L.Trotsky, *The Stalin School of Falsification*, New York 1962, pp.109-22

4. *CC Minutes, op.cit.* pp.136-8, 300

5. *ibid.* pp.139-41

6. *ibid.* p.150

7. O.H.Radkey, *The Sickle under the Hammer*, New York 1963, pp.66-7

8. Bunyan and Fisher, *op.cit.* p.190

Chapter 3: The Dissolution of the Constituent Assembly

1. Lenin, *Works*, Vol.24, p.99

2. *ibid.* Vol.26, p.20

3. Browder and Kerensky, *op.cit.* Vol.3, p.1695

4. *ibid.* p.1729

5. Trotsky, *On Lenin, op.cit.* pp.105-6

6. O. H. Radkey, *The Elections to the Russian Constituent Assembly of 1917*, Cambridge (Mass.) 1950, pp.16-17

7. *ibid.* p.20

8. *ibid.* p.36

9. *ibid.* p.37

10. Radkey, *The Sickle under the Hammer*, op.cit. p.344
11. Radkey, *The Elections to the Russian Constituent Assembly of 1917*, op.cit. p.38
12. Lenin, *Works*, Vol.26, p.380
13. Radkey, *The Sickle under the Hammer*, op.cit. p.301
14. See T.Cliff, *Lenin*, London 1975, Vol.1, p.116
15. Lenin, *Works*, Vol.26, pp.379-83
16. *ibid.* Vol.30, pp.257-8
17. *ibid.* p.263
18. *ibid.*
19. *ibid.* pp.266-7
20. K.Marx and F. Engels, *Selected Correspondence*, London 1942, pp.433-4
21. K.Marx, 'Address to the Communist League, 1850', Appendix to F.Engels, *Revolution and Counter Revolution in Germany*, London 1933

Chapter 4: The Peace of Brest-Litovsk

1. Lenin, *Works*, Vol.21, p.404
2. *ibid.* Vol.26, pp.444, 447-8
3. *CC Minutes*, op.cit. p.173
4. Lenin, *Works*, Vol.26, p.451
5. *CC Minutes*, op.cit. pp.177-8
6. *ibid.* p.174
7. *ibid.* p.179
8. *ibid.* pp.189-91
9. *ibid.* p.194
10. V.I.Lenin, *Sochineniia*, 1st edition, Moscow 1924-5, Vol.15, p.626
11. J.W.Wheeler-Bennett, *Brest Litovsk: The Forgotten Peace*, London 1938, p.237
12. *CC Minutes*, op.cit p.205
13. *ibid.* pp.210-11
14. *ibid.* pp.212-15
15. Lenin, *Works*, Vol.27, p.37
16. *ibid.* p.39
17. *CC Minutes*, op.cit, p.216
18. Lenin, *Works*, Vol.27, pp.19-20
19. *ibid.* pp.23-4
20. *ibid.* p.29
21. *ibid.* p.65
22. *CC Minutes*, op.cit. pp.218-25
23. Lenin, *Works*, Vol.27, pp.68-9
24. Bunyan and Fisher, op.cit. p.523
25. *ibid.* pp.523-4
26. *Leninskii sbornik*, Vol.11, pp.59-61
27. *ibid.* p.89
28. *ibid.* p.42
29. Trotsky, *My Life*, op.cit. pp.380-1
30. Wheeler-Bennett, op.cit. p.170
31. *ibid.* p.196
32. *Piatii sozyv vserossiiskogo tsentralnogo ispolnitelnogo komiteta sovetov rabochikh, krestianskikh, krasnoarmeiskikh, kazachikh deputatov: stenograficheskii otchet*, Moscow 1919, p.248
33. Lenin, *Works*, Vol.33, p.95
34. *ibid.* p.98
35. Trotsky, *On Lenin*, op.cit. p.103-4

Chapter 5: The Transition from Capitalism to Socialism

1. Lenin, *Works*, Vol. 27, pp.230-1
2. K.Marx and F. Engels, *Selected Works*, London 1942, Vol.2, p.504
3. S.E.Cohen, *Bukharin and the*

Bolshevik Revolution, a
Political Biography 1888-
1938, London 1974, p.90
4. K.Marx, F.Engels and
F.Lassalle, *Aus dem liter-
arischen Nachlass von K.
Marx, Fr. Engels und F.
Lassalle*, Stuttgart 1902, Vol.3,
pp.435-9; in D.Ryazanoff (ed.),
K.Marx and F.Engels, *The
Communist Manifesto*, New
York 1963, pp.184-5
5. K.Marx, *The Cologne Communist Trial*, London 1971,
p.62
6. Lenin, *Works*, Vol.25, p. 329

7. *ibid.* pp.330-1
8. *ibid.* p.337
9. *ibid.* pp.341-2
10. *ibid.* Vol.27, p.148
11. *ibid.* Vol.28, p.214
12. *ibid.* pp.424-5
13. *ibid.* Vol.29, p.69
14. *ibid.* p.74
15. *ibid.* p.206
16. *ibid.* p.208
17. *ibid.* Vol.10, pp.253-4
18. *ibid.* Vol.30, pp.330-1
19. *ibid.* Vol.28, pp.72-3
20. *ibid.* Vol.30, p.202
21. *ibid.* p.518

Chapter 6: 'We Need State Capitalism'

1. M.Philips Price, *My Reminiscences of the Russian
Revolution*, London 1921,
p.212
2. Chamberlin, *op.cit.* Vol.1,
p.416
3. Serge, *op.cit.* p.212
4. *ibid.* p.236
5. Chamberlin, *op.cit.* Vol.1,
p.418
6. Bunyan and Fisher, *op.cit.*
pp. 649-50
7. See T.Cliff, *State Capitalism
in Russia*, London 1974
8. Lenin, *Works*, Vol.27, p.301
9. Carr, *op.cit.* Vol.2, pp.88-9;
Bunyan and Fisher, *op.cit.*
pp.621-2
10. Lenin, *Works*, Vol.27,
pp.245-6
11. *ibid.* p.248
12. *ibid.* pp.248-50
13. *ibid.* pp.249, 350
14. *ibid.* pp.268-9

15. *ibid.* p.212
16. *ibid.* p.349
17. *ibid.* p.271
18. *ibid.* p.212
19. *ibid.* Vol.26, p.500
20. *ibid.* Vol.27, p.231
21. *ibid.* p.515
22. *ibid.* pp.258-9
23. *ibid.* Vol.20, pp.152-4
24. *ibid.* Vol.27, pp.335-6
25. *ibid.* p.294
26. *ibid.* p.337
27. *ibid.* pp.338-9
28. *ibid.* pp.295-6
29. *ibid.* p.340
30. *ibid.* p.301
31. *ibid.* pp.213-4
32. *ibid.* p.396
33. *ibid.* p.475
34. *ibid.* p.218
35. Marx and Engels, *Selected
Correspondence, op.cit* p.493
36. Cliff, *State Capitalism in
Russia, op.cit* pp.124-41

Chapter 7: War Communism (1918-1921)

1. V.Brügmann, *Die russischen
Gewerkschaften in Revo-
lution und Bürgerkrieg 1917-*

1919, Frankfurt a/M 1972,
p.140
2. M.Dobb, *Soviet Economic*

Development Since 1917,
London 1948, pp.84-5
3. Serge, *op.cit* p.137
4. Dobb, *op.cit.* p.90
5. V.P.Miliutin, *Istoriia eko-
   nomicheskogo razvitiia SSSR*,
   Moscow–Leningrad 1929,
   p.115
6. Brügmann, *op.cit.* p. 247
7. L.N.Kritzman, *Die
   heroische Periode der grossen
   russischen Revolution*,
   Frankfurt a/M 1971,
   pp.101-2, 208
8. *ibid.* pp.97-8
9. *ibid.* p.80
10. *ibid.* p.293
11. K.Leites, *Recent Economic
    Development in Russia*,
    Oxford 1922, pp.152, 199
12. J.Bunyan, *The Origin of
    Forced Labor in the Soviet
    State: 1917-1921*, Baltimore
    1967, pp.173-4
13. Brügmann, *op.cit.* p.151
14. Kritzman, *op.cit.* p.252
15. *ibid.* p.254
16. *ibid.* p.283
17. *ibid.* p.265
18. *ibid.* p.273
19. *ibid.* p.276
20. *ibid.* p.216
21. Chamberlin, *op.cit.* Vol.2,
    pp.100-1
22. Dobb, *op.cit.* p.100
23. Chamberlin, *op.cit.* Vol.2,
    p.105
24. Kritzman, *op.cit.* p.287
25. Lenin, *Works*, Vol.30, p.228
26. F.Lorimer, *The Population of
    the Soviet Union, History and
    Prospects*, Geneva 1948, p.41
27. Kritzman, *op.cit.* p.288
28. *Lenin and Gorky: Letters,
    Reminiscences, Articles*,
    Moscow 1973, p.163
29. V.Serge, *Conquered City*,
    London 1976, pp.89-90
30. V.Serge, *Memoirs of a Revo-
    lutionary, 1901-1941*, London
    1963. p.79
31. *ibid.* p.101
32. Lenin, *Works*, Vol.35, p.333
33. A.Ransome, *Six Weeks in
    Russia in 1919*, London 1919,
    pp.68-9
34. Lenin, *Works*, Vol.32, p.22
35. Dobb, *op.cit.* p.114
36. Lenin, *Works*, Vol.29,
    pp.137-8
37. *ibid.* Vol.30, pp.108-9
38. *ibid.* pp.284-5
39. N.I.Bukharin, *Economics of
    the Transformation Period*,
    New York 1971, p.146
40. C.Clark, *The Conditions of
    Economic Progress*, London
    1940, pp.79, 83, 91, 98
41. Lenin, *Works*, Vol.33, pp.62-3
42. *ibid.* p.58
43. *ibid.* p.57
44. *ibid.* pp.84-6
45. L.Trotsky, *The First Five
    Years of the Communist
    International*, London 1953,
    Vol.2, p.266
46. Lenin, *Works*, Vol.32,
    pp.233-4
47. *ibid.* p.343

Chapter 8: The Heroic and the Tragic Intertwine

1. Lenin, *Works*, Vol.30, p.437
2. *ibid.* p.454
3. *ibid.* p.288
4. *ibid.* p.297
5. *ibid.* Vol.32, p.154
6. L. Trotsky, *Problems of
   Everyday Life*, New York
   1973, p.163

7. Reed, *op.cit.* p.12
8. Serge, *Year One of the Russian Revolution, op.cit.* p.362
9. Chamberlin, *op.cit.* Vol.2, p.340
10. J. Maynard, *The Russian Peasant: and Other Studies,* London 1942, pp.102, 139
11. L.Trotsky, *The Revolution Betrayed,* New York 1937, p.181
12. K Marx and F.Engels, *Collected Works,* London 1976, Vol.3, p.263
13. Trotsky, *Problems of Everyday Life, op.cit.* p.53
14. Trotsky, quoted in I.Deutscher, *The Prophet Armed,* London 1954, p.407
15. Lenin, *Works,* Vol.29, p.74
16. *ibid.* pp.154-5

17. *ibid.* Vol.30, p.518
18. *ibid.* Vol.33, p.24
19. *ibid.* Vol.32, p.361
20. *ibid.* p.327
21. Bunyan, *The Origin of Forced Labor in the Soviet State, op.cit.* p.98
22. K.Marx, *The German Ideology,* London 1940, p.69
23. Trotsky, *Problems of Everyday Life, op.cit.* p.54
24. Trotsky, *The First Five Years of the Communist International, op.cit.* Vol.2, p.120
25. Lenin, *Works,* Vol.28, p.72
26. *ibid.* Vol.27, p.341
27. *ibid.* p.498
28. *ibid.* Vol.33, p.306
29. *ibid.* p.605
30. *ibid.* p.279
31. *ibid.* Vol.32, p.224
32. Shakespeare, *Macbeth*

Chapter 9: The Proletariat under War Communism

1. Ia.S.Rosenfeld, *Promyshlennaia politika SSSR,* Moscow 1926, p.37
2. Brügmann, *op.cit.* pp.215-6
3. *Vtoroi vserossiiskii sezd professionalnykh soiuzov,* Moscow 1921, p.138
4. Lenin, *Works,* Vol.29, p.158
5. *ibid.* Vol.33, p.26
6. *ibid.* p.256
7. Kritzman, *op.cit.* p.217
8. *Trudy II vserossiiskogo sezda sovetov narodnogo khoziaistva,* Moscow 1919, p.251
9. Kritzman, *op.cit.* p.218
10. *Trudy I vserossiiskogo sezda sovetov narodnogo khoziaistva,* Moscow 1918, p.434
11. *Chetvertii vserossiiskii sezd professionalnykh soiuzov,* Moscow 1921, p.119

12. M.H.Dobb and H.C.Stevens, *Russian Economic Development Since the Revolution,* London 1928, p.189
13. Lenin, *Works,* Vol.29, p.555
14. *ibid.* Vol.33, p.65
15. *ibid.* Vol.32, p.199
16. *ibid.* p.411
17. *ibid.* Vol.33, pp.23-4
18. R.Arskii, 'Trade Unions and Factory Committees', *Vestnik narodnogo kommissariata truda,* February-March 1918. Quoted in F.I.Kaplan, *Bolshevik Ideology and the Ethics of Soviet Labour,* London 1969, pp.129-30
19. A.Pankratova, *Fabzavkomy i profsoiuzy v revoliutsii 1917 goda,* Moscow–Leningrad 1927, p.238
20. *Izvestiia,* 27 April 1918.

Quoted in Bunyan and Fisher,
op.cit. p.619
21. Bunyan, *Origin of Forced
Labor in the Soviet State,*
op.cit. pp.20-1
22. *ibid.* p.26
23. P.N.Amosov *et al.,*
*Oktiabrskaia revoliutsiia i
fabzavkomy,* Moscow 1927,
Vol.2, p.188
24. *Pervii vserossiiskii seze
professionalnykh soiuzov,*
Moscow 1918, p.235
25. *ibid.* p.243
26. *ibid.* pp.369-70
27. *ibid.* p.374
28. Akhapkin, *op.cit.* p.50
29. J.Bunyan, *Intervention, Civil
War and Communism in
Russia, April-December 1918,*
Baltimore 1936, pp.405-6
30. *Trudy I vesrossiiskogo sezda
sovetov narodnogo khozi-
aistva, op.cit.* p.10
31. *Chetvertii vesrossiiskaia konferentsiia professionalnykh
soiuzov,* Moscow 1923, p.28
32. Kritzman, *op.cit.* p.135

33. N.Bukharin and P.Preobraz-
hensky, *The ABC of Com-
munism,* London 1969, p.448
34. *Sobranie uzakonenii i rasporiazhenii rabochego i krestian-
skogo pravitelstva,* 1919,
No.14, Art.163 (hereafter
sited as SUR)
35. *SUR,* 1919, No.18, Art.204
36. Bunyan, *Origin of Forced
Labor in the Soviet State,*
op.cit. pp.163-4
37. M.Dewar, *Labour Policy in
the USSR: 1917-1928,* London
1956, pp.48-9
38. Lenin, *Works,* Vol.30, p.312
39. *ibid.* pp.333-4
40. Kaplan, *op.cit.* p.359
41. Lenin, *Works,* Vol. 29,
pp.423-4, 426-7
42. Dewar, *op.cit.* p.61
43. Lenin, *Works,* Vol.30, p.499
44. *ibid.* Vol.32, p.412
45. *Odinnadtsatii sezd RKP(b),*
Moscow 1936, p.109
46. Lenin, *Works,* Vol.31,
pp.364-5

Chapter 10: War Communism and the Peasantry

1. Cliff, *Lenin, op.cit.* Vol.1,
pp.211ff., 224-5
2. Lenin, *Works,* Vol.10, p.191
3. *ibid.* Vol.32, p.251
4. *ibid.* Vol.30, p.506
5. *ibid.* Vol.29, p.359
6. *ibid.* Vol.27, p.232
7. *ibid.* Vol.24, p.23
8. *Kommunisticheskaia partiia
sovetskogo soiuza v rezoliutsiiakh i resheniiakh sezdov,
konferentsii i plenumov TsK,*
7th edition, Moscow 1953
(hereafter cited as *KPSS v
Rezoliutsiiakh*), Vol.1,
pp.341-2
9. *O Zemle,* Moscow 1921, p.9

10. Lenin, *Works,* Vol.28,
pp.175-7
11. *ibid.* p.342
12. *SUR,* 1919, No.4
13. J.L.H.Keep, *The Russian
Revolution: A Study in Mass
Mobilization,* London 1976,
p.414
14. A.M.Bolshakov and
N.A.Rozhkov, *Istoriia khoziaistva rossii v materialakh i
dokumentakh,* Leningrad
1926, Vol.3, p.248
15. P.Lezhnev-Finkovskii, *Sov-
khozy i kolkhozy,* Moscow–
Leningrad 1928, p.61
16. Lenin, *Works,* Vol.27, p.337

17. Keep, *The Russian Revolution*, op.cit. p.462
18. *Izvestiia TsK RKP(b)*, No.8, 2 December 1919. Quoted in R.H.Rigby, *Communist Party Membership in the USSR, 1917-1967*, Princeton 1968, p.106
19. O.A.Narkiewicz, *The Making of the Soviet State Apparatus*, Manchester 1970, p.60
20. Ia.A.Iakovlev (ed.), *K voprosu o sotsialisticheskom pereustroistve selskogo khoziaistva*, Moscow 1928, pp. 3, 7
21. Kritzman, op.cit. p.73
22. Lenin, *Works*, Vol.32, p.277
23. *ibid.* p.341
24. *ibid.* Vol.26, p.503
25. *ibid.* pp.503-4
26. *SUR* 1917-1918, No.35; Bunyan, *Intervention, Civil War and Communism in Russia*, op.cit. pp.460-2
27. *ibid.* p.464
28. Lenin, *Works*, Vol.27, p.397
29. *ibid.* pp.437-9
30. *SUR*, 1917-1918, No.43; Bunyan, *Intervention, Civil War and Communism in Russia*, op.cit. pp.472-3
31. Lenin, *Works*, Vol.29, p.157
32. Kritzman, op.cit. pp.135-9
33. A. S. Pukhov, *Kronstadtskii Miatezh 1921 g*, Leningrad 1931, p.8
34. C.Betelheim, *Class Struggles in the USSR: First Period: 1917-1923*, New York 1976, p.233
35. B. Pilnyak, *Mother Earth and other Stories*, London 1972, p.20
36. Lenin, *Works*, Vol. 29, p.299
37. Maynard, op.cit. p.104
38. Marx and Engels, *Collected Works*, op.cit. Vol.7, p.520
39. *The Trotsky Papers*, edited by J.M.Meijer, The Hague 1971, Vol.2, pp.485-565
40. *Kolkhozy vo vtoroi stalinskoi piatiletke*, Moscow 1939, p.1
41. *ibid.*
42. Lenin, *Works*, Vol.30, p.112
43. *ibid.* Vol.29, pp.359, 369

Chapter 11: The Withering Away of the State?

1. Lenin, *Works*, Vol.25, p.402
2. *ibid.* pp.412, 463
3. *ibid.* pp.487-8
4. *ibid.* p.472
5. *ibid.* p. 489
6. *ibid.* p.429
7. *ibid.* p.448
8. Akhapkin, op.cit. p.157
9. *Sezdy sovetov RSFSR v postanovleniakh i rezoliutsiiakh*, Moscow 1939, p.218
10. J.Towster, *Political Power in the USSR: 1917-1947*, New York 1948, p.209
11. *ibid.* pp.157-9
12. Lenin, *Works*, Vol.30, p.237
13. *Sedmoi vserossiiskii sezd sovetov rabochikh, krestianskikh, krasnoarmeiskikh, i kazachikh deputatov*, Moscow 1920, pp.261-2
14. Towster, op.cit. p.246
15. G.V.Vernadsky, *A History of Russia*, New York 1944, p.319
16. *SUR*, 1917-1918, No.12, Art.79
17. *SUR*, 1919, No.53, Art.508
18. O.Anweiler, *The Soviets: The Russian Workers, Peasants and Soldiers' Councils, 1905-1921*, New York 1974, p.235
19. J.V.Stalin, *Works*, Moscow 1952-5, Vol.4, p.220

20. Latsis, *op.cit.*
21. W.Pietsch, *Revolution und Statt: Institutionen als Träger der Macht in der Sowjetrussland (1917-1922)*, Cologne 1969, p.94
22. *ibid.* p.95
23. *ibid.* p.96
24. *ibid.* pp.114-5
25. Lenin, *Works*, Vol.33, p.176
26. *SUR*, 1922, No.4, Art. 42
27. Lenin, *Works*, Vol.25, p.389
28. *ibid.* Vol.26, p.272
29. *ibid.* Vol.24, pp.100-1
30. Bunyan and Fisher, *op.cit.* pp.298-9
31. Rigby, *op.cit.* pp.417-18 *Growth of the Red Army*, Princeton 1944, p.102
32. *The Trotsky Papers*, *op.cit.* Vol.1, pp.799-800
33. Fedotoff-White, *op.cit.* p.105
34. *ibid.* p.99
35. *ibid.* p.91
36. *The Trotsky Papers*, *op.cit.* Vol.1, p.29
37. *ibid.* p.208
38. *ibid.* p.118
39. L.Trotsky, *Kak vooruzhalas revoliutsiia*, Moscow 1923, Vol.1, p.235
40. Fedotoff-White, *op.cit.* p.90
41. Pietsch, *op.cit.* p.137
42. Lenin, *Works*, Vol.31, p.178
43. Kritzman, *op.cit.* p.233
44. Lenin, *Works*, Vol. 29, pp.32-3
45. *ibid.* p.183
46. *ibid.* Vol.33, p.77
47. *ibid.* Vol.36, p.557
48. *ibid.* p.566
49. *ibid.* Vol. 33, pp.428-9
50. Bukharin and Preobrazhensky, *op.cit.* p.240

Chapter 12: The Establishment of the Bolsheviks' Political Monopoly

1. Lenin, *Works*, Vol.23, pp.325-6
2. *ibid.* Vol.25, p.450
3. *ibid.* p.440
4. *ibid.* p.404
5. *ibid.* pp.487-8
6. Sukhanov, *op.cit.* pp.528-9
7. Carr, *op.cit.* Vol.1, p.183
8. Bunyan and Fisher, *op.cit.* p.359
9. *ibid.* p.361
10. *ibid.* p.220
11. Radkey, *The Sickle under the Hammer, op.cit* p.291
12. *ibid.* p.491
13. Serge, *Year One of the Russian Revolution, op.cit.* p.230
14. *SUR*, 1917-1918, No.44, Art.536
15. Lenin, *Works*, Vol.28, pp.190-1
16. M.Gorky, *Untimely Thoughts: Essays on Revolution, Culture and the Bolsheviks, 1917-18*, New York 1968, pp.85-6
17. *ibid.* p.88
18. Stalin, *op.cit.* Vol.4, p.138
19. Carr, *op.cit.* Vol.1, p.171
20. Lenin, *Works*, Vol.28, pp.212-3
21. *ibid.* Vol.29, p.151
22. Getzler, *op.cit.* p.200
23. L.Schapiro, *The Origin of the Communist Autocracy*, New York 1965, pp.123, 125-6
24. P.Avrich, *The Russian Anarchists*, Princeton 1971, pp.195-6
25. Bukharin and Preobrazhensky, *op.cit.* p.436
26. Serge, *Year One of the Russian Revolution, op.cit.* p.336

27. *KPSS v rezoliutsiakh*, Vol.1, pp.446-7
28. ibid. pp.600-1
29. ibid. p.627
30. ibid. p.469
31. Rigby, *op.cit.* pp.417-18
32. ibid. pp. 470-1
33. Lenin, *Works*, Vol.33, p.135
34. ibid. Vol.26, p.260
35. ibid. Vol.29, p.183
36. ibid. p.559
37. ibid. Vol.36, p.561
38. *Dvenadtsatii sezd RKP(b)*, Moscow 1923, pp.41, 207
39. Bunyan, *The Origin of Forced Labor in the Soviet State*, op. cit. p.251
40. *Vosmoi sezd RKP(b)*, Moscow 1933, p.250
41. *Deviagii sezd RKP(b)*, Moscow 1934, p.307
42. Trotsky, *The First Five Years of the Communist International*, op.cit. Vol.1, pp.99-100
43. M. A. Waters (ed.) *Rosa Luxemburg Speaks*, New York 1970, p.394
44. ibid. pp.389-90
45. ibid. p.391
46. ibid. p.375
47. ibid. p.369
48. ibid. p. 394
49. ibid.
50. Lenin, *Works*, Vol.32, p.25
51. ibid. Vol.33, pp.306-7, 314
52. Serge, *Year One of the Russian Revolution*, op.cit. p.264

Chapter 13: The Transformation of the Party

1. See Cliff, *Lenin*, op.cit. Vol.2, pp.160-1
2. Rigby, *op.cit.* pp.241-2
3. Lenin, *Works*, Vol.30, p.498
4. *Izvestiia TsK RKP(b)*, 24 March 1920
5. *Desiatii sezd RKP(b)*, Moscow 1933, pp.29-30, 76
6. *Odinnadtsatii sezd RKP(b)*, op.cit. p.443
7. ibid. p.422
8. Rigby, *op.cit.* p.109
9. *Izvestiia IsK RKP(b)*, January 1923
10. Narkiewicz, *op.cit.* p.61
11. Rigby, *op.cit.* p.245
12. *Izvestiia TsK RKP(b)*, 2 December 1919
13. Lenin, *Works*, Vol.30, p.71
14. Rigby, *op.cit.* p.78
15. Lenin, *Works*, Vol.28, p.61
16. ibid. Vol.29, pp.32-3
17. ibid. Vol.30, p.485
18. ibid. Vol.29, p.265
19. ibid. Vol.32, p.355
20. *KPSS v rezoliutsiiakh*, op.cit. Vol.1, pp.623-4
21. Lenin, *Works*, Vol.33, p.254
22. *KPSS v rezoliutsiiakh*, op.cit. Vol.1, pp.446-7
23. Rigby, *op.cit.*, p.77
24. Lenin, *Works*, Vol. 24, pp.432-3.
25. *Izvestiia TsK RKP(b)*, March 1922
26. Pietsch, *op.cit.* p.133
27. *Izvestiia TsK RKP(b)*, 24 March 1920
28. *Odinnatsatii sezd RKP(b)*, op.cit. p.420
29. Lenin, *Works*, Vol.28, p.257
30. *KPSS v rezoliutsiiakh*, op.cit. Vol.1, pp.442, 463
31. ibid. p.525
32. *CC Minutes*, op.cit. pp.126-251
33. Pietsch, *op.cit.* p.153
34. R.H.McNeal (ed.), *Resolu-*

tions and Decisions of the Communist Party of the Soviet Union, Toronto 1974, Vol.2, p.13
35. Lenin, Works, Vol.30, pp.443-4
36. KPSS v rezoliutsiiakh, op.cit. Vol.1, p.500
37. Lenin, Works, Vol.30, p.444
38. Vosmaia konferentsiia RKP(b), Moscow 1961, p.221
39. Desiatii sezd RKP(b), op.cit. p.56
40. Izvestiia TsK RKP(b), 5 March 1921
41. Dvenadtsatii sezd RKP(b) op.cit. p.207
42. Izvestiia Tsk RKP(b), March 1923
43. KPSS v rezoliutsiiakh, op. cit. Vol.1, p.509
44. McNeal, op.cit. Vol.2, pp.11-12
45. Odinnadtsatii sezd RKP(b), op.cit. pp.277-8
46. J.B.Sorenson, The Life and Death of Soviet Trade Unionism, 1917-1928, New York 1969, pp.167-9

47. K.Marx and F.Engels, Sochineniia, Moscow 1955, Vol.3, p.33
48. Pilnyak, op.cit. p.145
49. I.Libedinsky, A Week, London 1923, p.42
50. ibid. p.47
51. ibid. p.99
52. Desiatii sezd RKP(b), op.cit. p.52
53. ibid. p.54
54. ibid. pp.62-3
55. ibid. pp.56-7
56. Carr, op.cit. Vol.1, p.188
57. A.G.Löwy, Die Weltgeschichte ist das Weltgericht, Vienna 1968, p.111
58. R.V.Daniels, The Conscience of the Revolution: Communist Opposition in Soviet Russia, Cambridge (Mass.) 1965, p.129
59. Lenin, Works, Vol.31, p.336; Serge, Year One of the Russian Revolution, op.cit. pp.366-7
60. Cliff, Lenin, op.cit. Vol.2, p.169

Chapter 14: Lenin and the Military Front

1. The Trotsky Papers, op.cit. Vol.1, pp.107-9
2. Lenin, Works, Vol.28, p.195
3. Trotsky, My Life, op.cit. p.447
4. Lenin, Works, Vol.29, p.71
5. Trotsky, My Life, op.cit p.452
6. ibid. p.454
7. ibid. pp.454-5
8. Trotsky, Kak vooruzhalas revoliutsiia, op.cit. Vol. 2, Book 1, pp.388ff.
9. Stalin, op.cit. Vol.4, pp.345-6
10. L.Trotsky, Stalin, London 1947, pp.329, 332
11. Lenin, Works, Vol.32, p.173

12. C.Zetkin, Reminiscences of Lenin, London 1929, p.20
13. The Trotsky Papers, op.cit. Vols.1 and 2
14. See Cliff, Lenin, op.cit. Vol.2 pp.369-75
15. The Trotsky Papers, op.cit. Vol. 1, p.589
16. B.Souvarine, Stalin, London 1939, pp.222-3
17. Trotsky, My Life, op.cit. p.414
18. Lenin, Works, Vol.26, pp.470-1
19. ibid. Vol.27, p.95
20. ibid. p.98

Chapter 15: The Rise of the Communist International

1. V.I.Lenin, *Collected Works* translated from the fourth Russian edition (henceforth referred to as *Works*), Vol.21, pp.33-4
2. *ibid.* pp.40-1
3. See further T.Cliff, *Lenin*, London 1976, Vol.2, Ch.1
4. N.K.Krupskaya, *Memories of Lenin*, London 1970, p.285
5. Lenin, *Works*, Vol.24, p.24
6. *ibid.* Vol.26, pp.470-1
7. *ibid.* Vol.27, p.95
8. *ibid.* p.98
9. *ibid.* Vol.29, p.153
10. *ibid.* Vol.31, pp.397-8
11. *ibid.* p.457
12. *ibid.* Vol.21, p.330 ,
13. L.Fischer, *The Soviets in World Affairs*, London 1930, Vol.1, p.32
14. B.Lazitch and M.M.Drachkovitch, *Lenin and the Comintern*, Stanford 1972, Vol.1, pp.31-2
15. Lenin, *Sochineniia*, 2nd edition, Vol.24, p.128. Quoted in Carr, *op.cit.* Vol.3. p.74
16. *Vosmoi sezd RKP(b)*, Moscow 1939, pp.501-4
17. Lenin, *Works*, Vol.28, p.475
18. J.Degras (ed.) *The Communist International (1919–1943): Documents*, London 1956, Vol.1, p.26
19. Lazitch and Drachkovitch, *op.cit.* p.77
10. H.Gruber (ed.) *International Communism in the Era of Lenin: a Documentary History*, New York 1972, p.81
21. *Sedmoi sezd RKP(b)*, Moscow 1923, p.138
22. Lenin, *Works*, Vol.28, pp.476-7
23. *ibid.* Vol.29, pp.306-7
24. E.H.Carr, *The Bolshevik Revolution, 1917-1923.* London 1953, Vol.3, p.128
25. *ibid.*
26. Lenin, *Works*, Vol.29, p.307
27. *ibid.* p.493
28. Degras, *op.cit.* Vol.1, pp.50-3
29. J.Braunthal, *History of the International*, London 1967, Vol.2, p.168
30. *ibid.* p.184
31. W.H.Crook, *The General Strike*, London 1931, pp.240-3; *ibid.*

Chapter 16: The Proletarian Assault Rebuffed – the Need for a New Policy

1. Trotsky, *The First Five Years of the Communist International*, New York 1945, Vol.1, pp.176, 294
2. Lenin, *Works*, Vol.29, p.227
3. Lazitch and Drachkovitch, *op.cit.* p.112
4. Lenin, *Works*, Vol.30, p.354

5. *ibid.* Vol.31, p.111
6. Lazitch and Drachkovitch, *op.cit.* p.113
7. *ibid.* pp.115-6
8. Lenin, *Works*, Vol.31, pp.249-50
9. P.Frölich, *Rosa Luxemburg – Ideas in Action*, London 1972, p.281
10. P.Broué, *Révolution en Allemagne, 1917-1923*, Paris 1971, p.218
11. *ibid.* pp.219-20
12. J.P.Nettl, *Rosa Luxemburg*, London 1962, Vol.2, p.758

13. Quoted in Cliff, *Lenin*, *op.cit.*, Vol.2, p.261
14. Lenin, *Works*, Vol.25, p.312
15. *ibid.* Vol.29, p.396
16. Broué, *op.cit.* pp.864-5
17. See T.Cliff, *Lenin*, *op.cit.* Vol.2, pp.6, 10-11
18. See T. Cliff, *Rosa Luxemburg*, London 1968, pp.51-2
19. Nettl, *op.cit.* Vol.2, p.752
20. Frölich, *op.cit.* p.279
21. I.Deutscher, 'Record of a Discussion with Heinrich Brandler', *New Left Review*, September-October 1977, p.48

Chapter 17: The Comintern: A School for Tactics

1. Lenin, *Works*, Vol.31, p.21
2. *ibid.* p.26
3. *ibid.* p.62
4. *ibid.* p.37
5. *ibid.* pp.68-9
6. *ibid.* p.77
7. *ibid.* p.70
8. *ibid.* Vol.30, p.55
9. *ibid.* pp.87-8
10. *ibid.* Vol.29, pp.562, 565
11. *ibid.* Vol.31, pp.56, 58-9
12. *ibid.* p.93
13. *ibid.* pp. 59-60
14. *ibid.* pp.53, 55
15. *ibid.* p.55
16. Cliff, *Lenin*, *op.cit.* Vol.1, pp. 257-8
17. Lenin, *Works*, Vol.31, p.80
18. *ibid.* pp.95-6
19. *ibid.* Vol.29, pp.325-6
20. *Der Zweite Kongress der Kommunistischen Internationale*, Hamburg 1921, p.370
21. Degras, *op.cit.* Vol.1, pp.110-1
24. *Der Zweite Kongress der Kommunistischen Internationale*, *op.cit.* pp.14-5

23. *ibid.* p.8
24. J.T.Murphy, *New Horizons*, London 1941, p.152
25. Cliff, *Lenin*, *op.cit.* Vol.1, p.126
26. *Der Zweite Kongress der Kommunistischen Internationale*, *op.cit.* pp.407-8
27. Lazitch and Drachkovitch, *op.cit.* p.254
28. *ibid.* p.255
29. Degras, *op.cit.* Vol.1, pp.154-5
30. Cliff, *Lenin*, *op.cit.* Vol.1, pp.211-27
31. *ibid.* Vol.2, p.217
32. Degras, *op.cit.* Vol.1, pp.156-61
33. *Der Zweite Kongress der Kommunistischen Internationale*, *op.cit.* p.318
34. *ibid.* p.561
35. Lenin, *Works*, Vol.31, pp.144-51
36. *ibid.* p.244
37. Marx's Introduction to the 1882 Russian edition of the Communist Manifesto: K.Marx and F.Engels, *Selec-*

ted Works, Moscow 1951,
Vol.1, pp.23-4
38. Lenin, *Works,* Vol.31, p.453
39. *ibid.* pp.206-7
40. *ibid.* pp.206-11

41. Degras, *op.cit.* Vol.1, p.172
42. *Der Zweite Kongress der Kommunistischen Internationale, op.cit.* p.695
43. *ibid.* p.300

Chapter 18: Lenin, Bolshevism and the Comintern

1. Degras, *op.cit.* Vol.1, p.164
2. Broué, *op.cit.* p.865
3. A.Rosmer, *Lenin's Moscow,* London 1971, p.77
4. *ibid.* p.51
5. Cliff, *Lenin, op.cit.* Vol.1, p.256
6. Engels to Marx on 7 October 1858, and Engels to Kautsky on 12 September 1882, Marx and Engels, *Selected Correspondence,* London, 1942, pp.110, 351
7. Lenin, *Works,* Vol.22, p.301 194
8. T.Cliff, 'Economic Roots of Reformism', June 1957, in *A Socialist Review,* London 1964, pp.48-58
9. Lenin, *Works,* Vol.28, pp.292-3
10. *ibid.* Vol.29, p.310
11. *ibid.* Vol.31, pp.21-2, 91
12. V.Serge, *Memoirs of a Revolutionary, 1901-1941,* London 1963, p.107
13. R.Wohl, *French Communism in the Making, 1919-1924,* Stanford 1966, p.355
14. *Der Zweite Kongress der Kommunistischen Internationale, op.cit.* p.79
15. *ibid.* p.315
16. *ibid.* p.340
17. Murphy, *op.cit.* p.150
18. *Bulletin of the IV Congress of the Communist International,* Moscow 1922, No.20
19. Degras, *op.cit.* Vol.1, p.258

20. *ibid.* p.165
21. Braunthal, *op.cit.* Vol.1, p.108
22. *Der Zweite Kongress der Kommunistischen Internationale, op.cit.* p.238
23. Lazitch and Drachkovitch, *op.cit.* p.19
24. L.J.Macfarlane, *The British Communist Party: Its Origin and Development until 1929,* London 1966, p.139
25. Broué, *op.cit.* p.825
26. Deutscher, 'Record of a Discussion with Heinrich Brandler,' *New Left Review, op.cit.* pp.50-1
27. *Der Zweite Kongress der Kommunistischen Internationale, op.cit.* p.382
28. L.Trotsky, *History of the Russian Revolution,* London 1934, p.558
29. *ibid.* p.315
30. Serge, *Memoirs of a Revolutionary, op.cit.* p.177
31. Broué, *op.cit.* pp. 826-7
32. *ibid.* p.830
33. Lazitch and Drachkovitch, *op.cit.* p.455
34. P.Levi, *Unsere Weg,* quoted *ibid.* p.509
35. *ibid.* p.159
36. Serge, *Memoirs of a Revolutionary, op.cit.* p.187
37. Lenin, *Works,* Vol.33, p.430
38. *ibid.* p.431
39. L.Trotsky, *The Third International After Lenin,* New York 1936, p.159

Chapter 19: The Grafting of Bolshevism Fails

1. Wohl. *op.cit.* p.82
2. *ibid.* p.91
3. ibid. pp.218-9
4. *ibid.* pp.438-9
5. *ibid.* p.174
6. *ibid.* pp.89-90
7. *ibid.* p.96
8. *ibid.* p.307
9. Braunthal, *op.cit.* Vol.2, p.193
10. Wohl, *op.cit.* p.218
11. *ibid.* p.288
12. *ibid.* pp.407-8
13. D.W.Urquidi, *The Origins of the Italian Communist Party, 1918-1921*, Columbia University Ph.D, 1962, Preface, pp.1-2
14. *ibid.* p.390
15. *ibid.* pp.390-1
16. *ibid.* pp.306-7
17. *ibid.* p.393
18. *ibid.* p.394
19. *Il Soviet*, 3 October 1920. Quoted in Urquidi, p.269
20. *Il Soviet*, 21 September 1919. Quoted in Urquidi, p.54
21. *Bulletin of the IV Congress of the Communist International, op.cit.* No.12
22. *ibid.* No.2
23. *ibid.* No.11
24. Urquidi, *op.cit.* p.102
25. Curt Geyer's interview with R.Loewenthal, 'The Bolshevization of the Spartacus League', *International Communism*, St. Antony's Papers, No.9, London 1960, p.57
26. R.Fischer, *Stalin and German Communism*, London 1948, pp.174-5
27. Trotsky, *The Third International after Lenin, op.cit.* p.89
28. W.D.Angress, *Stillborn Revolution: The Communist Bid for Power in Germany, 1921-1923*, Princeton 1963, p.145
29. *ibid.* pp.146, 149
30. *ibid.* pp.156-7
31. H.Malzahn in *Protokoll des III Kongresses der Kommunistischen Internationale*, Hamburg 1921, p.251
32. Broué, *op.cit.* p.484

Chapter 20: Britain and Bulgaria: Two Antipodes

1. K.Marx and F.Engels, *On Britain*, Moscow 1962, p.582
2. Quoted in H.Collins, 'The Marxism of the Social Democratic Federation' in A.Briggs and J.Saville (eds), *Essays in Labour History, 1886-1923*, London 1971, p.55
3. W.Kendall, *The Revolutionary Movement in Britain, 1900-1921*, London 1969, pp.60-1
4. B.Holton, *British Syndicalism, 1900-1914*, London 1976, pp.179-80; L.J.Macfarlane, *op.cit.* pp.18-19
5. Holton, *op.cit.* p.172
6. Lenin, *Works*, Vol.22, p.180
7. Kendall, *op.cit.* p.388
8. J.Hinton, *The First Shop Stewards' Movement*, London 1973, p.183
9. *ibid.* pp.199-200
10. *ibid.* p.300
11. Degras, *op.cit.* Vol.1, p.4

12. First published by the Sheffield Workers' Committee,
1917, and reissued by *Plebs*,
London 1972
13. R.Challinor, *The Origins of
British Bolshevism*, London
1977, pp.18, 40, 121, 151
14. Holton, *op.cit*. p.56
15. *ibid*. p.60
16. *ibid*. p.139
17. *ibid*. p.66
18. Challinor, *op.cit*. pp.120-1
19. R Challinor, *John S Clarke*,
London 1977, p.25
20. Hinton, *op.cit*. p.131
21. T.J.Murphy, *Preparing for
Power*, London 1972, p.106
22. Challinor, *The Origins of
British Bolshevism*, *op.cit*.
p.157
23. Murphy, *New Horizons*,
op.cit. p.116
24. By far the best study of this
movement is Hinton's book,
op.cit.
25. Hinton, *op.cit*. pp.196-212
26. *ibid*. p.212
27. *ibid*. p.287
28. *ibid*. pp.223-33
29. J.Hinton's introduction to
T.J.Murphy; *The Workers'
Committee*, London 1972,
p.5, and Hinton, *op.cit*.
Ch.10
30. M.Woodhouse and B.Pearce,
*Essays on the History of
Communism in Britain*, London 1975, p.38
31. Hinton, *op.cit*. p.302
32. *ibid*. p.307
33. *ibid*. p.276
34. See Challinor, *The Origins
of British Bolshevism*, *op.cit*.
pp.176-80, 190-2
35. T.Bell, *Pioneering Days*, London 1941, p.176
36. V.I.Lenin, *On Britain*, Moscow, pp.423-4

37. *ibid*. pp.538-9
38. *ibid*. p.528
39. Macfarlane, *op.cit*. pp.198-9
40. *ibid*. p.55
41. Lenin, *On Britain*, *op.cit*.
p.540
42. Kendall, *op.cit*. p.400
43. *ibid*. p.423
44. *ibid*. p.274
45. Macfarlane, *op.cit*. p.71
46. J.Klugmann, *History of the
Communist Party of Great
Britain*, London 1960, Vol 1,
p.198
47. *ibid*. p.77
48. Challinor, *The Origins of
British Bolshevism*, *op.cit*.
p.201
49. *ibid*. p.196
50. Kendall, *op.cit*. p.190
51. Challinor, *The Origins of
British Bolshevism*, *op.cit*.
p.199
52. Murphy, *Preparing for
Power*, *op.cit*. p.184
53. See Cliff, *Lenin*, *op.cit*. Vol.1,
pp.30-1
54. Carr, *The Bolshevik Revolution*, *op.cit*. Vol.3, p.145
55. Serge, *Memoirs of a Revolutionary*, *op.cit*. p.178
56. J.Rothschild, *The Communist Party of Bulgaria:
Origins and Developments,
1883-1936*, New York 1959,
p.39
57. Cliff, *Lenin*, *op.cit*. Vol.1,
p.179
58. Rothschild, *op.cit*. pp.41, 80,
95
59. *ibid*. pp. 41, 80
60. *ibid*. p.44
61. *ibid*. p.96
62. *ibid*. p.80
63. *ibid*. pp.119-20
64. Gruber, *op.cit*. p.349
65. *ibid*. p.352
66. Degras, *op.cit*. Vol.2, p.50

67. Rothschild, *op.cit.* pp.122-3
68. Gruber, *op.cit.* pp.359-60
69. Rothschild, *op.cit.* pp.141-2
70. *Pravda*, 9 October 1923; a translation appeared in *Internationale Presse-Korrespondenz*, 15 October 1922
71. Rothschild, *op.cit.* pp.152-6
72. *ibid.* p.134
73. *ibid.* pp.150-1
74. *ibid.* p.147
75. Degras, *op.cit.* Vol.2, p.212
76. Stalin, *Sochineniia*, Vol.7, p.293; Carr, *Socialism in One Country*, *op.cit.* Vol.3, p.410
77. Rothschild, *op.cit.* p.260
78. *ibid.* p.41
79. *ibid.* p.95
80. *ibid.* p.106
81. *ibid.* pp.55, 95
82. Cliff, *Lenin*, *op.cit.* Vol.1, p.238
83. *ibid.* pp.320-1, 365
84. Rothschild, *op.cit.* p.54
85. *Der Zweite Kongress der Kommunistischen Internationale*, *op.cit.* p.557
86. Lenin, *Works*, *op.cit.* Vol.18, pp.586-7
87. Rothschild, *op.cit.* p.115
88. See *ibid.* pp. 22-3, 108-10, 154

Chapter 21: The Great Cover-Up

1. Gruber, *op.cit.* p.286
2. *ibid.* p.288
3. P.Levi, *Unser Weg*, pp.55-6. Quoted in H.Gruber, 'Paul Levi and the Comintern', *Survey*, London, October 1964
4. Degras, *op.cit.* Vol.1, p.218
5. Trotsky, *The Stalin School of Falsification*, New York 1962, p.335
6. Serge, *Memoirs of a Revolutionary*, *op.cit.* p.140
7. Lenin, *Works*, Vol.42, pp.319-23
8. *Protokoll des III Kongresses der Kommunistischen Internationale*, *op.cit.* pp.184-5
9. *ibid.* pp.295-8
10. Broué, *op.cit.* pp.520-2
11. *Protokoll des III Kongresses der Kommunistischen Internationale*, *op.cit.* pp.479-83
12. *ibid.* pp.650-1
13. Trotsky, *The First Five Years of the Communist International*, *op.cit.* Vol.1. pp.276-7
14. *ibid.*
15. Lenin, *Works*, Vol.32, pp.468-74
16. K.Zetkin, *Reminiscences of Lenin*, London 1929, pp.32-3
17. *ibid.* p.31
18. Degras, *op.cit.* Vol.1, pp.230-9
19. J.Degras, 'United Front Tactics in the Comintern, 1921-1928,' *International Communism*, St. Antony's Papers, No.9, p.10
20. Trotsky, *The First Five Years of the Communist International*, *op.cit.* Vol.1, p.122
21. Angress, *op.cit.* p.196 A.Rosenberg, *A History of the German Republic*, London 1936, p.392.
22. *Bulletin of the IV Congress of the Communist International*, *op.cit.*, Nos. 14-15
23. H.R.Isaacs, *The Tragedy of the Chinese Revolution*, London 1938, p.51

Chapter 22: The Bolshevik Regime in Crisis

1. L.N.Kritzman, *Die heroische Periode der grossen russischen Revolution*, Frankfurt a/M, 1971, p.166
2. *Desiatyi sezd RKP(b)*, Moscow 1933, p.214
3. *ibid.* p.454
4. Lenin, *Works*, Vol.32, pp.20-1
5. *ibid.* p.37
6. *ibid.* p.24
7. *ibid.* p.48
8. *ibid.* p.25
9. *ibid.* p.50
10. *ibid.* p.204
11. *Desiatyi sezd RKP(b)*, *op.cit.* p.214
12. L.Trotsky, *My Life*, New York 1960, pp.465-6
13. Lenin, *Works*, Vol.32, p.172
14. S.Singleton, 'The Tambov Revolt (1920-1921)' *Slavic Review*, September 1966
15. P.Avrich, *Kronstadt 1921*, New York 1974, p.35
16. *ibid.* p.37
17. *ibid.* p.39
18. Serge, *Memoirs of a Revolutionary*, *op.cit.* p.123
19. Avrich, *Kronstadt 1921*, *op.cit.* p.42
20. *ibid.* p.45
21. *ibid.* p.42
22. *ibid.* pp.46-7
23. *ibid.* pp.89-90
24. *ibid.* p.93
25. *ibid.* p.69
26. *ibid.* pp.163-4
27. *ibid.* pp.179-80
28. *Desiatyi sezd RKP(b)*, *op.cit.* p.253
29. Avrich, *Kronstadt 1921*, *op.cit.* p.184
30. Lenin,*Works*, Vol.32, p.279
31. L.Trotsky, *The Revolution Betrayed*, New York 1935, p.96
32. Lenin, *Works*, Vol.32, p.192
33. *ibid.* p.215
34. *ibid.* p.224
35. *ibid.* p.225
36. *Odinnadtsatii sezd RKP(b)*, Moscow 1936, p.468
37. Lenin, *Works*, Vol.32, p.43
38. *ibid.* Vol.42, p.275
39. *ibid.* Vol.32, p.169
40. *ibid.* p.178
41. *ibid.* pp.258-9
42. *ibid.* p.244
43. *ibid.* Vol.33, pp.281-2
44. *ibid.* Vol.32, p.261
45. *ibid.* p.243
46. *Desiatyi sezd RKP(b)*, *op.cit.* p.540

Chapter 23: The New Economic Policy

1. *Leninskii Sbornik*, Vol.7, p.363
2. *ibid.* Vol.35, p.175
3. Lenin, *Works*, Vol.31, p.505
4. L.Trotsky, *The New Course*, New York 1943, p.63
5. Lenin, *Works*, Vol.32, p.133
6. *ibid.* p.156
7. *ibid.* p.229
8. *ibid.* p.326
9. *ibid.* Vol.33, pp.172-3
10. *ibid.* p.59
11. *ibid.* p.275
12. *ibid.* p.113
13. *ibid.* pp.112-3
14. *ibid.* Vol.32, p.350
15. *ibid.* p.225
16. *ibid.* p.236
17. *ibid.* pp. 277-8
18. *ibid.* pp.95-6

19. M.Dobb, *Soviet Economic Development since 1917*, London 1948, p.143
20. *ibid.* p.183
21. *ibid.* p.42
22. *ibid.* pp.46-7
23. *ibid.* pp.89-90
24. *ibid.* p.93
25. A.Nove, *An Economic History of USSR*, London 1972, p.114
26. Carr, *The Interregnum*, *op.cit.* p.75
27. *ibid.* pp.77-8
28. *Sedmoi vsesoiuznyi sezd profsoiuzov*, Moscow 1927, p.373
29. *ibid.* p.243
30. Carr, *The Interregnum*, *op.cit.* p.85
31. Lenin, *Works*, Vol.42, pp.375-7
32. *Stenograficheskii otchet piatogo vserossiiskogo sezda professionalnykh soiuzov*, Moscow 1922, p.82
33. *Kommunisticheskaia partiia sovetskogo soiuza v rezoliutsiiakh i resheniiakh sezdov, konferentsii i plenumov TsK*, 7th edition, Moscow 1953 (hereafter cited as *KPSS v rezoliutsiiakh*), Vol.1, p.606
34. M.Dewar, *Labour Policy in the USSR, 1917-1928*, London 1956, pp.99-100
35. *ibid.* p.102
36. Carr, *The Interregnum*, *op.cit.* p.73
37. J.B.Sorenson, *The Life and Death of Soviet Trade Unionism, 1917-1928*, New York 1969, p.201
38. J.V.Stalin, *Works*, Moscow 1952-5, Vol.5, p.364
39. Carr, *The Interregnum*, *op.cit.* p.94
40. E.H.Carr, *Socialism in One Country*, London 1958, Vol.1, p.101
41. L.Leonov, *The Thief*, London 1931, pp.54, 57-8, 116
42. W.Duranty, *I Write as I Please*, New York 1935, p.138
43. *ibid.* pp.147-8
44. I.Ehrenburg, *Julio Jurenito*, London, 1958, p.295
45. Lenin, *Works*, Vol.32, p.429
46. *KPSS v rezoliutsiiakh*, *op.cit.* Vol.1, p. 574
47. Lenin, *Works*, Vol.32, p.447
48. *ibid.* Vol.42. p. 327
49. *ibid*, Vol.33, p.116
50. *ibid.* p.160
51. *ibid.* p.280
52. *ibid.* Vol.36, p.571
53. *ibid.* Vol.33, p.274
54. *ibid.* p.276
55. *ibid.* pp.286-7
56. *Odinnadtsatii sezd RKP(b)*, *op.cit.* p.83
57. *ibid.* p.134
58. *Dvenadtastii sezd RKP(b)*, Moscow 1923, p.133
59. L.Trotsky, *The Challenge of the Left Opposition (1923-5)*, New York 1975, pp.149-50
60. Lenin, *Works*, Vol.33, p.279
61. *ibid.* p.288

Chapter 24: The Defeat of the German Revolution

1. Angress, *op.cit.* pp.285, 350
2. E.Anderson, *Hammer or Anvil*, London 1945, p.91
3. Broué, *op.cit.* p.679
4. *ibid.* pp.698-700
5. Rosenberg, *op.cit.* p.194
6. Fischer, *op.cit.* p.293
7. *ibid.* pp.291-2

8. Broué, *op.cit.* p.710
9. Angress, *op.cit.* pp.371-2
10. Anderson, *op.cit.* pp.92-3
11. Angress, *op.cit.* p.302
12. Broué, *op.cit.* p.554
13. *ibid.* p.706
14. Fischer, *op.cit.* p.260; Degras, *op.cit.* Vol.2, pp.17-18
15. Broué, *op.cit.* p.715
16. Carr, *The Interregnum, op.cit.* p.201
17. Angress, *op.cit.* pp.392-3
18. *Protokoll des Fünfte Kongress der Kommunistischen Internationale, op.cit.* Vol.2, p.713
19. Angress, *op.cit.* pp.339-41
20. Broué, *op.cit.* p.718
21. Trotsky, *The First Five Years of the Communist International, op.cit.* Vol.2, pp.347, 349-50
22. Trotsky, *The Stalin School of Falsification, op.cit.* pp.195-6
23. Lenin, *Works,* Vol.26, p.181. See Cliff, *Lenin, op.cit.* Vol.2, Ch.19, 'Lenin Calls up the Insurrection'
24. I.Deutscher, *The Prophet Unarmed,* London 1959, pp.111-12
25. Angress, *op.cit.* p.400
26. Deutscher, 'Record of a Discussion with Heinrich

Brandler', *New Left Review, op.cit.* pp.51-2, 76
27. Angress, *op.cit.* p.430
28. *ibid.* pp.434-5
29. Fischer, *op.cit.* p.337
30. Carr, *The Interregnum, op.cit.* p.222
31. *Bulletin of the IV Congress of the Communist International, op.cit.* Nos.14-15
32. Lenin, *Works,* Vol.25, pp.285-6
33. R.Fischer, *op.cit.* p.312
34. Angress, *op.cit.* pp.396-7
35. Trotsky, *The New Course, op.cit.* pp.49-50
36. L.Trotsky, *Lessons of October,* New York 1937, p.23
37. Carr, *The Interregnum, op.cit.* pp.230-1; W.Korey, *Zinoviev on the Problems of World Revolution, 1919-27,* Columbia University Ph.D. Thesis, 1960, p.174
38. Trotsky, *The Third International after Lenin, op.cit.* p.100
39. Degras, *op.cit.* Vol.2, p.87
40. *ibid.* p.77
41. Trotsky, *The Third International after Lenin, op.cit.* p.95

Chapter 25: Lenin Fights for his Life-Work

1. Lenin, *Works,* Vol.35, p.454
2. *Leninskii sbornik,* Vol.35, p.172
3. Lenin, *Works,* Vol.45, p.249
4. Trotsky, *My Life, op.cit.* p.475
5. Lenin, *Works,* Vol.42, p.492
6. *ibid.* p.621
7. *ibid.* Vol.45, p.497
8. *ibid.* Vol.42, p.418

9. *ibid.* p.600
10. Quoted by L.A.Fotieva, *Iz vospominanii o Lenine,* Moscow 1964, pp.28-9
11. Lenin, *Works,* Vol.45, p.601
12. *ibid.* Vol.33, pp.460-1
13. *ibid.* p.458
14. *ibid.* Vol.45, p.606
15. Carr, *The Bolshevik Revolution, op.cit.* Vol.2, pp.310-11

16. Lenin, *Works*, Vol.33, p.426
17. *ibid.* p.501
18. Carr, *The Bolshevik Revolution*, op.cit. Vol.2, p.372
19. Lenin, *Works*, Vol.31, pp.514, 516
20. *ibid.* Vol.35, p.475
21. *The Trotsky Papers*, edited by J.M.Meijer, The Hague 1971, Vol.2, pp.745-9
22. Lenin, *Works*, Vol.36, p.598
23. *ibid.* Vol.45, p.593
24. Trotsky, *The First Five Years of the Communist International*, op.cit. Vol.2, pp.270-1
25. Lenin, *Works*, Vol.29, p.194
26. *Desiatyi sezd RKP(b)*, op.cit. pp.163-8
27. *KPSS v rezoliutsiiakh*, op.cit. Vol.2, p.562
28. *The Trotsky Papers*, op.cit. Vol.2 pp.347-9
29. *Odinnadtsatii sezd RKP(b)*, op.cit. pp.72-5
30. Lenin, *Works*, Vol.42, pp.602-3
31. R.Pipes, *The Formation of the Soviet Union: Communism and Nationalism, 1917-1923*, Cambridge 1964, p.271
32. Lenin, *Works*, Vol.42, pp.421-3
33. P.N.Pospelov *et al.*, *Vladimir Ilyich Lenin, Biografiia*, Moscow 1963, p.611
34. Trotsky, *The Stalin School of Falsification*, op.cit. pp.66-7
35. Lenin, *Works*, Vol.33, p.372
36. *Dvenadtsatyi sezd RKP(b)*, op.cit. p.150
37. Lenin, *Sochineniia*, 5th edition, Vol.45, p.710. Quoted in M.Lewin, *Lenin's Last Struggle*, New York 1968, p.153
38. Lenin, *Works*, Vol.42, p.485
39. *ibid.* p.486
40. *ibid.* pp.605-6
41. *ibid.* pp.607-8
42. *ibid.* pp.610-11
43. *ibid.* Vol.42, p.493
44. *ibid.* Vol.45, p.607
45. *ibid.* p.608

Chapter 26: Fighting to the Last Breath ...

1. *KPSS v rezoliutsiiakh*, op.cit. Vol.1, p.533
2. I.Deutscher, *The Prophet Unarmed*, London 1959, p.47
3. Lenin, *Works*, Vol.33, pp.353-4
4. *ibid.* p.490
5. *ibid.* pp.490-1
6. *ibid.* p.494
7. Trotsky, *The Stalin School of Falsification*, op.cit. p.72
8. 'Letter to the Congress', Lenin, *Works*, Vol.36, p.593
9. *ibid.* pp.596-7
10. *ibid.* Vol.33, p.482
11. *ibid.* pp.484-5
12. Trotsky, *The Stalin School of Falsification*, op.cit. pp.73-4
13. Lenin, *Works*, Vol. 36, pp.594-5
14. Lenin, *Sochineniia*, 5th edition, Vol.54, pp.674-5. Quoted in Lewin, op.cit. pp.152-3
15. Lenin, *Works*, Vol.36, p.596
16. Cliff, *Lenin*, op.cit. Vol.1, p.115
17. Lenin, *Works*, Vol.45, pp.607-8
18. *ibid.* Vol.32, p.34

Chapter 27: The Final Defeat

1. Trotsky, *My Life, op.cit.* p.482
2. *ibid.* p.486
3. Stalin, *op.cit.* Vol.5, pp.261-2
4. *Dvenadtsatyi sezd RKP(b), op.cit.* p.563
5. *ibid.* p.526
6. Stalin, *op.cit.* Vol.5, p.271
7. *Dvenadtsatyi sezd RKP(b), op.cit.* p.577
8. *ibid.* p.96
9. Stalin, *op.cit.* Vol.5, pp.209-10
10. *ibid.* p.223
11. *KPSS v rezoliutsiiakh, op.cit.* Vol.1, pp.719-23
12. Stalin, *op.cit.* Vol.5, p.240
13. *The Trotsky Papers, op.cit.* Vol.2, pp.813-5
14. Trotsky, *The Challenge of the Left Opposition, op.cit.* pp.312-3
15. Trotsky, *My Life, op.cit.* p.481
16. *ibid.* pp.481-2
17. *ibid.* p.537
18. Trotsky, *The New Course, op.cit.* pp.27, 37
19. Trotsky, *The Challenge of the Left Opposition, op.cit.* pp.154, 161
20. Deutscher, *The Prophet Unarmed, op.cit.* p.93
21. Trotsky, *Stalin, op.cit.* pp.242-3
22. A.Soboul, *The French Revolution. 1787-1799*, London 1974, Vol.2, p.422
23. *ibid.* p.439
24. Deutscher, *The Prophet Unarmed, op.cit.* pp.106-7
25. Trotsky, *Stalin, op.cit.* p.387
26. *ibid.* pp.403-4
27. Trotsky, *My Life, op.cit.* pp.508-9
28. Stalin, *op.cit.* Vol.6, pp.47-53
29. Carr, *The Interregnum, op.cit.* p.349
30. R.H.McNeal, *Bride of the Revolution: Krupskaya and Lenin*, London 1973, p.242
31. Lenin, *Works*, Vol.25, p.385
32. F.Engels, *The Peasant War in Germany*, London 1927, pp.135-6
33. Lenin, *Works*, Vol.36, p.595
34. Cliff, *Lenin, op.cit.* Vol.2 p.xi
35. E.A.Preobrazhensky, *From NEP to Socialism: a Glance into the Future of Russia and Europe*, London 1971, p.99
36. *ibid.* p.116
37. See further Cliff, *Lenin, op.cit.* Vol.2, pp.136-9
38. M.A.Waters (ed.), *Rosa Luxemburg Speaks*, New York 1970, p.395

Chronology

Events occurring before 1 February 1918 are dated according to the Julian as well as the (western) Gregorian calendars; events occurring later are dated according to the Gregorian calendar only.

1917

25 October / 7 November: Overthrow of the Provisional Government in Petrograd; Kerensky flees. Second Congress of Soviets, with Bolshevik majority, opens in Petrograd.

26 October / 8 November: Organization of new Government of People's Commissars, consisting exclusively of Bolsheviks; promulgation of decrees nationalizing the land and proposing immediate peace negotiations to all belligerent powers.

27 October / 9 November: Kerensky starts to move on Petrograd with General Krasnov, who commands a force of a few hundred Cossacks. Beginning of fighting between the forces of the Provisional Government and of the Soviet in Moscow.

29 October / 11 November: Unsuccessful uprising of Junkers in Petrograd.

30 October / 12 November: Fighting with Kerensky's troops on the outskirts of Petrograd.

1 November / 14 November: Flight of Kerensky and capture of Krasnov.

2 November / 15 November: Victory of the Bolsheviks in Moscow. General Alekseev, former Commander-in-chief of the Russian Army arrives in the Don Cossack capital, Novo-Cherkassk, and sets about forming the Volunteer Army, which later becomes the most formidable of the anti-Bolshevik military forces.

4 November / 17 November: Withdrawal of some prominent Communists from the Council of People's Commissars and from the Central Committee of the Communist Party as a protest against Lenin's uncompromising attitude toward inclusion of representatives of other Socialist parties in the Government.

7 November / 20 November: Ukrainian Rada, which has seized power in Ukraine, publishes Third Universal, asserting its right to exercise state power until the convocation of the Constituent

Assembly. Soviet Government orders Commander-in-chief Dukhonin to begin peace negotiations.

9 November / 22 November: Dukhonin dismissed for refusing to obey orders of Soviet Government; Bolshevik Ensign Krilenko appointed Commander-in-chief.

13 November / 26 November: Decree establishing workers' control over all industrial enterprises.

18 November / 1 December: Agreement between Bolsheviks and Left Socialist Revolutionaries, as result of which representatives of latter Party enter the Government.

19 November / 2 December: Kornilov, Denikin and other Generals, imprisoned in Bikov, near Moghilev, for participation in the Kornilov revolt, escape and make for the Don Territory, where they become leaders of Alekseev's Volunteer Army.

22 November / 5 December: Preliminary armistice agreement signed.

2 December / 15 December: Conclusion of armistice with Central Powers.

4 December / 17 December: Soviet Government addresses ultimatum to Ukrainian Rada, demanding that it cease disarming revolutionary troops and permitting Cossack units to pass through Ukraine to the Don.

7 December / 20 December: Organization of the Cheka – the All-Russian Commission for Combating Counterrevolution, Sabotage and Speculation.

9 December / 22 December: Beginning of peace negotiations in Brest-Litovsk.

13 December / 26 December: Organization of Ukrainian Soviet Government, challenging the authority of the Rada, in Kharkov.

14 December / 27 December: Decree nationalizing the banks.

23-31 December / 5-13 January 1918: Third Congress of Soviets.

1918

5 January / 18 January: The Constituent Assembly opens; reveals an anti-Bolshevik majority.

6 January / 19 January: Constituent Assembly dispersed by commander of the sailors and soldiers appointed to guard it.

7-14 January / 20-27 January: First Congress of Trade Unions.

8-9 January / 21-22 January: Extraordinary sessions of the Central Committee concerning the Brest-Litovsk parleys; both Lenin's proposal (sign annexationist peace) and Trotsky's (no peace, no war) outvoted in favour of Bukharin's proposal (wage a revolutionary war against the Germans).

10-18 January / 23-31 January: Third Congress of Soviets.

12 January / 25 January: Ukrainian Rada issues Third Universal, declaring Ukraine independent.

16-23 January / 29 January-3 February: Bolshevik rebellion in Kiev, finally suppressed by Ukrainian troops.

28 January / 8 February: Kiev occupied by Red Army.

29 January / 9 February: Representatives of the Rada sign separate peace with the Central Powers.

30 January / 10 February: Trotsky, as head of the Soviet peace delegation, issues statement refusing to sign peace, but declaring the war ended and the Russian army demobilized.

18 February: Germans, beginning broad advance, occupy Dvinsk. Extraordinary session of the Central Committee; at morning session Lenin outvoted by Trotsky and Bukharin supporters; at evening session Lenin's motion for immediate peace adopted after Trotsky swings his support to Lenin.

19 February: Soviet Government agrees to sign peace.

20 February: Decree for formation of Red Army.

22 February: At session of Central Committee, Trotsky proposes asking Allies for aid against Germans and tenders his resignation as Commissar of Foreign Affairs; Lenin, absent, sends note approving 'receipt of support and arms from Anglo-French imperialist brigands;' Trotsky's recommendation adopted by a 6 to 5 vote. Soviet Government receives new German peace conditions.

23 February: The Council of People's Commissars and the Bolshevik Party Central Committee agree to sign the peace.

25 February: Rostov and Novo-Cherkassk, the centres of the anti-Bolshevik movement in the Don Territory, occupied by Red Troops; the small Volunteer Army retreats southward and moves into the Kuban Territory.

2 March: German army occupies Kiev, restores Government of the Ukrainian Rada.

3 March. Signature of Peace of Brest-Litovsk.

6-8 March: Seventh Party Congress.

8 March: the Bolsheviks adopt the name 'Communists'.

12 March: Government moves from Petrograd to Moscow.

13 March: Trotsky appointed War Commissar.

14 March: Red troops occupy Kuban capital, Ekaterinodar, after flight of the local Cossack Government.

14-16 March: Fourth Congress of Soviets.

15 March: Fourth Congress of Soviets ratifies the Peace of Brest-Litovsk. Left Socialist Revolutionaries leave Soviet Government as protest against the signature of the Treaty.

6 April: Japenese descent in Vladivostok.

9 April: Proclamation of the independence of Trans-Caucasia.

15 April: Turks take Batum.

23 April: Decree nationalizing foreign trade.

29 April: Germans dissolve Ukrainian Rada; General Skoropadsky proclaimed Hetman of Ukraine with dictatorial powers.

6 May: Insurgent anti-Soviet Cossacks occupy Novo-Cherkassk.

8 May: Germans and Cossacks occupy Rostov.

25 May: Beginning of open hostilities between the Soviets and the Czecho-Slovaks; the latter occupy Cheliabinsk.

26 May: The Trans-Caucasian Federation breaks up into the three independent states of Georgia, Armenia and Azerbaidzhan.

28 May: Czecho-Slovaks seize a number of towns in Eastern Russia and Siberia.

29 May: All-Russian Soviet Executive Committee introduces partial conscription for the Red Army.

8 June: Czecho-Slovaks occupy Samara, making possible creation of anti-Bolshevik Government, headed by Socialist Revolutionary members of the Constituent Assembly. Anti-Bolshevik Government created in Omsk, in Siberia.

11 June: Institution of the Committees of Poor Peasants.

17-19 June: Unsuccessful rebellion against the Soviet regime in Tambov.

20 June: Assassination of prominent Petrograd Communist, Volodarsky, by a Socialist Revolutionary.

28 June: Nationalization of large industries.

4-10 July: Fifth Congress of Soviets adopts Constitution.

6 July: German Ambassador, Count Mirbach, assassinated by Left Socialist Revolutionaries in Moscow; rebellion of the Left Socialist Revolutionaries. Town of Iaroslav seized by insurgents acting under the direction of Boris Savinkov.

11 July: Muraviev, commander of Soviet troops on the Volga front, turns against the Bolsheviks and tries to send troops against Moscow; is shot when his troops refuse to follow him.

16 July: The former Tsar and members of his family shot in Ekaterinburg.

21 July: Iaroslav captured by Soviet troops.

2 August: Allied occupation of Archangel and organization of anti-Bolshevik Government of North Russia.

6 August: Czecho-Slovaks and anti-Bolshevik Russians capture Kazan, high point of their advance.

14 August: Small British force under General Dusterville occupies Baku after Bolshevik Soviet regime has been ousted by the population.

15 August: Volunteer Army, under leadership of General Denikin, captures the capital of the Kuban Territory, Ekaterinodar.

26 August: Volunteer Army occupies Novorossisk, gains access to the sea.

30 August: Fanya Kaplan fires at and wounds Lenin; Uritzky, prominent Petrograd Communist, killed by a Socialist Revolutionary.

4 September: Soviet Commissar for the Interior, Petrovsky, publishes appeal for 'mass terror' against the bourgeoisie.

8-23 September: Representatives of anti-Bolshevik Government of Siberia and Eastern Russia meet in State Conference at Ufa; agree to create central authority in the form of a Directory of five persons.

10 September: Red Army captures Kazan; turning point of campaign on Volga.

14 September: Turks occupy Baku after departure of British; great massacre of Armenians.

20 September: Execution of twenty-six Baku Commissars in the desert between Krasnovodsk and Askhabad by order of the Trans-Caspian authorities.

8 October: Red Army captures Samara.

6-9 November: Sixth Congress of Soviets.

9 November: Revolution in Germany.

13 November: Soviet Government annuls Treaty of Brest-Litovsk. Ukrainian nationalists, under leadership of Petlura, raise revolt against Hetman in town of Belaia Tserkov.

18 November: Admiral Alexander Kolchak proclaimed Supreme Ruler, vested with dictatorial powers, after military coup d'état in Omsk and arrest of Socialist Revolutionary members of the Directory.

21 November: Soviet Government nationalizes internal trade.

27 November: Provisional Soviet Government of Ukraine proclaimed, as first step toward new Bolshevik occupation of Ukraine.

14 December: Ukrainian nationalist troops under Petlura occupy Kiev; Hetman Skoropadsky flees. Red Army, moving westward into former zone of German occupation, occupies Minsk.

1919

3 January: Soviet troops, advancing in western and southern directions, take Riga, capital of Latvia, and Kharkov, the largest city of Eastern Ukraine.

16-25 January: Second Congress of Trade Unions.

6 February: Red Army captures Kiev, capital of the Ukranian nationalist regime.

15 February: General Krasnov, Ataman of the Don Territory, resigns and is succeeded by General Bogaevsky, withdrawal of Krasnov leaves Denikin in supreme command of anti-Bolshevik forces in south-eastern Russia.

2-7 March: First Congress of the Communist International in Moscow.

13 March: Kolchak's army, launching drive toward Volga, captures Uta.

18-23 March: Eighth Congress of the Communist Party.

21 March: Soviet regime established in Hungary.

6 April: Red Army enters chief Ukranian port, Odessa, after its evacuation by French forces of occupation.

10 April: Soviet troops, invading Crimean peninsula, occupy Simferopol.

26 April: Kolchak's offensive stopped before reaching Volga as a results of defeats in the Buzuluk and Buguruslan regions.

7 May: Ataman Grigoriev, leader of Soviet troops which were destined for offensive against Rumania, begins rebellion; issues anti-Bolshevik and anti-Semitic manifesto to the population.

15-17 May: Huge pogrom carried out by Grigoriev troops in town of Elizavetgrad.

19 May: Denikin takes offensive against Soviet troops on southeastern front; his cavalry breaks through Red front near Iuzovka.

4 June: Partisan leader Makhno breaks with Red Army command; dissatisfaction among Makhno's followers and other Red troops helps White Army of Denikin to win decisive victories in the Don Territory and in the Donetz coal basin.

9 June: Ufa retaken by Red troops; Kolchak's retreat continues.

12 June: Fort Krasnaia Gorka, near Petrograd, betrayed to Northwestern White Army by its commanding officers.

16 June: Krasnaia Gorka retaken; threat to Petrograd averted.

25 June: Denikin captures Kharkov.

30 June: Continuation of Denikin's advance marked by capture of Tsaritsin and Ekaterinoslav.

1 July: Soviet troops, pushing forward on Eastern Front, take Perm.

25 July: Red Army occupies Cheliabinsk; retreat of Kolchak's troops becomes increasingly disorderly.

27 July: Grigoriev killed by Makhno.

1 August: Fall of Hungarian Soviet Government.

10 August: Denikin's cavalry General, Mamontov, breaks through front, begins long raid in rear of Soviet armies on Southern Front.

18-21 August: Mamontov holds Tambov.

23 August: Denikin seizes Odessa.

30 August: Red Army evacuates Kiev; Petlurists march in.

31 August: Denikin's forces push Petlurists out of Kiev.

25 September: Anarchists throw bomb into headquarters of Moscow Committee of Communist Party; a number of Communists killed and wounded.

11 October: Iudenitch starts drive on Petrograd.

14 October: Denikin occupies Orel: high point of his advance.

20 October: Red Army retakes Orel.

22 October: Iudenitch pushed back from suburbs of Petrograd. Tsarskow Selo and Pavlovsk.

14 November: Red Army takes Kolchak's capital, Omsk.

17 November: Soviet troops on Southern Front occupy Kurks; Denikin's resistance begins to crumble all along the line.

5-9 December: Seventh Congress of Soviets.

12 December: Red Army captures Kharkov.

30 December: Red troops take Ekaterinoslav.

1920

3 January: Red Army occupies Tsaritsin.

4 January: Kolchak abdicates as Supreme Ruler in favour of Denikin.

8 January: Red Army captures Rostov, seat of Denikin's Government; Denikin's Army retreats south of the Don.

15 January: Kolchak handed over to the Political Centre in Irkutsk by Czecho-Slovaks who were guarding him.

16 January: Allies Supreme Council raises the blockade of Soviet Russia.

2 February: Signature of Peace with Esthonia.

7 February: Kolchak shot by decision of the Revolutionary Committee in Irkutsk.

10 February: Beginning of organization of 'labour armies' with a view to utilizing Red Army soldiers for productive work.

19 February: Fall of Northern Government in Archangel.

17 March: Red Army occupies Kuban capital, Ekaterinodar.

27 March: Soviet troops, pursuing demoralized White Army of Denikin, take port of Novorossisk.

4 April: Denikin resigns command of armed forces of South Russia, nominating General Baron Peter Wrangel as his successor.

3-6 April: Third Congress of Trade Unions.

27 April: Red Army captures Baku; Azerbaidjan Soviet Government organized.

29 April-5 May: Tenth Congress of Communist Party.

6 May: Poles enter Kiev.

7 May: Soviet Government concludes treaty with Georgia, recognizing its independence.

6 June: Wrangel, after reorganizing his army, begins movement northward from the Crimea.

8 June: Budenny's Cavalry Army, raiding in rear of Poles, seizes Berditchev and Zhitomir.

12 June: Red Army retakes Kiev.

11 July: Red Army, on the offensive of the Polish Front, captures Minsk.

14 July: Soviet troops occupy Vilna.

21 July / 6 August: Second Congress of Communist International.

31 July: With view to creating a Soviet regime in Poland a Revolutionary Committee, headed by communists of Polish origin, is established in Belostok.

1 August: Red Army takes Brest-Litovsk.

15 August: Polish forces south of Warsaw launch counter-offensive.

21 August: Success of Polish counterstroke marked by recapture of Brest-Litovsk and general retreat of Red Army from the Vistula.

21 September: Beginning of Russo-Polish peace negotiations in Riga.

12 October: Signature of preliminary peace treaty with Poland.

20 October: Beginning of final offensive against Wrangel.

2 November: Wrangel's Army retreats into the Crimea.

11 November: Red Army storms the Isthmus of Perekop, the approach to the Crimea.

14 November: Wrangel evacuates the Crimea.

29 November: Soviet Government issues decree nationalizing small industries.

Index

period, 59-60, 74-5, 79-80;
deteriorates as a result of
malnutrition and exhaustion of
workers, 85-6
Land decree, 8-9, 35
Larin,U., 7
Lashevich,M., 196
Latsis,M.I., 18
Left Communists, 39-51
Lenin,V.I., on prospects of Bolsheviks
retaining power, 1; issues many
decrees, 5-6; strict chairman of
Sovnarkom, 5-6; decrees part of his
Collected Works, 6; did not see
many decrees published over his
signature, 7-8; drafts decree on
peace, 8; drafts decree on land, 8-9;
pinches SR programme, 9; drafts
decree on right of national self-
determination, 9; drafts decree on
workers' control, 10; drafts decree
on right of recall, 10; involved in
trivial administrative matters,
11-12; aided by primitive sectarian
organization, 12; on Red Terror,
17-19; badly wounded in attempt on
his life, 18-19, 166; robbed, 20-1;
Mensheviks and SRs demand his
(and Trotsky's) exclusion from
coalition of all socialist parties,
23-8; opposes coalition government
with Mensheviks and SRs, 23-8; in
minority in Central Committee on
question, 25; puts ultimatum to
Right Bolsheviks, 27-8; prior to
October revolution calls for early
convening of Constituent
Assembly, 30; hesitates whether to
hold elections to Constituent
Assembly, 31-2; for dispersal of
Constituent Assembly, 34; on
relation between Constituent
Assembly and Soviets, 34-6; on
towns leading countryside, 36-7;
prior to October revolution argues
for revolutionary war, 39; after
October argues for accepting
German peace terms, 39-41; for
marking time until victory of
German revolution, 39-40; his peace
policy rejected by majority of
Central Committee and Party,
41-51; rebukes Zinoviev and Stalin
who used non-internationalist
arguments in support of peace
policy, 42-3; for accepting military
aid from Britain and France, 44-5
argues in press for peace policy,
45-7; wins Central Committee for

same, 48-9; wins Party for same,
49-51; opposes Stalin's suggestion of
expelling Left Communist leaders
from Party 49; his peace policy –
principled and realistic, 53-4; learns
from Marx and Engels regarding
transition period, 55-9; charting
transitional demands prior to
October revolution 60-2; on
workers' control, 62; on long and
complicated transition period, 62-6;
on human nature changing in
transition period, 63-4; on
creativity of masses as key to
transition, 64-6; state capitalism as
content of transition period, 66-71;
state capitalism and peasantry, 69,
76-7; on need for bourgeois
specialists, 71-2; privileges of
technicians are concessions to
capitalism, 72-3; on one-man
management, 73-5; on Taylorism,
75; on petty bourgeois counter-
revolutionary threats during
transition period, 76-7; on threat of
counter-revolution from
intelligentsia, 78-80; on need to
strengthen proletarian dictatorship,
78-9; on lice threatening the
revolution, 89-90; his very frugal
life-style, 91-2; defines War
Communism as real communism,
93-4; redefines War Communism as
unavoidable siege economy, 96-9;
on miracles of organization and
heroism of proletariat, peasantry
and Red Army, 100-1; on Bolsheviks'
unpreparedness to govern, 104; on
proletarian perseverance as
guarantee for victory, 104-5; on
need for realism – neither
pessimism nor optimism, 104-5; on
stench of old society poisoning the
new, 107; on revolution as a 'leap to
freedom', 109; on means and ends –
proletarian dictatorship and
freedom, 110; on bureaucratic
degeneration of state, 111-12; on
decimation of proletariat during
civil war, 113; on proletariat
becoming more petty bourgeois,
113-14; on the decomposition of the
proletariat, 115; on militarization of
labour, 125-6; on statification of
trade unions, 126; on subbotniks,
127; on the proletarian nature of
the state undermined by
decomposition of the proletariat,
128-9; on distinction between

proletariat and peasantry, 130, 144; on need to organize large farms, 130-2; on organizing agricultural workers, 133-4; on food requisitioning, 133-4; on Poor Peasant Committees, 134-7; on peasantry gaining from revolution far more than proletariat, 143; on withering away of state, 144-5; on dictatorship of proletariat as consistent democracy, 145-6; on decline of VTsIK, 148; on need to limit power of Cheka, 152-3; for soldiers' committees and election of officers in army, 153; on great number of bourgeois officials in state apparatus, 158; on dictatorship of proletariat or of Party, 161-2, 174; for relaxation of measures against Right SRs, 166-7; conciliatory attitude towards Mensheviks, 168-9; for tightening screws on Right SRs and Mensheviks, 169; on need of workers to defend themselves against state, 178; on distorted relationships between party and state, 178; on mobilization of party members whenever regime threatened, 180; on need to purge careerists from party, 182-3; on scarcity of veterans in party, 184; on relation between Politburo, Orgburo and secretariat on the one hand and Central Committee on the other, 186; Lenin, the party and the proletariat, 193-4; supports Trotsky against 'military opposition', 195-6; disagrees with Trotsky on military strategy and proved largely wrong, 197-203; for evacuation of Petrograd, 199-200; for march on Warsaw, 200-2; on international nature of revolution, 204-5, 208-9; on role of Second International, 207-11; on need for a new International, 207-8; on imminence of revolution in Europe, 208-14; at founding congress of Comintern, 212-13; on historical role of Comintern, 213-14; on Hungarian Soviet Republic, 218-21, 246; against adventurism during July days, 225; on international significance of Russian revolution, 230, 259; on compromises, 231-2; on Communists in parliamentary elections, 232-5, 297; on Communists and the trade unions,

235-6; on training of Communist leaders, 236-7; and the Bavarian Soviet Republic, 237-8; on agrarian question, 244-6; on national and colonial question, 246-8; drafting '21 Conditions', 248-51; and Kautsky, 252, 259; and the aristocracy of labour, 257-8; on Zinoviev's character, 267, 419; criticizes Comintern as too Russian, 270-1; and foundation of British CP, 296-300; and affiliation of British CP to Labour Party, 397-9; and P. Levi, 318-19, 321-4; and Märzaktion, 318-19, 321-5; and trade union debate, 329, 331-5; and Kronstadt uprising, 340; and 'Peasant Brest', 340-1, 347; for banning factions in party, 341-4; and NEP, 345-51, 361-4, 396-7; on state capitalism, 348-9; on Ustrialov, 363-4; on rising bureaucracy, 363-4, 413-18; his health, 394-6, 408, 411; industry while on sickbed, 395; in defence of monopoly of foreign trade, 397-9; on economic planning, 400-3; on Great Russian chauvinism, 403-411; on Georgia, 406-11; turns to Trotsky for an alliance against Great Russian chauvinism, 411; attacks Stalin's Great Russian chauvinism, 411; on bureaucracy in Rabkrin, 413-15, 418; turns to Trotsky for alliance in fighting against bureaucracy, 416-17; his testament, 417-22; on Stalin, 418-21; on Trotsky, 418-19; on Kamenev, 419; on Bukharin, 419; his death, 434; his cult, 434-6

Levi,P., on propaganda nature of Spartakusbund, 226; gets rid of ultra-lefts in KPD, 227-8; on Comintern emissaries in Italy, 269; and Märzaktion, 279-80, 317-18; expelled from KPD, 317-18; and Lenin, 318-19, 321-4

Libedinsky,I., 190-1

Lice, threat to revolution, 89-90

Liebknecht,K., 214, 223-4, 279, 387

Lloyd George,D., 214

Lomov,G.I., 5, 43-4, 46, 50

Ludendorff, 52-3

Lukacs,G., 242

Lunacharsky,A.V., 5, 23-8

Luxemburg,R., against substitution of party for proletariat in power, 176; party monopoly will lead to withering away of the soviet, 176-7; substitution of party for class caused by isolation of Russian revolution, 177-8; and founding congress of Comintern, 221-3; against boycotting National Assembly, 221-2; against leaving the trade unions, 222; opposes January 1919 uprising in Germany, 224; her organization a loose propaganda group, 226-7, 279; her fatalism, 254-5; and international significance of Bolshevism, 260, 442

Maksimovsky,V.N., 191
Mann.T., 291
March on Warsaw, 201-3, 239-41
Makhlevsky.J., 201
Marriage law, 11
Martov.L., on popularity of Bolshevik regime, 2; calling for a coalition government of all socialist parties, 3; leaves the Soviet, 4; on helplessness of 'third camp', 169
Marx,K., on 'pure democracy', 38; on communist society, 93-5; on equality not compatible with poverty, 95; on revolution as only way to transform proletariat, 106; 247-8
Märzaktion, 316-26
Mayakovsky,V.V., 108
Means and ends – proletarian dictatorship and freedom, 109-12
Mensheviks, 1-2; in Second Congress of Soviets, 3; leaving Soviet, 4; organizing strikes against Bolshevik government, 15-17; demand a coalition government of all socialist parties with exclusion of Lenin and Trotsky, 23-8; faring badly in election to Constituent Assembly, 32-4; reject decrees on land, peace and workers' control at Constituent Assembly, 35; the press unfettered, 167-8; support Bolshevik regime critically, 168; suppression 169-70
Menzhinsky,V.R., 6-7
Meyer,E., 267
Miliutin,V.P., 4, 23, 28
Militarization of labour, 124-6
Molotov,V.M., 184
Monopoly of foreign trade, 397-9
Muir,J., 292
Murphy,J.T., 261, 287, 292, 294-5

Nogin,V.P., 4, 13, 23-8
Norwegian CP, 211, 217

Obolensky,V., 43
One-man management, 73-5

Ordzhonikidze,G.K., 195, 407-11, 417, 419

Pankhurst,S., 233, 297
Peace decree, 8, 35
Peasantry, land decree, 8-9; distinction from proletariat, 36-7, 129-30, 144; and state capitalism, 69, 76-7; complusory requisition of grain, 87-8, 133-4; effect on Jacobin centralization of state, 105, 138-43; and organization of large farms, 130-2; decline in stratification of, 133-4; Poor Peasant Committees, 134-8; resistance to compulsory requisitions, 137-8; contradictions in attitude to Bolsheviks, 138; affecting moods of proletariat, 142-3; affect moods in Party, 143; gained from revolution more than proletariat, 143; increased social weight compared with proletariat, 143; under NEP, 349-52
Petukovsky,S.S., 6-7
Piatakov,G.L., 43, 46, 49-50, 419
Pilnyak,B., 138, 190
Planning, 397-400
Plekhanov,G.B., 35
Potorovsky,M.N., 46, 50
Preobrazhensky,E.A., 43, 50, 365, 439-40
Prokopovich,S.N., 1
Proletariat, versus peasantry, 36-7, 129-30, 144; exhibits miracles of organization and heroism, 99, 101; thirst for culture, 101-3; its perseverance guarantee for victory, 104-5; its being a tiny minority of population undermines democracy, 105-6; tolerates dictatorship against itself, 106; its heroism intertwines with backwardness, 106-7; overburdened with dead weight of past, 106, 108; decomposition of proletariat affects party, 108; decimation during civil war, 113; becoming petty bourgeois, 113-14; decomposition of proletariat and collapse of workers' control, 115-18; militarization of, 125-6; subbotniks, 126-8; its decomposition affects socialist nature of state, 128-9; organizing agricultural proletariat, 130-3; disappearance of agricultural proletariat, 133-4; gained from revolution less than peasantry, 143; has to defend itself from state, 178; its relation to party and to Lenin, 193-4; see factory committees, trade